CAMPDEN

A New History

CAMPDEN

A New History

by Members of CADHAS

Edited by
Allan Warmington

Campden and District Historical
and Archaeological Society

2005

Published by CADHAS - Campden and District Historical and Archaeological Society
The Old Police Station, High Street, Chipping Campden, Glos. GL55 6HB

Cover design by Vale Press Ltd

Vale Press Ltd

Printed and bound in Great Britain
by Vale Press Ltd, Willersey

ISBN 0-9550866-0-4

Dedicated to the Memory of
Geoffrey Powell
Soldier, Historian and Writer
and successively
Chairman, Vice President and President
of CADHAS

Some changes benefit Campden and its people. Many do not. ... But the core of the town is the same as ever it was, people with deep roots in the place, fiercely proud of it and of their origins. Incoming residents, and the writer speaks as one himself, are privileged to live in such a town. Their lives are supported, and often prolonged, by its quality. They receive much. Let them remember to give as well, not just in money but in love, care and respect, and with humility.

Geoffrey Powell, *The Book of Campden*

Despite the efforts of certain of its practitioners, history is fun.

Geoffrey Powell, *Why History?*

Publication of this book has been assisted by grants from :

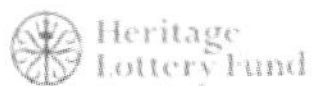

and by gifts from :

Campden & Chorleywood Food Research Association
Cotswold House Hotel
Robert Welch Associates
Lloyds TSB plc
Cutts of Campden

CONTENTS

ILLUSTRATIONS

FOREWORD

Chipping Campden has had its history written on more than one occasion, but in each succeeding generation new information is gathered, and we approach the past in a different way. This new book brings together the work of a number of different contributors, and the Campden Historical Society deserves credit for recruiting authors and coordinating their efforts to produce a coherent and continuous account of the town from earliest times until the twentieth century.

Readers will find accounts of the familiar landmarks in the town's history, though often seeing them from a new angle. The foundation of the borough, the flourishing of William Grevel, the 'flower of wool merchants', the influence of Baptist Hicks and the Noel family are all here, as are Dover's games and the 'Campden Wonder' when William Harrison returned from captivity in 1662. The Campden Guild and the rise of tourism in recent times complete the familiar aspects of the town's history. New dimensions for this reader included the dispute arising from the gift of pigeons to a girl singer in the thirteenth century, the connection between the parish church and the monks of Chester, the revival of Dover's games in the eighteenth and nineteenth centuries (leading to much moralistic disapproval), the vandalising of the German field gun in 1919 (showing that people rejected excessive gloating over victory), and the story of the Polish 'displaced persons' in local camps after World War II. A most valuable addition to the history of Campden, which will surely stimulate new research, is the publication of part of the map of 1722.

Every reader will find some episode that will interest them. I was pleased to read about the strange accommodation of the Grammar School scattered around the town at the beginning of the twentieth century, when my mother attended as a scholarship pupil. She had many memories of her education, but did not seem to find it odd that pupils had to move from building to building in the town centre. It was also a pleasure that Herbert Finberg's time in the town as a printer is remembered. He was my predecessor but three in the Department of English Local History, and he wrote some important essays about Gloucestershire's early history, and much else besides.

Chipping Campden was (and is) an important town in the north Cotswolds which served a large rural area stretching over the hills to the south, and into the valley to the north. It has developed its own special character and institutions, and has attracted many enterprising and creative people. Its curving main street, its harmonious buildings, and setting in a valley give it a special atmosphere. This book celebrates an attractive place, but it also accepts realistically that the town had its share of poverty and crime. I hope that it will be widely read.

Christopher Dyer
Professor of Regional and Local History,
University of Leicester.

INTRODUCTION AND ACKNOWLEDGEMENTS

This book was inspired by our late President, Geoffrey Powell. He believed that all the research that had been carried out by members of CADHAS during its first 20 years could lead to a new perspective on Campden which should be captured in book form. He wrote a short paper at the beginning of 2000 setting out the case for a New History of Campden, outlining its contents and suggesting the form and the procedures to be followed. He then gathered together a group of CADHAS members and in his own persuasive way enthused them all in taking part in the venture. Each member of the group undertook to research and draft a particular section of the book, and occasional meetings were held under Geoffrey's guidance to discuss progress. His death at the end of 2004 was a great loss to us, but he was able to see and comment on the first complete draft.

The main contributors to the book, apart from Geoffrey himself, were Celia Jones, Tim Jones, Vanessa Rigg, Allan Warmington and Jill Wilson, with other contributions from Dennis Granger and David Vince The team has also made wide use of the draft of and notes towards an unfinished history of the last hundred years in Campden (Campden Remembered) written by the late Carolyn Mason, and we are grateful to her executors for allowing us to make use of this valuable material.

The authors do not claim this to be a definitive history of Campden. Each contributor has emphasised matters within his or her own interests and competences. Further, because of the number of authors there are differences in style between the various sections of the book, which, we hope adds to its attractiveness.

Throughout the time the book has been in production, we have had constant help from many people. Although it is invidious to mention just a few names, some people stand out. Diana Evans has spent many hours proof-reading and conscientiously checking over the typescript and has found many inconsistencies which we were able to correct before the book went to print. Jenny Bruce, with her great knowledge of the photographic archive of CADHAS, has also worked uncomplainingly and far beyond the call of duty, in helping us choose illustrations for the book and advising us on sources. Bob Jones provided a house style and has read the page proofs with his usual competence. Frank Johnson and Carol Jackson have both given extensive advice and provided materials and Frank Mottershead had given much help with the 20th century. Then there are the interviewees who are mentioned in the text, who gave very generously of their time. We should like to thank, too, the individuals and organisations that have lent, and given us permission to use, illustrations in their possession. Where no acknowledgement is made, the pictures are from CADHAS Archives. We should also like to thank the staff of Campden Library, Gloucester Record Office, the Leicester, Leicestershire and Rutland Record Office, Kent Archives Office, the BGAS Library, Sandon Estate Archives, Castle Ashby Archives, The Ashmolean Collection and Cheltenham Art Gallery and Museum for their invariable helpfulness.

Readers will note that we have referred to the parish throughout as 'Campden', and have only used the term 'Chipping Campden' when referring to the market area or the old tightly constrained borough. That was the custom right up to the end of the 19th century and beyond.

Geoffrey wrote in February 2000 that the book should be both readable and academically sound, of value to future scholars. We hope we have fulfilled these aims. We hope, too that readers in Campden and beyond will take it upon themselves to make additions and corrections to the book. CADHAS regularly publishes its research periodical, Notes and Queries, which is ideal for such contributions.

A.W.

PART I: CAMPDEN BEFORE THE CONQUEST

1

Early Settlers: Celts, Romans and Saxons

The small market town of Campden lies in a bowl-shaped valley on the northern tip of the Gloucestershire Cotswolds. A little to the north is the Warwickshire boundary, close to the west is Worcestershire and not far to the east is Oxfordshire.

The hills that can be seen above the roofs of the High Street houses are of oolitic limestone of the Jurassic age, laid down under the sea a little less than 200 million years ago.[i] The fine cream or honey-coloured stone from the quarries on Westington Hill has been used for building at least since Norman times. Fossils are regularly found in the ploughland and pastures of the upper hillsides. Below the limestone an impervious bed of Lias clay provides a spring-line. The brooks originating here join eventually to form the stream, now known as the Cam,[ii] while other brooks rise further south and flow eastwards out past Broad Campden. The valley sides of these limey clays have been used as arable land for many centuries, perhaps since before the arrival of the Romans. The alluvium below the river-bed at the very bottom of the valley consists of up to 35 feet of deposits: glacial outwash, gravels and more recent peats.[iii] Here meadows have existed for hundreds of years.

The Cotswolds have been inhabited on and off for up to 12,000 years, though surviving evidence of human activity is available for less than half that time. The earliest people were hunter-gatherers, and the Cotswolds were probably settled in the Mesolithic period, up to 7,000 years ago. An occasional Mesolithic flint has been reported. A Neolithic flint scraper found in ploughland above the town[iv] suggests the possible presence of early agriculturalists in the neighbourhood, perhaps 5,000 years ago. None of these finds have been found *in situ* so no more is known at present.

Close to Campden, at Weston-sub-Edge, a Middle Bronze Age axe (dating from 1400 - 1000 BC) has been found. A Bronze Age socketed axe has been found within the parish,[v] and the later Iron Age hill-forts at Willersey Hill, two miles west, and Meon Hill, some way to the north-east, also show that the area was inhabited from time to time before the Romans arrived. The last Iron-Age people, the Celts, arrived in about 450 BC. There were a number of Celtic tribal groups or kingdoms in Britain: the local clan, whose land stretched from north Somerset up to the borders of Worcestershire, being the Dobunni. Celts lived mainly on farms and in small villages and it is very likely that they settled in the sheltered valley of Campden, though they have left no clear evidence.

Bronze Age socketed axe discovered in Campden. The basal loop would have been used to help in tying the axe-head to the wooden haft. Length 11cm. ***(By kind permission of Cheltenham Art Gallery and Museum)***

There are a number of long-distance trackways in Britain dating from the pre-Roman period, many of them running across high ground. One is the former road running from near Andoversford and passing near Roel, Lynes Barn and Stumps Cross, to the Cross Hands, from where it probably ran down the hill through Broad Campden and on by Ebrington Hill towards Banbury. Another track lies along Kingcombe Lane and on past Meon Hill to a crossing of the Avon at Salford Priors.

At the time of the Roman invasion in AD 43 Britain was a comparatively wealthy place; it was trade as well as expansionism that drew the Romans. They stayed for 400 years, constructing their towns, villas and roads and bringing their own culture to this island. A major Roman road built to control a first century frontier zone is the Fosse Way, which passes Campden about four miles to the east. A later long-distance road passed right through the Campden area. Ryknield Street, parts of which are also known since Saxon times as Buckle Street, runs from Bourton-on-the-Water to Wall in Staffordshire. Until the mid 20th century it formed nearly two miles of the south-western boundary of Campden parish.[vi]

Left: The line of Ryknield Street along the former Campden/Broadway boundary
Right: Roman coffin found in the Kingcombe Lane area c1969, near the site of a probable Romano-British farmstead, and believed to be of the 4th century
(By kind permission of Clive Lockyer)

A scatter of potsherds and the occasional Roman coin picked up in ploughland suggest that there were Roman settlements in Campden. More extensive archaeological study would probably provide more conclusive evidence of this. Two Romano-British farmsteads may have existed in the 2nd and 3rd centuries AD. A Roman villa has been excavated at Ebrington[vii] and more distant settlements are known at Dorn and elsewhere on the Fosse Way. Antiquarian writers mention finds of Roman pottery in the area, and some pottery found in the Kingcombe Lane area was recently identified as Roman.[viii] On the same site in 1969 a local farmer found a coffin dated from the 4th century.[ix] This seems to suggest some form of Roman or Romano-British settlement, probably a Roman Villa or a temple. It may be significant that these finds lie on the Campden—Weston-sub-edge boundary and near the ancient trackway. The remains of a Roman villa are said to have been found near Battle Bridge in the 1840s during the building of the railway,[x] and there are clear signs of another in Broad Campden. All the evidence would point to a fair degree of settlement locally during the Roman period.

With the withdrawal of Roman imperial protection in the 5th century, the Roman villas probably became native Romano-British farms. Left unprotected, these people had to organise their own defences, and they did this partly by the settling of Irish and Saxon mercenaries. Saxon mercenaries were based at Bidford-on-Avon around AD 400: a march of three hours from Campden along Ryknield Street.

Yet Anglo-Saxon settlers took another 200 years to reach this part of the country. This is the most elusive period of British history. The British and later the Saxons reverted to building in timber rather than stone and traces of their buildings have disappeared. However, by the late Anglo-Saxon period the appearance of the northern Cotswold hills may have been very similar to that of later medieval times. The hills had originally been covered with woodland, which was still plentiful in north-eastern Gloucestershire. On the higher parts of the oolitic limestone uplands arable agriculture appears to have given way to a mixture of pastureland and woodland. Sheep-rearing was carried out on the hills by the middle of the Anglo-Saxon period and that hastened the clearance of trees.

The area now covered by most of Worcestershire, Gloucestershire and parts of Warwickshire and Oxfordshire was occupied by a mixed Anglian and Celtic people called the Hwicce. This area was once a separate kingdom but later it became a sub-kingdom and later still just a province of Mercia. A bishopric of the Hwicce was established at Worcester in AD 680 and the bounds of the medieval diocese of Worcester probably show the extent of the Hwiccian kingdom. It is likely that the British people who formed the core of this kingdom had a continuing Christian tradition from late Roman times. However, by the late 7th century Christianity had become established in the Roman rather than the Celtic tradition. Many minsters were established in the diocese of Worcester. Their estates often covered an area much larger than the parishes of modern England. Blockley is a good example of a minster church with a large parish and it is possible that Campden and Ebrington were initially served spiritually by the church at Blockley rather than by their own priests.

By the early 10th century the local administration of justice and the collection of taxes had become the responsibility of the hundreds. The hundreds may also have had a military function, with each being expected to supply a certain number of men for the *fyrd* or army of the king. Campden, and a score of other lay estates, were grouped together to form the rather scattered Witlai Hundred,[xi] which was combined with the neighbouring Chelthorn Hundred during the 11th or 12th century into the early Kiftsgate Hundred, later to be vastly extended. The meeting place of both Witlai and Kiftsgate hundreds was probably at the Kiftsgate Stone just off Kingcombe Lane in Weston Park. It was customary to put such meeting places along areas of 'no mans land' as, for instance, on estate boundaries.

Early English settlement patterns had varied. Frequently a Saxon *ceorl*, or independent farmer, would with his family and retainers occupy a farm of as much as 100 acres (known in the early days as a hide). In other cases a number of families would come together in a small hamlet or village where land would be divided between them. From this developed the typical pattern of settlement during the Anglo-Saxon period. Each estate held by a *thegn* or an earl would have consisted of one or more settlements of agriculturalists paying service to their lord. Many estates locally were held by the church, but Campden seems always to have been in lay hands. By the early 11th century it had come into the hands of probably the most powerful family in England. Godwin, Earl of Wessex, or his son Swein, seems to have acquired Campden about that time. He held it until his death, when it was inherited by Godwin's other son, Harold Godwinson, who later, as King Harold II, was killed at Hastings in 1066.

We know very little about Campden in the late Saxon period. This contrasts with many of the neighbouring parishes. Blockley, Broadway and Willersey for example had been held by Benedictine monasteries for the past two or three hundred years. Monasteries kept close and detailed records, and, for instance, Blockley (held by the Bishop of Worcester) has records that can be traced back to the 9th century, and even places like Willersey (which was held by Evesham Abbey) and Broadway (held by Pershore) have charters from the 10th century in which the extent and the boundaries of the manor are defined.[xii] The manorial records of lay lords, on the other hand, have often disappeared. There is just one reference to Campden before the conquest, in a Mickleton charter dated 1005 giving the bounds of that parish.[xiii] The Mickleton-Campden boundary still runs along the brook behind Hillsdown until it meets the Weston-sub-Edge boundary near Paul's Pike, a point the charter calls *Campsaeten gamaere ac Westham* or 'the boundary of the Camp people and Westham' [the west homestead, now known as Weston-sub-Edge]. This, and a 10th century boundary charter of Broadway, confirm that the boundary of Campden manor in the early 11th century was already set. It remained virtually unchanged as the parish boundary until the mid 20th century.

Probably at that time there were three or four settlements, for instance at Broad Campden, Berrington and Westington, which had been grouped together under one lord, but we have no record of how the manor developed before the Norman Conquest. The estate acquired the name Campden during the Anglo-Saxon period, but even the derivation of the name is not clear. The dene, or *denu* element seems to refer to the steep valley in which Broad Campden brook runs, and it is generally thought that *camp* is a Saxon word derived from the Latin meaning 'enclosure'. Westington is so called as it is the homestead lying to the west of the principal hamlet of [Broad] Campden, and Berrington (or *Byrigton* in its earlier form) is the homestead in the stronghold, or fortified enclosure.

Notes

i Hadfield, Charles & Mary (ed), *The Cotswolds: A New Study* (David & Charles, 1973) Ch 1 passim

ii 'Cam' is a 20th century back formation from 'Campden'. See Smith A.H. *The Placenames of Gloucestershire* (1964) 237-8

iii Noted when testing was being undertaken prior to pile-driving at Noel Court and other sites in Calf Lane

iv CADHAS Archives 2000/067/E. See Hadfield op cit 76-7

v Described as a socketed axe of the late bronze age, of a regional style: the Ewart Park phase. It is now in Cheltenham Museum collection (1944:56). Illustrated in Saville, Alan (ed) *Archaeology in Gloucestershire* Cheltenham Art Gallery & Museum & BGAS (1984) 123

vi Saville, Alan (ed), *Archaeological Sites in the Avon and Gloucestershire* Cotswolds Committee for Rescue Archaeology in Avon, Gloucestershire and Somerset, Survey No. 5 (1980) 15

vii Ball, Stephen 'Ebrington - a Brief History' *CADHAS Notes & Queries Vol II 7-8*

viii Saville op cit 123 & Fig 5

ix *Cotswold Journal* 8th January 1970

x Potter, F.Scarlett, *The Ilmington Hills* 143; Shakespeare Trust Record Office: F.S.Potter Papers Ref ER82/9 and ER87.2

xi By the late Saxon period the church was powerful in this area: the abbey, abbot and monks of Worcester together held as much as 40 per cent of what later became Worcestershire and C.S. Taylor has calculated that by the 8th century about a quarter of Gloucestershire had been granted to the Church. In most parts of the country hundreds were contiguous areas of a number of neighbouring estates. In the northern part of the Hwicce province, however, the church at Worcester had grouped all its many scattered estates into one large triple hundred, known collectively as Oswaldslow. This stretched from Kings Norton in the north, to Blockley, Evenlode and Church Icomb in the south, with many dozens of manors in between. Worcester's example was followed by other local churches, such as Pershore and Deerhurst, so that the hundreds map of the Hwicce province had become very complicated, as also later did the boundaries of counties.

xii e.g. Birch, *Chartae Anglosaxonicae* (BCS) 274 & 482; or Kemble, *Codex Dipl.* (KCD) Vol 3 Appx 274 for Willersey; BCS 1282 or KCD 570 for Broadway

xiii *KCD* 714

PART II: MEDIEVAL CAMPDEN

2

Norman Lords of the Manor

Campden at the time of the Conquest in 1066 was very different from today's bustling town. There were three or four agricultural settlements, each about a mile apart, in the places we now know as Broad Campden, Westington, and Berrington which had probably originally been settled in the early days of Anglo-Saxon settlement. At some time during the Anglo-Saxon period they had been grouped together into one estate under one lordship, under the name Campedene, but they still retained their individual identities. One can imagine groups of wooden houses built on rising land near the brooks in each place, each with its own fields of arable land, its meadows, pastures and woodland, and two of them with large areas of grassland on the top of the hills, used as sheep runs. Where Chipping Campden High Street now stands were either arable fields or meadows sloping down to the brook, probably belonging to the Berrington settlement.

The Domesday Book, compiled in 1086 on the orders of William the Conqueror, provides an indication of Campden's character twenty years after the conquest.[i] The record states that :

> In Witelai hundred. The earl *[Hugh of Chester]* holds Campedene. Earl Harold held it *[before the Conquest]*. There are 15 taxable hides there. In the demesne 6 plough teams; and 50 villeins and 8 bordars with 21 ploughs. There are 12 serfs and 2 mills worth 6s 2d. There are 3 female serfs. It was worth £30, now £20.

Campden at that time was already a fairly important manor. It had the fifth largest population in Gloucestershire.[ii] It is hard to say what the population actually was because only heads of families were enumerated. The 50 villeins were customary tenants tied to the land, and the 8 bordars were small holders; they would all have had families, as probably would the serfs. Some of the villeins could have had servants working for them, too. Also resident in Campden would have been the lord's bailiff and other officers, and probably some labourers would have been working on his demesne lands. Although a market was not established in Campden for another 100 years, a few independent traders and craftsmen were probably living in the hamlets. Altogether, then, the total population in 1086 was probably over 300 souls.

There are indications that the seat of the manor at that time, where the lord and his agents had their residence, was at Broad Campden, then the largest and most important of the three settlements. Berrington, where the manor house was moved a hundred or a hundred and fifty years later, was much smaller.[iii]

As we have seen, in late Saxon times the manor of Campden was held by a powerful absentee lord. This was a fate it was to continue to have for the next two hundred years and more. After the defeat of King Harold at the Battle of Hastings, William granted Campden (and others of Harold's estates) to a Norman earl, Hugh d'Avranches, whom he had made earl of Chester. Hugh was nicknamed Lupus, the Wolf, partly because of the ravages he made in Eastern England during his progress north after the conquest. He was one of the most powerful of William's followers, and held many manors in Cheshire and throughout the Midlands and eastern England. These properties gave him 'numerous peasant tenants scattered over a wide area, while Chipping Campden was an estate of some significance'.[iv] The same authors suggest that his possessions were planned as chains of demesne manors, each one day's drive from the next. Campden is at the end of one chain running from Chester through Macclesfield, Leek, Repton and Coventry to Campden.

Campden had a strategic position at the southernmost end of this trail of manors and was a source of wool and other agricultural produce for the earl. From the late 12th century onwards it was, from time to time, a place where the king stayed during his progressions through England and was no doubt visited rather more often by the earl himself.[v]

Campden was held by the earls of Chester for 165 years, though with a few significant breaks. Being always among the most important magnates in the country, these earls were deeply involved in politics and in the foreign and domestic struggles characteristic of the reigns of the Norman kings, and, although it was so distant from Chester, Campden itself must have been influenced by their activities.

Earl Hugh's son, Richard, the second Norman Earl of Chester, was lost in the White Ship disaster in 1120, when the king's son and many of his companions drowned on their way home from France. Neither of the next two earls seem to have held Campden: a break that may have occurred during the chaos of

Stephen's reign. The Chester earls and the Earl of Gloucester were both involved in the disputes that tore the country apart at that time, sometimes apparently as foes and sometimes as allies, and at some stage Campden seems to have been taken into the hands of the Earl of Gloucester. However, the fourth Chester earl, Ranulf de Guernon, married Gloucester's daughter, and in 1140 that earl granted the manor of Campden to his daughter, thus restoring it firmly to the Chester line.[vi] Indeed, it was excised completely from the Honor of Gloucester, for as late as 1214 the only places in the shire to be specifically excluded from the overlordship of a new Earl of Gloucester were the castle, town and forest of Bristol and the town of Campden.[vii]

One after-effect of the Chester—Gloucester marriage was that in 1150 Combe (where Campden House now stands) was granted to the recently founded abbey of Bordesley, near Redditch. This grant, by Ranulf de Guernon, was confirmed after Ranulf's death by his widow and son and later still by other earls.[viii] Details of Combe's existence under Bordesley are given in Appendix II.

A much more significant break in the tenure of the earls of Chester occurred in 1173 as a result of a rebellion by some English and Breton earls against Henry II. One of the chief rebels was the next earl, Hugh de Kyvelock. The uprising was quickly defeated, Hugh was captured at Dol, and all his lands were, as was usual in such events, taken into the king's hands.[ix] The king did not generally administer such lands himself, and in the case of Campden the manor was held for the king by a man named Hugh de Gondeville.[x]

De Gondeville was an important man in the kingdom: he was 'ranked among the highest in the court'.[xi] During the 1170s he was one of the four tutors of the 'Young King' (Henry II's eldest son).[xii] Without doubt, he did more for the manor in the ten or fifteen years that it was in his charge than the earls of Chester had done in the previous hundred years. In particular, he formalised, if he did not establish, a weekly market and almost certainly began to lay out the site where the town of Chipping Campden now stands, with its burgage plots running back from the wide High Street, and bulging in the centre to take the market stalls. Campden's graduation to the status of a borough probably dates from this time. Unfortunately the first charter has been lost, but it is thought to have been granted about 1185. Hugh de Gondeville's tenure of the manor is also noteworthy in that he founded a new chapel of St Katherine in his manor, endowed it with land and appointed its chaplains.[xiii]

Earl Hugh de Kyvelock was released from prison in 1177 and most of his lands were returned to him[xiv] but for some reason Campden seems to have remained in the hands of the king, at least until Hugh de Gondeville died, somewhere between 1186 and 1189. Earl Hugh's son and successor, Ranulf de Blundeville, seems to have regained possession quietly about 1190. This Ranulf was the most powerful of all the Norman earls of Chester. He has been called variously 'the flower of English chivalry' and 'almost the last relic of the great feudal aristocracy of the Conquest'.[xv] He was Earl of Chester for more than forty years, during four reigns, and he held Campden for most of that time.

Ranulf became active in the Crusades in the 1220s and led at least one campaign.[xvi] No doubt some Campden men were called upon to fight in the Crusades and in some of the other wars of the period.[xvii] But, more significantly, Ranulf further divided Campden. Originally he had been married to Constance, who, as those familiar with Shakespeare's King John will know, was the mother of Prince Arthur, King John's rival for the throne. In 1198 he divorced Constance and married again. As part of the wedding transactions much land was exchanged between Ranulf and his new wife's guardian, a Breton nobleman, William de Feugieres.[xviii] In the course of this, Ranulf, with King John's consent, granted Broad Campden to William, who thereupon granted the land to one of his own knights, Guiomar le Breton, or Brito.[xix] From that time on, for almost four hundred years, Broad Campden was separated from the rest of the manor, although the lords of Broad Campden always paid homage to the lords of Campden[xx].

There was one other short break in Ranulf's tenure of Campden. In May 1204 he borrowed 200 marks (£133) from the king[xxi] as part of a huge ransom demanded for the redemption of the constable of Chester, who had been captured during the wars in France. In return he pledged as surety the manors of Great Tew in Oxfordshire and Campden, both of which were temporarily taken into the king's custody. Once again the king handed Campden over to a third party to hold for him. A letter to the sheriff of Gloucester from King John's justiciar, Geoffrey fitz Peter, reads as follows:

> We command you that you should cause our venerable priest, H. Archbishop of Canterbury, to have the manor of Campden with its appurtenances, because he will answer therefor at our exchequer at our command and at our will.[xxii]

The manor remained in the hands of the archbishop, presumably until the loan had been repaid by Ranulf, or until the amount of the loan had been recovered from the revenues of the two manors. We do not know when that was, but Ranulf appears to have regained Campden in due course and he held it without further interruption until his death in 1232.

So, with a few breaks and with the loss of some parts of the manor, Campden had been held by the one family of Norman lords ever since the Conquest. However, despite his two marriages, Ranulf died without any surviving offspring and so his vast estates had to be divided between the heirs of his four sisters. Campden fell to the son of his second sister, Mabel, the dowager countess of Arundel, whose husband and elder son, the third and fourth earls, had both been killed in the Crusades fighting alongside Ranulf. Campden, together with Barrow-on-Soar in Leicestershire, Coventry, Olney in Buckinghamshire, and, a little later, Leeds, all passed to her younger son, Hugh d'Albini, the fifth Earl of Arundel.

Hugh was still a minor and it was ordered that 'the aforesaid manors be retained in the hands of the king on behalf of the said earl and kept safe'.[xxiii] The king granted the income of Campden 'for the current year at a rent of 100 marks, to wit 50 marks at Easter and 50 marks at Michaelmas' to Walter le Fleming of Southampton.[xxiv] This Walter was a leading citizen of Southampton, the owner of many houses and warehouses there, a merchant and ship owner and a bailiff of the town. One connection between the town and Walter is that Campden was at that time exporting wool to the continent via both Bristol and Southampton. Walter le Fleming's ships often carried wool into France and Italy and brought back wine.

There are incidents that took place a few years earlier which associate Walter with Ranulf de Blundeville. In 1229 the inexperienced King Henry III, under pressure from his nobles in Normandy and Brittany, had mounted a military campaign against the French King, Louis IX. He had assembled a large and enthusiastic army at Portsmouth, but the campaign was frustrated, allegedly because the authorities failed to assemble the necessary transport fleet or to provide other essential supplies. The impetuous young king on the quay at Portsmouth, in the words of an 18th century historian,[xxv] 'branded the minister with the name of traitor and drawing his sword, would have killed him on the spot had it not been for the interposition of the earl of Chester'. In August a ship belonging to Walter le Fleming and carrying a cargo of wool was ordered to be arrested in Jersey and returned immediately to Portsmouth for the service of the king.[xxvi] And in September either this or another of Walter's ships, called 'La Haytee' was requisitioned there for the use of the Earl of Chester in the invasion.[xxvii] Eventually however the whole operation had to be abandoned until the following year.

Hugh d'Albini, only a few years younger than the king, was also a young man in a hurry and wanted to gain control of his lands. In November 1233 the king issued an acknowledgement that Hugh 'has made a fine with the king for 2,050 marks [£1,366] to have seisin [i.e. possession] and tenure of the king, until he is of lawful age, of all the lands and estates' which he had inherited from his brother, and also those 'which were of R. the earl of Chester and Lincoln, his uncle, and which remain in the custody of the king by reason of his age'.[xxviii]

So Walter le Fleming's tenure of Campden only lasted one year. The short tenure did, however, cause one hiccup that seems rather typical of Hugh d'Albini's various transactions. The following letter was written by the king in August 1234:

> The king to Hugh de Albini, greeting. Be it known that when we granted to our beloved and faithful Walter le Fleming the revenues of the manor of Campden we granted it to him with all its appurtenances, and he then received none of the hay *[fenum]* in that manor. A certain servant of yours kept his hay back from him in this, the eighteenth year of our reign, so he declares.
>
> Wherefor we command you that you should make recompense to him for his hay for the aforesaid year, paid for, as much as is due and assized on the men of the borough of Campden; and in the same way with his other arrears you will permit the said Walter to collect them without impediment, nor to have recourse to bring his complaints to us again.[xxix]

The hay referred to was probably not the hay itself but the revenues that the lord would have expected to receive from the crop of hay in his demesne — possibly the assessed revenues of the meadows. Hugh's servants could hardly have allowed the manor to be denuded of the hay crop needed for fodder for that winter.[xxx]

Hugh d'Albini's tenure of Campden was not of long standing: he died ten years later, while still in his twenties. Outside Campden he became rather notorious. He was excommunicated by the Archbishop of Canterbury for hunting with dogs on the Archbishop's lands, and was thus prevented from carrying out his hereditary duties as cup bearer at the queen's coronation,[xxxi] — an honour retained to this day by the Duke of Norfolk and Earl of Arundel. He seems to have been rather litigious, too. Another incident was the attempt, mentioned later, to deprive the Abbot of Chester of the advowson of the church at Campden — one which eventually failed.

Like his uncle before him, Hugh d'Albini died without issue. Once again his estates were divided between the husbands of his four sisters. This time just two estates, Campden and Barrow-on-Soar, fell to his sister Nichola, who had married Sir Roger de Somery.[xxxii] Sir Roger was a favourite of King Henry III.[xxxiii] He already held more than thirty estates and the family's fortune included coal and iron mines in Dudley and, apparently, some early iron works. As a knight he served with the king in campaigns in Wales and 'beyond the seas'. He was richly rewarded for services to the royal cause during and after the rebellion of Simon de Montfort.[xxxiv]

The disposal of his lands and estates after Sir Roger's death in 1273 was a little complicated. Most of his lands were taken into the king's hands until his young son should attain his majority.[xxxv] However, Campden and Barrow, which had come to Sir Roger through his first wife from the Albini inheritance, were treated differently. They were to be inherited in equal portions by Nichola's four surviving daughters, or in effect by their husbands.[xxxvi] So, by a curious coincidence, Sir Roger was the third successive tenant-in-chief of Campden to have his estates inherited by and divided between four female heirs. However, the vast Chester estates had been so reduced by the previous two deaths that when Sir Roger died his inheritance was of only two manors, which were to be divided between four heirs. This division created immediate problems, and Campden, already reduced by the loss of Broad Campden and Combe, was no longer to be a manor in the hands of a single lord. It was to remain shared between two or more tenants-in-chief for the next 250 years and more.

Notes

i Moore, John (ed), *Domesday Book - Gloucestershire* (Phillimore, 1982)

ii Its Domesday population was exceeded only by Gloucester, Winchcombe, Tewkesbury (which already had a market) and the royal manor of Thornbury.

iii For a discussion of this point, see Warmington, 'Where is Campden?', *CADHAS Notes & Queries IV 1, 11*

iv Davies, R.H.C. & Barraclough, G., 'The Earldom of Chester & its Charters', *Jnl of Chester*

Arch. Soc, Vol 71 1991 55-57. The reference to Chipping Campden is rather anachronistic. "Chipping" was not applied to the borough until the 13th century. Earl Hugh held other manors in Gloucestershire, including Bisley and Westonbirt.

v Lewis, C.P., 'On the formation of the Honor of Chester' : *Jnl of Chester Arch. Soc, Vol 71* 1991 45: states that 31 per cent of tax assessments from Earl Hugh's lands came from King Harold's estates; 11 manors (including Campden) had been worth more than £15 before the Conquest.

vi For a discussion of this problem, see Davies & Barraclough, op cit 33

vii Hardy, T.D. (ed): *Rotuli Litteratum Clausarum* (Records Commission 1833) 10 John; and Barnes, P.M. and Slade, C.F., *A Medieval Miscellany for D.M. Stenton* (Pipe Roll Soc NS6, 26)

viii Dugdale, *Monasticon Anglicanum* (ed Caley, Ellis & Bandinel) Vol V 140ff.

ix See Stubbs, W. (ed), *Chronica Rogeri de Hovendon* (Rolls Series, 1869) Vol II 51ff; Stubbs, W., (ed): *Gesta Regis Henrici Secundi* (1867) Vol I 57.

x There are some difficulties in saying exactly who Hugh de Gondeville was. There seem to have been three or four men living in the 12th and early 13th centuries who bore this name — possibly all members of the same family. Our de Gondeville seems to have been the most renowned of them.

xi Warren, W.L., *Henry II* (London 1973)

xii Both Rushen and Whitfield rather libel de Gondeville by associating him with the murder of Thomas à Beckett. This seems unlikely. The only reference to him in relation to Thomas is in about 1165, after Thomas had gone to Flanders and France to be received by King Louis. Louis, as a means of gaining an advantage over the English king, recommended Thomas to the Pope. King Henry II thereupon sent a delegation to make representations to the Pope. The delegation included the Archbishop of York, four bishops, and eight others, including Hugh de Gondeville. The mission was not successful as the Pope avoided either meeting it or appointing a legate to meet it.

xiii *Register Wulstan* Vol I, fol 121a

xiv Warren, W.L., op cit; and W.Stubbs (ed): *Chronica Magistri Rogeri de Hovedene*, Vol II 118

xv Stephens, L. (ed), *Dictionary of National Biography* (London 1881) Vol V 267

xvi Ormerod , George, *A History of the County Palatinate and City of Chester* (London 1819) Vol I 27, 33-41

xvii There is no direct evidence of Campden men serving in the Crusades during de Blundeville's time, but in 1275 *Reg. Giffard* includes a letter from the Bishop of Worcester referring to William Calf and Richard and William Pope, Crusaders 'who are much troubled by Julian of Campden'.

xviii Ormerod, op cit 38-41

xix Hardy, T.D. (ed), *Rotuli chartarum in Turri Londonensis* (Records Commission London 1837); 1 John, 1199, 21

xx For some details of Broad Campden's succession during its separation from the rest of Campden, see Appendix II

xxi Hardy, T.D. (ed), *Rotuli de Liberate* (London 1844); 5 John 29 May 1204 .103

xxii *Rot Litt Claus* 5 John 14b; *Calendar of Patent Rolls* (Records Commission 60 Vols) 6 John m12. (p 9) *(de terris normanie datis)*. Possibly connected with this is a letter the king wrote the same year to Hugh de Nevill, his justice of the forests, saying he had released the Earl of Chester from paying 25 marks that Nevill had exacted from his men of Campden 'for a certain amercement *[fine]* of the forest' and commanded him to free Ranulf from the debt. *Rot.Litt. Claus.* 6 John memb 21 (1204) 1

xxiii *Close Rolls* (HMSO 6 vols 1900-1937) 22nd November 1232

xxiv *Cal Pat Rolls* 1232 m9 dated 24th November

xxv Russel, W.A., *A New and Authentic History of England* 168

xxvi *Close Rolls*, 13 Henry III m6

xxvii *Close Rolls*, 13 Henry III 1229 m4d

xxviii *Excerpta e Rotuli Finum* (HMSO) 18 Henry III m11 (1233)

xxix *Close Rolls* 1234

xxx This letter makes a curious distinction between the manor of Campden, the whole of which had been held by Walter, and the borough, whose burgesses were to make good the debt to him. It is difficult to explain why this was.

xxxi See Stenton, D.M., *English Society in the Early Middle Ages* (Penguin Books) 29 For a full description see *Red Book of the Exchequer* Vol 2; 758 *'de servitus magnatum in die coronationis Regis et Reginae'*

xxxii See *Close Rolls* 27 Hy III, pt II, (1243) 100; 116; *Close Rolls* 1244 248-252; *Cal Pat Rolls* 1243 Nov 27 408

xxxiii See for instance *Close Rolls* 1266, 211, where he is given two stags from Kinver Forest; p267 where the king grants him 40 oaks for timber for the damages which he sustained in the service of the king; and 273 where he is pardoned a debt of £100 owed to the exchequer. He was one of six people (together with the Bishops of Exeter, Bath and Worcester and others) charged with 'procuring what is deemed necessary for the reformation of the peace of the land' and to decide what was to happen to the estates of those disinherited as a result of the war.

xxxiv Roger and Nichola had a number of offspring. We cannot be sure how many, but we know that Nichola gave him at least four daughters. Further, it appears from a document in the *Patent Rolls* of Henry III in 1257 that they had sons. The document testifies that 'Walter, son of Roger de Somery, lost his left ear by some evildoer in the forest of Clarendon, and not on account of any felony'. There is no other trace of Walter in the printed records, apart from this certificate of good character and he seems to have died before his father. There are other documents in the *Close Rolls* of 1261 and 1262 referring to Ralph, son and heir of Roger de Somery 'recently deceased'. Nichola also died, some time after 1243. Sir Roger then married again. By his second wife, Amabel, a widow, he had a young son, Roger junior, who was still a minor when his father died, in 1273.

xxxv C. Roberts (ed), Cal. *Genealogicum* (HMSO 1865 2 vols Hy III & Edw I) 1 Edw I 196; *Cal Close Rolls* (HMSO 40 vols 1900 - 1937) 1 Edw I, Memb 3; Memb 11; 2 Edw I Memb 1

xxxvi *Cal. Genealogicum* 55 Hy III, 151; & 1 Edw I 196

3

Everyday Life: 1066 - 1300

In the first two hundred years after the Conquest conditions of life in England changed radically. Population increased rapidly, housing and diets improved, and farm crops were modified. The Saxon system of serfdom, where a minority of men were tied strictly to one lord, was replaced, some serfs gaining the status of small customary tenants while others became paid labourers working on the lord's demesne. At the time of the Conquest most peasants in the Campden hamlets probably lived in single storey wood-framed and thatched houses, not very substantial, with earth floors, each on its own small plot of land, and surrounded by farm buildings to house the crops and animals. Their diets would have consisted mainly of rye bread, potages of peas, beans and oats, together with vegetables from their garden plots, dairy produce and only the occasional dish of meat. The main drink was locally brewed beer.[i]

Westington Forge, an example of a medieval cottage, demolished in the late 20th century
(Jesse Taylor/G of H Trust)

Between the 11th and 13th centuries wheat began to replace oats and rye; the wood framed houses, filled in with wattle and daub, began to be built on more solid stone foundations, and most houses in Westington and Berrington would have been of three 'bays' measuring about fifteen feet by forty five feet, accompanied by storage barns and sheds for the animals. By the late 13th century some of the more prosperous peasants' houses were being built of stone up to the rafters. A hundred years later a few two-storey houses may have begun to appear in the hamlets. An example of a stone 13th or 14th century house was the cottage and forge in Westington, demolished in the last years of the 20th century.

Patterns of agriculture had not changed much since Anglo-Saxon times. Each peasant family had between fifteen and thirty acres of land in strips of about an acre each, scattered in the fields around each settlement, half of them lying fallow and the rest growing cereals and pulses in a pattern strictly controlled by the community. Families were tied to their pieces of land by customary rules and each family was required to provide up to three man-days of labour each week (more at harvest time) on the lord's demesnes. Life in the hamlets was physically hard, but as prosperity increased some labour dues began to be commuted to money payments made to the lord.

Apart from the two large arable fields in each hamlet, there were hay meadows near the streams on the boundaries with Ebrington and Paxford. There were pastures where cows and oxen grazed, and much woodland producing timber for housebuilding, fencing, and firewood. Finally, on the extensive grass lands on the hills, sheep, many owned by the lord and others by peasants, grazed in summer, to be brought down during the winter into sheep cotes or to graze on the fallow, thus manuring it for the next season.

But the most striking change occurred in the late 12th century, with the enterprising lordship of Hugh de Gondeville. No doubt during the century after the Conquest groups of traders and craftsmen had come to Campden and the manor was already becoming a centre of local trade for the smaller manors round about.[ii] Hugh finally established a weekly market in about 1185, and with it came in merchants and artisans, many from a distance, to trade and to settle.

The formal establishment of the borough and the laying out of the town meant a revolution in the way of life in Campden. Up to the early 12th century the church, the manor house and lord's court were probably at Broad Campden; there were a few craftsmen in each hamlet, who, as well as farming, could erect or thatch a house, weave cloth, sew a coat, make a plough or forge an axehead. Now the new town had been planned and built, with its main street on the slope above, and running parallel to, the brook between Westington and Berrington, and intruding into Berrington settlement. The town street, made wide enough to accommodate stalls on market days, may at first have been shorter than it is today, but eventually it ran from today's Sheep Street corner as far as the pool that stood at the bottom of Church Street. On the top side of the street narrow plots, known as burgage plots, were laid out, running back as far as the slopes of Hoo Field and occupied, subject to customary rents and services, by merchants and artisans who had the status of burgesses, or townspeople with full rights to practise their trade. Other, smaller, plots were developed on the lower side of the street, running down towards the brook.

Chipping Campden from the air, 2001. The original town plan consisting of a broad high street and burgage plots laid out in the late 12th century can still be discerned.
(A Commission Air photograph. By kind permission of the Campden Society)

This completely altered the complexion of Campden and by 1200 the town had begun to take on the physical structure it has to this day. The peasants now formed only a minority of the inhabitants of the manor and had suffered some rearrangement of their land. Berrington in particular suffered by the intrusion of the market so close to its settlement. The establishment of the new town shifted the manor's focus from Broad Campden to the borough. The lord's court, and with it the church, moved to a prominent site above the town in Berrington. This made it easy for Ranulf de Blundeville, a few years after he had regained Campden, to grant Broad Campden away to the guardian of his new wife.[iii]

Most of the houses in the new town would still have been wood framed and thatched, though quite soon some of the richer merchants may have been building in stone. There was a change in the kind of people who lived in the borough, too — often incomers: merchants or craftsmen, making their living by buying or selling, baking, brewing, weaving or practising other non-agricultural crafts. Some owned smallholdings known as crofts, or orchards, and one or two had agricultural land in Westington as well. Moreover, these new people had many more freedoms than the peasants beside whom they were living.

No 12th century charter has ever been found, but its existence is confirmed by the grant in 1216 to Ranulf de Blundeville of an annual three-day fair in the town on St James's Day (25th July) and the next two days.[iv] In 1247, soon after Roger de Somery became lord of Campden, a charter of King Henry III[v] granted him and his heirs free warren (the right to take game) in his demesne lands in Campden with a weekly market at Campden and the same yearly fair. More formally, in 1249 Henry issued a confirmation of the 12th century grant of the borough, reading as follows :

> Letters Patent confirming: the grant that Hugh de Gundevill made to the burgesses of Campeden concerning their burgages in the borough of Campeden and the grant that Ranulfus sometime earl of Chester made to the same burgesses, that they and all who should come to the market of Campeden should be quit of toll, and that if any of his free burgesses of Campeden should fall into his mercy he should be quit for twelve pence unless he should have caused bloodshed or felony.
>
> And the grant that Roger de Sumery has made to the aforesaid burgesses there that they and their heirs and all those who come to the market and fair of Campeden should be quit for ever of all kinds of tolls and customs pertaining to the said market and the said fair and that they should have

for ever the same liberty from tolls and customs pertaining to the aforesaid market and the said fair as they had in the time of the aforesaid earl.[vi]

So a burgess, once established in the borough of Campden and paying a small rent of a few pence a year, had the liberty to carry out his trade free of all tolls, and the maximum amount the lord could fine a burgess in his own court was 12d. A second fair, on the eve, the feast and the morrow of St George's Day (23rd April), was to be granted by Edward III in 1360 or 1361.[vii]

The lord's rule in Campden, so distant from Chester, may have been fairly tolerant. However, the inhabitants of the town and manor were subject to his court for rents, local taxes and other dues, for the regulation of labour services and the occupation of land. Penalties could be imposed for breaches of these customs — limited in the borough, as we have seen, to 12d. There was indeed a system of mutual obligation, the tenants owing rents and services to the lord, while the lord's rights were also restricted by custom.

The lord was represented by his steward or bailiff who collected the rents and other dues, organised the work on the demesne and presided at the lord's court. There would have been a number of other officers around him, some of them local men, some drawn from Chester, as well as servants about the household. The lord held demesne lands which he farmed himself, and which in Campden seem to have lain separately from the peasants' open fields, and consisted of some 300 acres of land, possibly running along the east side of the brook from near Westington towards the Paxford boundary.

For offences other than those dealt with by the lord, the judicial system was quite sophisticated. For minor offences, such as assaults or petty thefts, there was the hundred court, where cases from about a dozen manors were disposed of, traditionally at the Kiftsgate Stone in Weston Park. This was presided over by the sheriff or one of his officers, with judgments given by a jury of twelve local worthies. For example, in a 14th century case tried in Kiftsgate Hundred and dated about 1361, the jury found that Richard Cantare of Caumpeden 'by force of arms at Caumpeden unjustly seized and carried away 6 horses and 1 cart value 100 shillings from Adam Plays against the peace'.[viii]

The king's court, meeting in Gloucester or Worcester under one of the king's itinerant justices, would try the more serious cases, up to and including murder. In Gloucester in 1221 it was found that Reginald Rug, a thief, had killed another thief in the field of Campden. He had fled but was then hanged for another offence. In another case Ralph Walensis had killed Hugh Pondevske and fled.

He was sentenced to be outlawed but it was testified that he had died.[ix] In the same year Thomas de la Hethe was taken by indictment for thefts and other evil deeds. The jurors found that he had sheltered Howe Golightly, a known thief who had been hanged at Campden, and that he had stolen sheep and plough beasts and other things. He was sentenced to hang.[x] In 1257 Patrick of Campeden was held in prison in Gloucester for 'the death of two strangers found in the field of Mikleton'.[xi] Even the wealthy freeman William of Westington was accused of murder in 1267 by 'certain of his rivals' but after an inquiry set up by the king he was found not to be guilty.[xii]

Cases of national concern and much civil litigation would be heard in the King's Bench Division in London. Commonly cases are reported of widows coming to court to secure a proportion of their husband's land as dower. In the mid 13th century Earl Ranulph de Blundeville disputed with the abbot of Pershore over a common pasture called Coteswand or Codeswaud [Cotswold] on the border between Campden and Broadway — a dispute which led to the king ordering a perambulation of the border by the sheriffs of Gloucestershire and Worcestershire and the defining of the boundary between the two places along a ditch called Meredich.[xiii] During the lordship of Sir Roger de Somery another perambulation of the same area took place and the sheriffs were to report to the justices at the next assizes.[xiv]

Not that everything was ruled by law. There were frequent revolts and rebellions, not only of the aristocracy but also of common people. In 1233 a revolt of barons in the west of England against the appointment of a new justiciar led King Henry III to send an army to suppress it. In August that year parties of armed men from Herefordshire seem to have been roaming in the vicinity of Campden, and letters were written by the king warning the bailiffs of Gloucestershire and neighbouring counties to prepare for a visit of the king and his army to Gloucester.[xv] He also wrote letters stating that 'armed people were roaming through the county of Gloucestershire' and the sheriff was commanded that all men of the hundreds of Winchcombe and of Slaughter who were sworn to arms ... should come to Campden, and others to Cirencester, 'in such a way that no-one goes through those towns armed but that with their horses and harness they should be arrested and safely detained. And, if it is not possible to arrest the said men they should raise a hue and cry and they should be followed from town to town until they are so arrested.'[xvi]

The 'hue and cry', or pursuit and capture of the felons by the people, seems to have been successful for later the same month the king wrote to the sheriff of Gloucester saying that twelve men, many bearing Herefordshire names, 'taken and detained in our prison at Gloucester, who were found in part of Kampeden bearing arms amongst themselves against our peace, have found for us ... pledges from the county of Hereford', and they were to be released.[xvii]

However, such events were exceptional, and for the most part Campden people lived quietly, working on the land, or trading or practising their crafts in the borough.

Following Sir Roger de Somery's death in 1273, detailed inquisitions were made into the part of Campden he had held. Local juries sat and produced breakdowns of all the inhabitants, the sources of income and the division of the revenues and services among the four heirs.[xviii] These inquisitions mean that today we have a vivid picture of Campden in the late 13th century. The surveys list between 135 and 140 households, representing a population of perhaps 600 or 700.[xix] The population had changed in character since the Domesday survey almost 200 years earlier. Relative stagnation in the tied agricultural population had been accompanied by a flourishing of commercial activities and the establishment of the large trading population in the new town.

Sir Roger's demesne consisted of his own house (said to be only partly built), with its garden and a dovecote, about 320 acres of arable land, 20 acres of demesne meadow and 70 acres of copse or spinney, a fishpond, and three and a half mills. The lord also had the right to have 1,000 sheep on the common pasture. The annual value of the whole of the demesne was calculated to be £29 11s 6d. Meadows, with the hay they produced for feeding cattle in winter, were obviously valuable and the land was valued at 2s an acre as compared with only 4d an acre for arable land. The copse, or spinney, was the area where timber and firewood could be gathered and pigs and possibly cows would be put to graze. The three mills were probably even then on the sites of Westington Mill, the Town Mill off Calf Lane and Berrington Mill. The half mill could possibly have been on the site of the present Silk Mill, which had a mill pool attached right up to the beginning of the 19th century.

The most likely location for the lord's new house would seem to be the knoll in Berrington near where Sir Baptist Hicks built his own magnificent house in the 17th century. This may be confirmed by the fact that a hundred years after this survey one of the lords of Campden, Thomas de Lodelowe, was resident in Berrington. From a later reference, too, it seems probable that this new or rebuilt manor house was adjacent to the Chapel of St Katherine founded nearly a hundred years earlier by de Gondeville: an inquisition on the death of one of the earls of Gloucester who held part of Campden refers to 'the chapel of St Katherine in the court of the lords of Campden'.[xx]

What of the rest of the population? There were just three free tenants in 1273: William of Westington, William Calf and Robert Caspy, all occupying land in Westington, each of them paying suit at the lord's court once a year and paying quarterly dues in respect of the land they occupied. The rents they paid varied: William of Westington paid 12s a year for two virgates (60 to 65 acres) he held 'by charter',[xxi] William Calf paid 3s and half a pound of pepper, also for two virgates, and Robert Caspy half a pound of pepper for one virgate and a croft. The payment of pepper — the origin of the term 'peppercorn rent' — shows how valuable a commodity it was in those days, and it may indicate the trading activities of those two men. Presumably these men were relatively free to move as they wished, and their obligations to the lord were correspondingly light. By medieval standards people like William of Westington would have been prosperous and influential members of society, with servants to work their land and provide for them. William Calf and Robert Caspy also held rich burgages in the borough and were probably merchants. They would also have had responsibilities in town, hundred and shire. Both regularly served on the juries of Kiftsgate Hundred, especially for matters concerning the villages immediately around Campden.[xxii]

Five other free men occupied burgages or messuages [houses] 'of the manor of Campden' in the more ancient boroughs of Winchcombe and Gloucester; one was Richard the Provost — possibly the provost or reeve of Campden, who superintended the work of the manor.

The hamlets were mainly populated by the customary tenants, the successors of Domesday's villeins. These people worked the land with their families. There were 22 such tenants in 'Westington-on-the-Wold', most of them holding one virgate (about 30 acres) of land, scattered in strips. There were 13 customary tenants, mainly with smaller holdings, in 'Byriton-in-the-Marsh'. Each was required to pay the following in money or in labour services, for each virgate he held:

> Money payment *[rent]* by the year 4.6d; certain works between the Nativity of St John the Baptist *[24th June]* and the feast of St Michael *[29th September]*, to the value of 6s 2d; three ploughings made for the lord, value 1d each; six bedreps *[reaping services]* made in the Autumn valued at 1 1/2d each; tallage *[tax]* paid in addition, which, for the 'average' tenant, in 'common' years was reckoned at 1s 8d, though they may be taxed at the will of the lord.

So the value to the lord of the works and payments a tenant made was 13s 4d for each virgate he held. Then there were other payments, for instance a fine on marriage, and maybe a heriot (the gift of a beast paid to the lord by the heir on death). In addition the church took its tithes and payments for such events as funerals. To pay these dues, and to buy clothes and other necessities, he would have had to sell some of his produce or do further work for wages.

Altogether these customary tenants, or customars, held 31 virgates of arable land (somewhere about 950 acres, 680 in Westington and 270 in Berrington). So, with casual proceeds the lord got a little under £21 in revenues and services from customars. The obligations owed by these thirty-five householders were onerous, as can be judged from information in a later inquisition. For when a later lord of Campden, John de Lodelowe, died in 1295, the duties of the customary tenants were set out in more detail:[xxiii]

> And each virgate ought to work from the feast of St John the Baptist up to the feast of St Michael for four days in the week, viz. Monday, Tuesday, Wednesday and Thursday, unless feast days intervene when they shall happen; and the work of each virgate is worth 5s; price of each day's work from the feast of St John the Baptist up to the Gule of August 1d, and from the said day up to the feast of St Michael, 1 1/2d...

So up to 52 days of labour were due to the lord each summer from each tenant who held a virgate. In addition there were ploughing and harvesting services to be done in autumn and winter. Each virgate still paid 4s 6d a year rent in 1295. However, by 1314 the amount of labour services owed and their value was somewhat reduced.[xxiv] Then each villein had to pay 4s a year in rent and undertake 42 days of manual work and two bederepes or harvesting services. Life was hard for a peasant in those days, especially one with a small family: the larger the family, the more labour was available to work one's own land as well as the lord's demesne.

Further down the scale were smallholders. Compared with the four 'bordars' in the Domesday survey, just two 'cottars' are recorded in Campden in 1273, one of them paying 16d and the other 8d each year. Nothing is known of these two but their names: Emma the Gardener and Alexander Mire.

The holders of burgages and messuages in the borough were much freer of obligations to their lord than the customary tenants. Their rents and other obligations were light, though they were liable to be assessed from time to time for other dues. They were also liable to fines for breaches of commercial regulations or for other misdemeanours, and presumably they had to pay for the privilege of taking up a burgage in the first place. The borough was already a self-regulating institution and the more important burgesses would have been much involved in its administration, as they certainly were in the administration of the hundred and county.

The majority of Campdonians, even in 1273, were attached to the borough rather than the manor. About one hundred such people are recorded. The jurors calculated that these hundred people held 75½ burgages and 21 messuages. Rents varied, though most of the full burgages paid between 10d and 20d a year, the messuages a few pence only. Altogether these holdings were valued at £4 15s 10d a year, plus one pound of cummin (another spice that, like pepper, was valuable enough to be acceptable as rent). In addition there were 40s worth of incidental payments. So, from the point of view solely of direct revenue, the borough with 100 burgesses was far less valuable to the lord than the manor with its 35 customars.

Most burgesses were probably traders, shop-keepers and craftsmen. According to the surveys, five of them held shops or stalls and one held a 'holte' or enclosure — possibly a piece of woodland. Some burgesses may have been more in the nature of agricultural smallholders than of urban traders or craftsmen. Those like William Calf or Robert Caspy, who, as we have seen, held agricultural tenancies in Westington as well as the most valuable burgages, were no doubt wool, corn or cloth merchants rather than petty traders. Those with stalls or booths seem more likely to have been small market traders.

To make up the whole population there were the lord's bailiff and his officers, servants and labourers. The free tenants and larger burgesses at least would have had servants, as would some of the more prosperous peasants. There would also have been a few labourers living in the borough.

As would be expected, the borough had many people from outside Campden; not only from local villages like Alice of Badsey, Robert of Aston, Walter of

Blockley, William of Saintbury and Cecilia of Ilmington, but names of more distant places like John de Lyneham, William de Monmouth, and William de Bello Loco [Beaulieu?]. Some families in the borough seem to have originated outside England, like the Frauncevs, the Quincys and possibly Fressant. Was this the influence of the wool trade?

There are disappointingly few occupational names in the borough but a number of office-bearers can be identified. Henry the Clerk (of the market) who would have been in charge of weights and measures and general market regulation, Geoffrey the Bedell would have been the messenger or town crier, and Robert the Messer may have been in charge of the market place. In Westington and Berrington there were the cottar, Emma the Gardener (celebrated, no doubt, for growing vegetables), Richard the Smith and two 'le Messers', one of whom had become 'the Hayward' by the time of the later surveys. In agricultural settlements, the messer held a minor office of ensuring the security of the fields and meadows and may have assisted the hayward who was in charge of fences and enclosures.

The tenants in the hamlets were tied to their land, but among them were incomers from neighbouring villages. In Berrington lived Robert of Quinton and Richard of Norton, and in Westington there were Walter of Condicote, Richard of Brailes and William of Tyw (Great Tew in Oxfordshire which had been held by Ranulf de Blundeville). The character of the two hamlets is reflected in the names of some of the tenants. So Westington-on-the-Wold had a Gilbert by-the-Grove and Geoffrey by-the-Elm, whereas Berrington-in-the-Marsh had Thomas by-the-Slough and Alexander Mire. Other peasants' names, like Sparrowhawk, Partridge and Russell [the redhead] are nicknames descriptive of those men or their forebears.

So we have a picture of everyday life in Campden two hundred years after the Conquest. The borough was growing in prosperity and importance and outsiders were coming in to trade. The people in the hamlets were also becoming richer, though being tied to the land they were much more stable than the borough population. Campden was not, however, a closed community and some effects of contact with life outside will now be looked at.

Notes

i Many of the facts in the next few pages have been drawn from Dyer, Christopher, *Making a Living in the Middle Ages* (Yale UP, 2001) Chapters 4 - 6.

ii For instance the charter granting land to the new chapel of St Katherine includes one piece of land running from 'the messuage of Serlo the Cook to the house of Herbert Salins deacon of the mother church'. This would appear to indicate a street already laid out.

iii *Rotuli Chartarum in Turri Londinensis* 1 John, 1199, 21. Although now separated from the rest of Campden, the village, first as Little *(Parva)* Campeden, and later Brode Campeden, retained its original cognomen.

iv *Rot Litt Clausarum*, 1216 2 Hy III 361

v *Cal. Charter Rolls* (HMSO 6 vols,1903-1927) 31 Hy III m3, 1247 (251)

vi *Cal. Charter Rolls* 33 Henry III memb 4 (1249) (47)

vii *Cal. Charter Rolls* 34-35 Edw III Mem 6; May 26 (166)

viii *Gloucs Peace Rolls* 1361-68 60 & 77

ix Maitland, F.W. (ed), *Pleas of the Crown for the Country of Gloucs* 1221 (HMSO 1884)- Villata de Campeden 21 & 23

x Selsdon Assoc Series Vol 59 1221-2 No. 767

xi *Close Rolls* 1257 m 15

xii *Cal Patent Rolls* 1267 117 and 158

xiii *Curia Regis Rolls* 1224 No 2403 & 1330 No 4; Castle Ashby Archive op cit Deed No 1; Feet of Fines No 164, 8th June 1225

xiv *Close Rolls* 1254-5 39 Henry III m14d. (183)

xv *Close Rolls* 1233 317

xvi ibid 3rd August 313

xvii ibid 24th August 251

xviii See *Cal Chan Inq p.m.* 1 Edw I, No 15; *Chan Inq p.m.* 1 Edw I No 48A; *Cal Close Rolls*, 2 Edw I, Memb 10. A 16th century copy of the first of these inquisitions is on display in the Court Room at the Police Station, Campden.

xix These surveys exclude Broad Campden and Combe, which had been granted away by earlier lords.

xx *Chan Inq p.m.* 8 Edw II No 68. Madge, S.J. (ed), *Abstracts of Inq. post mortem for Gloucestershire* pt IV 142 (inquisition at Tewkesbury on death of Gilbert de Clare the Younger). The whereabouts of the chapel is confirmed in the proceedings of a court case in 1612, where Lionel Cranfield refers to 'one other parcell of grounde whereon a chapell some tyme was buylt, lyinge neare the mannor house of Campden aforesaid'. (See Whitfield, Christopher , 'Lionel Cranfield and the Rectory of Campden' *BGAS Trans. 1962* Vol lxxxi 112 and 115)

xxi In *Cal Charter Rolls* 45 Henry III (30th January 1260/1) William de Radingis, king's sergeant, and his heirs are granted 'the land at Westinton, co. Hampshire, which he previously held of the king's bail for life'. There does not appear to be a Westington in Hampshire, and this may be the charter concerned.

xxii William Calf, for instance, sat on inquisitions into the death of Ralph Musard of Saintury in 1273, and of John le Strange in 1276. Robert Caspy sat on two inquisitions into Ralph Musard's death in 1273, and into Henry de Penebrigge and Walter Giffard, Archbishop of York, both of Weston sub Edge, in 1279. (See Madge,S.J.,; op cit)

xxiii *Chan inq.p.m.* 23 Edw I No 29; .Madge, S.J (op cit) Pt IV 167-8

xxiv *Chan inq.p.m.* 35 Edw I No 47 and 8 Edw II No 68

4

1300 - 1540: Disease, Division, Dishonesty

From the early 14th century, after two hundred years of prosperity and growth, things began to change. A series of bad harvests was followed in the 1340s by the onset of the Black Death. Right through till the 15th century high death rates and falling crop yields led to social and economic disruption and increased poverty. The economy stagnated and population fell. Although the borough seems to have maintained its prosperity as the wool trade grew, the dramatic effect of the Black Death can be seen in a fall in the amount of land that was in cultivation and a corresponding fall in the value of the whole manor.[i] It can also be detected in the succession of the lordships of Campden. From the middle of the 14th, and particularly in the 15th century, the tenants-in-chief tended to die young and to leave small children as heirs. No doubt this trend was even more pronounced in the general population.

However, what was tragedy for some families was opportunity for others, and there grew up during the 14th and 15th centuries a group of wealthy yeomen who, together with the tradesmen and merchants in the borough, took advantage of the slackening hold of the lords and the growing freedom of the market to accumulate wealth. Feudal society was breaking down and relationships were freeing up. From the 15th century onwards most lords and many merchants gained the right to entail their houses and lands in favour of their elder sons, and other land began to be exchanged freely by sale or lease between individuals. Whatever the effects of climate and disease on agriculture, the prosperity of the borough, and therefore of Campden taken as a whole, benefited from the new conditions, and by the middle of the 15th century there were a number of very prosperous figures trading in the town.

For some 250 years after the death of Sir Roger de Somery Campden was divided and held by a succession of minor lords. At the inquisitions on Sir Roger's death in 1273 the jurors went to great trouble to divide his estate equally between the four heirs. The jurors calculated the annual value of Campden to be £61 4s 03/4d and the share allocated to each tenant was calculated to be £15 6s 01/4d. Each heir was to receive a quarter of the annual value of the messuage, garden and dovecote and of the rest of the demesne. In the manor each was made lord over a certain number of named tenants. Likewise in the borough the rents from burgesses were allocated in such a way that equality in revenue was achieved.

Of Sir Roger's four successors, Sir John le Strange, who died in 1275, soon after succeeding, was a member of an important marcher family and held many lands in Shropshire and in Norfolk.[ii] Henry de Erdington's family, according to Canon Bartleet[iii], had for generations been tenants in the de Somery's Erdington manor. He seems to have been related to Egidius de Erdington, a Justice in Eyre, or circuit judge.[iv] Henry, however, gave up his lordship of Campden very soon after succeeding to it.

Walter de Sully seems to have been an associate of the earls of Gloucester.[v] He died in 1286 and although his son Raymond did homage for all his father's lands,[vi] Gilbert de Clare, then Earl of Gloucester, later claimed and gained possession of this portion of Campden.[vii] Finally, Sir Ralph de Crumwell was one of Sir Roger's executors and the husband of his eldest daughter. Little other information is to be found on him. Like le Strange he seems to have been abroad when he succeeded.[iii]

As is only to be expected, the succession of Campden over the next three hundred years is somewhat complicated. Briefly, by 1286 one half of the manor was in the hands of one Sir John de Lodelowe. Lodelowe and his descendants were wool merchants; and their descendants remained lords of this half of the manor for the next 200 years. Through a complicated series of successions the other half came to be held by Sir Richard Stafford in 1347, and from then on Campden was divided into these two moieties: the Lodelowe (or Ludlow) manor and the Stafford manor, until in the 16th century it was reunited under Sir Thomas Smyth. Further details of the succession from 1273 to 1544 are given in Appendix I.

Education developed throughout this period. From the 13th century onwards the influence of the Church and of Chester Abbey in particular, may have created a number of educated Campden men. In the late 13th and early 14th centuries a number of townspeople, including Hugh Proude, Roger Faytur, William Calf and Thomas Fraunceys, all of whose families were recorded as burgesses in the 1273 surveys, were ordained as sub-deacons and often promoted to become deacons or priests. Whether they were trained in Campden by a local rector or in Worcester or Chester we cannot know.

A considerable number of men with the surname Campeden became chaplains, parsons or clerks in different parts of the country. To take just two names, Master Henry of Campeden, Rector of Grimsby, was given wine and robes by Henry III and is described in 1253 as the king's physician.[ix] He was clearly a Campden man as after his death his daughter, Isabella, claimed land in Campden (presumably Broad Campden) against Robert Russell.[x] And Walter de Campeden, who seems to have been a favourite of Edward III's Queen, Philippa of Hainault, was made a guardian of the young John of Gaunt and his brother in 1356.[xi] Ten years later, when John, now Duke of Lancaster, went to Gascony with an army, Walter was one of those responsible for any debts he incurred,[xii] and some years later still, Walter, along with the Bishop of Winchester, the Bishop of London, the Earl of Arundel and others, were to have the keeping of all John's castles for one year should he die.[xiii] Several score other men surnamed Campeden held churches in many parts of the country at this time. Some of these at least were Campden natives. Others may have been monks at Chester who had taken on the surname Campeden.

Despite these evidences of education there is no positive record of any school in Campden until some time about 1440, when John Fereby, or Feryby, a Citizen of London and Commissioner of the Peace for the county of Surrey, and Margery his wife, granted lands at Lynham near Shipton- under-Wychwood for the purpose of establishing a 'ffreeschole' in Campden. Any other connection between John Fereby and Campden is unknown, though it has been suggested that he was born nearby. Most of the references to him are in connection with London or Surrey.[xiv] He died in late 1441 and among the lands left to his wife were 'Hunchewyke [Hinchwick], Maresden [Marston?] and Codesdon [Cutsdean]' in the county of Gloucester. No contemporary documentation about the founding of the school subsists, but it is generally accepted that his lifetime grant was for the foundation of Campden Grammar School and that it was established from the beginning on the site of the old Grammar School building in High Street.

There was contact with life outside Campden, not least through the administration of justice. Among the problems the manor faced was, apparently, corruption among officials. When Edward I came to the throne he set up a commission in every hundred to inquire of the local jurors who rightly held the land and also to discover what corruption existed on the part of royal officials.

In the 1274 'Hundred Rolls', as the reports of this commission are known, corruption by the sheriff and his officers seems to have been a constant source of complaint and, especially in Kiftsgate Hundred and in the neighbouring hundred of Holeford and Greston, the jurors make some outspoken comments. For instance:

> *Item* Of those who took money from anyone whatever through the execution of his office etc. ... They say that all bailiffs commonly do this.

And there were many accusations against Walter de Bokyng, the undersheriff:

> They say also that Walter Molindarius *[the miller]* of Caumpeden was accused by Adam de M'lave, bailiff of Caumpeden of the death of a man and was sent to Gloucester castle and was imprisoned in that place and was delivered by Walter de Bokyng for 20 shillings which he gave to him.
>
> They say also that Henry de Bars and Thomas le Wise seized Robert Faber of Paxford on the kings road between Mickleton and Caumpeden and took from him 8 shillings and led him away to Gloucester castle and imprisoned him there. Walter de Bokyng did not wish to deliver the same until he gave him 20 shillings. ...
>
> They say that Peter de Chavent, the sheriff of Gloucester and Walter de Bockyng enforce four sessions of the hundred of Kyfft' where they were never accustomed to come, nor should they, except twice in a year. And he takes before him both the free men and customars if they do not come to his summons. ... And for that they amerced *[fined]* the town of Caumpeden twenty shillings and caused Walter Molinarius of that town to be distrained of one horse price ten marks and he was still detained.[xv]

One incident is reported by both hundreds and in other places as well :

> They say that Thomas de la Vyse, then bailiff of Kistesgate stopped four waggons carrying twelve sacks of wool and took from them sixteen shillings and allowed the same to depart and carry that wool through Oxford, they do not know to which part.[xvi]

This bribe was taken at a time when there was a prohibition on the export of wool. The jurors also made a curious report about Richard de Clifford, the king's escheator (the official who looked after estates in the king's hands) and the fishpond of Campden:

> They say that master Richard de Clyfford made a right to fish in the vivarium of Caumpeden for his dinner. They say also that lord John de Extraneus *[John le Strange]* made a right to fish in that place in the said vivarium while it was in the hands of the lord king ...[xvii]

That is how the jury of Kiftsgate Hundred reported the incident. What it appears to mean is that while the manor was in the king's hands, after the death of Sir Roger de Somery, both the escheator and John le Strange took it upon themselves to take fish illegally from the vivarium. Greston jury claimed further that the escheator had laid waste to (that is, damaged) the pond and fleeced the men of Campden.

It may be that resentment against the sheriffs and their men caused a reaction by the people. In 1328 the sheriff of Worcester won an action against some Campden men :

> Robert de Warr' sheriff of the king receives 50 pounds for damages against Richard Mantill of Westington and five others of that town and John West of Broad Campden and 6 others of that town in that they impeded the same sheriff from holding his tourne.[xviii]

The tourne was the twice-yearly court the Sheriff held in each hundred. But it was not only the sheriff and his men who were corrupt :

> They say also that the town of Caumpeden has an assize of bread and ale by what warrant they do not know nor for how long. They say also that a marshal of the lord king came to the market of Caumpeden to see false measures corrected and good ones retained; after the withdrawal of the itinerant marshal they once again resumed the false and dismissed the good against the provisions of the marshal.[xix]

It appears also that Campden had trouble with visits from powerful men and their retainers. The jury reported an incident of what we might call a breach of the peace, or at least disorderly conduct:

> They say that men of the earl of Gloucester were staying in Caumpeden in the time of Henry the king before the king who now is; when the bailiff of Caumpeden heard that horses of the earl were in the town he told them that they should come for hay for the earl's horses and the earl's men sent two of their grooms after hay. Going there they came to where girls and boys were singing for pigeons and one of the grooms said that one of the girls sang well and gave her pigeons. This was heard by Nicholas Calf and Thomas le Prute *[two senior burgesses]* who had put up the pigeons and they said that he lied and she should not have the pigeons. They threatened the groom with a stick and struck him; this was heard by the earl's men and they came with bows and other arms to rescue the groom. At this the young men of Caumpedene and Westindone came and mingled themselves with the earl's men and each wounded and maltreated the other. Meanwhile one of the earl's men shot one of the town of Caumpeden with a barbed arrow after which the men of Caumpeden proceeded to the place where the earl's men were staying and broke into their house and feloniously entered and indeed came upon and seized two

> of the men of the county and imprisoned them until they should have the felon. The felon was imprisoned. Afterwards the earl's men came to Caumpeden and a man named Munda with three servants seized the aforesaid felon by force and took him away. Afterwards Simon le Beier came with his men, invaded the house of John Thole and there seized a certain book price 20 shillings and took it away and other minor things which things they do not know. This done they seized Robert Caspi, William Calf, Henry Clerk and Thomas le Prute and led them away to Hamile and there detained them until they made a fine of six score pounds of which 15 pounds was relaxed.[xx]

Nearly all the Campdonians named in this curious report were prominent townspeople.

Another of the burdens on the people of Campden during the whole medieval period was the occasional call to entertain the monarch. Medieval kings spent much of their lives travelling about the country, staying in castles or hunting lodges or on the estates of their favourites. While on tour they would be accompanied by all the apparatus of government, and, as well as dispensing justice, they would administer the country from wherever they were staying. In Campden this would be the lord's house, where food, wine and entertainment would be provided at great expense, much of which would presumably be borne by the townspeople.

Campden, held until 1232 by one of the most powerful lords in the country and a prosperous market town, received some of these royal visitations. It was often the case that letters, commands or writs were issued from where the king was staying and from these we can trace the route of his journeyings. Campden was certainly visited by King Henry II in 1185 when it was held by his courtier, Hugh de Gondeville. Richard I spent so few weeks in England during his reign that he probably saw very little of the country. King John, however, visited Campden at least once, en route from Oxford to Feckenham Forest in July 1215, and there are records of six letters that he witnessed while here.[xxi] John's son, Henry III, visited Campden at least three times — in May 1220, June 1229, and January 1233, writing letters or issuing writs on each occasion.[xxii]

After this Campden was held by lesser lords. There is no evidence of visits by Henry after Ranulph de Blundeville's demise, or by King Edward I. Edward II spent five days at the Bishop of Worcester's messuage in Weston-sub-Edge in February 1322, during the Lancaster rebellion, and sent many letters from there calling men to arms and ordering the arrest of rebels, including John Giffard of

Brimpsfield, a kinsman of his host. King Edward III visited Campden at least twice, in December 1327 and in January 1330, when the lordship of Campden was shared between the Earl of Gloucester and the wool merchant, Bogo de Lodelow.[xxiii]

Finally, one event occurring about this time must have been the talk of the town. This was an inquisition about the discovery and later disappearance, in about 1343, of buried treasure. There are a number of references to this in the records; the following is an extract from the most detailed:

> Regarding an inquiry upon discovered treasure :
>
> The king to his beloved and faithful Peter de Greece and John de Charyngworth, greetings.
>
> Know that we have appointed you to make an inquiry by the oaths of good honest and lawful men of the county of Gloucester through whom the truth of the matter can best be known, what malefactors and disturbers of our peace have seized and carried off no mean treasure discovered at Caumpeden concealed beneath the ground which concerns us by reason of the dignity of our Kingdom; and into the hands of which person or persons the said treasure fell and what person or persons offered counsel, assent or aid for this and into the hands of which person or persons the said treasure now is and how and by what means, and of all other points in the future relevant to the full truth.[xxiv]

Nothing further is known of this treasure, what it consisted of or where it was originally found.

To summarise, life in medieval Campden was a mixture. The population was subject to strictly regulated customs and a well developed and understood framework of laws, duties and obligations in which everyone had their place. Most no doubt submitted to this order and suffered the inconveniences. But they also experienced violence, corruption and other criminal activities, including even murder. One could assume that crime increased over the centuries as regulation began to break down, society was disrupted by the Black Death, and market influences (trade, freedom of movement, buying and selling of property, and so on) began to take over. Human nature will always take advantage of circumstances and this district at that time is no exception.

Notes

i When Sir John Strange died in 1276, his moiety was calculated to be worth £25 6s 52d a year, approximately double the quarter share he had inherited. Twenty years later, when John de Lodelow died, the annual value was still £20 5s 0d. However, in 1376 when Thomas de Lodelow died it was said to be only 20 marks (£13 6s 8d) and by 1394 it had fallen to £10.(Madge, S.J., *Ipm's for Gloucestershire* Vol IV 99/100; Vol IV 167/8; Vol VI 101; Vol VI 174/5). When Richard Stafford died in 1380 the annual value of the other half of the manor had also fallen to £10. By 1504 the stated value had risen again to 20 marks.

ii He was the son of John le Strange de Knokyn, an earl marcher who had served under King John at Poitou and at various times had been made constable of the castles of Montgomery, Shrewsbury, Bridgnorth and Chester. (*Patent Rolls* 13 & 16 November 1261; 7 Mar 1265; *Close Rolls* 1262 & 1263 passim); John seems to have been abroad, presumably on the king's service, at the time of de Somery's death. (*Close Rolls* 1274 says 'The king has committed this purparty to John to hold until his return to England ...')

iii Bartleet, Rev S.E., 'The Manor and Borough of Campden' *BGAS Transactions 1884*

iv He became tenant in chief of the manor of Erdington, and also of Shawbury in Shropshire and Corfe Mullen in Dorset. (*Close Rolls* 27 Jun 1282)

v *Close Rolls* 47 Henry III (1263). The letter granting him the de Somery lands ends cryptically 'to be held until Whitsuntide next, on condition that the said Walter shall go to the king's subjects supplying his place in England in the mean time to do what ought of right to be done in their behalf'.(*Close Rolls* 1274)

vi *Cal Fine Rolls* Feb 26 1286

vii *Pleas Edw* I Rot. 31 *(Cott Ms Tiberius A vi 49)* as cited by Rushen, Percy C., *The History & Antiquities of Chipping Campden* (2nd Edition, 1911)

viii *Cal. Close Rolls* 1274 states 'The king has taken the fealty .... upon condition that he come to the king on his arrival in England to do what ought to be done of right in this behalf'.

ix *Close Rolls* 1247, 1252 and Cal Patent Rolls 1253 memb 20 p 169 Jan 2nd

x *ibid* 1254 m7d (p 140)

xi *Cal Pat Rolls* 1356 October 23rd

xii ibids 1366 November 6th

xiii *ibid* 1366 November 6th; 1373 May 11th

xiv In 1422 John Fereby, king's clerk, was granted the manor of Whitley in Surrey and three months later made Parker of the parks there. In 1441, then controller of the household, he was again granted the same manor; in 1433 he and Margery his wife had been granted the manor of West Horsley, and he was given a number of duties in the county. *Cal Pat Rolls* 1422 Dec 15th and 1423 Feb 24th; 1433 March 20th; 1436 Oct 28th; 1439 Mar 16, May 17th and Dec 8th; 1440 Nov 26th; 1441 Feb 18th; 1441 March 9th. Although no record has been found connecting John Feryby with Campden, a Robert Feryby was granted a shop in 1427 'at the east of the shops opposite the Holy Cross' in Campden and a place in Sheppestret. Another lease to him is dated 1457. (Castle Ashby Archives, *53 Deeds relating to Chipping Campden* Nos 46 & 47)

xv *Rotuli Hundredorum Com Gloucs* (Rec. Com. 1812-18) 1274 passim

xvi ibid 174; 172; Abbey of Winchcombe Landboc xxiii Note 3

xvii *Rot Hundredorum* 1274 op cit 172; 174; 1278 182

xviii Placit' Abbrev' (Rec. Com. 1811) 317. (rot 71) Worcs.

xix *Rot Hundredorum* 1274 op cit 174; 1278 182

xx ibid 1274 174

xxi *Rot. Lit. Pat.* 1215 150b; *Rotuli de finibus* 17-18 Johann, 1215-16 Memb 8; and *Rot Chart in Turr.Lond* 17 John 1215 memb 6 xxii *Close Rolls* 4 Hy III 417b *Patent Rolls* 4 Hy III; *Cal of Liberate Rolls* 13 Hy III 135 and *Close Rolls* 1229, 183 m9; *Cal liberate Rolls* 17 Hy III, 194

xxiii *Cal of Close Rolls* Dec 16 1327 190; *Cal Close Rolls* 6 Edw III July 28/9 1330, 481, 580,583

xxiv Rymers *Feodera* II II 1219 ; *Letters & Acta Publica* 1343 An 17 Edw III

5

The 1381 Poll Tax and Some Characters in the Wool Trade

A picture of life in Campden towards the end of the 14th century can be gained from the 1381 Poll Tax returns. When Richard II came to the throne the expense of his wars against the French led to the imposition of poll taxes on the population. During the first few years these were of only a few pence each but in 1381 changes were made. Every town and village in the country that year had to raise the equivalent of three groats (one shilling) for every member of the population over 15 years old (other than genuine paupers). Within this constraint, people were to pay according to their wealth. Somewhat like the limits on Council Tax bands of the 1980s and 1990s, however, no one was to pay more than £1 and no one less than a groat.

The 1381 returns for Gloucestershire have survived and have recently been published. Campden borough and its three hamlets were each assessed separately and we have a clear view of the adult population at that time.[i] Chipping Campden (the borough) had 309 adults, Broad Campden 78, Westington 55 and Berrington 41, a total of 483 adults, or a total population of possibly 800 to 1,000 people. Campden then was slightly smaller than Cirencester, but considerably larger than either Northleach or the ancient borough of Winchcombe. Almost all the people living in the three hamlets were families of peasant farmers or their servants. Broad Campden had two 'frankleyns', or freeholders, both named Weoley; in Westington there was a clerk and in Berrington one 'armiger' or squire: Thomas Lodelowe, one of the lords of the manor. None of these more prosperous men paid more than 2s 0d or 2s 6d in tax.

In the large population of the borough the situation was different. Among the few tradesmen and merchants whose occupations are given there were four butchers, four tailors, three cobblers, two weavers, two drapers, two masons, a carpenter, a cooper and a smith, as well as six brewers (five of them women) and two innkeepers. There were also a number of merchants, one of whom, William Grevel, cited as a wool merchant, paid the large sum of 13s 4d in tax (thus by himself relieving about twenty poorer families from the burden of finding the whole 12d). Of the other richer men, one of the innkeepers paid 8s and the other 4s 6d, one draper paid 8s and so did a man called Peter Smyth. Robert Calf, designated as a farmer, paid 4s 6d, Richard Campion 5s 6d, and another farmer in the borough paid 4s 6d. These larger contributions meant that of the 309 tax payers in the borough, some 77 of the least well-off were lucky enough to pay the minimum of one groat and many more paid only 6d or 9d. In the poorer hamlets, where there were not the rich men to share the burden, very few got away with paying less than the standard 12d and only one, a woman servant in Berrington, paid the minimum. In the south east of the country the seeming inequity of this poll tax led directly to the peasants' revolt, though there is no evidence of unrest in this part of the country.

One reason for the prosperity of the borough was the growth of the wool trade, which peaked in importance in the 15th century. From Saxon times the Cotswolds had been noted for the production of wool. Cotswold sheep were renowned and their long wool was much in demand on the continent. The lords of Campden kept sheep on the common pasture on the hills and most peasants had customary rights to keep a given number of sheep there. After Campden's market developed it became a centre for the collection of wool from the villages around, and eventually from as far afield as Wales. Several townspeople became wealthy wool merchants, or more properly wool mongers: i.e. those who bought wool from the producers, collected it together and sold it on to the 'Merchants of the Staple' who travelled to wool towns all over the country, collecting the wool and exporting it, generally via the Staple town of Calais, to the Low Countries or to Italy.

Wool was the most profitable commodity traded in Campden, as in the country as a whole. It is not clear to what destinations Campden wool was sent. The Cely family of London merchants, who exported Cotswold wool through Calais, sold mainly to Flanders and the Low Countries, but their main contact was in Northleach and there is only one mention of Campden in the whole of their published papers. It could be, from the evidence of William Weoley's difficulties mentioned below, that most Campden wool went to Florence. Indeed, in one letter the head of the Cely family, writes in 1480:

> I have not as yet packed my wool at London nor have I not bought this year
> a lock of wool for the wool of Cottyswolde is bought by Lombardys ...[ii]

The export of wool was extremely important to the economy of England during the 14th and 15th centuries and privileges were given to those engaged in it. One of the most striking is a series of identical Letters Patent issued in 1395 to several hundred wool merchants, wool mongers, wool buyers, woolmen and others, mainly living in the Midlands or eastern England, apparently giving them a licence to indulge in dishonest practices at the expense of foreigners. The following is a local example:

> Pardon and remission to William Grevell of Campedene wool merchant of all contempts, transparencies, frauds, deceits and unjust and excessive weighings and purchases of wools contrary to statute whereof he is or may be indicted, and also of all ransoms, imprisonments due therefor or forfeiture incurred thereby. [iii]

A number of wool trading families stand out in the medieval history of Campden. This William Grevel is the best known. He lived here in the late 14th century. Tradition has it that the house known as Grevel House that stands in the High Street was built by him; and he has a magnificent brass in the chancel of the church, where he is described as 'the flower of the wool merchants of all England'. Little is known of Grevel's ancestry though Rushen, the early 20th century Campden antiquarian, believed William's family was of Norman or Flemish extraction.[iv]

However, by late in the 14th century William Grevel, his wife Marion and father Richard Grevel were all members of the Guild of the Holy Trinity in Coventry, which was a centre of the wool trade.[v] His name first appears in Campden in the 1360s. In 1362 he obtained a right to the lands and tenements of William Dalby after the death of Dalby's wife. Dalby was another merchant incomer who had acquired a lot of property in Campden during the 1350s but had then died.[vi] Five years later Grevel relinquished to Walter Belamy messuages called Dalbyes Lyn and Coumbesplace and a shop in Schoprewe as well as rents of cottages in Broad Campden.[vii] Already he was wealthy enough to be exchanging property in the town. In 1397 he was among a large group of men who lent money to the king (in his case 300 marks).[viii] The *Inquisition post mortem* taken on his death[ix] (an enquiry customarily taken upon the death of a landholder) shows that in Campden he held 14 messuages and two virgates of land from the lords of the manor.

Grevel's House, Chipping Campden.

Grevel House from an engraving by F.L. Griggs, 1909

But most of the lands he acquired were outside Campden. He had clearly accumulated considerable wealth through his dealings in wool, for in 1386 he was able to buy some land at Sezincote and in 1387 he purchased the lordship of the manor of Charlton Kings. In the last years of the 14th Century he acquired land in Upper and Lower Pillerton, Warwickshire, and the manors of Charingworth, Welford and Weston-on-Avon, and nearby Milcote, where he built a house in which he lived during the last years of his life. He married twice. His first wife, Marion, died in 1386, and he then married Joan, sister of Sir Philip Thornbury. He had at least seven children from his two marriages, two of his sons, John and Ludovic [Lewis] being his principal heirs. In Kent Archives Office is a long and complicated settlement showing William Grevel entailing all the above properties, as well as Meon, and lands in Lower Lemington, Mickleton, Ilmington, Ullington, Pebworth, Longborough and elsewhere on his many heirs.[x] By his will he left the residue of his personal property to his widow (who later married Edward Benestede),[xi] his son John and one other executor. He died in 1401 and was buried in Campden Church, possibly in the North Aisle.

The Grevels were associated with the earlier wool merchant family, the Lodelowes, who had held half of Campden as lords of the manor from the late 13th century. William Grevel's daughter, Alice, married Edward Lodelowe, who became lord of half the manor in 1391. John Grevel and Alice were the executors of Edward's will.

William Grevel does not seem to have taken much part in the civic life of the town and his name rarely appears either as juror or as witness to bonds or leases. He does, however, seem to have been a benefactor to the church during his lifetime. In his will he left 100 marks 'for the work to be done' in the church and £200 to maintain four chaplains celebrating mass in the church daily for ten years. It is probable that some rebuilding of the church at that time was due mainly to his generosity. One wonders, too, whether some of the masons working on the church may have been responsible for work on the contemporary Grevel House.[xii]

William's son John Grevel became escheator for Gloucestershire early in the 15th century and later sheriff of the county. He remained closely associated with Edward Lodelowe until the latter's death and seems to have continued in the wool trade. Another son, Ludovic, held the Campden lands and messuages for a time and later passed them on to his son Robert,[xiii] but he spent the rest of his life in Oxfordshire. Branches of the Grevels (or Grevilles as they became known) remained lords of Sezincote, Lower Lemington and the estates bordering Warwickshire up to the 17th century, and descendants of William became earls of Warwick. In Campden, however, the name is renowned because of Grevel House, the Grevel brass in the church and the fact that he financed part of the structure of the early 15th century work in the church of St James.

Another family who became traders and wool merchants were the Weoleys, who were living in Broad Campden during the last half of the 13th century.

They later moved into the borough and were still here in the 16th century. There were clearly several branches of this family in Campden during the 14th century, some trading mainly in wool and helping to administer the town and hundred, some farming, and some participating in the violence and lawlessness that were endemic.

Unlike William Grevel, the Weoleys played their full part in the administration of Campden. William, John and Simon de Weleye all appear as jurors in the late 13th and early 14th centuries. They seem first to have acquired land in Broad Campden, possibly as tenants of the Greinvilles, for in 1307 Katherine, widow of Richard de Greinville, unsuccessfully claimed rents from William de Wyleigh in Broad Campden as her dower,[xiv] and in 1313 Thomas Attwell of Hodinton, a chaplain, granted to 'Henry de Weley of Brodecampedene' and Sybil his wife some houses and land in the town of Brodecampedene.[xv]

In the 1327 Subsidy Roll, Henry Weoley was living in Broad Campden and a John Weoleye in Westington. Henry Weoley was the founder of the senior branch of this family, who developed into wealthy merchants. He did, however, have one brush with the law — a complaint was made that in 1314 twenty-one named individuals, including Henry de Weleye, had assaulted Thomas Bisshope at Campeden and carried away his goods. What the cause of this was — probably a market fracas — is not known.[xvi]

There is no doubt that there was a significant amount of crime at this period, some of it violent. Two members of a minor branch of the Weoley family seem to have been involved in many incidents during the 1340s and 1350s, both in and outside the district. John de Weoleye and his son appear often in the records. In 1337 one Geoffrey de Aston, the parson of Mickleton, complained that eight named men, including three clerks or chaplains, and John de Weleye of Broad Campden, assaulted him at Mickleton and carried away his goods.[xvii] This John de Weleye seems to have been a servant of the Abbot of Eynsham, a powerful lord who then held Mickleton manor. This, and the presence of several clerics, suggests the abbot may have been the instigator of the assault. In 1340 in a possibly connected incident, the Abbot of Eynsham complained that the vicar of Tetbury had broken down the abbot's door at Tetbury, carried away his goods, charters, writings and muniments, and assaulted four men, including again John Weleye of Campden, his servant, and imprisoned them until he had 'made a writing in £100 for their deliverance'.[xviii]

A John Weleye (probably either this man or his son) seems to have served in the army in France. Seven years after the last incident two Letters Patent were granted to 'John Weleye, son of John Weleye of Chepyinge Campeden' pardoning him because of 'good service in the war in France' (probably at the Battle of Crecy) for 'all homicides, felonies, robberies and trespasses committed, and for any consequent outlawries' on condition that he did not withdraw from the king's service without special leave.[xix] This pardon was repeated the same year and again in 1351, 1352 and 1354, the last three being issued at the request of the Duke of Lancaster and citing a particular robbery from William Gilbert.[xx] It seems that army service could be a way of avoiding the consequences of crime.

John Weleye, son of John Weleye of Chepyngcaumpeden, was again indicted in 1358, together with a monk of Eynsham Abbey and a clerk, for entering Eynsham Abbey and stealing chalices of silver and gold, books and vestments.[xxi] The following year he and seven others, including this time the Abbot of Evesham and John Proude of Campden, abducted one Thomas Iweyn at Ludyngton, Warwickshire while he was under the king's protection.[xxii] Three years later, however, John was again pardoned for these crimes and any consequent outlawry 'for good service done' in France, this time in the company of Richard de Stafford, one of the lords of Campden.[xxiii]

John Weleye's father seems to have been involved in the same kind of activity. In 1354 'John Weleye of Chipping Campden the elder' was accused with others that at Mickleton they broke into the Abbot of Eynsham's close and house and drove away 4 mares, 2 colts, 24 oxen, 12 cows, 16 heifers, 100 swine and 200 sheep, worth in all £100, that they entered his warren and carried away hares, conies, pheasants and partridges, and assaulted his men and servants.[xxiv] One wonders why the abbot, victim of this huge foray, was the focus of so much theft and violence, in Mickleton and elsewhere over some thirty years. John Weoley the elder was pardoned of his outlawry in 1356[xxv] and again in 1366, apparently for an unpaid debt of £40, 'he having now surrendered to the Flete prison'.[xxvi] In 1374 a writ was issued to the Sheriff of Worcester to seize John Weleye of Campeden the elder, whom the bishop had excommunicated for contumacy, or refusal to conform to a ruling of the church.[xxvii] John seems to have appealed, but with what effect is not known.[xxviii]

Despite the activities of their kinsmen, the respectable branch of this family prospered. William Weoley, the great grandson of Henry of Broad Campden, is the best known Campden member of the family. He became an important wool merchant, one of the successors of William Grevel. He died in 1450, has a brass in St James's church and almost certainly contributed money towards its reconstruction. He was married to Alice, daughter of William Bovy, a weaver of Campden. His status may be judged by the fact that in granting him letters of marque (a licence to take reprisals) in 1440[xxix] against a Florentine wool trader, the king states that he himself had written repeatedly on the subject. This judgment, for the huge sum of £1,080, was against an agent of the wool trading company of Albertini of Florence. It was repeated in 1442 and 1445[xxx] since, as the letter from the king says, it was

> being repelled and delayed by various pretences, protestations and other frivolous and unjust allegations and by undue favour, neglect and delay on the part of the said *[Florentine]* magistrates .....

The importance to the country of wool exports may be gathered from this correspondence. The letters of marque are only to have full effect 'on the lapse of the protection granted for three years to the said merchants' and 'provided always that letters of safe conduct of the king already granted to Florentines be not infringed by these present letters of marque'. This protection to the Florentines seems to have been continually updated, so that the letters of marque were not of much practical use to William. In 1445 he was given exemption for life from being put on juries, assizes, inquisitions, etc., and from being made mayor, sheriff, or any of a dozen other offices.[xxxi] After his death, his son, Thomas, disposed of his father's lands 'in the town and fields of Chipping Campden, Berrington and Little Compton' to a group of four men, whence they passed by gift to a succession of beneficiaries,[xxxii] and were possibly used to finance the rebuilding of the church.

However, it is William's great-great-great-grandson, Richard, who is perhaps the best known member of the family outside Campden. He had moved to London and it was he who as Master of the Founders Company of London presented to the company in 1631 a Venetian painted glass goblet which to this day is drunk from by the new Master at his swearing-in ceremony at which time a solemn declaration penned by Richard is read.

Rather like the Weoleys, the Calf family, after whom Calf Lane is named, was also prominent in the town in the 13th and 14th centuries, as farmers and probably also wool merchants. In 1273 William Calf was a free tenant of the manor and also held an important burgage in the borough. A descendant, Philip Calf, paid 12d subsidy there in 1327 and Robert Calf was in the borough in 1381. Robert, son of John Calf, obtained a messuage and a croft called Giffard's Croft in 1350. It is not clear whether the Calfs were also engaged in the wool trade but they were clearly an influential family in the town over at least three centuries.

There were many other, less well known merchants living in Campden during the 15th century. William Gibbyes (who held some of William Weoley's property) and John Lethenard are both described on brasses in the church as merchants living in Campden. Though little more is known about them, it is most likely that they also contributed towards the rebuilding of the church during that century. There were Gibbs living in Campden in every century from the 16th to the 20th, though there is no evidence of their connection with William Gibbyes. The name Lethenard appears only rarely in the records, once as 'constable' witnessing deeds (one in company with William Weoley and another townsman, William Skytter). He may, however, be identified with John Leynard, who was a trustee of the will of William Skytter, and a relative of Richard Leynard, who was associated in the wool trade with William Bradway.[xxxiii] William Bradway is rather better known. He died in 1480 and left not only 100 marks towards the work in the church but also the fine altar cloths described in Chapter 6. These are only a few among the many traders and merchants who made up the population of Chipping Campden during its era of greatest prosperity.

Notes

i Fenwick, Carolyn C., *The Poll Taxes of 1377, 1379 and 1381*, 276 & 282-285

ii Malden H.E., *The Cely Papers*-(Camden Soc 3rd Series) 29th October 1480

iii *Cal Pat Rolls* 1395 Oct 16th (627). This seems to have been a general amnesty and there is no evidence that Grevel had committed any offence in fact.

iv Rushen, Percy C., *The History and Antiquities of Chipping Campden* (2nd edition 1911) 20 A Simon Grivel and a Thomas Grivel were living in Campden in 1273, each having a small holding of half a burgage and in 1314 a Peter de Grevel was accused with others of assault and robbery. None of these appear among the relatively few more prosperous burgesses who paid subsidy in 1327, and they are probably unconnected.

v Harris, Mary Dormer, (ed). *Register of the Guild of the Holy Trinity, Coventry*, 1935, 50 & 89

vi Castle Ashby Archives op cit Nos 19, 20, 22, 23, 30, 31, 32

vii ibid No 33
viii *Cal Pat Rolls* 1397 Aug 25th (179) and Sept 20th (180)
ix *Chan Inq p.m.* Ser I; 3 Hy IV No 33
x *Cal. Pat. Rolls*, 1405-1408, vol. 111, m. 16, Dec. 5
xi ibid, 1405-408, vol. 111, m. 32, Dec.1, 1405; Close Rolls 1405 Dec 1st 7 Hy IV
xii I am grateful to Mr Morris Barton for this suggestion.
xiii *Cal. Pat. Rolls*, 1401-1405, vol. 11, m. 27, Oct. 1402
xiv *de Banco Rolls* Trin & Easter 1 Edw II; Mich 3 Edw II (1307 & 1309)
xv *Cal of Ancient Deeds* (PRO 1890) Vol IV A7407 Friday of St Valentine 7 Edw II (1313)
xvi As an illustration of some of the civic duties carried out by local people we may cite the following. In 1347 a John de Weleye was appointed with the sheriff of Worcester and others, to arrest and bring to the Tower of London a 'large number of disturbers of the peace' who intended to enter the house of the vicar of Tredington, the king's clerk, 'despoil him of the church and carry away tithes, profits and faculties'. Some time earlier 'the evil doers came armed, entered houses by force of arms and collected tithes and profits of the church and consumed them ...' The following month an enlarged commission still including John de Weleye, was set up because when the first had ordered a sitting in the vicar's house 'a large number of evildoers' entered the house and 'prevented them from entering and placed pennons of arms on the walls'. The sheriff raised a hue and cry and proclaimed that all in the county should help, but no one did so, and 'many cherish and nourish the evildoers and outlaws to the utmost'. The commissioners were therefore ordered to take the evildoers and everyone who lent aid to them to the Tower of London. Anyone who refused to help them in this was to be put in the nearest gaol. How effective this order was is unclear. *(Cal Pat.Rolls, 20 Jun and 5 Jul 1347)*
xvii *Cal Pat Rolls* 1337 Memb 36d 10th Sept.
xviii ibid 1340
xix ibid January 20 1346/7
xx ibid 1351 Feb 17; 1352 Aug 26; 1354 April 8th
xxi ibid 1358 Nov 21
xxii ibid 1359 Sept 4th
xxiii ibid 1361 Feb 1st
xxiv ibid 1354 Feb 1st
xxv ibid 1356 Nov 7th
xxvi ibid 1366 March 3rd & May 10th
xxvii Griffiths, W.C.L., *Reg sede vacante* fol 177
xxviii ibid. fol 175
xxix *Cal Pat Rolls* 1440 March 28 (398)
xxx ibid 1442 June 28 (88)1442 Oct 12 (150) and 145 May 24 (363)
xxxi ibid 1445 July 16 (351)
xxxii *Confirmation of gift*, 1490, Leicester RO DE3214 341/1 Details of later generations of the Weoleys are given, together with a family tree, in Rushen, op cit 21 - 24.
xxxiii Rushen op cit 14

6

The Church in the Middle Ages

Campden's fine parish church standing on its knoll in Berrington and visible for many miles around is, with Northleach and Cirencester, one of the best of the Cotswold's so-called 'Wool Churches'. Its present appearance dates largely from the 15th century, but it was probably erected on the site of a smaller 13th century church. The magnificent Perpendicular tower, built at the very end of the 15th century, bears a strong resemblance to that of Gloucester Cathedral. It is perhaps the finest tower of any parish church in the county.[i]

It has hitherto been generally assumed that a church has occupied this site since Norman times, if not before. Percy C. Rushen, the doyen of Campden's historians, declared that there was a church in Norman times and probably in Edward the Confessor's time, too. He admits however that it can only be supposition that it occupied the present site.[ii] F.E. Howard, woodworker and church historian, wrote in the first known church guide, 'Undoubtedly there was a church there in Norman times',[iii] basing this conclusion mainly on the fact that 'practically every tiny Cotswold hamlet seems to have had its church rebuilt in Norman days'.[iv] A slightly earlier but anonymous description of St James's had declared that there was 'probably a church there in Saxon times' and mentions several Norman incumbents by name.[v]

Later church guides follow Howard, some stating that the Norman work merely amounted to 'a corbel from the corbel table built into the south walls of the sacristy',[vi] and others affirming the 'Norman corbel of a muzzled bear in the Muniment Room' as the sole survival of Norman work.[vii] Of greater stature is the *Gloucestershire and the Cotswolds* volume of the Pevsner guides, which refers to an alleged 13th century extension of the 'Norman chancel', and states that 'fragments of earlier work survive', including that 'muzzled bear corbel'.[viii] None of these authorities gives any clear evidence about 'the earlier and Norman Church'[ix] before elaborating in detail on its later Perpendicular glory.

The existence of any church on this site earlier than the 13th century is questionable. We know that a church dedicated to St Mary did exist in Norman times, but the earliest building in Campden of which there are any remaining traces is the Norman Chapel in Broad Campden, which dates from the late 11th or early 12th century. The largest part of the population at that time lived in Broad Campden and it would be only logical for the church and probably the seat of the lord to have been there. This was a hundred years before the town itself came into existence and the centre of population moved a mile and a half north. Rushen reminded his readers that 'an earlier ecclesiastical structure' at Broad Campden might have been the early church. This supposition, however, he immediately rejects.[x] Rushen seems to have forgotten that the town did not exist until the late 12th century.

For the first hundred and forty years after the Conquest there is no information either about a church or about the priest here. Half a century after the Conquest the manor of Campden became associated with Chester Abbey. Hugh d'Avranches, the first Norman earl of Chester, had re-established the despoiled St Werburgh's Abbey in Chester in about 1093, and he provided that after his death or that of his wife, the abbey was to receive the reversion of the tithes of about a dozen of his manors, including the tithes of Campden. These tithes were defined as the 'direct tithes, not only of the produce [i.e. the grain] but also of foals and calves, of pigs and lambs, of butter and cheese and of all things from which tithes ought to be given in these my manors'.[xi]

From then on, right up till the dissolution of the monasteries, the association of Campden and its church with St. Werburgh's Abbey was continuous — not always, it must be said, to the benefit of Campden. About 1150 Earl Ranulf de Guernon renewed or confirmed his predecessor's grant of the tithes,[xii] and in about 1190 Pope Clement III gave a confirmation of the abbey's possessions and privileges which included 'the tithes of all things from which tithes ought to be given of the demesnes of these manors: Frodsham, Weaverham, Lache, Rocester, Coleshill, Campden ...'[xiii] All the early references connecting St Werburgh's with Campden concern the grant of tithes.

When Hugh de Gondeville set up the market in Campden he also established, in about 1180, a new chapel of St Katherine with its own chaplains. The foundation charter to 'the blessed Virgin Katherine' (of Alexandria) endowed the chapel with three named hides of land in Westington. There were to be two chaplains, each holding half the revenues from the three hides, and each was to give a pound of incense annually to the mother church, to whom all chaplains were to swear fealty.[xiv]

Hugh de Gondeville had a motive for building his chapel in or near to the new town and appointing and paying its priest. If the mother church was still in Broad Campden a new place of worship in the town, or nearby in Berrington, would have been convenient both for the lord and his household and for the townspeople as a whole. The land at Broad Campden and with it the Norman Chapel, was granted away to William de Feugieres about fifteen years after the foundation of St Katherine's. The existence of the new chapel no doubt made this easier, and it is probable that the mother church was later relocated to Berrington.

The doorway of the Norman Chapel, Broad Campden, possibly the original church of Campden *(Jesse Taylor/G of H Trust)*

The ecclesiastical history of Broad Campden after its excision from the manor is difficult to follow. However, by 1240 the Norman Chapel had fallen into the hands of Tewkesbury Abbey and seems to have remained in their possession, now dedicated to St Mary Magdalene, until the dissolution, though there are very few references to the chapel either in the Tewkesbury annals, or elsewhere. After the dissolution it seems to have fallen into disuse and for some hundreds of years existed as a barn or other farm building. We suggest that this 'Norman Chapel' was the original church of Campden and it was only in the 13th century, after the borough and market had become firmly established, that another church was newly built in Berrington.

Brasses of William Grevel, wool merchant and his wife Marian *(Jesse Taylor/CADHAS)*

Of 13th century work in the present church there is plenty. The south doorway, the blocked lancet window to its west, together with a piscina at the end of the south aisle suggest that the fabric of this aisle, though later refaced, dates from about 1260, and that there was an altar at the end. Work on the lower part of the north chapel is probably of the same date, together with its archway into the chancel, the tomb recess in the latter probably marking its eastern end.[xv] From these details it is possible to visualise the outline of the church as it then was: a nave with a south aisle, and a north chapel leading into a shorter chancel but probably no south chapel or north aisle. Such an arrangement was quite common in the 13th century.

Over the next two to three centuries the outward appearance of the church, then dedicated to the Virgin, grew in both size and beauty. Towards the end of the 14th century the chancel was extended to its present length, the fabric and buttresses of a north aisle were added, together with the crypt below it. Also added was a south porch — to be expanded in the 17th century, with a school or priest's room overhead, said to have been one of Baptist Hicks's gifts to the church.[xvi]

It was during the 15th century that the church reached its present Perpendicular magnificence, at first sight seemingly built as a single entity. For this we can be grateful to the munificence of the merchants, traders and townspeople of Campden during that century. Three benefactors are known by name: William Grevel, William Weoley and William Bradway, all merchants, who died respectively at the beginning, the middle and the end of that century. All of them left money in their wills specifically for the new work in the church,[xvii] and most probably contributed during their lives as well. There were many other donors in the town, both merchants grown rich from the profits of trade (among them William Gybbes and John Lethanard,[xviii] whose brasses lie today in the chancel) and traders and ordinary people in the town.

William Grevel, who died in 1401, left one hundred marks 'towards the work to be done' *[ad opus faciendum]*[xix] and these funds are thought to have contributed to the construction of the north aisle. There are said to have been mullets — part of the Grevel arms — in the windows of the north aisle. It has been suggested that Grevel was buried in this aisle and that his brass in the chancel, proudly boasting him as 'the flower of the wool-merchants of all England', was originally on his tomb there.[xx] The architecture of the south aisle, and the south wall with its windows and battlements, indicates they were probably rebuilt about 1450; they could well have been financed by the Weoley family, who were then at the peak of their prosperity. A brass commemorating William Weoley lies in the chancel next to William Grevel's.

William Bradway's will of 1488 states 'I bequeath to the building of the nave and body of the same parish church 100 marks.'[xxi] And it was during the final decades of the 15th century that the old nave was replaced by the lofty new one, with its clerestory windows and battlements, inserted between the earlier north and south aisles — delicate engineering work indeed. Characterised by its eight tall octagonal fluted piers, joined by low arched arcades below those clerestory windows, it is similar to the nave of Northleach church, probably completed between 1450 and 1470. Other similarities between the two churches suggest that Northleach's master mason probably moved on to Campden.[xxii]

Finally, the west door and that magnificent tower, dominating Campden, were added at the turn of the 16th century, the latter probably replacing an existing structure.

Apart from the brasses of four 14th and 15th century merchants, and a number of interesting tombs (most post-reformation, but one dating from the 13th century) Campden church contains other medieval treasures. A cope of about 1400 seems to have been in the church's possession throughout; and a large and virtually complete set of 15th century altar hangings is thought to be another of William Bradway's bequests: 'to every altar in the said church a chasuble of white damask with all the apparel thereto belonging'.[xxiii] Both cope and altar hangings are now displayed inside the church.

Part of a set of altar hangings. The dossal shown here, and the frontal, are believed to be the only surviving purpose made set of English medieval altar hangings

Incidentally, the charter founding St Katherine's provides us with the name of the first vicar of Campden of whom we have any record — Osmund the Priest. Precisely where the chapel was is not clear. However, its charter says the chapel was established 'in my court of Campeden' and later inquisitions speak in terms such as 'the chapel of St Katherine within the court of the lords of Campden' which may mean it was located in Berrington, where Hugh's successors established a new court.[xxiv] Indeed, some confirmation of this is provided by evidence given in a 17th century court case, where Sir Baptist Hicks cited as among the lands belonging to the rectory 'the parcell of grounds wherein by the supposal of the said bill a chapple was sometime built'.[xxv] However, while the advowson (the right to appoint a priest) of the mother church was in the hands of the Abbot of Chester at least from about 1200, the right to appoint chaplains to St Katherine's belonged to the lords of Campden for the next three hundred years and more, it being taken in turns between the various holders during the time that the manor was divided.

There is some controversy about when Chester Abbey first got the advowson of the mother church. About 1190, after de Gondeville's death, Campden was repossessed by Earl Ranulf de Blundeville, and he confirmed the living of the church of St Mary at Campden to Stephen the Clerk [the parson] 'as is attested in the charter of Abbot Robert and the community at Chester who had bestowed the aforesaid church on him'.[xxvi] This is the first explicit reference to Chester having appointed an incumbent to Campden church. It has been inferred that this abbot, Robert de Hastings, had only recently acquired the advowson and that it was probably Ranulf de Blundeville who had granted the privilege.[xxvii] If this is so, and it is not certain, this grant may have followed the creation of St Katherine's chapel. As the advowson of the chapel was now in the hands of the lord of the manor, the gift of St Mary's church could be handed over to the abbot.

The abbot's possession was not always unquestioned and some of the events in the 13th century may confirm that there was a change of circumstances at that time. The manor of Campden was inherited in 1232 by the young Hugh de'Albini, the fifth earl of Arundel. Soon after Hugh came of age and took full possession of the manor, he seems to have tried to deprive St Werburgh's of the advowson. No doubt in most of the manors held by Hugh, he also held the advowson, as this was the usual practice. It may have seemed wrong to the new young lord that an abbey in Cheshire, in which county the earl had no lands, was not only entitled to the tithes, but also appointed the priest to the mother church of one of his manors. There followed several hearings in the king's court at Westminster over this attempt, but eventually, in 1238, Hugh agreed to grant and release to the abbot and his successors all rights and claims that he and his successors had in the church at Campden.[xxviii]

In the same year, as though in support of the abbot's claim to the advowson, the Bishop of Worcester certified to the Justices of the King's Bench that the abbot and community of Chester were the true patrons of the church at Campden and that he had accepted the abbot's nominee, R. de Stainsby, as clerk and rector of the church there.[xxix] He ordered that the new rector be inducted and given possession of the church.[xxx] It is possible that de Stainsby was the first clergyman appointed to Campden since the manor had been inherited by the new earl and possibly the first since a new church had been built in Berrington.[xxxi]

Disputes over the right to appoint an incumbent were not uncommon at that period and the Albini challenge was not unique. In the 1280s the Bishop of Worcester initiated a series of disputes over the advowson in which he tried to appoint his own chaplain, Adam of Avebury, to the rectory against two successive appointments by the Abbot of Chester. This involved much opposition locally, action in the ecclesiastical courts, the sequestration for a time of the profits of the church, and the successive excommunication of many of the participants. For over two years there were two competing incumbents in Campden, one appointed by the Abbot of Chester and the other by the Bishop of Worcester, whose motive seems to have been to find a parish for his chaplain. After three years the Bishop eventually gave way.[xxxii]

One curious event was that a licence was given in 1270 to the rector of Campden 'to erect a small refuge for Matilda of Campden, without the order or habit of a nun, in the churchyard of the parish church, without injury to the bodies of the dead resting there'. Whereabouts in the churchyard this refuge was is unknown: there is no trace of it remaining.[xxxiii] We know no more about this lady, but this was a time when anchorites and anchoresses were revered by the ordinary people as particularly holy.

By the late 12th and into the 13th and 14th centuries, ecclesiastical affairs in Campden were somewhat complicated. While Campden was then in the diocese of Worcester, the advowson of its church and the tithes for the whole manor and borough belonged to the Abbey of St Werburgh's of Chester, in the diocese of Lichfield. In addition, the lord of Campden had his own chapel of St. Katherine of which he held the advowson and financed its priest. From the mid-13th century, the Norman Chapel at Broad Campden was held by Tewkesbury abbey, and the abbey of Bordesley held the land at Combe with the duty of establishing a cell of monks there.

It is not surprising that this caused complications. There were disputes over land between the Abbot of Bordesley and the people of Campden. On 7th June 1250 a dispute was settled between Abbot William of Bordesley and Peter, the parson of Campden, in which it was noted that the abbot 'only paid a yearly nominal pension of 2 marks for the tithes of the grange of Combe, and so if he obtained other lands in the same parish [of Campden] he should pay the full tithes from them'.[xxxiv] There was thus a distinction between Combe and the rest of Campden in the collection of tithes.

One factor that may possibly have influenced Hugh d'Albini's claim to the tithes and the advowson of the church in the 1230s is the fact that the abbots of Chester were beginning to exploit the revenues obtainable from Campden. At various stages from the early 13th century on, the tithes and other revenues of Campden were used by the abbots of Chester, often for the rebuilding or restoration of the fabric of their abbey; sometimes, it appears for less deserving or less reputable purposes.

A number of letters about Campden were written by abbots of Chester to the ecclesiastical authorities. A little before 1200 Abbot Robert de Hastings petitioned the Archbishop of Canterbury and the Bishop of Worcester to be allowed to 'appropriate' the living of Campden church, in partial recompense for the abbey's loss of land at Ince in Cheshire through inroads of the sea, and the loss of the church of Holywell and other places after their capture by the Welsh princes.[xxxv] About this time Abbot Robert assigned many of the tithes he received, together with 'ten shillings yearly from Campden, and whatever can be obtained from the Church of Campden' to the restoration of the fabric of the abbey.

The practice of appropriation of parish revenues was common at this period, though it normally required papal, or at least episcopal, approval. Appropriation was quite valuable. It gave the abbey not only the tithes from every family living in the parish, but also parishioners' payments for burials and other services performed by the church, altar offerings and many other forms of income. It has been shown that even where an abbot was lord of the manor, his 'spiritual' or parish revenues could be much greater than the lay revenues he received as lord of the manor.[xxxvi] When an abbey appropriated the spiritual revenues of a parish, the usual practice was to appoint a 'vicar' to the cure of souls in the place, and give him a small pension, or at best only a fraction of the tithes for his maintenance, while the rest of the parish revenues were used for monastic purposes. What arrangements St Werburgh's made for a priest at Campden subsequent to the appropriation is not known, although sixty years after this the incumbent is still called 'rector': a designation normally given to one who was entitled to the tithes and other offerings. However, the appropriation of the living seems to have persisted for at least 150 years.

During the 14th century, and under successive abbots, the community at Chester, in common with many Benedictine abbeys, became rather notorious for dissolute living, culminating in the enforced resignation and imprisonment of one of its abbots. Two diocesan visitations were made, in 1315 and 1323. The Visitors found, for instance, that the abbot, and probably the monks too, had hunting dogs which ate the food reserved for distribution to the poor; that the prior regularly went hunting and used bows and arrows; that the abbot had too many personal servants — one cause of the abbey's increasing indebtedness; that he held 'feasts' at times when there was no justification, ate meat in his apartment on fish days and invited certain favourites among the brethren to his chamber for 'recreation and refreshment'; that drinks were often taken after compline; that the sons of rich men were supported by alms set aside for the poor; that monks sometimes wore 'fashionable clothes,' or, 'thinking themselves of more importance and better standing than others wear belts and knives unnecessarily ornamented ...'. A number of monks were deprived of their offices by the Visitors, and three of them were accused of 'incontinence and violence', one of these being forbidden 'to talk with any woman, not even his own relations'. The abbot himself was said in 1323 to have his 'well-known bodily weaknesses' and hence two austere coadjutators were deputed to act with him.[xxxvii]

The revenues of Campden seem to have played their part in financing these and other practices. In 1332 a royal licence was granted to Chester Abbey to appropriate Campden church.[xxxviii] Even in 1340 the income of Campden church, now entirely under the control of Chester, seems to have been assigned directly to the cellarer of the abbey.

However, another appeal was made in the same year to the Bishop of Worcester and the Pope, it being stated that:

> The Monastery has lost by inundation of the sea, 30 carucates of land in Bromburgh, Eastham, Whiteby and Ines [Ince] of the yearly value of £100 and the manors of Brocton, Issard and the church of Holiwell in Wales by reason of the wars between the Kings of England and Princes of Wales. The belfry and most of the church are dangerously out of repair.[xxxix]

These, of course, were the very same reasons as in the letter of a hundred and fifty years earlier. However, the Bishop confirmed the appropriation, and this was itself confirmed by the Pope in 1345.

In 1379 the income from Campden was transferred from the cellarer to a new chantry, established for the benefit of the souls of the incumbent abbot and his monks. This chantry, where masses were to be said continuously for the souls of the late abbot, the present abbot on his death, and any monks who might die in future, was to be financed wholly from revenues arising from Campden church.[xl] Campden seems over this period to have been contributing to the material comforts as well as to the spiritual needs of the community at Chester.

At the dissolution St Werburgh's lost all its possessions. In 1541, however, just a few years after the dissolution, Henry VIII founded new episcopal sees at Gloucester, Chester and elsewhere, and granted Chester Cathedral the tithes, rectory and advowson of Campden that had formerly belonged to the abbey. A few years later, however, this charter was voided and in exchange for land the Cathedral gave up its rights in a number of churches, including Campden.[xli] The disputes that followed these events are outlined below in Chapters 8 and 12.

Notes

i Verey, David *Cotswold Churches* (Batsford 1976) 30 & 175
ii Rushen, op cit..118
iii Howard, F.E., 'Account of the Architecture of the Church' *A Guide to the Parish Church of Chipping Campden, Glos* (SPCK: Notes on Famous Churches and Abbeys No 40)
iv ibid
v Anon, `Church of St. James', Chipping Campden', *Gloucester Diocesan Magazine*, 1914, 137.
vi Verey & Brooks, *The Buildings of England : Gloucestershire 1: The Cotswolds* (Penguin Books 1986) 230
vii St. James's Church Guide, 2
viii Verey & Brooks, op cit 153
ix ibid 230
x Rushen, op cit.118
xi *Cartulary of Chester Abbey*, reprinted in Chatham Society, *Remains in Lancashire and Cheshire* NS Vol 79 (1920) 14,17,31; Birch,W. de Gray, *Jnl of Chester Archaeological & Historical Soc.* NS Vol III 1890, 1 - 25
xii *Remains* 53-55
xiii ibid 110
xiv Bishop Wulstan, *Register*, Vol 1 fol121 (a) quoted by Rushen op cit 113/4
xv Howard, F.E. op cit
xvi Personal knowledge
xvii William Weoley's will is unknown, but the fact that his brass exists in the church makes it likely that he also left a bequest.
xviii Rushen, op cit has sixteen references to the Gibbes, Gybbys or Gybbes families, extending over five centuries, together with pre and post Reformation mentions of Lethenards.
xix Verey, *Cotswold Churches* 31-2

xx ibid

xxi Powell, Geoffrey & Wilson, Jill, The Chipping Campden Altar Hangings, *BGAS Trans*, Vol CXV, 1997

xxii Verey & Brooks, op cit 230

xxiii Powell & Wilson, op cit

xxiv For instance the inquisitions on the deaths of Sir Roger de Somery in 1273 (*Cal Inq p.m.* 1 Edw I No 13) and Gilbert de Clare dated 12th August 1314 (*Cal Inq p.m.* 8 Edw II No 68).

xxv See Whitfield, Christopher, 'Lionel Cranfield and the Rectory of Campden' *BGAS Trans xxxi* 1962 114-5

xxvi *Remains*, Vol 79 Charter No 120 138

xxvii ibid. Editor's Note to Charter

xxviii *Feet of Fines Glos* Case 73 file 12 No 223; *Remains* Vol 79 Charter No 121

xxix *Remains* Vol 79, Charter No 122 f11d (8d)

xxx R. de Stainsby seems to have remained vicar here for some decades. In 1275 the Bishop of Worcester wrote to the deacons of Campden and Blockley about a debt paid by de Stainsby's proctor to Elizabeth Lady of Hoggindaston (Aston Magna) : *Reg Giffard* folio 6d Worcs Hist Soc 85 - quoted in Hockaday Abstracts.

xxxi There is a note in the Register of Worcester Priory that sometime in the mid-13th century the Abbot of Chester paid Worcester a 4s 4d pension for the church at Campden. See Hale, W. (ed), *Register of Worcester Priory* (Camden Soc Pubns VolXCI).

xxxii Warmington, 'A medieval dispute' *CADHAS Notes & Queries* Vol IV No 2

xxxiii *Reg Giffard* 18d Worc Misc 21 - quoted in Hockaday abstracts

xxxiv *Remains* Vol 79 p.139 Charter 123. see.also. *Trans Chester Hist Soc* NS 55 64

xxxv Ormerod, op cit Vol I 250; Vol II 12; Burns, R.V.H., *History of the Monks of Chester* 14 - 16; *Papal Letters* 1345 8 Kal Feb Avignon 166

xxxvi Hilton, R.H., *The Medieval Society: The West Midlands at the End of the Thirteenth Century*, (Weidenfeld & Nicholson, 1967). The value of Campden Church in 1291, according to the *Taxatio* of Pope Nicholas was 10s.

xxxvii Burne, Canon R.V.H., op cit

xxxviii *Cal Pat Rolls* 6 Edw III pt 1 M15

xxxix *Cal Pap Reg* 3 Fol 166

xl Burns, op cit. 98; ee also 'St Werburgh's Chantries in 1379': *The Cheshire Sheaf* December 1906 Notes 1179; 97-98 ; For example, every day a mass was to be said for the abbot and for the dead, each monk to celebrate this in turn for a week, and to receive 2s from the revenues of Campden church. On the anniversary of the abbot's death, the almoner was to receive 20s from the revenues of Campden church for the use of the poor, half to be distributed in white bread or money and the monks to have a pint of wine each out of the 20s 'in order that they may pray with more devotion'. Thirdly every year at Easter the cellarer was to pay the prior 13s 4d and each of the other monks, chaplains and professed 10s from the revenues of Campden church for the augmentation of their vestments, 'so that they may more devoutly serve God and pray for the soul of the abbot'.

xli *The Cheshire Sheaf* (Third Series, Vol II, Jan 1898) 7; Hemingway, Chester I. 316; Bp Gastrell, *Notitia Cestriensis* I, 67

PART III: THE 16th AND 17th CENTURIES

7

Sir Thomas Smyth and the Reunification of Campden

As we have seen, at the end of the 15th century the manor of Campden was still divided between the descendants of the heirs of the Stafford and Lodelowe families. However, the actual land holdings within the manor were far more complex. Leases and sub-leases, bequests in support of chantries, and other forms of transfer and disposal had resulted in a patchwork of tenures and holdings, perhaps even then difficult to disentangle. Change was rapid. However, at the dawn of Tudor England Campden showed no sign of the development which would occur in the next century.

Early in the 16th century Campden's four parts were surveyed for ostensibly military purposes but also for tax.[i] The 1522 survey provides another snapshot of the manor like those of 1273 and 1381, but great changes are visible. Henry VIII required knowledge of the number of able-bodied men who might be available for the militia in case of war with France, and what weapons and harness could be supplied. In addition he needed to have an indication of the probable sums that could be levied to pay for any war. Like the rest of Gloucestershire, Chipping Campden (probably with Berrington), Broad Campden and Westington each provided returns. Although Combe is not shown, the Abbot of Bordesley is listed with other churchmen at the head of the Chipping Campden list.

Since the survey covered the entire county it gives an opportunity to measure the parish of Campden against other towns and hamlets nearby. £2 was the lowest sum expected to contribute to a lay subsidy. Only Winchcombe exceeded Campden in the number of inhabitants with goods valued at £2 or more.

The survey provides an interesting but very incomplete view of Campden at this time. Those named on the lists were men able to bear arms (a total of 53), those possessing harness or weapons (two) and those with sufficient land or goods to be able to pay a levy should one be needed. Thus most women, children, and the feeble or elderly poor were omitted.

Taxation was levied at the place of residence so where the value of land is indicated without any goods it can be assumed that the land-holder was not resident. Using this criterion, none of the gentry was resident. Richard Tracy, gent, held land in Westington, George Samwel in Chipping Campden and John Russell and Sir Edward Grevyle in Broad Campden. The latter held but 7 shillings worth here but his estate in Charlton Kings was valued at £20 and five other holdings in the county were recorded. The richest man was Thomas Bonar[ii] of Chipping Campden, whose 20s worth of land was nothing compared to his £400 worth of goods. No-one else approached his wealth, William Blowar and Richard Nobill, the next richest having but £20 apiece.

The clergy were included, with the value of their land holdings and salaries. It was only some 20 years before the dissolution of the monasteries, and returns such as this showed only too clearly where much of the wealth lay.[iii] The land holdings listed for the clergy were valued at above £50 as against less than £20 for the lay holders. Whilst this survey was only partial and omitted much information, nevertheless it provides a backdrop for the dramatic changes in land ownership later in the century.

A further aspect of life in Campden at that time is shown by the differing value of the goods possessed by those listed in the return. In Westington 8 of the 11 men (mainly agriculturalists) listed possessed goods worth £2 or more. In Broad Campden only one of the eight listed had no assessable property. In Chipping Campden, however, 35 out of 79 fell below the £2 limit. Most, perhaps all, of these will have been sons, apprentices, journeymen and servants of the skilled craftsmen, artisans and merchants who made up the population of the market town. Twenty men, however, had £8 or more in goods.

Only one trade is mentioned: another Thomas Bonar 'tailor' with £2 worth of goods, so described no doubt to distinguish him from his rich namesake. However, the town would have been able to supply the district with a variety of goods and services: all the trades noted in the Poll Tax survey 130 years earlier would still have been there, and no doubt others besides, like a blacksmith, a collar-maker and a glover.

Every Wednesday a market was held in the wide High Street. People from the surrounding district flocked in to buy, sell and gossip and to take advantage of the many services not available in their own villages. Several times a year a fair[iv] was held where itinerant pedlars and specialist itinerant artisans sold less frequently needed items, in addition to agricultural produce, animals and other goods.

A single court in each hamlet and another in the town dealt with the necessary decisions involved in strip farming and husbandry in the hamlets, the business of the town and similar matters.[v] There is some doubt how far the town had changed in extent since the 12th century. The original town plan may well have allowed for growth. Gardens and closes unoccupied by dwellings occur in some of the earlier leases.

One important institution in the town was its school, situated in the High Street.[vi] Supported by the Fereby bequest it continued to provide free schooling for Campden boys. Those accepted were most probably the sons of the yeomen, the wealthier townsfolk, and minor gentry who might be intended for careers in the church, the law or other professions. The schoolmaster was also the chantry priest, and was proficient in Latin and the classics. One master's name is known before the 17th century: Sir Robert Glazeman in 1547, who received £8 a year. The title 'Sir' indicates that he was in holy orders. He is known only from the records of the commissioners sent at the time of the dissolution of the chantries.

When Thomas Smyth married Elizabeth, widow of Edward Smyth of Cressing Temple, Essex, probably in 1534, both parties may have congratulated themselves on an advantageous match. He had been for some time a page in the king's household. It seems likely that he had been amongst the royal entourage at the Field of the Cloth of Gold in 1520 and more recently, in 1532, he had accompanied King Henry VIII and Anne Boleyn on a state visit to Calais and Boulogne visiting King Francis I.[vii] His wife had been born Elizabeth Fitzherbert. She was heiress to one half of the manor of Campden and descendent of a line going back to Edward de Lodelowe.

Probably the only interest the previous holders of Campden had taken in their half of the manor was as a source of income. Sir Thomas, however, was to involve himself in the tangled maze of freeholds, leases and sub-leases within the entire manor, not just of the part he held by right of his wife.[viii] On 8th November 1544 he bought a substantial part of the estate of Christopher Savage, heir to the other half manor. As well as two woods, part of a close and other property, he acquired the entitlement to the rents from the town, the view of frankpledge and the leet of the manor of Campden, rights which made him responsible for good order and justice there. He was no longer just lord of one half of the manor but had gained some lordship rights over the entire manor of Campden, other than Broad Campden and Combe.

However, it seems that he needed to establish facts about the original manor. Even the precise extent of his wife's inheritance might have been unknown. In an illiterate age much would have depended on the testimony of the older members of the community who could vouch for customs and practices from time out of mind. So, possibly in order to prove his rights and entitlements, on 1st December 1546 he obtained Letters Patent from Henry VIII providing a certified copy of the writ and the inquisition findings that described the manor at the death of Sir Roger de Somery in 1273.[ix] This no doubt was an attempt to establish a base from which to reclaim rights and powers over his lands.

This takeover by a newcomer, however wealthy and with whatever rights he had through his wife, does not appear to have been welcome to some of the long-standing dignitaries of the town, who had been used to having their own way. Thomas Bonner, who had himself obtained a share of Christopher Savage's lands in 1544, together with others, eventually took action and sent their servants with weapons to prevent the Smyths' cattle being put out to graze in the common pasture of the New Leasow.[x] The town bailiffs were brought in and settled matters in favour of the Smyths and for a short while the cattle grazed contentedly, as they had every right to do. Overnight, however, on 23rd April 1545 the cattle were removed again, and once again the matter was settled by their being returned to the pasture.

This was not the end of the affair for on 20th June the cattle were not just turned out of the pasture but were impounded and Thomas Bonner produced a writ ordering the town bailiffs to hand them over to him. Up to this point Sir Thomas Smyth had been reasonably forbearing but, using his knowledge of the workings of the law, and no doubt his acquaintance with many of the judges and lawyers, he took legal action. A case was brought before Star Chamber accusing Bonner of forging the writ. The causes of this dispute are unknown. Possibly Bonner felt he had a genuine grievance; it seems from some correspondence 70 years later that the New Leasow was used for hay, and the grazing of cattle in Spring and Summer could have been against the custom of the manor.

Nevertheless, Sir Thomas Smyth was fully intent on receiving his due. The

Star Chamber proceedings between a page in the King's Chamber and a 'great ryche man'[xi] would have been the talk of Campden. Smyth, who probably knew and was known by most, if not all of the councillors sitting in judgment,[xii] made his point - he was not to be trifled with.

It is uncertain what passed between the two in the next year but on 14th February 1547 much of the land acquired by Thomas Bonner from Christopher Savage and subsequently passed by Bonner to his son Anthony, was granted to Sir Thomas Smyth. About the same time Smyth obtained 'a moiety of the manor, various lands, the advowsons of two chapels and a prebend' from Francis Savage.[xiii] Smyth was not yet done with the law, however, for a number of further Star Chamber suits are recorded during the next five or six years against William Sheldon,[xiv] Francis Savage, Anthony Bonner, John Bowkarr and Harry Langston amongst others, over such matters as felling trees and bushes. His London background and contacts seem to have encouraged Smyth to engage in litigation.

Some conflict persisted between Smyth as lord of the manor, and the town, over rights and privileges. The arrival of a firm and resident lord seems to have been a problem to those who had lived for so long under a laxer regime. During the period of the fragmented manor, the townsfolk, and to a lesser extent those in the hamlets, had probably been in the habit of running their own affairs and, no doubt, encroaching somewhat on the customary rights of the lords.

Sir Thomas Smyth seems to have been intent on restoring the powers and revenues of the lord of the manor. On 20th June 1555 he obtained from Philip and Mary yet further Letters Patent including copies of two more charters obtained by earlier lords of the manor.[xv] One was the charter granted by Henry III in 1247 to Sir Roger de Somery, giving the right of a Wednesday market and a fair. The other was the 14th century charter granted to Richard de Stafford, granting a second fair.[xvi]

The dissolution of the monasteries gave certain opportunities to leaseholders to acquire the land they occupied. In 1545 Sir Thomas Russell bought a large area in Broad Campden, previously held by Tewkesbury Abbey. Further changes and opportunities were to come. As foreshadowed in a commission of Henry VIII, Edward VI dissolved the chantries in 1547.

A substantial amount of property came eventually to Sir Thomas Smyth

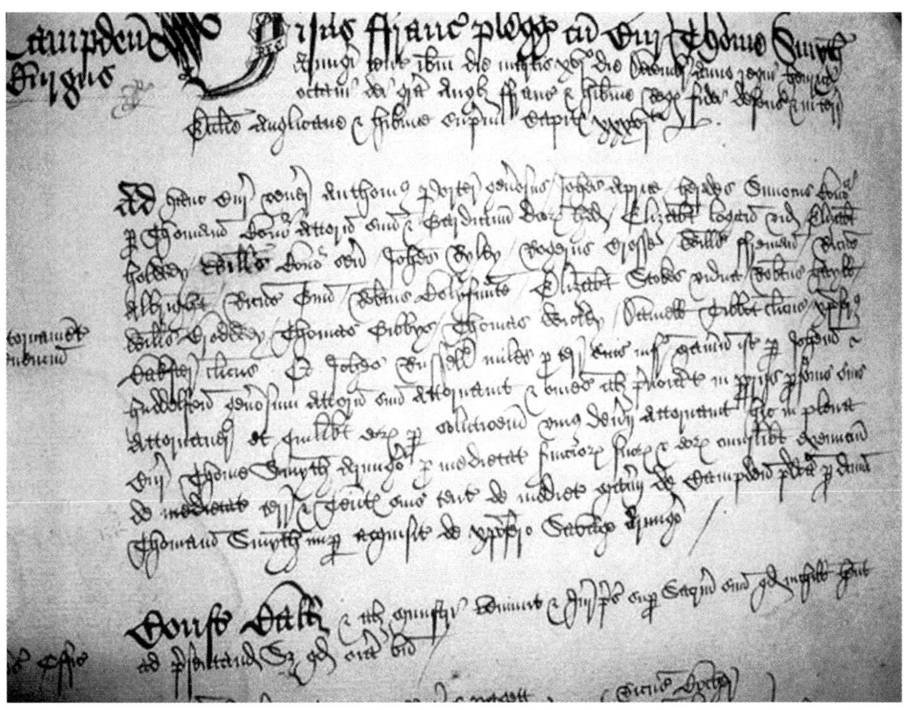

Part of a page from the Court Leet book of Sir Thomas Smyth. The heading reads (in Latin) 'Campden Borough : View of the Frank Pledge of Sir Thomas Smyth Esquire, on ...the 16th day of December in the 36th year of the reign of Henry VIII by the grace of God king of England France and Ireland and Supreme Head of the Anglican and Irish churches.' The book runs through four reigns, from the last years of Henry VIII to the early years of Elizabeth.
(By kind permission of Leicester, Leicestershire and Rutland Record Office)

following the seizure of the chantry lands by the Crown. A little before their dissolution he acquired the advowsons and revenues of the two chantries of St Katherine. Certain lands of the other dissolved Campden chantries were granted to a Henry Stapleton on 13 March 1549[xvii] and on the same day Thomas Smyth acquired them from Stapleton.[xviii] A further batch of chantry lands, again over a wide area but including several parcels within Campden parish, was acquired by two gentlemen on 25th March the same year.[xix] The named tenants included that 'great rich man' Thomas Bonner who held land from Holy Trinity and Our Lady's chantries. The detailed schedules listing these properties show that, although the rents for these lands had belonged to the chantries, the entitlement to the ground rents had remained with the manor. This meant that Thomas Bonner's holdings were due to pay 16d a year to Sir Thomas Smyth.

Sir Thomas Smyth took every opportunity to add to his holding by buying back lands within the manor as and when they became available and by leasing where he could. The augmentation of his lands was a lengthy process partly because he had to find the resources to pay for his acquisitions and partly because the disentangling and offering for sale of small parcels of land held by syndicates took time.

Elizabeth, Smyth's wife, died at about this time and he married another widow, Katherine Winter, née Throckmorton. In 1553 Thomas and Katherine were granted Combe Manor, to be held in chief from the king at one fortieth of a knight's fee. Bordesley Abbey, which had held Combe, had been dissolved in 1538.

In 1569 the tragic death of his eldest son and heir occurred. Henry Smyth, a young student lawyer, hanged himself in the Temple, London. His story, enhanced by moralising on the unwisdom of relapsing from the reformed Protestant religion back to Rome, was included as a cautionary tale by John Foxe, the martyrologist, in his Actes and Monuments in 1563.

The number of Smyth's children is not completely certain. The rhyme that used to be recited in the 18th century by the sexton when showing visitors the Smyth tomb, in its prime position at the northeast corner of the chancel of the church, is of interest but patently inaccurate:

> Little pretty Betty, Dorothy and Anne,
> Mary and Mosselyn, little Gizzy Ganne,
> Richard and Robert, Geoffrey and John,
> Edward and William, and little pretty Tom.
> These are all Mr Smyth's children everyone
> Besides two stillborn infants, a daughter and a son.

Henry is omitted, perhaps because he was a suicide, and so is Cassandre who died before her father. Gizzy Ganne is Grisogon who married Andrew Jenour of Alfriston Hall in Essex. These, with Thomas who died young, were children of his first marriage. His second family included his heir, Anthony, also omitted from the rhyme, and Richard, Lucius, Paul, Daniel, Elizabeth, Anne and Catherine.[xx]

Katherine died on 25th July 1574 and Sir Thomas did not marry a third time. In 1577 he began to make appropriate provision for his family after his own death. The only surviving child of his first marriage, Grisogon, was given one fourth of his estate, disentailed on condition that she and her husband should sell it to Anthony Smyth, his principal heir, if he so desired. Somewhat later, in 1622, he leased to two of his younger sons at a peppercorn rent 'a cornmill adjoining the Coneygree' (at that time being occupied by Anthony) and certain woods and dwellings standing on Court Piece. This gave them in effect an income of £40 a year each and seems to have been a way of ensuring their inheritance. Provision was made also for certain named servants to have the use of specified parcels of land, Anthony Smyth being required to allow 'quiet enjoyment' to them.[xxi] In view of Anthony's future actions it might be thought that his father was already well aware of his son's shortcomings.

The Smyth monument, in the north-east corner of the chancel
(Jesse Taylor/CADHAS)

Smyth's own tenure of land was not entirely with quiet enjoyment however. In the period from 1579 to 1587 he had faced a suit in Chancery brought by Thomas Procter and others over land in Broad Campden. In 1587 he himself took action, bringing a suit in Chancery against widow Bridgett Bonner. He had been denied access to his mill (presumably Berrington Mill) across a close she held, and claimed loss of profits. Her defence was that since her son, Anthony, was a minor the close and other lands were in the hands of the Crown. Nevertheless, she admitted that free access to the mill had previously been given to all tenants of the manor across the close. 'Ote Close' had been enclosed some 35 years earlier and the mill had been built five years before that.

On 31st October 1593 Sir Thomas Smyth died in Ocle, Herefordshire, perhaps when visiting his daughter Elizabeth, wife of Hugh Walshe of Ocle. Anthony, his eldest surviving son, from his second marriage, succeeded to the main part of his property.

The manor was now once again a single entity after more than three hundred years of division; but much remained to be done. Parts of the manor were still in other hands, and the town dignitaries were not yet won over to the idea of a single and resident lord and landowner. The burgesses' right to control of the town was clear, but outside that boundary the influence of the parishioners had been curtailed by his wresting back of manorial rights and powers. It would take someone with a different approach to resolve the simmering discontent. Unfortunately Anthony Smyth, the new lord of the manor, was not that person.

Notes

i Hoyle, R.W. (ed), *The Military Survey of Gloucestershire 1522*, (BGAS Gloucestershire Record Series Vol 6 1993)

ii This is almost certainly the Thomas Bonner with whom Thomas Smyth had dealings a few years later.

iii Hoyle, op cit 226-7. Lands belonging to the Abbot of Chester, rector, £28; Edward Gyffard, vicar, vicarage worth £16; Abbot of Bordesley £6 13s 4d; salaries: William Sharpe, curate £6 13s 4d, three chantrists £6 each, one chantrist £4 13s 4d

iv Two annual fairs held on St George's day (23rd April) and St James's day (25th July) were granted to the lords of the manor in the13th and 14th centuries but a later charter granted in 1605 granted to the bailiffs and burgesses two fairs to be held on Ash Wednesday and St Andrew's day (30th November). Whether these were in addition to the two medieval fairs, or were a replacement is not clear. Originally each lasted three or four days and began on the eve of the set date.

v The proceedings are recorded in a Court Leet book covering the period from the last years of Henry VIII to the beginning of Elizabeth's reign, now deposited in Leicester Record Office. (Leics R.O. DE3214 1 (673))

vi Cook, Robert, *Chipping Campden School* (Drinkwater 1990)

vii It is possible that he came either from a Campden family or was closely related to that family.

viii His duties as a member of the royal household for some while may have prevented him from beginning to take an active role in the management of the estate. During the later stages of the siege of Boulogne in 1544 Thomas Smyth, there in attendance on the king, was knighted and granted arms. These were given by Garter King of Arms on 4th September. It may be that this marked the end of his continuous royal service for later the same year Sir Thomas Smyth began his planned acquisition of lands in Campden.

ix This certified copy includes the first of the inquisitions outlined in Chapter 3 above. The copy is from 1543/4 or later, since it gives the full titulary of Henry VIII adopted in that year. A copy of this document is displayed in the Court Room of the Old Police Station in Chipping Campden High Street. (Gloucs R O D2635)

x This seems to be one of the leasows to the west of the upper part of Hoo Lane.

xi Rushen op cit 28, quoting Star Chamber Proceedings

xii Sitting in the court of Star Chamber might be "the lord chancellor and the lords and other of the Privy Council, so many as will, and other lords and barons which be not of the Privy Council and be in the town, and the judges of England, specially the two chief judges', according to the contemporary lawyer Sir Thomas Smyth (not believed to be any relation) in his *De Republica Anglorum*; quoted by Elton, G.R., *The Tudor Constitution, Documents and Commentary*, (CUP 1962), 164.

xiii '... royal licence to Francis Savage to alienate to Thomas Smythe a moiety of the manor of Campden alias Chepyng Campden, and land ... there and in Brodecampden, Westington and Burrington ... and advowsons of the two chantries or free chapels of St Katherine, and of the prebend of St Katherine in Campden, except the water mill called the Over Mill in Westington.' (PRO *Pat. Roll*; 38 Henry VIII 10m.35; quoted by Josephine Griffiths)

xiv On this dispute, see Warmington, Allan, 'The Land at Combe and the Dissolution' *CADHAS Notes & Queries* Vol 3 No 1

xv A certified copy of the two charters from the Rolls of Henry III and Edward III (referred to in Chapter 3) giving the rights of the lord of the manor and listing a Wednesday market, and annual fairs. It is dated from the reign of Philip and Mary, and was probably written between 25th July 1554 and 19th July 1555. A copy of this document is displayed in the Court Room of the Old Police Station in Chipping Campden High Street. (Gloucs R O D2635).

xvi It is possible that the two fairs were held in the wide street of Leysbourne, then outside the town and within the lord of the manor's own lands. If so, the market would have just extended throughout the entire space of the High Street and Leysbourne. However, the market dues would be paid separately to the town and the lord of the manor. There is no direct evidence for this but it is considered possible by analogy with other towns.

xvii Henry Stapleton paid £1028 9s 2d for a large number of lands widely distributed. The full list is very detailed, for example including '... one yard of land and a barn and close lately in tenure of John Prat and afterwards of Thomas Smyth esq in the field called Byrrington in Champden *[sic]* parish Glouc which belonged to the late chantry called the First Chantry *[prime cantarie]* ...' (*Cal Patent Rolls* Edward VI, Vol V, 294-5.)

xviii Gwilt, Charles Perkins, *Notices relating to Thomas Smyth of Campden and Henry Smyth Sometime Alderman of London*, (1836) 10

xix Thomas Watson of 'Daglynworth' Gloucestershire and William Adys of Worcestershire, bought for £1306 0s 3d a considerable number of properties including some that had been part of the endowments of the chantries of Second St Katherine's, Holy Trinity and St Mary's (*Cal Patent Rolls* Edward VI Vol II, 187). Other records show that the purchase of lands in this way was a long drawn-out process. The request to purchase is dated 23rd February and the grant 24th April.

xx The rhyme perhaps related only to the carved figures of his family surrounding his monument in St James's church. The arms of both wives are given separately, impaled with his. This does not explain the omission of several of his offspring.

xxi Leics RO DE3214 267/23

8

Land Controversies and Disputes

Having inherited the manor of Campden and the greater part of his father's wealth in 1593, Anthony Smyth managed his affairs so ill that within six years he was finding it necessary to borrow money. At that time there was no banking system to provide means of borrowing, but a number of rich men were prepared to lend against the security of landed property — at a high rate of interest. For London merchants this was a profitable addition to their business, and for the wealthy gentry and titled men for whom, because of their rank, trade was not an option, it was one form of business open to them. It was a lucrative pursuit, even though the risk of bad debts was high, as the sums to be repaid considerably exceeded the amounts actually loaned. In a very few years Anthony Smyth's estate became encumbered with a greater and greater burden of debt.

As early as 1600 a consortium of lenders including Ralph Sheldon of Weston Park, Warwickshire, John Throgmorton of Lyppiatt, Gloucestershire, and a London lawyer had loaned a large sum against the security of the manor house of Campden, its demesne lands, other lands and the rectory and tithes of the parish.[i]

It was easy to fall further into debt. A loan requiring the repayment of £500 is recorded in 1599.[ii] In May 1602 this debt fell due on the death of the lender. Unable to pay, Anthony Smyth offered the sum of £210 (two hundred guineas), possibly the original amount borrowed, by November of the same year and repayment of the entire £500 was deferred until the following May.[iii]

Anthony Smyth seems to have fallen into the trap of borrowing more to pay off earlier debts as further loans were obtained from a number of other parties. Soon he appears to have been obtaining money from a large number of sources at high repayment rates. A summary in 1604 includes £1,000 due for £630 borrowed, two amounts of £300 for loans of £210, £500 for £315 owed, £800 for a debt of £525, and £400 against the sum of £210 borrowed. These debts appear to be in addition to a sum of £7,000 payable to Sir William Bond and Sir William Wythens, against the security of the manor of Campden, and perhaps also to £4,200, owed to Henry Adams.[iv] This situation had not escaped the notice of several wealthy men.

Meanwhile one of the ways in which Anthony Smyth attempted to restore his fortunes is alleged to have been downright theft. As the story is known only from the side of the townsfolk it cannot be said whether he considered that he had right on his side. It seems that in 1605 one of the bells in the tower of the parish church had cracked and the churchwardens decided to have it recast. The bell was taken down and the valuable pieces of bell-metal worth 100 marks were locked in the church awaiting the arrival of the carts to remove them to the bell-founder's premises the following day. For some reason the townspeople were uneasy: perhaps there had already been some argument about the ownership of the bell. They set two sturdy fellows armed with staves within the church to watch overnight.

Suddenly at midnight three of Anthony Smyth's servants, 'of bad repute' according to the subsequent Star Chamber proceedings, burst in to take the metal. Following a 'most cruelle assault' they were forced to flee and found refuge in the manor house close at hand. The constable's attempt to arrest them came to nothing as he was refused admittance. Next day two of the men were taken and bound over but the third was still protected, Anthony Smyth flying into 'a great rage and furie' with the constable and throwing him out. Nevertheless, his debts at this time were so great that even if he had gained possession of the bell-metal, its value would have been but a drop in the ocean. It was becoming increasingly evident that there could only be one end.[v]

The townsfolk of the borough seem to have become thoroughly hostile to some of the activities of Anthony Smyth, which no doubt they saw as interfering with their long-established privileges. They therefore took advantage of the arrival in 1603 of a new king to establish once and for all their powers and privileges. In 1605 the burgesses of Chipping Campden sought and obtained a royal charter from James I, defining in great detail exactly how the town should be governed.[vi] The cost of this enterprise would have been substantial in fees and other expenses, especially without any assistance in the way of influence or finance from the lord of the manor. Ceremonial was not overlooked. Two silver maces were bought for the two sergeants-at-mace appointed to serve the bailiffs.[vii] How all this was paid for was not, perhaps, made clear to the townsfolk at the time, but a later revelation suggests that the money had been embezzled from a charitable fund.[viii]

Part of the heading of the 1605 Charter granted by James I to the bailiffs and burgesses of Chipping Campden ***(By kind permission of Leicester, Leicestershire and Rutland Record Office)***

The first bailiffs and elected burgesses of the borough and the first High Steward were named in the charter. John Price, bailiff, was to be prominent a little later in a dispute between Sir Baptist Hicks and Lionel Cranfield; William Damporte, the other bailiff, was involved in a scandal over the funding of the school. Nicholas Overbury, first High Steward, was almost certainly the father or grandfather of Sir Thomas Overbury, the local magistrate at the time of the Campden Wonder in 1660.

In this same year the bailiffs of Chipping Campden, no doubt bolstered by their newly confirmed status, instituted proceedings in the Star Chamber against Anthony Smyth who was also a local justice of the peace. They alleged that for five years he had let off people accused of breaking the peace and even petty criminals, for bribes.[ix] There is no doubt that there was considerable ill-feeling between Smyth and the town. Anthony Smyth was being attacked from all sides.

At this time of transition Campden and the surrounding district were largely self-sufficient economically, as was normal in the early 17th century. The open fields, pastures, orchards and closes, together with the gardens of the inhabitants provided fresh food and the town offered the services to supply most manufactured needs. The weekly Wednesday market in the borough brought in people with produce to sell and all those from round about needing supplies, goods and services. It seems probable that even local tobacco would have been on sale from the fields of the Vale and perhaps Westington Hill.[x]

Early in 1610 a Londoner, Lionel Cranfield,[xi] having purchased (securely, as he thought) the rectory and tithes of Campden from a consortium appointed by the Crown, sent his agents to discover the facts about the manor. They responded with a wealth of information that provides an astonishingly detailed snapshot of the place in the early 17th century.[xii]

The three hamlets of Broad Campden, Westington and Berrington were exhaustively described. The majority of the holdings were held on the usual form of lease, for the lives of three successive family members. Each holder of land was named, together with the other 'lives' included in the lease. The houses and property were described in considerable detail, and the area of land held, the annual rent, the yearly value and the estimated purchase price were given. The names and holdings of 17 families are named in Broad Campden, holding 20 yardlands; there were 16 families in Westington with 24 yardlands; and 25 in Berrington with 13 yardlands. Just as in 1273, Berrington people each held less land that those in the other hamlets.

The demesne lands, certain freehold lands and the glebe were described, as were the amount and annual value of crops in each hamlet. A separate list showed the names of the inhabitants of the borough with the amount of the yearly ground-rent payable by each. About 100 names of residents and shopkeepers are listed in the borough, with another 45 holders of closes and tenements there. All in all Lionel Cranfield had a substantial amount of information on which to make his decision. Indeed the information is so detailed that it may possibly have been in his mind to purchase the whole manor.[xiii]

Even during the period of this survey, Anthony Smyth was continuing to borrow against his lands. In 1606 he mortgaged Grange farm (probably Combe) to Sir William Bond and Sir William Wythens.[xiv] By this time they appear to have been the major creditors and had wisely remortgaged much of the lands involved.

A 1608 Survey of men fit for military service[xv] supplements the Cranfield Survey and shows a busy town capable of handling most local requirements. Five butchers are recorded. Their by-product, leather, was handled by a tanner and a currier (leather dresser). A glover, who would have made gloves for hedgers and other agricultural workers, presumably acquired his supplies from them, although high quality leather for special orders might have been brought from further afield. The two shoemakers would also have made use of local supplies. Harness for horses and for draught oxen was the concern of the collarmaker. Horse-collars were made to measure for each horse. Amongst the wide variety of work carried out by the four smiths would have been shoeing horses.

Nine tailors are named. A major local product was hemp and one tewgarer is recorded, whose job it was to treat the hemp ready for the roper or for onward sale. Grain would have been ground locally in the mills; and two millers are listed. Three bakers are named and, since ovens were not to be found in most houses or cottages, they would have baked dishes brought in by townsfolk as well.

Four maltsters used local barley to make one of the basic ingredients for beer, but only one innkeeper is recorded. This does not mean that the town was without beer- and ale-houses. The Limitation of Taverns Acts of 1553 and 1590 had laid down that there might be only one tavern (which provided overnight accommodation) in a town or city, apart from named exceptions, such as Bristol. Two victuallers, who would have made and sold ale, are recorded. No other ale or beer makers are named; but it is likely that, as in subsequent centuries, many of those engaged in other trades also made ale or beer as a side venture. Two coopers kept them supplied with new barrels.

Building work employed a number of craftsmen: four masons, two carpenters, one pargeter (plasterer), a glazier and four slaters. Stone from the local quarries was used for most building, but the stone used for roofing and flagged floors came from a little further afield. Most houses in both town and hamlets were thatched but, on some larger town houses, new stone roofing slates were used.

Wool was still of importance, though less so than formerly. Four weavers, two fullers and two dyers may have produced sufficient cloth for both local needs and for sale at one of the annual fairs. In about 1617 a royal proclamation limited the sale of wool except through certain 'staple' towns and this seriously affected the local wool trade. The Corporation petitioned unsuccessfully to have Campden added to the list, with the full support of Sir Baptist Hicks.[xvi]

Not everything could be supplied from local resources, however. The chapman, or peddler, would have provided small items like needles and ribbons that it would not be economic to make in Campden. A haberdasher and a hatter supplied other items, many of which they may have made from materials brought in from elsewhere. The single mercer in this market town would have been a retail trader. His shop is likely to have supplied sugar, dried fruits and other luxury items to the local gentry. Letters and parcels could be dispatched to or received from London by the Shipston carrier.

When fairs took place travelling tradesmen and sellers of a wide variety of goods would converge on the town, together with those wishing to buy or sell livestock and others providing entertainment. Stalls and shops would have been set up in the wide market street and customers would stream in from considerably further afield than for the usual weekly market.

It is likely that some sort of jollifications were held in the locality from much earlier times but it was not until about 1612 that a group of gentry, led by Robert Dover, co-ordinated them into the annual event still known as Dover's Games or the Cotswold Olympicks. The open ground on which the games are held, Dover's Hill as it is known today, is actually in the parish of Weston-sub-Edge. However, being on the hill above Campden, it seems always to have drawn a large proportion of the contestants and spectators from this parish. Endymion Porter of Aston-sub-Edge was amongst the initiators of the Games and is said to have persuaded King James himself to donate a cast-off suit of clothing, or at least a hat and some other items, to be worn by the master of ceremonies.[xvii] As a Groom of the Bedchamber he would have been in an excellent position to have made such a request successfully.

By 1636 the annual event had become so well known amongst local and London gentry that a book of poems in praise of Dover and his Games was published.[xviii] Contributors included Ben Johnson and Michael Drayton. Since he lived so near at Stratford-upon-Avon, it has been suggested that William Shakespeare may have been a spectator in its earliest years.[xix] In *The Merry Wives of Windsor*, written in 1602, Shakespeare has Slender refer to Page's greyhound being 'outrun on Cotsall', which may confirm that sports were held nearby even before Captain Dover brought them together.

At this time the possession of landed property provided far higher social status than mere wealth, however vast. Thus an encumbered estate was marketable, often perforce if the impoverished owner could not meet his obligations. Potential buyers were likely to seek detailed information in advance about estates that might thus become available, to establish a value in absolute and annual revenue terms.

Cranfield was not alone in eyeing the manor of Campden. An immensely wealthy London mercer, Sir Baptist Hicks, was also seeking a prime seat in the country. How he assessed the manor is unknown since no records of a survey survive. He seems not to have acted openly but through agents. Whatever the means, by or during 1609 the manor was effectively already in the possession of Sir Baptist, though the formal transfer of the property seems only to have taken place two years later.

Anthony Smyth had died before Sir Baptist Hicks's purchase of his lands was complete.[xx] It seems probable that Sir Baptist bought up most of Smyth's debts and mortgages piecemeal and finally made his widow and son, Thomas, an offer for what remained.[xxi] It has been suggested that Sir William Bond and Sir William Wythens had been acting as his agents in buying up these debts, small and large, over some years. Cranfield's purchase of the rectory and tithes in 1609,[xxii] however, proved a bone of contention since he found his right to the tithes and the rectory lands was challenged by Sir Baptist Hicks, who had, in his own opinion, bought the rectory from Smyth. Many of the events in the dispute between Lionel Cranfield, the vicar and Baptist Hicks over the tithes of Campden are documented by a series of letters mainly between Cranfield, John Price, his agent and George Bonner, his attorney.[xxiii] Eventually the case was brought to court but it seems that it was resolved, perhaps by a deal out of court.

Little of this financial and legal activity would have been known to the inhabitants of the parish, except that from time to time different and changing landlords sought payment of rents, tithes and ground-rents.

Apart from these unseemly quarrels between neighbours, the letters from John Price give a view of aspects of local life. Several of the letters to Cranfield were sent by the Shipston carrier but urgent communications, particularly from George Bonner, travelled by a servant as messenger. Several times the carrier also took gifts of cheeses from Mrs Price. Apart from hay, crops mentioned include beans, wheat and barley. The best time to sell the barley 'which is but ffytting for mawlting' is discussed and said to be winter, 'the tyme of mawlte makinge'.[xxiv] The possibility of Mr Fleetwoode, a local landowner, inclosing land at 'Kinghome' is mentioned.[xxv] The rental obtained per yardland in Westington is 33s 4d whereas only 30s was offered in Broad Campden, 'Brode Campden mene are verrye back[w]arde'.[xxvi]

It seems that Sir Baptist obtained formal possession of the manor in 1611.

This is suggested by a lawsuit in which he was the plaintiff in the Trinity term of 1611, following the death of Anthony Smyth in Cirencester. It was common practice to establish transfer of property or confirm ownership by common agreement amongst all those concerned through a fictitious lawsuit. This appears to be such a case, since the other parties were the widow Joan Smyth and a number of gentlemen including Sir William Bond and Sir William Wythens and his wife, and the case related to the manors of Westington, Chipping Campden, Broad Campden and Berrington. The *Inquisition Post Mortem* of Anthony Smyth confirms that the formal sale of the manor to Sir Baptist occurred after the former's death.[xxvii] It is perhaps significant that Sir Baptist's various gifts to the church and town and the building of his new manor house do not begin until after this event. The new pulpit is dated 1612 which is also the traditional date for the beginning of work on the almshouses, the new manor house and the water supply from Westington Hill. These will now be described.

Notes

i Although as is made clear later, it is doubtful if the tithes and rectory were actually held by Anthony Smyth.

ii Leics R.O. DE3214 427/1

iii Leics R.O. DE 3214 427/2

iv Leics R.O. DE3214 491/4 and 341/6

v Whitfield, Christopher, *A History of Chipping Campden* (Shakespeare Head Press 1958), 89-90

vi Strictly speaking the document was not a charter but 'Letters Patent'. However, it has been familiarly referred to as a charter by earlier historians and this tradition is followed here. The original document was rediscovered in 2003 after having been lost for 130 years and more. The following year a copy was placed on display in the Court Room of the Old Police Station in Chipping Campden. (The original is in Leics R.O. DE3214 156.)

vii Briefly it established 26 burgesses, 14 being capital burgesses and 12 being inferior burgesses. Two of the capital burgesses were to be elected as bailiffs each year on the Wednesday before Michaelmas. Election to fill vacancies in the body of burgesses was by all the remaining burgesses from the townsmen and was for life. The 2 serjeants at mace were elected by the bailiffs. A steward, with knowledge of the law, was elected and paid by the burgesses. The 'charter' named all of the first bailiffs and burgesses and the steward. The corporation had power to make and enforce laws and penalties within the borough and to try, amongst other things, cases for amounts up to £6 13s 4d.

viii See Chapter 9 page 74

ix Whitfield, Christopher, *History* op cit 88-9

x The Penguin *Atlas of British and Irish History*, 133, shows the tobacco growing areas in Gloucestershire. The closest shown to Campden was on the hills to the south and west. Tobacco growing in this country was made illegal in 1619, though it did continue in some places until the 1630s.

xi Lionel Cranfield (1575-1645) merchant adventurer and mercer of London; became an MP in 1614 and held a succession of offices under the crown, including Lord Treasurer in 1621; created Earl of Middlesex in 1622. From the early 1600s was associated with Sir Edward Greville, who became indebted to him and from whom in 1622 he obtained the manors of Welford and Weston-on-Avon, Sezincote and Greville's own mansion, originally built by his ancestor, William Grevel, at Milcote.

xii *Survey of Campden carried out for Lionel Cranfield 1607-1609* Kent Archives Office; U269/1 B4; Transcription in CADHAS Archives 1995/1R

xiii Indeed, in March 1609/10 Cranfield bought Grevel House and certain other lands and properties in Berrington and Westington from his agent, John Price, for £800. (*Articles of Agreement between Edward Greville ... and Lionel Cranfield*; Kent Archive Office; U269/1 T19

xiv Gwilt, Charles Perkins, *Notices relating to Thomas Smith of Campden and Henry Smith, Sometime Alderman of London*, (1836), 12-13

xv Smith, John, *Men & Armour for Gloucestershire in 1608*, (Alan Sutton 1980). The listing includes only those men with armour and those physically capable of service in the militia. The main occupation is given in most cases but, judging from the trade directories of the next two centuries, many will have had secondary or even tertiary minor occupations as well. In addition, should the sole person in a particular trade have been unfit for war service, he would not have been listed. Similarly female occupations, seamstress for example, are not included. Nevertheless the list is sufficiently comprehensive to give a fair picture of the town.

xvi Rushen, op cit 43/4 quoting *State Papers* May 1617 26

xvii A suit of the king's clothes might well have been wearable by most people since 'He was of a middle stature, more corpulent through his clothes than in his body, yet fat enough, his clothes ever being made large and easy, the doublets quilted for stiletto proof, his breeches in great pleats and fully stuffed: ...' Weldon, Sir Anthony, 'The Court and Character of James I,' (1651) included in Millward, J.S. ed. *Portraits and Documents Seventeenth Century,* Hutchinson Educational (1961)

xviii Vyvyan, E.R (ed), *Annalia Dubrensis Upon the yeerely celebration of Mr Robert Dover's Olimpick Games upon Cotswold Hills*, with 32 contributors; reprinted The Tabard Press (1970)

xix Burns, Dr Francis, *Heigh for Cotswold; A History of Robert Dover's Olimpick Games*, Robert Dover's Games Society revised edition (2000) 9

xx Anthony Smyth's death seems to have occurred about the same time as Sir Baptist's purchase of the manor. He had certainly died by 1611.

xxi Several of Smyth's major creditors were known associates of Baptist Hicks. It has been suggested that Hicks worked through these men as agents. He wanted Campden as the future seat for his family and to provide a name for the title he foresaw would shortly be his and does not seem to have looked on it as a possible business proposition like Cranfield.

xxii Prestwich, Menna, *Cranfield: Politics and Profits under the early Stuarts*, (Clarendon Press 1966) 78; Whitfield, Christopher, 'Lionel Cranfield and the Rectory of Campden,' *Trans. BGAS* Vol. LXXXI, 100. Further details of this dispute are given in Chapter 9.

xxiii Whitfield, Christopher, 'Lionel Cranfield'. op cit 100; *Correspondence* in Sackville Papers, Kent Archive Office U269/1 B4 and B 8-10. Trancriptions in CADHAS Arch 1995/1R

xxiv Kent Arch Off U269/1 B8 & B9 : Letter 15th September, 1610; John Price to Lionel Cranfield. (Trans-criptions in CADHAS Archive 1995/1R)

xxv ibid: letter 11th March, 1610/11; John Price to Lionel Cranfield. Supposedly, this refers to Kingcombe.

xxvi ibid: letter 4th June 1611; John Price to Lionel Cranfield

xxvii Gwilt, Charles Perkins, op cit 12-13. The other two gentlemen were William and Edward Baber.

9

Sir Baptist Hicks Makes His Mark

Sir Baptist Hicks was a wealthy London mercer. Born in 1551, he was knighted the day before the coronation of James I & VI, was created Viscount Campden after his purchase of the manor and became Baron Hicks of Ilmington in 1628. He inherited the family business at the Sign of the White Boar in Soper Lane, off Cheapside, and sold rich stuffs — taffetas, velvets, silks — to the Court and to wealthy merchants. It is likely that many of the magnificent fabrics to be seen in the portraits of the period came from his shop. Money-lending to king and court provided a lucrative income and a source of influence.[i] As a magistrate he was the donor of the new Middlesex Sessions House, known as Hicks Hall. His younger brother, Sir Michael Hicks, was confidential secretary to Sir Robert Cecil, and this connection, as well as his experience as a magistrate, may explain his appointment as foreman of the jury, in 1606, at the trial of Father Garnet, who was accused of being the instigator of the Gunpowder Plot.

His many formal benefactions to Campden were recorded at length after his death. They include the almshouses, the Market Hall and many gifts to the church as well as the re-endowment of the grammar school. Moreover, an unrecorded but significant economic benefit must have come from the building of his great mansion, old Campden House, and the associated works. The previous manor house was adjacent to the church in Berrington and probably within the same enclosure as the new building. There is no record of any major rebuilding works by Sir Thomas Smyth and so the shell of his house could well have been standing for some centuries. It may have been of half-timbered construction in accordance with the late medieval tradition.

The old manor house appears to have been completely demolished by Sir Baptist. No physical indications have been found of the old building, and no archaeological excavations have taken place. It is possible that the clearance of the area to level and extend the terrace on which the new house was built swept away the foundations of the old. Alternatively, some of the tales of tunnels under Campden House may have their origin in the burial of parts of an earlier building under the raised terrace. A further possibility may also be worth considering since the large building, now known as the Court House in Calf Lane, does not seem to fit in with the alignment of the new house and the almshouses. Its building history is not well-established and it might in part predate Sir Baptist's major works. Although now faced with stone, almost certainly by Hicks, it could incorporate an earlier edifice, perhaps a barn or even the previous manor house.

It is not certain when Sir Baptist took the decision to build a completely new house. It is not impossible that the availability of high quality stone for such a project may have influenced him in his choice of Campden as a residence. The new house was designed to be in the forefront of contemporary fashion as was appropriate for someone with his wealth and connections. He had decided that Campden would be the principal seat of his family and he planned accordingly. His place in society was not such as to permit a 'prodigy house,' though he was wealthy enough to have afforded it. Nevertheless, his intention was to indicate his wealth and importance by producing a jewel of a house in the setting of a beautiful town and countryside.

Study of the house is hampered since no accounts or other records of the actual building works survive and even the precise plan and appearance of the house is uncertain. The earliest drawings of the house and its gardens date from about one hundred years after it was burnt down and differ in important details. The present ruins are all that remain after the removal of reusable stone in later centuries.

Nevertheless, the steps involved in the design and building of a great house can be reconstructed. In the early 17th century such works were planned and carried out without the assistance of an architect. Master masons worked out with the client what was required. Plans and information were exchanged between masons and, more importantly, between different clients planning and carrying out projects. As late as 1660 the advice given to those proposing to build a new house was to:

> ... make use of whatsoever you have either observed, or heard to be excellent elsewhere, then if you be not able to handsomely contrive it yourself, get some ingenious gentleman who has seen much of that kind ... to do it for you, and to give you a design of it on paper, though but roughly drawn, ...[ii]

A major new house being planned and built at the same time as Sir Baptist's was Hatfield House. Sir Robert Cecil did not destroy the large Elizabethan building within the same grounds but built his magnificent palace with long prospects on higher ground nearby. Since Sir Michael Hicks, the brother of Sir Baptist, was Cecil's confidential secretary there would have been no problem in gaining the most up-to-the-minute information on exterior and interior design and fashion. Sir Baptist's circle of London merchants and members of the court could also have been a source of further architectural advice based on experience.

The stone used was local, very probably from Westington Hill. The quarries there had been in use since at least medieval times and are still the source of high quality limestone. The master mason has not been identified but it is possible that he was a member of the White family.[iii] Other materials for the house would have been brought from further afield. Timber for roofs, floors and joists and the fine oak for panelling could not have been obtained locally. Glass may even have been brought from London.

Employment for a wide variety of labourers, artisans and tradesmen would have continued for several years. The enterprise was so substantial that it would have affected most of the population of the parish. Although the churchwardens' accounts[iv] do not survive before 1626, when the house had been completed, it seems probable that most of the specialist artisans and tradesmen were then still in business and could well figure amongst those employed in the first few years. Amongst these was Abraham White, mentioned above, William Lane the glazier, Thomas Whitefield the plumber and William Cale perhaps a blacksmith who made keys, hinges and other items. In addition local shopkeepers and suppliers, such as William Horne, who was paid for nails by the churchwardens, and John Milles who provided boards and joists, may perhaps have provided goods for Sir Baptist's work. The carrying of stone and timber would have required the hire of a large number of carts and horses.

It is clear that the house was typical of the Jacobean period: three main stories with dormers to the attic floor above. The principal façade lies on a terrace facing a formal garden at a lower level. At either end of the terrace was placed a small 'banqueting house', a place where Sir Baptist and his guests would retire after dinner for fruits and sweetmeats and for conversation. The quality of work and design of these pavilions, neither of which was destroyed in the fire, gives an idea of the standard of workmanship and the decorative features of the main building.

The principal floor of the interior was panelled in accordance with current fashion. Furnishings were equally of high quality and many, especially the fabrics, are likely to have been brought from London. The total cost of the house was said to be £29,000 and the furnishings £15,000.

The decoration and arrangements for the interior of the house can be pictured from a description of Sir Baptist's London mansion in Kensington, also known as Campden House, built at much the same time. A 19th century guide to ancient houses includes the following:

> Faulkner in his *History and Antiquities of Kensington* describes the entrance hall as lined with oak panelling, and as having a great archway leading to the grand staircase. The great dining room in which Charles II supped with Lord Campden, was richly carved in oak, the ceiling being stuccoed, and ornamented with the arms of the Campden family. The chief attraction of this room, however, was the tabernacle oak mantel-piece, consisting of six Corinthian columns supporting a pediment, the intercolumniations being filled with grotesque devices, and the whole supported by two caryatidal figures finely carved.

Descriptions of the state apartments in the same work suggest that his country home was also magnificently decorated with rich plaster-worked ceilings and stained glass in the windows.[v] In accordance with contemporary fashion, the house overlooked a formal terraced garden and below that a terrace of orchards above a water garden. This utilised a stream to form a canal and water parterres.

However, more water was needed, both for the house and to provide fountains in the water garden. At the time Sir Baptist was planning and building his house in Campden, Sir Hugh Myddelton was engaged in the construction of the New River to bring Hertfordshire spring water 38 miles into the City of London. The expertise to provide a good, clean and safe supply of water for his house was therefore available. Sir Baptist's engineers tapped a number of springs on Westington Hill on the opposite side of the valley, where the oolitic limestone lies above an impermeable layer and there is spring water of excellent quality. The Conduit House, which was built beside the road, still today collects spring water in a trough and allows it to depart through lead piping down into the valley. The surplus overflowed to fill troughs both near the Conduit House and lower down the hill in Westington street. The main supply, under pressure since it originated much higher than the house, was led under the fields, across the stream and into the house and gardens. It is entirely possible that, like Henry

VIII's Hampton Court Palace, Campden House had running water as high as the second floor. Fountains in the lowest part of the garden would have reached quite a height. A branch supply led a small surplus to a bowl outside the almshouses for the benefit of the inhabitants.

Sir Baptist Hicks did not overlook the environs of his new mansion and the opportunity to impress others with his status. The access for a visitor from London would be along the road at the top of Westington Hill beside the quarry, and was planned to be a dramatic approach. Continuing down the lane towards Campden a turn in the road still provides a sudden view across the valley with the church and town below and Meon Hill in the distance beyond. The white stone of the new house must have been striking from that point. The gardens with their fountains would have been equally apparent. A little further, and the small but beautifully crafted Conduit House, then equally white and new, gave an indication of the expensive attention given to the provision of a pure water supply.

From this point on, however, the house itself was less visible and would not be seen except in tantalising glimpses until the very last moment. At the foot of the hill, the cottages and farmhouses of Westington showed the beginning of a prosperous community and displayed the generosity of the landowner whose water supply filled the troughs for cottagers and animals alike. Then into the narrower confines of Sheep Street Lane and the turn to the wide market area of the High Street. Again the prosperity of the town would be apparent and the new stone Market Hall, emblazoned with its donor's arms, would require admiration. The visitor would next turn right at the junction of the High Street and Leysbourne avoiding the pool there. Ahead would be a new stone wall with, on the right, a large but plain stone building, which, closer, would be seen to be but for stabling and other farm purposes. Swinging left he would see the new almshouses, again adorned with the donor's arms, and, at last the church and an elegant gatehouse. Only on passing through the gate and turning right would the house be visible in its entirety. Sunday worship in the church would continue to display his wealth and power as the visitor wondered at the superb Jacobean pulpit with its sounding board, the lectern, even then a valuable antique, and the east window, emblazoned with the Hicks arms in stained glass. Even one of the bells was his gift.

His wealth, gifts to town and parish, not to mention the money paid out for his building works, enabled him to enjoy a friendlier standing than either of his predecesors with many of the inhabitants. It seems that he was approached to help sort out a problem causing division in the Town. The 15th century grammar school in the High Street had been continuing to educate the boys of the town and district since the dissolution of the chantries. The land bequeathed by the Ferebys continued for decades to provide, by rents, the money needed to pay the schoolmaster each year. These rents had been rising, but the schoolmaster's salary remained unchanged. The surplus was intended to be used for the poor but the trustees had found other uses for the money.

By the 1620s the misappropriation of funds was becoming a scandal. Even the original lands at Lyneham in Oxfordshire had been disposed of in exchange for others. It appeared that one of the remaining trustees from the time of Sir Thomas Smyth, fifty years earlier, by now very old and blind, had at some point been duped into handing over the title deeds to the Lyneham lands. The new trustees, including Thomas Bason alias Butcher, William Damport and Anthony Jarrett, had exchanged them for other land at Barton-on-the-Heath, no doubt receiving a cash consideration for the transaction.

The case, brought by, among others, Sir Baptist, the vicar, and 300 poor inhabitants, was heard in the Court of Chancery. Their complaint, that the defendants had obtained the deeds by fraudulent means and had retained moneys for themselves, was upheld. The trustees' defence appears to have been that at least some of the money retained had been used for the benefit of the town by building a bridge and paying for the expenses of obtaining the Town Charter in 1605. The court's decision, given in 1627, was that they should account for all the money received, and were not to set expenditure against it other than for the original educational and charitable purposes of the bequest.[vi] Sir Baptist is credited with having re-endowed the school further. The following year is the traditional date for the addition of a new room to the grammar school building. The ornate fireplace there includes a bust, variously said to be either of Fereby or of Hicks himself.

Baptist Hicks did not cease extending his properties after purchasing Campden. Locally he bought land at Weston-sub-Edge, Ebrington, Ilmington and Charingworth. Further afield, Exton Hall and the manors of Exton, Horn and Whitwell, in Rutland, were bought in 1614-1615 and the manor of Hampstead in 1620.

Despite all his care to ensure his title to the property was sound, Sir Baptist's holding of the manor of Campden was to be challenged. Sir Paul Banning, the son of one of those who had lent money to Anthony Smyth, had discovered documents amongst his father's papers purporting to transfer to him the manor of Campden as surety for loans, with the loans apparently still outstanding. He demanded that Sir Baptist hand over the manor, since he held title. Over the next few years a number of people took the opportunity to throw doubt on Hicks's title to various lands and properties. He seems to have been prepared to settle these out of court by payments of money as compensation. The Banning case however lasted from 1616 to 1624, at the end of which the Court of Chancery found for Sir Baptist, and Sir Paul Banning was ordered to assign any rights he might have in the manor. This he did early in 1625.[vii]

During these long years, Sir Baptist had continued with his business interests and with his public duties. He served as MP for Tewkesbury for a number of years until 1628 when he was 'called to the Upper House' as Viscount Campden.[viii] In Campden a number of leases and other documents show that he, or his agent, continued with estate business. The traditional date for his building of the stone Market Hall is 1627. This probably replaced an earlier building, perhaps timber-framed.

From the Hicks monument. The fine carving of the effigies of the richly robed Sir Baptist and Lady Elizabeth Hicks has been attributed on stylistic grounds to Nicholas Stone (1586-1647), one of the most celebrated sculptors of this period.
(By kind permission of the Chipping Campden Camera Club)

The building of the almshouses, also replacing an earlier building, has been mentioned above. Sir Baptist's will included a perpetual annual payment of £140 a year for its upkeep and the support of the 6 poor men and 6 poor women within. The church had not been forgotten. As well as the Jacobean pulpit, he had given the magnificent lectern, a 15th century brass falcon, probably Flemish; and in 1623 he had acquired the advowson from the Crown.[ix] A pair of silver-gilt bowls was presented to the church in 1626; he received a couple of chickens in return from the grateful churchwardens.[x] His arrangement with the churchwardens for the use of the south chapel by his family in perpetuity was agreed in 1629, the year of his death.[xi] The final details of the monument that stands in the centre of that chapel must have been designed after he had been created viscount in 1628, since he and Lady Elizabeth are shown wearing their robes and coronets. It is in the style of, and has been attributed to, the sculptor Nicholas Stone, although documentary evidence has not been discovered.[xii]

On 12th October 1629, Sir Baptist Hicks, Viscount Campden, signed his will and six days later he died. Campden had changed dramatically in appearance and in many other ways during his quite short tenure of the manor. His superb manor house and other buildings and munificent gifts and bequests to the town, the poor and the church, together with the continuing benevolence of his heir, Lord Edward Noel, made it appear to the inhabitants of the district that the future was assured. Sir Baptist and his wife, Elizabeth May, had been married about 1574, long before his purchase of the manor of Campden or other estates. They had two surviving daughters at the time of his death: Juliana (or Julian) and Mary. Both had married well: Mary to Sir Charles Morrison of Cassiobury and the elder, Juliana, to Lord Edward Noel. It is said that each had received the enormous sum of £100,000 as dowry on her wedding. Unusually, as there was no male heir, the Crown permitted Sir Baptist's titles to descend in the female line, and so Edward Noel became the second Viscount Campden.[xiii] The Dowager Lady Elizabeth survived her husband for some fourteen years.

Baptist Hicks's elder daughter, Lady Juliana, is sometimes said to have had her home in Campden for some years and to have been much attached to the town. But the evidence for this is sparse and largely traditional. Born in 1585, married in 1605 and widowed in 1643, she died at the age of ninety-five. She may never have lived in Campden House itself. In fact, her parents themselves probably spent little time there: they had two houses in London, where most of his interests lay, and her mother disliked the country.[xiv] It is possible that Juliana lived in the house for some years after her father's death and that after the Civil War she lived either in the Court House or in an undamaged wing of the main house. The western end of the garden, runs down to the gateway into the fields, now known as 'Lady Juliana's Gate'. But Sir Baptist had bought Exton Hall and manor in Rutland for her and her husband, and Lord Edward already owned Brooke House also in Rutland. That is where she died, in about 1680.

The Noel monument. Sir Baptist Hicks's daughter, Lady Juliana and her husband, Lord Edward Noel are shown standing on the Day of Judgement, having risen in their shrouds. So far the sculptor is unknown. ***(By kind permission of the Chipping Campden Camera Club)***

The fact that Lady Juliana commissioned the magnificent standing memorial in St James's Church to her husband and herself, next to her parents' tomb, does suggest a knowledge of and affection for Campden — a conclusion supported by the fact that she reserved to herself the presentation to the vicarage and the 'placing of men and women in the beadhouse [the almshouses] there'.[xv] The famous traveller Celia Fiennes was another who knew Campden, describing its 'pretty church...built all of stone' and the tomb of the 'little Viscountess Campden who lived to a great age'. However, in none of the various accounts of 'The Campden Wonder' is there firm evidence that Lady Juliana lived here at the time.

In 1629, when Sir Baptist died, the surviving children of Juliana and Edward were Baptist, Henry and Penelope. Baptist, the eldest son, was married on Christmas Day 1631 to Lady Ann Fielding.[xvi] Penelope died in May 1633 at the age of 22, and is buried in the family vault. Her monument, a bust by Francesco Fanelli,[xvii] is on the east wall of the chapel. It is said that she died of septicaemia through pricking her finger when embroidering with dyed silks. Further deaths followed. None of Lady Ann's three children survived to reach a second birthday and she herself died in 1636. She also is commemorated by a bust on the east wall of the chapel.

Chipping Campden continued to prosper. The bailiffs and burgesses were well settled into their powers and all seemed set fair for continuing progress. National matters were to begin to impinge on the local community. The sole rule by Charles I brought changes to the system of taxation. The extension of Ship Money from the ports to inland towns brought a wave of protest. Lord Edward Noel was involved in meetings in Rutland, called to ask for a more equal assessment.[xviii]

In Campden a more urgent local issue was an outbreak of plague in 1635. It is likely that the market would have been cancelled and that haymaking, harvest and other agricultural matters would have been disrupted. In September the Sheriff of Gloucestershire informed the Privy Council that Campden was unable to pay their assessed amount as a result of the distress caused by the plague. Just over a week later he wrote again saying two more people had died in the previous week. Amongst those who died at about this time was the vicar, possibly another plague death. Another letter in early October indicates that the plague, which had appeared to be subsiding, had broken out once again. Even in November Campden was subsisting on £30 a week given charitably by neighbouring towns.[xix]

The uncertain state of the kingdom is perhaps reflected in a decision by the churchwardens in 1641. They decided that 'noe money shall be given to anie souldier or traveller' out of church funds: an indication of an increasing movement of people asking for assistance.[xx] The troubles that were to descend on Campden during the next years of Civil War would not be disposed of so easily.

Notes

i He was prepared to use royal influence to avoid holding office in the City and even paid a fine of £500 for not accepting nomination as Alderman. Nevertheless he became Master of the Mercers' Company in 1611.

ii Sir George Pratt; quoted in Airs, Malcolm, *The Tudor and Jacobean Country House - A Building History* (Sutton Publishing 1995) 50-1

iii The records of the building of the Canterbury Quadrangle at St John's College, Oxford, in 1636 mentions Robert, Abraham and Simon White, the latter two apparently masons of Chipping Campden. (*Oxoniensia*, vol. xiv, 1949, 64. Simon, born in 1619 would of course have been too young to have been involved in any of Sir Baptist's works, but his father, Abraham, and his kinsman, Robert, may well have been amongst those employed.

iv Bishop, Leighton (trans), *The General Accounts of the Churchwardens of Chipping Campden 1626 to 1907* (Campden Record Series, 1992)

v Timms, John and Gunn, Alexander, *Abbeys, Castles and Ancient Halls of England & Wales, South volume*, (Frederick Warne & Co. undated), 178-180

vi CADHAS Archives 2000/109/DS Vol; abstract of original decree held in Gloucs RO

vii Leics R.O. DE3214 195/7; DE3214 195/9; Writ to Sheriff of Gloucester & his certificate concerning the manor of Campden and Sir Paul Banning DE3214 195/8

viii Williams, W.R., *The Parliamentary History of the County of Gloucester*, (1898), 233-4

ix Hist. MSS: Comm: rep Earl Cowper - MSS 149. Sir Baptist's letter to one of His Majesty's Masters of Requests included the statement 'His Majesty loseth not anything by the donation'.

x Bishop, Leighton, op cit 3

xi He had previously paid for the repair and reroofing of the chapel. The work on the alteration to the arch to the chapel may have been done at this time. It is significant that it forms a frame for the Hicks monument when viewed on entering the church, rather than from just in front of the chapel.

xii Verey & Brooks, *The Buildings of England: Gloucestershire I, The Cotswolds*, op cit 155

xiii Lord Edward became 2nd Viscount Campden and 2nd Baron Hicks of Ilmington. He himself was created Baron Noel of Ridlington.

xiv Rushen, op cit 153

xv Leics RO DE3214 341/22 & 181/20: Lease of manor of Campden by Juliana to Baptist Viscount Campden, her son

xvi Daughter of William, Earl of Denbigh; her marriage portion is said 'not to have exceeded £3000.' Noel, Amelia F., *Some Letters and Records of the Noel Family*, (1910) 14ff.

xvii Verey & Brooks op cit . 155

xviii 16th June, 1636; Royal Comm. Hist. MS 5th report 402

xix Dom. Corresp. Off. 1635-6; 11th September, 21st September and 7th November (from Sheriff) and 7th October 1636 (from Henry Jay) (Quoted by Percy Rushen, op cit 51) One suggestion for the return of the plague in October was that a dead dog had been thrown into a growing hemp field a month before. When the crop came to be harvested the infection was able to spread again.

xx Bishop, Leighton, op cit 68 (10th July, 1641)

10

The Civil War: 'I Marched Straight to Cambden'

When King Charles raised his standard against his rebellious parliamentary subjects on 23rd August 1642, the war came as no surprise to the Noel family of Campden. As a Member of Parliament, Lord Edward Noel had been a witness to the arguments and growing tensions of the preceding two years. His son, Baptist Noel, MP for Rutland, was equally involved in the increasing polarisation between the king and parliament. As early as 1640 Lord Edward Noel had been one of six lords deputed to approach the City to obtain a loan of £200,000 on the king's personal security.[i] Presumably he was intending to use his late father-in-law's old business contacts in the city of London. He was not successful, as was only to be expected in view of the City's support for parliament. In all, just £50,000 could be raised and this only when the six lords had given their own personal bonds as security. Lord Edward raised the matter in parliament asking that they should themselves receive equivalent security from the king, since they were due to repay the loan in the October of the following year.

On the outbreak of war in 1642 Lord Edward joined the king, by whom he was commissioned to raise 500 horse. This would have been at his own expense, at least initially. Later a further commission required him to raise three additional regiments of horse and three of foot, but it is uncertain whether he had completed these tasks by the time of his death the following year. His first source of recruits would have been from his own tenantry in Campden and in Rutland. His eldest son, Baptist Noel, led a regiment of marauding Cavaliers based on the Exton manor in Rutland, that may well have been one of those raised by his father. These were to be a thorn in the flesh of the parliamentary forces in that area. It has been surmised that many were recruited from the Campden tenantry since they were known as the 'Campdeners'. However, since Baptist Noel inherited the title of Viscount Campden in March 1643 this name probably reflected his leadership.

Campden itself continued with daily life as far as possible, hoping that the war would remain at a distance. This proved impossible. The king's headquarters were at Oxford and most of his recruits and resources came via Worcester from Wales and the west. Parliamentary strongholds were Coventry, Warwick and Gloucester. The supply routes joining each of the warring parties thus crossed in or near Campden.[ii] It would not be a comfortable war for the inhabitants, unwillingly resident in such a strategic place.

This became obvious by September 1642. Parliamentary troops had entered Warwick in force. The Quarter Sessions had to be adjourned due to the noise of drums and trumpets, and the arrival of 800 soldiers could not but be alarming.[iii] No-one could have known that the next sitting of those Quarter Sessions would not be until 1648.

In October armies were marching close at hand. The battle of Edgehill on the 23rd was far nearer than Warwick. The sound of the field guns could well have been heard in Ilmington and might perhaps have been audible even in Campden.

Nevertheless, for the first few months things were relatively quiet. After Lord Edward died in the king's service in Oxford his body was brought back to Campden for burial in the family vault. His impressive monument was erected by his widow, Juliana, after the Restoration. Baptist Noel inherited the titles and estates in 1643, becoming third Viscount Campden.

The manor house, so recently built by Sir Baptist Hicks, was part of the dower of his widow, Lady Elizabeth. She, however, spent much of her time in Rutland, where she died in July 1643. It is, therefore, interesting that a joint funeral was held in Campden on 21st July for her and her grandson, Henry Noel, younger brother of Baptist, and his child, also Henry. Henry had been at home at Luffenham, Rutland in March when parliamentary forces had seized his house and taken him prisoner. Appeals to the House of Lords had been fruitless and Henry had died in prison.[iv] It had been necessary to obtain a pass from the parliamentary forces in July 'for carrying the bodies of Mr Henry Noel and his child to Campden in Gloucestershire'.[v] The three were interred in the family vault, already occupied by Sir Baptist Hicks and other members of the family.

Thereafter Campden House was from time to time occupied by royalist troops. In October 1643 a troop of about 300 royalist horsemen arrived in Campden and were quartered in houses in the town. Their leader, Lord Mollineux, was related to the family that had held part of the manor in the 15th century, and he and his officers may well have occupied the manor house. According to one of the London weekly newspapers, *God's Ark Overturned*, information about this came to Major Bridges, commander of the parliamentarian stronghold of Warwick Castle, who despatched a force to deal with them. The report states that they came :

> in the middle of the night, in the middle of the said town, suppriz'd most of them in their beds, and carried away prisoners to Warwick Castle, together with all their horses. There were between 30 and 40 of them that for some space stood stoutly to oppose our forces but they were soon quelled, and some of them slain in the fight.[vi]

Another account lists the officers taken and says that 100 horses were captured.[vii]

After her mother's death Campden became the dower of Lady Juliana. A number of leases and other documents show that the business of the estate continued as normally as possible during troubled times. A lease, dated in the same month as this night action, let premises to William Nutt, a tailor, for three lives or 99 years, indicating a certain confidence of both parties in the unchanging order of daily life.[viii] However, the loss of many able-bodied young men to the war is likely to have made agriculture more difficult. Markets continued to be held, but the quantity and quality of produce for sale varied. Shortages could occur without warning.

Fortunately Campden does not seem to have been on the route taken by entire armies. Nevertheless, skirmishing and ambushes took place in the vicinity as one side or the other seized an opportunity to inflict harm. In March 1644 Prince Rupert was informed that 'Wee have broken off three Bridges between Warwicke and Campden.'[ix] Later in the same month a company of royalist troops under the command of the Earl of Northampton was quartered not far from Campden when they were attacked by a larger force of Colonel Purefoy's forces from Warwick. This time Campden was occupied for at least one night by parliamentary troops.

In midsummer 1644 larger armies also were marching and counter-marching throughout the area. On the night of 5th June the king was at Moreton-in-Marsh and the following day he led his troops to Broadway and Evesham. The day after that Waller with a parliamentary army was at Broadway. This being about the time of the traditional Dover's Games it is hardly surprising that the vicar of Campden, William Bartholomew, decided they should be cancelled. Bartholomew has subsequently been branded a spoilsport Puritan for this decision. However, even if there had been a sufficient number of young men free to indulge in shin-kicking and other pastimes, the attempt to arrange a crowded public gathering in an area traversed by the soldiery of both sides would have surely been irresponsible.[x]

On 10th June Waller and his men were in Evesham; on the 16th the Royalists swept through that town, taking away one thousand pairs of stockings en route; and on the next day the king returned to Oxford 'over the Cotswold Downes where Dover's games were'. The parliamentary army remained at Evesham for a while until early July when the king returned through Moreton-in-Marsh, surprising Waller late on 3rd July. The next day, himself now in Evesham, the king wrote to parliament attempting a reconciliation. He received no satisfactory response to his offer of safe conduct to representatives. It was far too late for such a move to have any success.

Armies at that time depended very largely on foraging and on the resources of the locality they were travelling through. Supply trains were of most value to garrisoned strongholds but wagons of supplies could not easily keep in contact with rapidly moving troops. Moreover they were vulnerable to attacks and raids, thus needing difficult-to-spare guards. Thus Campden, in common with other towns and villages on or near the route of the marching columns, was expected to provide food and fodder. Paper receipts and promises to pay may have been given, but they were not always honoured in full, if at all, and in any case it required a dangerous journey to some distant place for reimbursement.

Towards the end of July 1644 Campden was taken by Captain Thomas Archer, who, calling himself 'governor of Campden', appealed to Colonel Massey, the parliamentary governor of Gloucester, for reinforcements to enable him to stay. In early August the Roundheads were still quartered here. Captain Archer wrote to the Earl of Denbigh, 'At this moment we are quartered in Campden, from whence we imploy parties out every day to gett contribution money in.' His superiors being unable to give him further support, he withdrew to Alcester about the middle of the month.

Both sides in the war were finding it more and more difficult to find both money and supplies. The problem of continuing to till the fields with men away, and of transporting produce and goods, with the roads made dangerous by foraging soldiers and informal bands of guerrillas, was having a devastating effect on the country as a whole. The previous few months in the Cotswolds had been particularly difficult and the harvests looked to be poor. Even the weather had been against the struggling farmers; the year began with much snow and mid May had seen an astonishing thunderstorm in the Midlands with giant hailstones. That year wheat rose to 61s 3d a quarter, higher than any year since 1631.[xi]

By now one way of obtaining money, food, forage and recruits was to divide up the areas controlled by one side or the other and place a small garrison at a central point with power to collect levies from the surrounding countryside. Certain unfortunate villages found themselves within the territory of more than one such centre. It made no difference whether the rival garrisons were on the same or different sides in the conflict: both would attempt to exact the due contribution.

To some extent the placing of a garrison in Campden might be beneficial in that it had but one such levy to provide, and might expect to receive a measure of protection from raids from the other side. On 30th November 1644 Prince Rupert was appointed commander of the king's army and one of his first acts was to direct that Campden House should be occupied and fortified. For the first time Campden was to be continuously occupied for a period of months. The new manor house, built by Sir Baptist Hicks, was to be the strongpoint, and near Christmas 1644 William Duggan and his men took charge on behalf of the king. He was disappointed with its potential for defence, writing 'the howse no wayes answers my expectations, beinge in my opinion neither of itselfe nor of any thinge I see about it tenable'.[xii] All the same he would do his best.

Whatever his view, parliamentary spies were keeping a watch on this activity. A report was sent to Samuel Luke, Scout-Master General, 'They are fortifying Campden house ...' The occupation of this strategic location would immediately alarm the parliamentary commanders in Warwick and Gloucester. Indeed they were so worried that other local houses might also be seized and fortified against them that they took the pre-emptive action of burning Milcote, the one time home of the wool merchant William Grevel, whose descendant Sir Edward Greville had recently been ousted from it by our old friend, Lionel Cranfield, now Earl of Middlesex.[xiii]

William Legge arrived, perhaps with reinforcements, and writing on Christmas Day to Prince Rupert, mentioned the dire shortage of provisions, saying that he feared 'a famine rather than an enemy'.[xiv] Neither Duggan nor Legge, however, was to remain in charge of the new garrison. Early in January

1644 Prince Maurice despatched Colonel Henry Bard to take charge.

Henry Bard was a colourful character, already known as an adventurer. Born of an old Norfolk family and educated at Eton and King's College, Cambridge he had already travelled as far as Paris before completing his studies. His travels thereafter, almost entirely on foot, took him across Europe into Turkey and through Palestine to Egypt. There he is said to have stolen a Koran, which he later presented to his old college. He was fluent in several languages and, indeed, must also have been capable of disguising himself in order to have travelled through the lands of the Sultan of Turkey at this time. The support of a wealthy brother, a London merchant, enabled him to live well thereafter.[xv] At the beginning of the Civil War he joined the king and came to the attention of Charles at Oxford in 1643. Placed in charge of a regiment at the battle of Cheriton Down that year he distinguished himself, but lost an arm and was taken prisoner.[xvi] In May 1644 he was freed and rejoined the king at Oxford, being created baronet in October of that year.

This then was the new governor of Campden and district. He lost no time in assessing the situation and sent an encouraging letter to Prince Rupert:

> May it please your Highnesse Excellency, I thought good to signify to you that I am here at Cambden *[sic]* House, with my forces, which I conceive will be very advantageous towards strengthening this association of your Highnesse, as we are taking great pains, with spades, mattocks, and shovels, 'planting the Gospel' and I am no longer happy than may wait upon your Highnesse.[xvii]

'Planting the Gospel' in this context meant fortifying the house as a strongpoint capable of withstanding an attack by the parliamentary forces. This was far from the doubtful attitude as to its capacity for being defended as expressed only days before by William Duggan. Curiously this letter seems to have fallen into parliamentary hands and to have caused a great deal of consternation. Notwithstanding Bard's statement about the defensive works being carried out, no evidence of any earthworks (which would have needed to be substantial) or other types of defence have been found associated with Campden House or its vicinity. Indeed it is doubtful if he could have achieved anything worthwhile with the number of soldiers with him even augmented by local labourers. It may be that, knowing that it could not be easily defended, his letter was a ruse intended to persuade the local parliamentary commanders of the uselessness of taking action against Campden House. If that were so he had misjudged Colonel Massey, parliament's governor of Gloucester, and the

Committee in London.

On 14th January 1645 the Committee of Both Kingdoms in London decided to order Colonel Massey 'to hasten against Campden House' and to authorise his employment of 1,000 foot and 1,300 horse, drawn from several garrisons. The following day detailed orders were sent to him and to the commanders of the other garrisons who were to supply troops.[xviii] The size of force proposed, considerably greater than the garrison of Campden House, would have been necessary if it was to succeed against the well-fortified, well-defended and well-supplied stronghold suggested in Bard's despatch. However, even had Bard planned to set up strong defences he would not have had time to build them and, as noted by William Legge, Campden House was not well supplied.

On 15th January, the day these detailed orders were being despatched, a London weekly newspaper, *Perfect Occurrences*, published both Bard's letter to Prince Rupert and the entire plan of action against Campden House. It was with some natural annoyance that Colonel Massey wrote back to the Committee that the plan could not be carried out 'by its publication beforehand in the London Mercuries'.[xix] He also asked on 22nd January, 'If upon less preparation and noise the enemy should be driven out of Campden House what is to be done with it, as I have no men to garrison it?'[xx]

The same report made it clear that he was being hard-pressed to control his existing surroundings: 'with our whole strength we cannot sufficiently guard this country, no quarter being free from their power ...' If Massey was in difficulties through shortage of men and supplies, Bard was perhaps in a worse position. The number of his men buried over the next weeks in Campden churchyard may indicate deaths through wounds received in skirmishes but also may be due to disease and malnutrition.[xxi]

Skirmishing there certainly was. Foraging parties were sent out round the countryside. Alcester, Tewkesbury and all the country round about were within Bard's purview and he was determined to obtain the monthly supplies of food, fodder and money demanded from each town, village and hamlet. A similar intention fired the governors of all districts, on both sides and throughout the country. Many, probably most, were ruthless. Few, however, have left behind such evidence of their activities.

By this time even without a war and the depredations of troops, the countryside would have been in near famine conditions after the previous year's poor harvest. Now the soldiers were desperate, but so also were the ordinary inhabitants. Nevertheless, failure to send the required supplies to the local governor could be construed as furtive support for the opposing cause, thus warranting severe measures. Several copies of Bard's fearsome standard letter, addressed to different communities, have survived:

> Know you that, unless you bring unto me at *[time and place specified]* the monthly contributions for six months, you are to expect an unsanctified troop of horse among you from whom, if you hide yourselves, (As I believe each of you has his hole), they shall fire your houses without mercy, hang up your bodies wherever they find them, and scare your ghosts into your drabbling garrison.[xxii]

He especially pointed out the difference between his unsanctified troopers and the Puritan horse who would sing hymns when on exactly the same errand. Although he and his men were regularly described as 'cormorants' no evidence for specific atrocities has survived in the records.

One local man made a stand against Bard and his Cavaliers. George Durant, vicar of Blockley, was a supporter of parliament. Indeed, long before the beginning of the conflict he had knocked into a ditch the local constable, who had asked him for his contribution to Ship Money. Now he refused to pay his contribution to the royalist cause. Bard acted. Durant's statement said, 'the Governor of the garrison threatened me with imprisonment and sending a partie of horse to take me from my house in the night'. He fled and made his way to London where it was stated on his behalf by Colonel Edward Freeman :

> ... George Durant Vicker of Blockley freely of his own accord sent in a very able horse to me beinge in armes for the Parlt. And also sent in the fund of £21, for the use of the state upon the publiq faith. ... And he, [Freeman] hath oftentimes received intelligence from him also of the strength of the Kinges party, whereby the better to avoid them ... the said Mr Durant sheltered and protected the parliament soldiers from the Kinges forces.[xxiii]

Bard may have had some suspicions about Durant's spying activities; he would certainly have been well aware through local gossip of his political views. He was probably glad to see the back of him.

The garrison at Campden House had without any doubt increased the difficulties experienced by the parliamentary forces in Warwick as well as Gloucester. Early in February John Bridges decided to take action from Warwick against Bard. However, by April the Royalists were still active along the opposing forces' principal route.

> I fear the way is something dangerous from Warwick to Gloucester. Some of Cambden's *[sic]* garrison went lately to Winchecombe, where they plundered them so there that the plundered had not a Sunday shift of clothes left them. All the cattle drove away.[xxiv]

Not all the encounters ended in favour of the Royalists. In the same month they were routed in a running fight near Warwick. Many of the king's soldiers were killed, the survivors fleeing to Campden and Evesham 'many without hats, others without Horses and few with Swords'.

The war was turning against the king and losses could no longer be made up from volunteers. Orders went out to the governors of districts ordering conscription. Henry Bard's standard order, circulated round the district, was in his usual forthright style:

> By vertue of an Order sent to me from his Highnesse Prince Maurice, I command you that you immediately send for the Pettie Constables ... and give order for the present impressing of 23 able souldiers for His Majesties Service, to kill and slay all [parliamentarian] committee men without exceptions; which men are to be delivered to Lieutenant-Colonell Bellingham in Evesham for his Highnesse use. And this shall be a sufficient warrant for you and your Brethren. Fail not, as you will answer the carrying of muskets your selves, and be made [to] fight against your Consciences.[xxv]

Now began the final manoeuvring of armies before the battle of Naseby. The king and his forces left Oxford and by 8th May 1645 were at Stow-on-the-Wold having joined forces with Prince Rupert. The next day they set out for Evesham. En route 300 of the garrison from Campden were withdrawn and the house was set on fire. Bard's laconic report just says 'Campden House is quit and fired.' Lord Clarendon's account, written after the Restoration, has been so often quoted that Henry Bard's tattered reputation was completely ruined:

> His Majesty reached Evesham and on his way drew out the garrison from Campden House, which had brought no other benefit to the public, than enriching the licentious governor thereof, who exercised an unbounded tyranny over the whole country, and took his leave of it by wantonly burning this noble pile which he had too long inhabited.[xxvi]

However eyewitness accounts tell a different story. Sir Henry Slingsby's Memoirs state:

> Before we started from [Campden en route to Evesham], the Prince [Rupert] had given command to Colonel Bard, Governor of Campden to march along with his regiment and lest the enemy should make use of the House for garrison when he had left it, being so near Evesham, ye Prince

> likewise commanded it to be burnt, which I set on a light fire before we marched off; a house as my Lord Cambden [sic] says that hath cost £33,000; in building and in furniture.[xxvii]

The king's Secretary, Sir Edward Walker, was less convinced of the need for the destruction, but also attributes the order to Prince Rupert.

> The King's Army marched to Evesham. By the way, the garrison of Campden House was drawn out, and the House (which cost above £30,000 the building) most unnecessarily burnt by Prince Rupert's Command.

Major George Purefoy, a parliamentarian commander from Warwick and a kinsman of the regicide Colonel William Purefoy, was swift to harass the rear of the royalist column and looked to seize the prize of Campden House. However, he arrived too late to take the house but had sufficient force to overwhelm the Royalists left to hold the town.[xxviii] A parliamentary report records:

> The enemy in the garrison at Cambden house ... being lately called thence to joyn with His Majesty's Army, a night or two before their departure turned their horses into the cornefields and committed many outrages against the Inhabitants, and when they had made such a devastation that nothing was left for them to destroy and spoyle they set fire of Cambden house it selfe, and burnt and consumed all the wainscots and other furniture of that brave house ...

So perished the fine mansion built by Sir Baptist Hicks. The present ruins give testimony to the intensity of the flames, for the Cotswold limestone turns pink when strongly heated and the inner surfaces of the remaining walls are in many places bright pink, showing the position of the wooden wainscotting. The house burned for a considerable time and it was said that Prince Rupert, at the rear of the king's army marching on the hills above the town travelled at night by the light of that fire.[xxix]

An impression of the appearance of the ruins almost fifty years later, in 1691, is indicated in a lease from Susannah, mother of the six-year-old 3rd Earl of Gainsborough, to Mary Rutter, a widow, that conveys to her:

> The Great Burnt Manor House together with the house called the brewhouse with the court on which it standeth, the burnt stables, the coach house, the passage towards strapyard, two porters' lodges with the court in which they stand, the court on the north side of the great burnt house, the rose garden, the bleaching garden and garden house standing therein, the pool ground, the poultry yard, the garden joining to the parsonage barne, the island contayning about halfe an acre lying on the east end of Robert Taylor's back, the Bridge Pool, Calves well pool, and the Stewpan, all with said brewhouse etc are part of and doo belong unto

the Great Burnt Manor House.[xxx]

Notwithstanding Clarendon's later remarks, which give the impression that Campden House was the only such incendiary event of the march, parliament was informed on 11th May 1645:

> The King's forces have burnt down divers houses between Oxford and Bristol, fearing we would make use of them ... and caused other men to pull down their houses, which otherwise they would have fired.[xxxi]

The withdrawal of royalist troops from the area left it wide open for the parliamentary forces to move in. As has been seen, Purefoy took Campden within hours of the departure of the garrison. A few days later Massey seized Evesham to receive a welcome from some of the inhabitants, two of whom wrote a letter to the House of Commons about this 'great service'.[xxxii] Meanwhile the king's forces, including Colonel Bard and the troops removed from Campden were approaching Leicester which they took by storm on 29th May.[xxxiii]

Royalist fortunes were never again so high. The disaster of Naseby on 14th June left the king's forces defeated and the whole south Midlands potentially open to parliament. Cromwell marched to secure the area, being in Warwick on 23rd June and in Stratford-upon-Avon on the following day. On the same day the parliamentary commander-in-chief, Fairfax, arrived in Campden with 11,500 troops heading towards Marlborough. They stayed but one night and their provisions, including bread and beer, were supplied from Stratford. The people of Campden could not, even in good times, have coped with such a horde and now after a succession of disasters must have been in despair. In late August Cromwell was again in the vicinity, at Evesham, and the king's soldiers were not far away. On 1st September parliament was informed that royalist troops had marched to Campden and their horse 'were about Campden on Saturday night'.[xxxiv] However, the royalist strength was rapidly collapsing and the king soon retired to Oxford, virtually defeated.

Notes

i *Calendar of State Papers (Domestic Series)* 96-7, 113, 134, 159

ii Tennant, Philip, *Edgehill and Beyond*, (Alan Sutton 1992), Introduction *passim* and Map 1, p.3

iii Warwick County Records Vol. II, Quarter Sessions Order Book 1637-1650 125 [Fo. 115], (1936)

iv 11, 14 March, 1 April 1643; Royal Comm. Hist. MS 5th Report, 76, 78-9

v 19 July, 1643, Royal Comm. Hist MS; House of Lords Calendar, 5th Report Part 1

vi Quoted by Tennant, op cit 203

vii *The Perfect Diurnal*, quoted by Whitfield, *History* (op cit) 122

viii Leics R O; DE3214 181/17

ix Quoted by Tennant, op cit 151

x Moreover any assembly of local people could well have been mistaken by the scouts of one or other of the opposing sides for an enemy force.

xi Stratton, J.M., and Brown, Jack Houghton, *Agricultural Records AD 20-1977*, (John Baker 1978). Wheat had reached 68s a quarter in 1631. For the next eight years, up to and including 1638, the price never fell below 53s 4d or rose above 58s. Thereafter the price fluctuated more widely: 1639 44s 10d; 1640 44s 8d; 1641 48s; 1642 60s 2d; 1643 59s 10d.

xii Quoted by Tennant, op cit. 203

xiii Porter, Stephen, *Destruction in the English Civil Wars*, Alan Sutton, (1994), 45; Prestwich, Minna, *Lionel Cranfield*, op cit 400-412

xiv Quoted by Warburton, *Life of Prince Rupert*, Vol. I, 516

xv *Dictionary of National Biography*

xvi Seymour, William, *Battles in Britain 1642-1746*, Sidgwick & Jackson, (1975), 74-5

xvii Quoted by Whitfield, *History*, 124

xviii *Calendar of State Papers, Domestic Series*, 1644-5

xix Quoted by Gilbert, John, *Military Government of Gloucester*, pp 132-3. 'Mercuries' was a colloquial term for newspapers, from Mercury, the Roman messenger of the gods.

xx Report by Colonel Massey to the Committee of Both Kingdoms; quoted by Whitfield, *History*, 126

xxi William Baxter, 24th January; Thomas Bowles, 27th February; Richard Soler and Thomas Sela, 9th March; 'Capitaine' Thomas Hall, 19th April; Robert Read, 3rd May; all 'king's soldiers'

xxii e.g. Tennant, op cit 207. Whitfield, *History* 125 amongst others also includes this eminently quotable letter.

xxiii Icely, H. E. M., *Blockley through Twelve Centuries*, The Paradigm Press (1984) 60

xxiv *Perfect Passages*, a London news weekly, 5th April, 1645

xxv To the High Constable of Tredington, late April or early May, 1645

xxvi Clarendon, Lord, *History of the Rebellion*

xxvii Quoted by Whitfield, *History* 128

xxviii Tennant, op cit 216. This is how Purefoy reported it. However there is a possibility that the Royalists he drove off comprised an ambush set by Bard, with instructions to strike and then withdraw swiftly.

xxix 'On Saturday last his Majesty in the evening went down by Broadway to Evesham; and Prince Rupert marched in the rearguard over Broadway hill by the light of Cambden House which they say was then on fire'. *Weekly Account*, a London news weekly, 12th May, 1645

xxx Leics RO, DE3214/132/15

xxxi Quoted by Tennant, op cit. 215

xxxii Proceedings of the House of Commons; letter from Mr Jo: Dormer and Mr Edm. Young, dated 26th May 1645

xxxiii Once again Bard distinguished himself in action, though wounded he 'then broke down the drawbridge, and made way for the horse to enter'. However, during the sacking of the town which followed 'in particular the late governour of Campden House gave command to ravish all and that he brag'd he had done it the same day several times'. Richards, Jeff, *The Siege and Storming of Leicester May 1645*, (2001), 187. For further information on Colonel Henry Bard, Viscount Bellamont, see *The Dictionary of National Biography*, also Wilson, Jill, 'Sir Henry Bard, Adventurer, Traveller, Soldier and Diplomatist,' *CADHAS Notes & Queries*, Vol. I, 5 & 15 and Wilson, Jill, 'Sir Henry Bard - Political Assassin?' *CADHAS Notes & Queries* Vol. III, 62

xxxiv '*Calendar of State Papers - Domestic series* 1645-1647

11

The Commonwealth, the Restoration and the Campden Wonder

By the middle of 1645 the outcome of the Civil War no longer seemed in question. Everyday life began to get back to normal. The eastern counties were now completely controlled by Parliament and more and more royalist supporters were slipping away to join those taking refuge overseas. Baptist Noel, third Viscount Campden, sought to join them. His house in Rutland was held by a parliamentarian commander and the manor house in Campden was a burned out shell. In September he sought the help of two other members of the House of Lords, both parliamentary supporters, to get a pass, but was unsuccessful.[i] By October he had found it necessary to 'enter into recognizance' to be ready to appear before the House of Commons at twenty-four hours notice.[ii]

In August 1646 he again petitioned Parliament, this time for his two guarantors to be discharged from the recognizance, as he had 'ever since behaved, so as to give no cause for suspicion, and has taken the national Covenant and Negative Oath'.[iii] Matters were not closed, however, for he subsequently had to make composition (a legal settlement) at the Guildhall in London. A memorandum of that occasion, dated 1st January 1648, noted that the plundering of Sir William Armyne's estate in 1643 should be taken into account.[iv] The case dragged on and several hearings took place in early 1651. At last on 8th March it was decided 'Lord Campden to be dismissed on entering into a bond of £10,000, for himself with two sureties of £5,000 each'.[v]

One final Civil War action involved Campden, on 20th March 1646, although its streets did not run with blood as did those of Stow-on-the-Wold the following day. The remnants of the royal army under Sir Jacob Astley were endeavouring to return eastwards to rejoin the king at Oxford. Shadowed by three parliamentary forces they toiled wearily up the Cotswold Edge on their way from Evesham. Above them, on Dover's Hill, they were watched by two parliamentary officers, Colonels Birch and Morgan, most of whose troops had been sent 'to ffeed and refresh themselves abundantly, which they did, from Cambdin'.[vi] So, once again, when barely recovered from the depredations of hungry soldiers, Campden found itself unwilling host to yet more.

The king was still at liberty in 1646, and, since no forces in the neighbourhood were likely to object, the bell ringers of Campden rang in celebration of the anniversary of his coronation. The churchwardens paid out one shilling for this.[vii] Matters of state thereafter did not touch the town directly for some considerable time. It may be supposed that some surviving sons made their way home and that the necessary agricultural and commercial activities began to return to normal. Dover's Games, morris-dancing and such-like worldly pastimes, however, remained banned.

War was renewed in the late summer of 1651 when the young Charles II was marching south with a force of wild Scots. After the defeat of the Royalists at Worcester on 3rd September, Charles escaped and the Roundheads sought him widely as the days passed.[viii] The escape of the young king and the search for him by parliamentary soldiers would have been the talk of market day on Wednesday 10th September, just a week after the battle. Cromwell himself had been at Evesham for three days[ix] and troops were in Stratford-upon-Avon and blocking the Fosseway at Moreton-in-Marsh.

The story of Charles's flight has been told many times. It was on Thursday 11th September that he travelled between Long Marston and Cirencester.[x] He was disguised as 'Will Jackson' the son of a poor tenant of Colonel Lane of Bentley Hall, Salop, escorting Jane Lane on a journey, ostensibly to visit relatives. Local traditions have it that they travelled through Campden and then via Longborough to join the Fosseway, perhaps near Stow-on-the-Wold. This is not improbable. As parliamentary troops were known to be in Moreton-in-Marsh, to join the Fosse Way south of Moreton would seem sensible. The continuation of the story: that Charles made a jocular remark to a local farmer in Campden High Street and only avoided temporary incarceration in the lockup by an abject apology, is in character but unsubstantiated.[xi]

Little information exists for the Commonwealth period apart from the *Churchwardens' Accounts*. The regular annual accounting for income and expenditure since the opening of the 'new booke' in 1626 had suffered during the Civil War and accounts were only presented intermittently until 1662. The inventory of 'Church goods' had previously been meticulously prepared each year and handed on from the retiring to the new churchwardens. The account for 1641 included 26 items beginning with 'two guilt Communion Boules with their Covers' and ending with 'two Church Lathers [ladders], whereof one is lent forth'.[xii] The list in 1657 consists of 9 items only, two being Bibles, not previously listed. The gilt communion chalices do not appear.[xiii] These must have been secreted somewhere safe since they reappear, together with many other items of lesser value, in 1662.[xiv] Only one ladder is then listed and it would seem that the one loaned some 20 years earlier had never been returned. A new long ladder was bought in 1662, no doubt in replacement.

Such evidence as there is suggests that Campden's place as a market town was beginning to recover during the Commonwealth from the damage and difficulties of the Civil Wars. Trade began to pick up and life to return to normal. Baptist Noel, however, was unable to visit: his movements were closely restricted as a 'malignant'. Moreover, his losses in sequestrated property, including Campden House, Kensington, and Brooke House, Rutland, together with the punitive fines he had been required to pay, had left him in straitened circumstances. No doubt the family steward, William Harrison, would have travelled to him and Lady Juliana from time to time, carrying information about the state of affairs in Campden and rents and other moneys. All would look forward in hope for better times to come.

In 1658 the church bells were rung on the death of Oliver Cromwell. The churchwardens tactfully recorded an expenditure of 5s 'for Ringing at the Proclaming of the late Protector',[xv] rather than saying at his death. His successor, however, had less than two years in power before, as Samuel Pepys wrote, 'All the discourse is that the king will come again, ... it is the wish of us all.'

The return of Charles II in 1660 was welcomed widely. But the actions and events of the past two decades could not be put aside and forgotten so easily. Many Royalists who had fled abroad would now be coming back home, seeking recompense for their period of exile, and others who had remained in England would be seeking to regain sequestered lands and revenues.

It has been suggested that the curious events of August 1660 in Campden had their roots in the aftermath of the Commonwealth. No proof has yet been found as to who or what might have been behind the strange disappearance of the elderly steward of the Noel estate. The story has been told many times under the name of 'The Campden Wonder', [xvi] and has been the basis of novels and plays right up to the present day. The earliest full source however is the account written by the local magistrate, Sir Thomas Overbury of Bourton-on-the-Hill, and published in 1676. Original gaol delivery records from Gloucester of 1661 and at least one broadsheet on sale in London in 1662 also relate to the strange happenings.

Stripped of the many unsupported additions made since 1676, the tale is as follows: on Thursday 16th August 1660 William Harrison, now aged about 70, long-time family employee and steward to Lady Juliana, walked away from Campden to collect rents in Ebrington and Charingworth, some two miles away, and vanished. Sir Thomas Overbury, who seems to have been the investigating justice, gives a remarkable amount of detail about the various searches, the building up of suspicion against John Perry, one of William Harrison's servants, and the latter's unexpected accusations of murder against his own mother and brother and his confession to assisting them. Both denied the charge vehemently and no murdered body or other certain evidence could be discovered. John Perry embroidered and added to his story whenever some new fact or suggestion was made to him, contradicting himself several times. The three, John and Richard Perry and Joan their mother, were brought up at the September assizes, since no-one could believe that an innocent man would accuse himself and his own blood relations. The judge refused to try them in the absence of a body, but they were also charged with an unsolved burglary at the Harrison house in the last days of the Commonwealth. Ill-advisedly, they admitted that charge, on the understanding that it would be set aside under the act of Indemnity and Oblivion recently passed by Parliament.

However, they were not released, since the question of the presumed murder of William Harrison had not yet been resolved. At the next assizes a different judge was not so nice in his interpretation of the law, and the three, found guilty, were sentenced to hang at the gibbet above Campden. Joan was hanged first, still protesting her innocence. It was believed that, as a witch, her death would release her sons from her spell and they would at last admit to their crime. Both died, even John saying at last that they knew nothing of the disappearance of the missing steward.

In August the following year William Harrison returned to Campden, alive and well, and telling a strange tale. His letter to Sir Thomas Overbury is included verbatim in the published account, but reads as though it has been rewritten at least once, possibly to omit certain information. His account of his kidnap by three men is full, as is that of his transport across southern England to the port of Deal. He even mentions overhearing the sum of £7 to be paid, as his captors negotiated with a ship's captain, named Wrenshaw.

Out at sea, in a ship filled with others 'in the same Condition', and healed of the wound received during his kidnap, Harrison told next of the arrival of three Turkish ships. He and the rest were handed over, taken to a port and sold as slaves. His purchaser, an elderly physician from Smyrna, set him to work in the still room, distilling medicines, or occasionally in the cotton fields. On the death of his master he took a silver bowl, made his way to the port, found sailors prepared to risk smuggling him away in return for the bowl, and eventually reached Lisbon. From there charitable help brought him to London.

He does not suggest why all this might have happened and he gives no information as to whom he went to on arrival in England. However, it is known that he was reinstated as steward by Lady Juliana and resumed his position as a trustee of the grammar school, of which, incidentally, Sir Thomas Overbury was also a trustee. It must be assumed that his full story satisfied the most searching questions from the Noel family and, no doubt, Sir Thomas. In London the merchants of the Levant Company and others who had travelled on diplomatic missions or for business would have been able to assess the credibility of his detailed account. The general populace of London, however, were quite certain it was all down to witchcraft as was explained in a broadsheet printed very soon after his arrival back in London, and a published ballad of about the same time.

Inevitably much has been written from that day to this on the question of what really happened. Speculation has ranged, from attempts to silence a witness, to the goings-on in, and the burning down of, Campden House in 1645; to the suppression of information in a case being prepared on behalf of Sir Baptist Noel, seeking return of the Kensington Campden House and restitution of other losses; to suggestions of magical practices and international secret societies. Many have attempted to prove that Harrison's story was completely nonsensical. However, apart from a few doubtful remarks by people not privy to any secret, the story seems to have been generally accepted at the time. Nevertheless, the careful gaps in Harrison's own account suggest that there was much more that could have been said as to who might have been behind his disappearance and the reason for it.

No point in his yarn has yet been disproved. The shortage of skilled craftsmen and women servants in the West Indies and in Virginia had led to a burgeoning trade in lured-away apprentices and servant girls from the London streets. The phrase 'spirited away' has its origins in this criminal activity. Cases in the Middlesex quarter sessions[xvii] over a period of many decades include those of 'spirits' involved in the trade. More than one case suggests that, for a fee, 'spirits' were prepared to send someone overseas to get them out of the way without the bother of a body. Thus the £7 overheard by William Harrison might have been the money being paid to the ship's captain to take him across the Atlantic.[xviii] He would have been able to return eventually, but too late perhaps for his evidence to be of any use.

At that period the Barbary Corsairs and other Turkish pirates were a scourge both to shipping and to coastal and island dwellers as far afield as Iceland. They raided along the south coast of England.[xix] The churchwardens' accounts of English churches include many briefs for the collection of money 'for the redemption of slaves'.[xx] William Harrison's bad luck seems to have been that he fell from the relatively gentle clutches of the 'spirits' into the hands of professional slavers, perhaps through a deal made by Captain Wrenshaw, to save himself, his own ship and his crew from an unequal and probably unwinnable fight.

The story has been told on the records that exist. Other pieces of information depend on gossip or second hand sources.

During this time, in Campden and in the country as a whole, matters gradually returned to normal. The Royal Arms were repainted on the wall of the church, at considerably greater expense than their removal. Expunged for 9d, now the wall was replastered for 7s, and £3 0s 6d was paid to the painter, with an additional 8d for bringing and removing his scaffolding.[xxi] The parishioners had made it clear that they remained loyal to the Crown.

News came from London that on 28th April 1661 the eldest son of Baptist Noel, 3rd Viscount Campden, had married a daughter of the Lord Treasurer and that his father had settled £8,000 a year on the couple. Campden House in Kensington had been recovered from sequestration and had been given to them.

The dowager Lady Juliana had retained Campden as her dower, though it is unlikely that she spent much time in residence. She is not mentioned at any point in the story of the disappearance of William Harrison: it might be expected that if present in Campden she would have been involved. In 1662 she leased the manor, together with associated lands in Weston-sub-Edge, Charingworth and Ebrington, to her son, Baptist, Viscount Campden, reserving to herself the advowson of the church and the placing of people in the almshouses.[xxii] Thereafter, leases of property in the manor are in the name of Lord Campden.

Since the Commonwealth period Campden's shops and tradesmen, like those in the rest of the kingdom, had suffered from a grave shortage of coins of small denominations. Little had been issued by the Mint over the past many years and no doubt some coins had been hidden for safe-keeping and never recovered.[xxiii] A new solution to the problem was found: merchants began to issue their own trade tokens and to take the opportunity to advertise their businesses at the same time. London engravers, some even Mint employees, produced the necessary dies. So it was that in Campden, towards the end of the 1650s, John Dickins, a draper, and John Moseley and William Yeate, mercers, issued their trade tokens.[xxiv] More token coins were subsequently issued by local tradesmen in addition to these three.

The use of tokens required trust by the customers who accepted them, and the number of token issuers in a town is to some extent a measure of that town's standing. With seven issuers, Chipping Campden comes fifth, equal with Winchcombe, out of 42 places issuing tokens in Gloucestershire and is in the middle rank of market towns in England at this time.[xxv]

From the trade tokens and other sources a number of trades and occupations in the latter part of the 17th century and the early part of the 18th can be established. All those present before the Civil Wars are found, with the additions of a barber-surgeon, a chandler or candle maker, and an ironmonger.

The town at this time begins to appear in itineraries although it was not then, and would never be, on a main route. Whereas in the 1540s, John Leland had barely mentioned 'Campden, seven-miles north-west of Stow' in his list of market towns of the Gloucestershire Wolds,[xxvi] John Ogilby's Road Book, published in 1675, included it on several routes.[xxvii] The form of the maps shows the road with drawings and occasional descriptions of the terrain. The detail is very clear even to the Conduit House on Westington Hill. Arable land is shown either side of the road coming towards Westington and pasture and arable beside what is now the Aston Road. It may be that the famous traveller

Celia Fiennes was using Ogilby's book when she passed through the town in about 1696, noting the view from the top of the hill 'from whence I could see a great distance'.

Notes

i Letter from Lord Campden: 'Belvoys, this 6 Sept 1645' asking Lord Denbigh 'to joyne with my Lord of Manchester in obtayning mee leave of the Parlament to come to London or Kensington ... and ... may have liberty (if I please) to go into Holland ...' Royal Comm. Hist. MS, Fourth Report 1874, Appendix, 272

ii Royal Comm Hist. MSS. 5th rep. App. 130

iii ibid

iv RCHM 7th rep. 1879; Calendar of House of Lords MS, 1a

v Council of State, Day's Proceedings; 5th February, 1st March, 3rd March, 8th March, 1651

vi 'Sir Jacob Astley came marching with his army in view, wee, lying on top of the hill neare Cambden, saw him march at least six miles together ... sent some 500 good horse and some ffew foote to make them spend their time and tire them; in the meantime the rest of our army to ffeed and refresh themselves abundantly, which they did, from Cambdin'. Colonel Birch, *Memoirs*. Sir Jacob Astley's force was defeated at Stow-on-the-Wold on 21st March, 1646.

vii Bishop, Leighton, op cit, entry for accounts of 11th November, 1645, f. 45, (76)

viii Ollard, Richard, *The Escape of Charles II After the Battle of Worcester*, (Constable 1986)

ix Gaunt, Peter, *A Cromwellian Gazetteer*, (Alan Sutton 1994), 227

x Ollard, Richard, op cit 62. The section of the journey between Long Marston and Stow-on-the-Wold is however described as 'uneventful'.

xi Being the day after market day; this makes the story somewhat less likely.

xii Bishop, Leighton, op cit fo 41v, (69). The silver gilt cups with covers are the pair presented by Sir Baptist Hicks.

xiii ibid fo. 51v, (85)

xiv ibid fo. 58, (97)

xv ibid fo. 53, (88)

xvi The principal source is Clark, Sir George (ed), *The Campden Wonder*, (OUP 1959), which includes the full text of the 1676 publication and other contemporary documents and comments, together with a number of articles on legal, psychological and other aspects of the case.

xvii Jefferson; John Cordy (ed), *Middlesex County Records* (Old Series) reprinted by the Greater London Council from the original edition of 1892. Volumes 3 and 4, covering the quarter sessions from 1625 to 1668, include 74 cases of kidnapping or 'spiriting'. Most were in respect of the abduction or enticement of apprentices and maidservants. One, Vol. 3, p 302, is of especial interest in that the abductee was no young servant girl but a married woman with child and an heiress 'to land' 'whereby hir husband ... may be much damnified by the loss of her'. This suggests that the organised gangs might also be prepared to remove human obstacles, without murder, on behalf of the unscrupulous, presumably at a price.

xviii Wilson, Jill, 'The Spiriting away of William Harrison', *CADHAS Notes & Queries*, Vol. 1, 62

xix Slaves taken in raids on Haimaey, Iceland, and Baltimore, Ireland, were sold in north Africa. The losses of English merchant ships eventually led the British government to pay 'protection money' to the ruler of Tripoli.

xx Bishop, Leighton op cit, 1692/3, 'for the Redempshon of captives 13s 9d'; 1700 £3 4s 0d 'being mony collected for the poor captives in Machanes' [Meknes, Morocco]. Other examples include: 'There was collected in Longborow [Longborough, Glos.] ye sum of ten shillings and two pence by virtue of a breife for ye redemptions of slaves in Turkey.'

xxi Bishop, Leighton, op cit f.55v (92)

xxii Leics RO DE3214 341/22 & 181/20: Lease of manor of Campden by Juliana to Baptist Viscount Campden, her son

xxiii For example a hoard hidden for safe-keeping in Weston-sub-Edge during the Civil War, found during building works in the late 20th century and now in the Corinium Museum, Cirencester.

xxiv John Dickins, d. 1657 (Drapers' Arms), and William Yeate, (Grocers' Arms); Thompson, R.H., ALA, *Sylloge of Coins of the British Isles*, part II, (Spink 1988); John Moseley, mentioned in late19th century newspaper query.

xxv Wilson, Jill, 'Campden in the Second Half of the Seventeenth Century - What was its County or National Importance?' *CADHAS Notes & Queries*, Vol. III 46-8. An eighth issuer is mentioned in *Gloucestershire Notes & Queries*, Vol. I, 347-52 but as no date is given and no other record of the coin has as yet been found, it has not been included.

xxvi Chandler, John, *John Leland's Itinerary - Travels in Tudor England*, Alan Sutton (1993), 188

xxvii In particular page 183 from Gloucester, via Cheltenham and Winchcombe to Campden. Some other pages include routes passing through Campden. Page 184 continues through Mickleton, Stratford-upon-Avon and Warwick to Coventry.

12

Churches, Chantries and Chapels

St James's Church in the 16th and 17th centuries was in its basic architecture much the same as it is today. The glass in the windows was different. The fragments of glass remaining and the description by the 18th century antiquarian George Ballard suggest that it was of several periods. The work begun in the 15th century by the rich townsfolk and wool merchants had been completed and the tombs of some of the benefactors were still in their original positions with their brasses, not, as now, in the chancel. It is possible that William Grevel's tomb was in the north aisle as a later record suggests that his arms were set in one of the aisle windows. No monument or brass of William Bradway survives, yet he had bequeathed a sum for the completion of the 'Navy' of the church.[i] Bradway, donor of the altar hangings, may perhaps have been buried between the two nave columns with brackets for a wooden tomb canopy. Analogy with the very similar bracketed columns at Northleach church suggests that this was their original purpose.

St James's Church, drawing by Constance Sparling, 1948
(By kind permission of the Vicar and Church Wardens)

The tower had been built to take bells and four at least are likely to have existed at this time.[ii] The portable property of the church is not easily established. It must have been well looked after, since a confession by one of the robbers who broke in about the time of Michaelmas in 1534 said that 'they took nothing thens, for there was nothing to be had'.[iii] Perhaps the altar hangings, robes, chalices and other items had been placed somewhere inaccessible because of the depredations of thieves at other churches.

After Henry VIII's schism with the Pope in 1534 the 48 freeholders of the Deanery of Campden acknowledged the change of headship of the English church without record of any objection. The Act for the Dissolution of the Lesser Monasteries followed in 1536.[iv] In 1538 one William Cave was called to account for failing to pay his dues to the church, and alleged that Sir John Jenks had said 'that there would soon not be four abbeys left in England'. William Cave and Sir John Jenks are not otherwise known, but their conversation 'at the churchwall' suggests that some people in Campden at least saw the Dissolution as a potential relief from payments to the church authorities.[v]

Five chantries had existed within the parish church: two chantries dedicated to St Katherine, otherwise known as Stafforde's First and Second; the Fereby Service or the Schoolmaster's Service; the Goode Service, which was also known as the 'Trynitie Service', and the Barnard Service, otherwise Our Lady Service.[vi] In only one case is there evidence that a special chapel was associated with a chantry.[vii] After the Dissolution, the priests of these four chantries were pensioned off by the state, receiving £5 each a year, and the lands taken from the dissolved chantries were sold by the Crown in 1549.[viii] Sir Thomas Smyth was the ground landlord of some of these lands and the opportunity was open for him to purchase them; they were conveyed to Smyth on 22nd May.

The property of the fifth Chantry, the Fereby or Schoolmaster's Service, was not sold with the rest, but the king's commissioners were 'empowered to assign lands for the support of a grammar school where such teaching was required by the foundation of the dissolved chantry'.[ix] The grammar school therefore continued to be funded by the income from the lands at Lyneham in Oxfordshire bequeathed by the Ferebys. The deeds for the property were held within the town as before and at some time in the next 20 or 30 years were kept by a man named Noble.

When the assets of Bordesley Abbey were taken over by the Crown in 1538, the lessees of the land at Combe were able to purchase it. Tewkesbury Abbey, which had a holding in Broad Campden, was dissolved in 1540. In 1545 James Gunter and William Lewis bought from the Crown certain tenements in Broad Campden, 'formerly belonging to the late monastery of Tewkesbury'. The next day these were sold on to Sir John Russell of Overtrensham, Worcs.[x] The Russell family had held the lordship of Broad Campden since the late 15th century.

Alabaster relief of the Trinity, of Nottinghamshire alabaster, and probably made in Nottingham, once the centre of a trade that supplied high quality work throughout Europe. It probably dates from the first half of the 15th century.

There were changes within the church, too. The removal of statuary, including the statue of the Virgin from the niche on the porch and an alabaster relief of the Trinity, was an obvious sign of the religious revolution of Edward VI's time. Equally the introduction of new service books and an English Bible made it very clear that the previous break with Rome had been only the beginning. The wills of members of the congregation changed in form. In March 1547 a 'shepard', John Hamlens, left his 'Sowle unto God and unto our Lady Seynte Mary' and Thomas Cockes later the same year used the same formula.[xi] Subsequent wills omit this standard opening.

The new Protestant church established by Edward VI was ended on his death in 1553, with the accession of Mary Tudor. Once again there is no indication of anything other than acquiescence by vicar and parish in Campden of any of these drastic changes. However, in London, Bishop Bonner, sometimes known as 'Bloody Bonner', was notorious for his harsh judgements and condemnations in the trials for heresy.[xii] It was said that he was an illegitimate child of George Savage, a priest thought to be related to the Savage family of Campden, whose mother had been sent away and married to a carpenter named Bonner, also related to the Campden family of that name.

Charitable assistance to the old and the poor appears to have continued. A will of 1549[xiii] includes a bequest of a 'peticote' to 'Mother Cowper of the Almes howse'. This might have been to a relative or friend but a bequest of 12d 'to each poor person in the almshouse' in 1580[xiv] is certainly an indication that the poor were not forgotten. It is uncertain when this almshouse had been built. There is no indication that it was a recent provision. Its location is equally uncertain, but it may be that the new building in Berrington built by Sir Baptist Hicks in the following century was on the same site.

At this time, the rectory of the parish church (which included the right to collect tithes) and the advowson (or right to appoint the incumbent) were considered two separate matters. St Werburgh's monastery at Chester was dissolved in 1537, but before the surrender came into effect the abbot had granted a lease of the Campden advowson to two laymen.[xv] The lease of the advowson was for two appointments only. Robert Fynch, appointed in 1544, was vicar until his death in 1549 and may have held more than one benefice, since several wills of this period mention 'Sir Richard Bannystur' as priest.[xvi] That year, William Radford, a successor of the original grantees, presented Sir Ralph Smythe as vicar. He was instituted on 14th August, having taken the obligatory oaths of Renunciation of the Bishop of Rome and of obedience to the Bishop of Gloucester. After this the advowson reverted to the Crown.

The lax state of the church at this time is apparent. Ralph Smythe did not appear at Bishop Hooper's visitation in 1551. The minister, Humphrey Hower, attended and had some problems in answering questions. He thought that the number of the Commandments was ten, had difficulty with the Apostles' Creed but could recite the Lord's Prayer satisfactorily. The number of communicants was 'about 485'. Things were little different in 1563 when the Consistory Court noted that no bible could be found in the parish church.

It is not certain when the change in the dedication of the parish church from the Blessed Virgin Mary to St James the Greater took place. It could have been after the accession of Edward VI or early in the reign of Elizabeth. The former is perhaps the more likely. The manor had been connected with St James since the 13th century, when the fair on his name day had been granted. The vestments belonging to the church, including the cope and some of the altar hangings continued to be used during Elizabeth's reign. The appliquè figures of the Virgin Mary and of the Angel Gabriel in the scene of the Annunciation were picked out and removed after the change in the dedication so that the frontal could still be used.

The people of Campden may not have considered the outward form of religious service to have been of great importance. The visitation of Matthew Parker, Archbishop of Canterbury, to Gloucestershire in 1563 noted that in Campden they talked through the service.[xvii] The church however continued its control over morals. A number of cases before the Consistory Court indicate that throughout the 16th century human nature remained unchanged, whatever the language or ritual in use. A case of defamation of character in 1543 involved the wives of several Campden men and other cases covered bastardy.[xviii]

The advowson was back in the hands of the Crown by 1570 on the death of Ralph Smythe, when Anthony Hyggens was instituted. He appears to have been unsatisfactory: records show that in 1572 the 'vicarage is in decay in default of the vicar'. Summoned to appear on 13th October the same year he failed to do so and 'was pronounced contumaceous', or obstinately disobedient. Moreover, 'the curate is an unrulie man; and serveth the parishioners with railing words'.[xix] Hyggens resigned in 1573, the Queen appointing Nathaniel Herford. Three years later he too resigned and Elizabeth appointed John Jennings. This ended a period of difficulties for the parish: Jennings remained vicar for the next forty years.

In the 1540s the question of the ownership of the rectory of Campden had come into dispute. In 1541 Henry VIII established the new Chester Cathedral and granted both the advowson and the rectory to the Dean and Chapter. The Crown then took them back on exchange for land. Shortly afterwards one John Booth stated in Chancery proceedings that a lease of the rectory had been granted to him by the Dean and Chapter before its surrender to the Crown. The case took some time but in 1544 John Booth is alleged to have been granted the rectory for 21 years from 27th December 1556.[xx]

When the 21 years came to an end in 1577, according to evidence given by Lionel Cranfield, it was granted to Sir Thomas Smyth, whence it passed on his death in 1593, to Anthony Smyth. However, on the death of Queen Elizabeth it seems to have reverted to the Crown.[xxi] A further dispute, already mentioned,[xxii] ensued when Cranfield, having acquired the rectory and tithes from the syndicate to whom it had been sold by the Crown, discovered that Sir Baptist Hicks also claimed that he had bought it, from Anthony Smyth.

There is nothing to suggest that any of the four vicars between 1570 and 1636 had puritan beliefs. Broad Campden however may already have been a home of dissent. Born there in 1581 and educated at Campden Grammar School, Robert Harris became a well-known puritan divine.[xxiii] His first sermon was preached in 1604 in Campden during the incumbency of John Jennings. It is recorded, however, 'that such were those times that in the greater town hee did not know where to procure a bible for the reading of his text. At length he was directed to the vicar there; the bible could hardly be found, being not seen some months before; at last it was found and the preacher furnished ...'[xxiv] This could not have occurred in a parish with a puritan vicar - or a large number of dissenting parishioners.

The ruling in 1635 by Archbishop Laud, that the altar table in all churches should be removed from the centre of the church, placed at the east end and railed in, was treated as a matter of importance. The *Churchwardens' Accounts* include a number of items that may be related to this increase in the ceremonial aspect of services.[xxv] The *Accounts* for 1636 include items relating to the provision of altar rails. Two of the churchwardens and a workman travelled to Stratford-on-Avon 'to view their Railes to make ours by Mr Bartholomew's appointment'.[xxvi] John Page was paid £3 10s 6d for making the rails and 'a sertivicate' confirming that they were in place was despatched to Gloucester. There is no direct indication that the installation of the rails caused controversy in the parish. However, by 1638 there is a record that a workman was required to mend the 'raile in the Chancel'[xxvii] though the cause of the damage is not known. Just before the outbreak of the Civil War, in the Accounts for 1641-2, the 'takeing downe the Railes' is recorded.[xxviii] This may however have been in connection with work on the paving of the Chancel, the preceding item on the page.

In 1636 '3 panes' (pans) to burn frankincense in church for 9d and six shillings-worth of 'frankinsense and Sweet Wood' were bought to burn 'in the time of visitation of sickness'. Plague struck Campden in this year and it may be no coincidence that the then vicar, Robert Lilley, died in that year.

There is a question over Lilley's successor. William Bartholomew[xxix] has been variously described as 'such an ardent Puritan that he was strongly suspected of Presbyterianism on the outbreak of the Civil War'.[xxx] On the other hand, his monument, set in the parish church by his successor and son-in-law, says that he was 'hammer of the Sectaries, defending undaunted the Orthodox Religion of the English Church and the Royalist party even in the worst of times'.[xxxi] His own personal views are still uncertain but a brief summary of his life and the events of his ministry may help illuminate a confused period.

Some time after his ordination in 1626[xxxii] he was appointed chaplain to Lord Edward Noel, the son-in-law of Sir Baptist Hicks. Bearing in mind that Lord Edward was to follow the king in the Civil War, it might seem unlikely that he would select a Puritan for this position. Bartholomew probably retained his post as chaplain to Lord Edward for some time after his appointment to Campden as the *Churchwardens' Accounts* indicate that a Richard Gostelo, presumably a curate, received the accounts in most years up to 1639. Although Bartholomew was present for the bishop's visitation in 1639 only Gostelo is recorded for 1640.

William Bartholomew appears to have done what he could to ameliorate the difficulties of the Civil War years. However, his appointment by Lord Edward Noel, and the support given to the royal cause by the Noel family generally, perhaps made it inevitable that he should be in trouble under a puritan administration. As early as 1647 William Bartholomew was facing charges brought by some of his parishioners to the Committee for Plundered Ministers — a committee set up by Parliament to examine the practices of ministers. From the surviving documents it seems that certain of the parishioners laid a complaint, 'a humble peticion,' which he was required to answer. The nature of the charges is not clear but cases brought against 'scandalous ministers' can usually be summarised as being insufficiently active in favour of puritan liturgy and being suspected of pro-royalist sympathies.

On 8th September the London Committee required the Gloucester Committee to 'certifie ... the articles exhibited before them, against William Bartholomew ... and his answers thereto, and the examinacions of witnesses on both sides'.[xxxiii] They were given three weeks to reply; and William Bartholomew was given the date of 7th October on which the case would be heard. On that day the case was deferred to the following Saturday and then, on 9th October, two Members of Parliament were named to expedite the hearing of the case.[xxxiv] It is said to have cost Bartholomew £200 to extricate himself though whether in fines or bribes is uncertain. However, he managed to retain his incumbency, unlike many other local clergy. An early 18th century historian said of him that he was 'miserably harassed by the Rebels'.[xxxv]

In the following year it is clear that Bartholomew and the parish were keeping very carefully within Parliament's instructions and ensuring that there was an official record. Great care is shown in the wording of certain subsequent entries in the *Churchwardens' Accounts*. The election of churchwardens was made 'Uppon publique notice given by Mr Bartholomew ... accordinge to the direccions in the ordinance of Parlament'.[xxxvi] The *Accounts* devote an entire page to a statement by the churchwardens confirming that 'the electynge and chosinge of Churchwardens' had been carried out by William Bartholomew 'accordinge to the direccions in the ordinance of Parlament'.[xxxvii] The requirement to know the will of parliament made it necessary later in the Commonwealth to purchase copies of the Acts of Parliament.[xxxviii]

Distant events in the lead-up to the Civil War are reflected in the *Accounts*. A 'proclamation from the kings majestie concerning the Scotts' was purchased for 4d in 1640. It seems that parishes were required to have such statements of royal policy read out — and to pay for the copies. The regular presentation of the *Accounts* was interrupted between 1642 and 1645 so it is not possible to say which were the further 'proclamacions', costing a total of 2s, recorded in the later accounts.

Every effort was made to keep parish matters as normal as possible during the Civil War. In past years the bells had been rung each year for the king's holiday (probably the anniversary of his accession or coronation), for the anniversary of the Gunpowder Plot, and whenever the bishop came on visitation. The ringers were supplied with beer on each occasion at the expense of the parish. Between 1642 and 1645 the bells were rung 'att 4 times', unspecified. As late as 1646 an item for ringing at the king's coronation is recorded.

Shortages are evident. Sums were paid for bread for the sacraments, which suggests that more puritan views were taking hold. Wine for communion was definitely in short supply. At Easter 1644 the sum of £2 11s 8d was expended on wine and a further 2s 8d 'for a horse and man to fetch the same'. Later 'Mr Izoid' was paid 3s 6d for metheglin, a type of spiced mead, 'to help out when wine was scarce'. On another occasion a man was paid 8d for 'going to Morton Henmarsh to look for wine'. A shortfall in the wine for the sacrament on two occasions was reported in the 1646 *Accounts* and £3 12s 2d for wine was listed in 1648, suggesting that a quantity had been bought at one time.

In the *Accounts* the removal of the painted Royal Arms from the wall of the church was recorded.[xxxix] Notwithstanding the execution of the king in 1649 and the formal setting up of the Commonwealth, it is not until the *Churchwardens' Accounts* presented on 11th April 1653, that the expenditure of 9d for washing out the Royal Arms is recorded. The same accounts also include the purchase of 'pouder and shott', an unusual item to say the least.[xl] Despite all his endeavours to comply with the new puritan regulations, William Bartholomew had nevertheless not come to the end of his difficulties with dissenters.

One of the changes in church services resulting from the new order of things was a substantial increase in the number and length of sermons. Known as 'lectures' they took place on some weekdays as well as Sundays. The *Accounts* for 1653 include £1 18s 6d for 'severall lectures'. Another reference relates to a market-day in 1659, when a burglary took place whilst William Harrison, Lady Juliana's steward, and his household were in attendance at 'the Lecture'.[xli]

Eventually the Commonwealth ended and the monarchy was restored in 1660. The fabric of the church does not appear to have been seriously damaged by wartime skirmishing or Puritan iconoclasm. The effigies within the church, of Sir Thomas Smyth and Baptist and Elizabeth Hicks, are unmarked. By the early 18th century it seems that the old stained glass windows in the north aisle were damaged but there is no indication of when this occurred. Extra expenditure on windows and glazing and on roof works and lead over the period of the Commonwealth and early in the Restoration suggest that there was some damage. Lead from the roof, for example, may well have been taken for lead shot.

Almost the last heard of William Bartholomew is in the few months following the arrival of King Charles in England. His sermon marking the event, *On a Strong Man evicted by a Stronger than He*, was published, dedicated to Lady Juliana. Later in August he is mentioned briefly in the account of the *Campden Wonder*.[xlii] The accused were brought to church on Sunday so that he might speak to them 'to persuade them to Repentance, and a further Confession'. A few weeks afterwards, on 11th October, he died. His death was later included in a collection of stories showing the fate of a Puritan who had deserted his faith: 'William Bartholomew, apostate minister at Campden, Gloucestershire, was struck dead on the first Lords Day on which he read the Service Book'.[xliii]

His successor as vicar was Henry Hickes, already vicar of Stretton-on-Fosse, who continued to hold both livings. Within a few years, certainly in or by 1667, he had married Mary Bartholomew, daughter of his predecessor. They lived at Stretton rather than at Campden. The Campden vicarage may perhaps have suffered damage during the Civil War. It may in later years even have been too small for his family: they had ten children.

Charles II had agreed before his return 'a liberty to tender consciences'.[xliv] Nevertheless, over the years, a number of Acts and other regulations were brought in to ensure that the clergy followed the approved liturgy and practices of the English Church. On 22nd August 1662, Henry Hickes signed the 'Declaration and Subscription' as required by the Act of Uniformity.[xlv] He seems to have been a model clergyman, fully prepared to fulfil all requirements of King and Church. Certain parishioners did not find it so easy however.

Dissent was widespread throughout the Cotswolds both during and after the Civil War and in Campden it can claim a more or less continuous existence since the 17th century. However, in the Compton Census of 1676, only 15 Non-Conformists are reported in Campden, out of an adult population of 790. There are many doubts about the reliability of this Census, but clearly Campden was then fairly strongly Conformist.

The law forbidding travelling on Sunday, except for the purpose of attendance at church services, was strictly enforced and a number of Quakers suffered by their refusal to attend their parish church. A Broadway man was fined ten shillings for Sunday travel when he passed through Chipping Campden on his way to a Quaker meeting in Broad Campden. On refusing to pay he was put in the stocks. Four inhabitants of Broad Campden were similarly punished for the same reason even though the meeting was within their own hamlet.

It was in the later years of the Commonwealth that local Quakers begin to enter the record. Ties between Blockley and Campden Quakers were close: a meeting took place in Campden (possibly in Broad Campden) in 1656. Only two names seem to be known among these early Quakers, both Blockley men: Edward Warner, a fuller, owner of the 'French' fulling mill in Blockley and brother to the William who gave the name Blockley to a suburb of Philadelphia; and John Norris, who lived at Pye Mill. Both were founding members of the Friends Meeting House in Broad Campden in 1663. Indeed they, together with four Campden men, bought the meeting house ('two bays of housing and an orchard.')[xlvi] from the owner, one John Hitchman and his wife Prudence, who also seem to have been Quakers. Fourteen years later it was enlarged. It seems likely that this house had previously been used for meetings.

The Quaker Meeting House in Broad Campden, dated 1603

The Restoration at first brought severe persecution. In 1660 soldiers burst into a Quaker meeting in Broad Campden and took prisoner many of those present.[xlvii] In 1682 the Chancellor of Gloucester personally vandalised the Broad Campden Meeting House, and distrained goods from members of its 'seditious conventicle'; one Gervais Harris was committed to prison for refusing to pay £30 for the release of livestock; a Paul Heron was another to suffer. Again three years later another local Quaker is recorded as undergoing distraint and a servant who interfered was threatened with a gun. In Evesham such oppression seems to have been even worse: there in 1660 eighty-three Friends had been jailed.[xlviii]

Men from other denominations also sometimes created a stir. The arrival of an itinerant preacher, William Simpson, in 1657, caused breaches of the peace. On the first occasion it was Sunday and the main part of the service in St James's church had finished, apart from communion. Simpson, supported by John North and Thomas Kite, announced that he proposed to speak to the people from the pulpit. The parishioners 'ran upon him and dragged him out'. In the churchyard he continued to demand to be allowed to speak whereupon he was 'dragged about the yard'.

On the following Sunday Simpson again disrupted the service and was sent to prison 'as a sturdy beggar'. He denied being a vagrant, saying he travelled 'in the service of the Lord'. Taken miles away by the constable, he later returned. Records elsewhere show he was similarly in trouble with the law in Evesham, Banbury and further afield.[xlix]

In the 1670s several groups of dissenters made application to meet in Campden. One was for 'the house of Samuel Horsman of Cambdon in Gloscestershire' to be used as a Congregational meeting place. Horsman was an apothecary and a capital burgess of the borough, and he owned a number of messuages, cottages and other properties in Campden. He died in 1701. His name may indicate the 'respectability' of some of the early local dissenters. Later, an M.A. of Trinity College, Cambridge, Mr William Davidson — 'a warm and useful preacher'[l] — was pastor of a congregation at Campden. He probably came to Campden about the time of the 1689 Act of Toleration and he received £26 a year for his services. At the Quarter Sessions in 1689 a Dissenters' Meeting House was registered at Chipping Campden, with William Davidson as Minister. This was to continue to be used, until 100 years later, when it became a Baptist chapel.

There is an enormous contrast in faith and practice between the 16th century and the 17th. In the immediate post-Reformation period the atmosphere was one of laxity and lack of enthusiasm, reflected in Campden by poorly-trained clergy, missing bibles, the dominance of powerful laymen and some ignorance on the part of congregations. Intellectual turmoil at the start of the 17th century led to the rise of Puritanism and radical convictions on the part of many. Many often intolerant sects emerged and dominated the period of the Commonwealth. After the Restoration the insistence of the bishops on uniformity led to dissension, and to a few years of persecution, until indulgences were granted from 1672, and the Act of Toleration was passed 17 years later. All this is reflected in the experience of Campden during this period.

Notes

i Powell, Geoffrey, and Wilson, Jill, 'The Chipping Campden Altar Hangings.' *Trans. Bristol & Gloucestershire Archaeological Society* CXV (1997), 233-43

ii Some bequests towards the upkeep of the bells include: Thomas Bonner, 6s 8d 1640/1; Richard ap Rice, 12d 1541; Richard Bochar (the younger), 4d 1545; Hunfrey Erys, 4d 1545; Richard Plume, 20d 1546.

iii *State Papers*, Henry VIII 96, 236 (quoted by Griffiths, Josephine ms unpublished). The date of Geoffrey Harley's confession is 24th September, 1535, saying the attempt took place 'about Mychaelmas laste' i.e. about 29th September, 1534.

iv 27 Henry VIII, Cap 28

v Quoted by Whitfield, *History* op cit 71. Sir John Jenks may be a curate, chaplain or chantry priest since holy orders was frequently indicated by the honorific 'Sir'.

vi Wilson, Jill, 'What Happened to Campden's Chantries?' *CADHAS Notes & Queries* Vol IV 59

vii Two fragments of an alabaster relief of the Trinity.

viii *Cal. Patent Rolls Edward VI*, Vol V. 149, 187, 189, 294-5

ix 'An Act whereby certain chantries, colleges, free chapels and the possession of the same be given to the King's Majesty' (1547: 1 Ed. VI, c. 14), quoted by Elton, G.R., *The Tudor Constitution, Documents and Commentary*, C U P (1962), 384

x PRO Parts for Grants 535. 1545 Jul 16: 37 Henry VIII; PRO Pat Roll 37. Henry VIII. Fo. 12M.22. quoted by Griffiths, Josephine, *Ecclesiastical Records of Campden* (unpublished)

xi Quoted by Griffiths, *Ecclesiastical Records* giving sources as Gloucs Diocesan Records No 85 Vol 3 and GDR No 149 Vol 4. The will of Thomas Cockes, dated 10th June 1547 and proved the following year commends his 'soule to God, to our Ladie Seynte Mary' and requests that his body 'be buryed in Churcheyarde of Campden'.

xii *Dictionary of National Biography*

xiii Will of Agnes Noble of Campden, Wydowe, 10th April 1549. Included by Griffiths *Ecclesiastical Records*

xiv Will of Anthony Bonner of Campden, gent., 2nd November 1580. Included by Griffith in *Ecclesiastical Records*, quoting PCC Arundell 43 as the source.

xv 1st October, 1537; 'Original Grant by Thomas, Abbot of the exempt Monastery of St Werburg of the City of Chester ... to John Birkened ..., marchount, and John Downe ... bocher, jointly and separately of the Advowson for the next vacancy of the perp(etual) Vicarage of ... Campden ...' [GDR 2.2; Doc 25; 1537 - quoted by Griffiths, *Ecclesiastical Records*]

xvi e.g. Richard Bochar of Campdenne, the younger, whose will, dated 1545, left 12d to 'Syr Richard Bannystur, my goostly father'. (GDR No 265, Vol 2, 1545; quoted by Griffiths, *Ecclesiastical Records*)

xvii Howes, Russell, 'The Reformation in Gloucestershire Parishes,' *Gloucester History No. 17 2003*, GLCC (2003), 14

xviii 1543 two cases; Mrs Grizegon Porter v. Anne Bollyfaunte, latter said that Elizabeth Pratt was an 'harrante hore' and Grizegon was no better. Mrs Elizabeth Pratt, wife of John, v. Thomasyn ap Rice, latter said Elizabeth was 'a strong hore, a naughty hore and an harraunte hore'. 1562; Robert Huggen had got Anne Wen (late his servant), with child. Penance imposed to appear in church for three Sundays 'bare footed, bare legged, wearing a white sheet' and to recite the Lord's Prayer. He was also to pay 20s in bread for the poor and 40s to the bailiff of Tewkesbury towards the repair of roads and bridges. 1572; Edmund Jarrett was excommunicated for deflowering Anne Gylles, his servant. [*BGAS Trans.* Vol 46, 219ff.]

xix Quoted by Griffiths, *Ecclesiastical Records*

xx Many years later it was alleged that Thomas Booth's title was fallacious since the original document had never been signed.

xxi Whitfield, Christopher 'Lionel Cranfield and the Rectory of Campden.' *BGAS Trans.* 1962, Vol. LXXXI, 100

xxii See Chapter 8 above

xxiii *Dictionary of National Biography*, which gives his date of birth as 1581 contrary to the 'received date' of 1578. It also says that he was born 'in a dark time and place' at Broad Campden. In 1642 he was chosen as one of the Puritan divines to advise Parliament. From 1648 he was President of Trinity College, Oxford, and died in 1658 before the end of the Commonwealth.

xxiv Warmington, Allan, *Seventeenth Century Dissent* (unpublished)

xxv Bishop, Leighton, op cit In both 1635 and 1636 'paid for a booke of Artikels,' ff 29, 29v. 31 In 1635 16s 4d was expended on 'a hood for Mr Lilly and for makinge thereof'.

xxvi ibid. f 31 This cost 5s

xxvii ibid, f 35v

xxviii ibid. f 42

xxix Vicar 1636-60

xxx Rushen, op cit 112. However no source is given for this statement.

xxxi 'Malleus Sectiorum, Orthodoxae Ecclesiae Anglicanae partium Carolinarum, pessimus licet temporibus, intrepidus assertor'. (My own rather free translation above.) It must be noted however that this monument may have been erected by his son-in-law and successor as vicar, after the Restoration.

xxxii He was born about 1604 and studied at Trinity College, Cambridge. Cambridge University, and indeed East Anglia, were areas where dissent had early taken hold so he may well have been exposed to these beliefs. Details of his education and subsequent career are recorded in Holdsworth, Donald, 'Two 17th Century Vicars of Campden - William Bartholomew & Henry Hicks, Father and Son-in-Law.' *CADHAS Notes & Queries* Vol. III 29-31

xxxiii Griffiths, op cit quoting BM Add. MSS 15671 236

xxxiv 'It is ordered that Mr Hodges and Mr Nathaniell Stephens ... doe ... write to the said (Gloucester) Committee to proceed speedilie and effectuallie to the hearinge and determininge of the said cause'. [Griffiths, op cit who quotes B.M. Add: MSS: 15671 236.]

xxxv Walker, J, *An attempt towards recovering an account of the numbers and sufferings of the clergy in the Church of England ...in the times of the Great Rebellion*, 1714, revised A.G.Matthews (1948), quoted by Holdsworth, op cit.

xxxvi Bishop, Leighton op cit fo. 45v, (77). '... Wee here present doe unanimously elect and choose ... which wee desire the Justices of the peace to confirme ...' 3rd April, 1648.

xxxvii ibid. fo 45, (77)

xxxviii ibid fo 52, (86) '3 bookes of the Acts of Parliament' - 1s 10d.

xxxix ibid. fo.48, 47, (81, 80) The accounts signed on 11th April 1653 were the first rendered since 1648 and covered all expenditure in the interim. The cost of 'washing out of Arms' was 9d. Other items included 'pouder and shott' bought by the sexton and 'a booke of thanksgivinge and a note from Parliament - 10d'. The largest item was £57 9s 10d paid to Richard Wells and William Lane the plumber for lead, solder, other materials and work. This suggests that amongst other repairs, lead from the church roof needed replacing.

xl ibid (80-1)

xli 'Mr Harrison had his House broken open, between Eleven and Twelve of the Clock at Noon, upon Campden Market-day, while he himself and his whole Family [household] were at the Lecture ...' Clark, Sir George, ed. *The Campden Wonder* (OUP, 1959) 21

xlii ibid 20

xliii *Annus Mirabilis, or Signs and Wonders in the year 1660*, Quoted in the F. Scarlett Potter Collection Shakespeare Trust RO [ER 82/9/5]

xliv Declaration of Breda 4/14 April, 1660; which continued 'no man shall be disquieted or called in question for differences of opinion in matter of religion, which do not disturb the peace of the kingdom'.

xlv The Uniformity Act 14 Charles II, Cap 4; 1662. This required the use of the Book of Common Prayer amongst other things. This Act did not achieve the desired result as many Presbyterian and Non-conformist clergy did not make the necessary declaration. The Five-Mile Act was introduced in 1665 and the Conventicle Acts in 1664 and 1670. These made it more difficult for clergy and others not conforming to the liturgy of the English Church to conduct services. These proving unsuccessful to stifle dissent the Test Act was passed in 1673.

xlvi Wood, Jack V., *Some Rural Quakers*, (William Sessions Ltd 1991) 74-75

xlvii Gloucs RO D1340/A/A1

xlviii Wood, op cit 43

xlix ibid 32-33

l Calamy, Dr Edmund, *The Nonconformists' Memorial*

PART IV: THE 18th AND 19th CENTURIES

13

Lady Dorothy's Map and the People of the 18th Century

If someone from the 21st century had been dropped into the High Street three centuries ago, a first glance would have shown few changes. Only the absence of familiar shop fronts and the architecture of house fronts might have surprised. The Market Hall would have looked just as it does today, as would the neighbouring Town Hall, except for the lack of a lobby and the addition of a small spire. On the other hand, to have ventured further would have revealed a rather different pattern of houses, roads and fields.

Most of this was already known, but evidence came to light when a detailed (but not quite accurately surveyed) map of the parish, drawn at a scale of ten inches to the mile and dated 1722, was found among the Noel family papers.[i] Commissioned by Dorothy, Countess of Gainsborough, the mother of the 14 year-old Earl, it shows a great number of the houses and cottages in Chipping Campden, Westington, Berrington and Broad Campden, including those in the small alleyways of cottages that ran back at right angles from so many of the High Street houses. This map is the earliest such survey of Campden yet found.

In the High Street itself and in Leysbourne, most of the burgage plots were individually drawn on the map with their gardens depicted as running through to Back Ends, Calf Lane or the brook. In much the same way nearly all the south side of what was then Sheep Street Lane is shown as built upon but with only four dwellings on the opposite side of the road. The east of Watery Lane[ii] is almost fully developed, but there are no more than half a dozen cottages opposite. Fifteen houses can be counted in Westington and some thirty-six in Broad Campden. In Littleworth (then part of Berrington hamlet) there are ten houses clustered around what is known now as Hoo Lane but a century ago as Littleworth Lane, a bridle road.[iii] Calf Lane ends by the 'Town Mill', as it did until the middle of the 20th century. Behind what is now the Noel Arms is shown a 'Bouling Green', a valued amenity sacrificed to new housing towards the end of the 20th century.

Aerial view of the old Bowling Green behind the Noel Arms, sadly closed for development in 1989.

The site of the present Tithe House, opposite the entrance to St. James's Church, is marked 'Tyth Yard', the site of a now destroyed ancient building, known within living memory as Parsonage Barn.[iv] To the south of it are shown the almshouses, marked as 'Hospitall', as they were then named.[v] On the north was the vicarage, reasonable in size at the time but much enlarged during the next hundred years, and then again by the Victorians. This resulted in it being far too big for the vicar at the start of the 20th century:[vi] the Victorian additions were later demolished, but even this did not prevent its being sold by the diocese towards the end of that century and its incumbent expelled to the stables. Its fine garden, still in the main existing, was designed by the famous Sir Joseph Paxton,[vii] renowned gardener and architect for the 1851 Great Exhibition.

Leysbourne must have seemed rather as it does today with two major exceptions. In the centre of the road, opposite a block of four cottages that were to be gentrified a century later into North End Terrace, is drawn a single isolated house; another and smaller one stood further down in the middle of the street at the junction with Cider Mill Lane. One, probably the larger, was demolished with the Countess's permission, soon after the map was drawn to make room for traffic.[viii] Many of Campden's closes are marked with their names, usually that of the occupier, and at the far end of Leysbourne is shown World's End Close, the area now known, rather more appropriately, as Wolds End.[ix] Of the other larger houses in Leysbourne, the south part of the convent and Staplers House (although then two cottages) appeared much as they do now, as did Stamford House, which in the 19th and early 20th centuries was the main farmhouse at that end of Campden, the cottages at either side housing its workers. The Stanley family who lived at Stamford House for 150 years or more, later worked the Town Farm, whose fields were on the left of Station Road.[x]

Until 1832, when it was piped underground down Leysbourne, the Scuttlebrook, which drained the Hoo and provided water for many of the cottages, ran into a large pond at the junction of Church Street. A causeway crossed that pond[xi] over which horsed traffic and pedestrians could pick their way. The piping for the stream, which then disappeared under Bedfont House and discharged into the main brook, was almost certainly constructed after the 1830 flood, one so serious that tradesmen's goods floated along the High Street. Coinciding with the death of King George IV on 20 June, it was long remembered as 'The King' s Flood' and as such was still known when the town was again inundated in 1901.[xii]

A closer look at the High Street would have revealed the Cotswold stone façades, the stone for it all quarried at Westington, punctuated by Tudor half timber, of which little now survives. The present beams and plaster of the Old King's Arms, are in fact a 20th century restoration by F.L. Griggs and Norman Jewson of a similar Tudor building.[xiii] However, the group of houses dropped into the High Street to the south-west of the Square, still showing traces of exposed timber-work, were certainly already there. North of the Market Hall and Town Hall, running from Cotswold House to the late 17th century Little Martins, is a row of late 18th and early 19th century houses. What stood there in 1722? Could it have been more half-timbered buildings?

In the same way, what was destroyed to make way for Bedfont House,

Campden's finest classical house? A late 17th century deed mentions a mansion on the south side of the High Street.[xiv] No trace of such a building now survives. Perhaps it was a medieval mansion destroyed to provide a site for the present Bedfont House. This is one of the glories of the High Street but it was not erected until some twenty years after the map was drawn.

Many of those cottages and similar dwellings in and near the High Street were thatched, straw being a cheap and natural material. Until the middle of the 20th century, Church Cottages in Cider Mill Lane were all thatched, as were those in Leysbourne and many in Watery Lane, the stonework of which suggests that they started life with only a single storey.

The map has also some delightful little drawings of several buildings, among them St James's Church, outwardly much as we see it now. Others show the gateway to the old Campden House, the Market Hall and the Town Hall — hence our knowledge of the spire on the last named. Although Campden House's gateway is delicately depicted, neither of the two banqueting houses appear, although a 'Walk' is shown as running between them. Of the ruins themselves there was then much more to be seen than now, as the robbing of material was to continue for a further century. As for the Court Barn, then used for threshing and storage, and only half its present size, its stonework would have looked very new, a fresh addition to the town.

The Market Hall was then invaluable to the farmers' wives, although such places were noted by an 18th century writer as being 'in winter chilling, and dangerous to the health of those who wait in them, especially women'.[xv] During the next century, however, it outlived its purpose and became a shelter for carts and wagons; even worse, its very existence lay under threat towards the end of the Second World War, when its then hard-up owner nearly sold it to the United States. It is just possible to excuse him: twenty years before, some townsfolk had favoured its demolition because no funds could be found to repair the decaying structure.[xvi]

From the map we can also learn more about the 18th century road system. From Broad Campden a track ran up the valley towards Campden Hill Farm (which was not then built); there it divides, one branch turning towards the Cross Hands and the other westwards through Stow Gate and marked 'To Stow'. From the Cross Hands, the Seven Wells road is shown as 'To Gloucester' and the present A44 is marked 'To Evesham' and 'To Oxford'. The Conduit is named as such and 'Conduit Lane' turns down into Westington. The Blockley road from Broad Campden is shown as leaving the main road at the back of Norman Chapel, rather than where Broad Campden Hill is now constructed. Most other roads are as now.

The present Campden House was then known as Combe and is shown as three separate buildings, one obviously its fine barn. The house was not then approached from Dyers Lane, but from the bottom of Blind Lane, with the road running up the valley from Westington Mill, passing the millpond to the north of the house. It was near on 150 years before its present main entrance was developed. Also shown is the back way in from the A44. Near there the Mile Drive (marking the border with Weston parish) is shown as a road branching off from Kingcombe Lane and running up to the Worcester road near Broadway Tower.

During the century after that map was drawn, the High Street buildings were to assume their present impact. As with North End Terrace, and the row of houses north of the Square, classical Georgian and Regency façades added dignity to what G.M. Trevelyan much later saw as 'The most beautiful village street now left in the island',[xvii] a perhaps hackneyed but rarely disputed claim. These taller houses with their gracious sashed windows replacing Elizabethan lattices, brought lighter and more airy rooms, although behind them lurked and often still do, Jacobean or even earlier rooms, unchanged since built. Nor did those new classical buildings conflict at all with the remaining 17th century or earlier façades, their balanced but natural harmony all the product of Westington Quarry. Even the Police Station, the Baptist Church and the extensions to the grammar school, the mid-19th century additions to the High Street, managed to blend with their neighbours. However, these new façades were a contrast indeed to the crammed, insanitary, sometimes disease-ridden, entries like Lodging-House Yard, George and Dragon Yard, Broad Entry, and Poppet's Alley, with their tiny overcrowded cottages running back into the burgage plots at right angles to and hidden by the High Street houses.[xviii]

Although the historian Ralph Bigland wrote about Campden in the 1780s of 'Marchandize and Manufactures of early days totally lost',[xix] this was not entirely so. It was agriculture, together with its business as a market town, that over the centuries kept the place prosperous. The High Street, lined with shops and craftsmen's workshops, their different trades and callings numbering at least

The Jacobean maces. The pair of brass-gilt maces by a London silversmith are hall-marked 1605. *(By kind permission of the Town Trust)*. The pulpit given in 1612 by Sir Baptist Hicks.

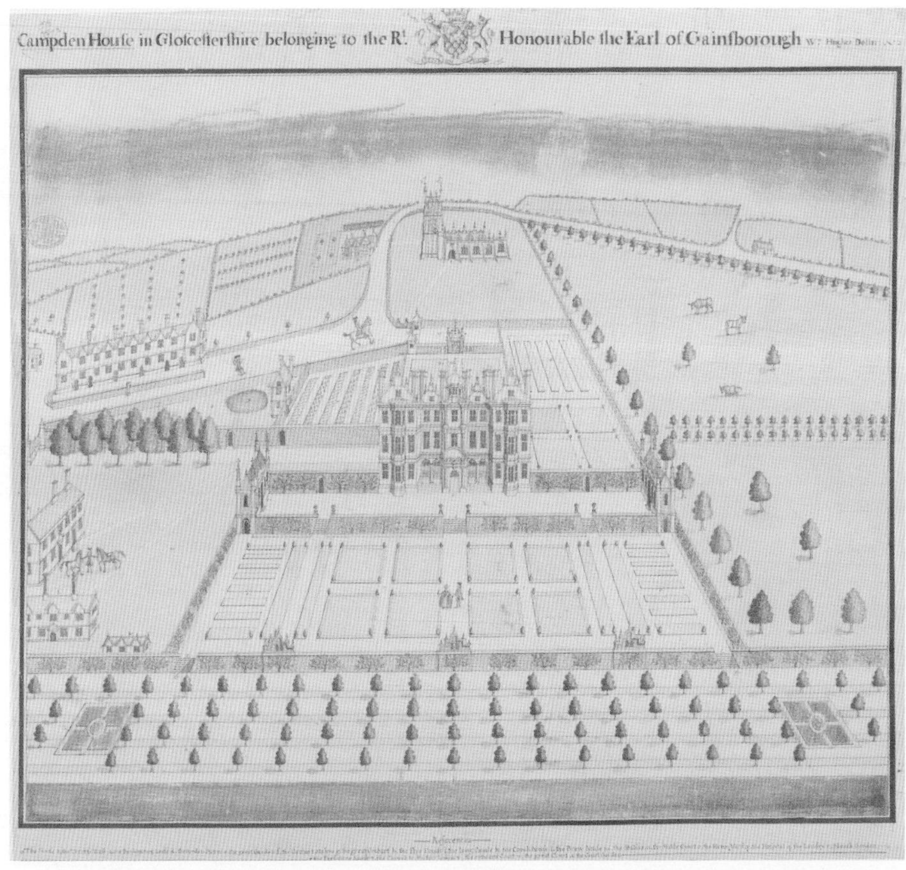

Old Campden House. This drawing dates from about a century after the manor house had been burned down but is likely to be relatively faithful as to its general appearance.
(By kind permission of the British Library)

A representation of the steamship patented by Jonathan Hulls in 1736
(By kind permission of Institute of Mechanical Engineers)

Sir Gerard Noel in 1824, a portrait in oils commissioned from
Sir Thomas Lawrence (1769-1830), fourth President of the Royal Academy
(By kind permission of Vale Press)

Rickyard at Lapstone Farm, watercolour by Margaret Calkin James, 1943. Calkin James, the designer, spent the war in Campden with her family and for 3 years lived at this farmhouse.
(By kind permission of Elizabeth Argent)

Market Scene with Punch, 1856 by the Worcester painter Edward Thompson Davis
(The original is currently in a private collection. Reproduced with kind permission of the owner)

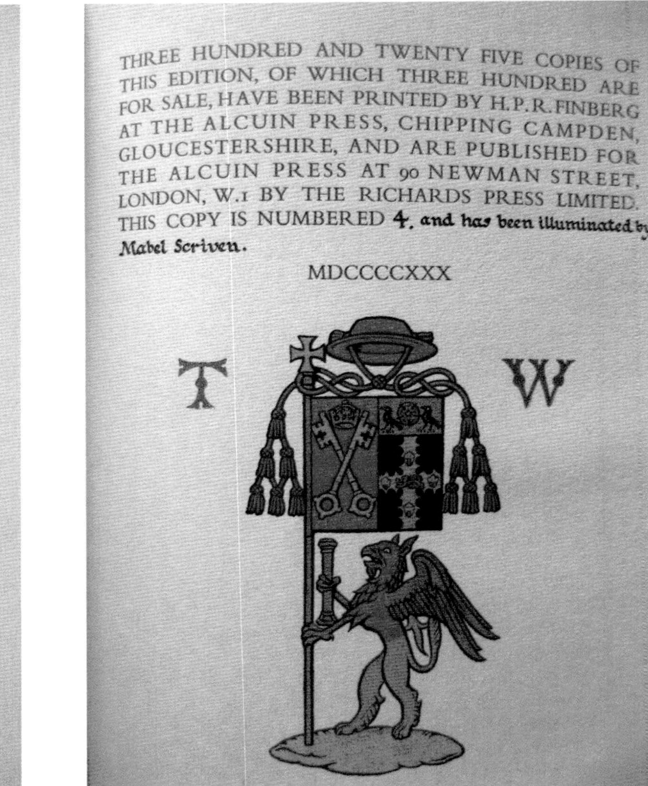

THE LIFE AND DEATH OF
THOMAS WOLSEY
the great CARDINAL of England
By GEORGE CAVENDISH

Newly printed at The Alcuin Press
Chipping Campden : MCMXXX

THREE HUNDRED AND TWENTY FIVE COPIES OF THIS EDITION, OF WHICH THREE HUNDRED ARE FOR SALE, HAVE BEEN PRINTED BY H.P.R. FINBERG AT THE ALCUIN PRESS, CHIPPING CAMPDEN, GLOUCESTERSHIRE, AND ARE PUBLISHED FOR THE ALCUIN PRESS AT 90 NEWMAN STREET, LONDON, W.1 BY THE RICHARDS PRESS LIMITED. THIS COPY IS NUMBERED 4. and has been illuminated by Mabel Scriven.

MDCCCCXXX

The title and end page of *The Life and Death of Thomas Wolsey* by George Cavendish showing the arms of the See of York and Thomas Wolsey designed by Paul Woodroffe and printed by the Alcuin Press, 1930. *(Private Collection)*

Little Miss Muffet, stained glass in Dover's House by Paul Woodroffe, c1926
(By kind permission of Audrey Wilkerson)

Wilson Garden under construction viewed from St James's tower, c.1983
(By kind permission of Ray Plested)

Poppet's Alley, an example of the 'crammed, insanitary entries' that existed behind the High Street houses until the mid- 20th century

twenty, attracted incomers from nearby villages to buy and sell and sometimes to work in the town.

It was not until the start of the 18th century that industry, commerce and agriculture began, to quote Trevelyan once again, 'moving forward unconsciously towards the industrial revolution'.[xx] Nevertheless, in 1712, ten years before that map was drawn, Campden had 401 dwellings, 258 in Chipping Campden itself, 40 in Berrington, 19 in Westington and Combe and 54 in Broad Campden; in 1801 the number was 405, almost exactly the same. Living in those houses in 1712 were 1,718 people; 1,700 were counted at the first national census held in 1801. During the following hundred years the population changed little except for a slight upward tilt in mid-century and a steady fall thereafter.[xxi] It was to stay almost constant for a further century until near the time of writing. Houses did proliferate but not the total population of the parish.

During the century that followed the surveying of Lady Gainsborough's map, minor industries began to take shape in the town, giving work not just to the men, but to their women and their children as well. Already the town had become famous for its stockings and soon many of the women were also making kid gloves or stays in their houses.[xxii] Throughout the century flax was an increasingly popular crop and its product was employing ever more people locally: by 1838 a flax mill was employing as many as 47 hands and the present Twine Cottages mark the site of a rope and bag workshop.[xxiii]

During most of the 18th century, of even greater importance was silk-throwing (the spinning of silk into thread), though it was never more than ancillary to Blockley's famous industry. Although thought to have been converted in the early years of the century, the first known mention of the Silk Mill itself (the future home of the Guild of Handicraft) appeared in the British Directory of 1793-4 with the entry that 'A silk mill under Mr John Franklin was recently established in the town', and went on to mention that its presence adds greatly to the advantage of its owner and his employees.[xxiv] The building, however, could be older and the attached house certainly is, so some business could have been carried out there before the silk-throwing. The mill was powered at first by the brook, the noise of its water-wheel echoing around the area.[xxv] Some thirty years later, horse had taken over from water power as the driving force, understandably so, as droughts can cut the brook's flow to a trickle. At the same time a twelve horse-power steam engine was being planned.[xxvi]

The building boom, first brought about by the restoration of Charles II, and continuing throughout the next century, also made work and brought money to the town. Mention has already been made of the fine Bedfont House, which was almost certainly built by Thomas Woodward, he who drew Lady Gainsborough's map and was the owner of Westington Quarry. Thomas Woodward was the head of the family of masons. He and his son Edward, both of whom are buried in Campden's churchyard, were to raise many distinguished buildings, both in their own county and nearby. Among them were the present towers of Blockley and Alcester Churches; St John's Church in Gloucester, together with the now lost Georgian façade of the nearby Bishop's Palace, St Mary's Church at Preston-on-Stour and probably the adjacent Foxcote Manor, and the fine Gothic revival work at Alscot Park near Stratford.[xxvii] Although the Woodwards seem to have been the most prominent building firm in the town during the 18th century, finding custom as they did far afield, there must have been many other individuals and small firms exercising their craftsmanship to complete the work of giving Campden High Street its present appearance.

What Campden lacked most at that time was a resident Lord of the Manor. The Gainsboroughs, who still owned most of it, had their main estates and residence in Rutland and ran Campden through an agent. After Lady Juliana's death in 1680, no Gainsborough is known to have had a house in Campden until the 19th century. Indeed, not until the early 18th century, when the Campden estates passed to Dorothy, widow of the third Earl and daughter of the 1st Duke of Rutland, is there evidence of a Gainsborough taking a close interest in the place. There was no longer a manor house suitable for a major landed proprietor. The old Campden House was in ruins and a mansion at Broad Campden, of which nothing is known other than its mention in leases, had disappeared a century or more before.[xxviii] It was in the mid-19th century that Combe (at various times known as Combe Farm or Combe House) was expanded in size to become a Gainsborough family home and the present Campden House.

Also lacking in Campden were squires, small landed gentry, or even mere gentlemen, people who were thought fit to add the distinction of 'Esquire' to their names. In 1811 the voters' list showed only two esquires living in Campden itself.[xxix] One was Richard Miles, who, no more than a grocer in

1784, had so increased his wealth that he could describe himself as 'Esquire' and quickly climb the social ladder. Living in the newly-built Cotswold House, he also owned Westcote and Miles Houses in the High Street and was about to develop North End Terrace. Other 'esquires' on the list were non-resident: James Roberts of Blockley, who voted as the owner of a house and land in Broad Campden, and Sir Gerard Noel Noel of Exton Hall, who did so through his ownership of lands and of the then tenanted Court House.

As late as 1844, only three men living in Campden itself could be called 'Esquire', one of them Samuel Hiron, a member of a very old Campden family whose members seem to have crossed all social boundaries. Otherwise only the vicar, the Rev Charles Kennaway, married to a Noel, and his curate, who was also headmaster of the grammar school, were admitted into the category of 'Nobility, Gentry and Clergy' in the Pigot Directory of Gloucestershire.[xxx] The local attorney, John Rood Griffiths, the owner of Bedfont House, and three surgeons, two of them also Hirons, were listed separately from the 'Shopkeepers and Tradesmen' as 'Professional Persons'. Surgeons, it should be said, had only just begun to graduate from 'trade' to such status. Although not listed as such, the lawyer, Rood Griffiths, living in the finest house in the High Street, would by then have been seen as a gentleman.

In Campden in 1712 there were 63 freeholders[xxxi] entitled to vote at elections. There were 64 of them in 1776, with four exercising their vote elsewhere, and 51 in 1811. The names of those voting at the latter two elections we know. Of these freeholders some held land that had in the past been sold by the Lord of the Manor, but a larger number were the owners of houses or shops in the streets of the Borough. Familiar some names still are: Cotterill, Ellis, Freeman, Haines, Hands, Hiron, Horne, Hulls, Izod, Stanley, Tidmarsh and Warner.[xxxii]

Campden was, in fact, a solidly middle class town by the 19th century, although the term was only just coming into use. As a chartered borough, the town itself was run by an oligarchy of its more prosperous residents — tradesmen and shopkeepers — watched over with varying degrees of enthusiasm and diligence by the Gainsborough agent. Among those who were moving into the middle class at the beginning of the century were the attorney-at-law, Edward Cotterill, owner of Bedfont House (soon to be sold to his successor, Griffiths), Richard Lambert, bailiff, and one of the three surgeons and apothecaries then recorded. There were also the doctors, four of them in

Campden at one time,[xxxiii] better educated and more respected than the surgeons. However prosperous their parents might be, the younger and less successful male members of often large families were obliged to earn their own living, at times by migrating elsewhere. Others took whatever work could be found locally. Hence one reason for Campden's great sense of community. There are several examples of Campden men of the time.

The Hiron family had been prominent in Campden since at least the beginning of the 17th century,[xxxiv] and Hiron is one of those names that constantly recur. By the 19th century they were a leading family, employing a couple of indoor servants,[xxxv] and soon to move into the professional classes. It was a time when the sons of such respectable families rarely became soldiers, but in 1809 Sergeant Robert Hiron was writing to his 'dear honoured Father' recounting in excellent English and a well-formed hand an accurate and detailed account of his regiment's part in the Battle of Talavera in the Peninsular War against Napoleon, and the hardships suffered by his comrades during the campaign. Which of the several Hirons was his father is not known, but Robert himself ended his days in the Royal Hospital at Chelsea.[xxxvi]

Another family whose prosperity ebbed and flowed was the Ballards. Campden's first known historian was George Ballard, whose paper on St James's Church, written in 1731, waited for forty years before being read by another historian to the Society of Antiquaries. This and other work brought him a post at Magdalen College with board and £60 annually. Almost wholly self educated and a chandler's orphaned son, Ballard had been apprenticed to a stay and habit maker in the town. But his great uncle had been a well-known local physician and his grandfather a wealthy yeoman.

Jonathan Hulls, near contemporary of George Ballard and son of a weaver and small husbandman, was another who rose in the world, in this case to national fame. An original thinker and deft mechanic, he was the first to conceive and patent the idea of applying steam power to propel a vessel. His prototype sadly failed in its trials on the Avon.[xxxvii] However, his name was to be so remembered by nautical engineers that two centuries later the bewigged portrait of this Campden churchwarden and mechanic was to hang in a stateroom of the famous liner *Queen Mary*.[xxxviii] Hulls also patented a number of other inventions, including a machine for weighing gold coins, and a slide rule.

The 1844 directory, listing as it does virtually all the shopkeepers and traders, reveals the extent of the services available, both to the residents of Campden itself, and to the people of the nearby villages and farms. Quite a few of those tradesmen needed to augment their living in other ways. There was but a single banker and one auctioneer, but of the five grocers in the town one worked also as postmistress, one as the registrar of births and deaths and two as druggists. There was also a full-time chemist and druggist. The clock and watch maker also retailed beer as did one of the four boot and shoe makers and two other shopkeepers. Of the five bakers, one was also a miller and one a flour dealer. There were two other full-time millers, seven butchers and four maltsters in business. Of craftsmen, there were two carpenters, one also an ironmonger, a single cabinetmaker, a cooper, a wheelwright, two braziers, one of them a tinsmith, one basket maker, two plasterers, one also a slater, one painter, two plumbers and glaziers, three stone masons, no fewer than eight tailors, two of them doubling as beer retailers and one as a draper, a turner and chairmaker, two saddlers and collar-makers, a silk-throwster and a wheelwright. Other shopkeepers included a couple of stationers, one also a hardware dealer, a further hardware man, a gardener and seedsman, together with a hairdresser who also held the post of town crier. Some of these named people did, of course, employ apprentices, assistants, journeymen and unskilled men and women, as well as other workfolk. It is hard to think of anything useful that could not at that time have been bought or made in Campden.[xxxix]

A Campden Bank Note from the 1790s

Sixty years earlier, the list of traders and merchants had read much the same except for the addition of a firm of milliners and a fishmonger; instead of the one banker and one attorney, three of each calling were then in practice.[xl] Nearby manor houses such as Foxcote, Northwick Park and Springhill would probably then have done more business locally in Campden. By the 1840s with better communications they could have looked further away to larger trading centres such as Stratford, Evesham or even London for luxuries and professional advice.

Notes

i Leics RO, DE3214 486/6 (Copy in CADHAS Archives 2002/052/M)
ii We prefer this long-established name for the street once also called Victoria Street, and now renamed Park Road.
iii Rushen, *History* 100
iv ibid 165
v Bigland, Ralph, in Frith, Brian (ed) *Historical Collection Relative to the County of Gloucester*, Part 1, Vol. 2, (BGAS, 1989) 279
vi Rushen, op cit 165
vii ibid
viii Leics RO, DE3214 41/11
ix Leics RO, DE3214 635/6. Sixty years ago people still argued whether it was `Wold's' or `World's'. Both have been used at one time or another.
x Stanley *Farm Ledger* Transcript by Diana Evans (CADHAS Archives 2004/129/DT
xi The `Cawsey Way is mentioned in an Elizabethan deed Leics RO DE3214/41/11.
xii Rushen op cit 82, 91
xiii Jones, Celia and others, *The Inns and Alehouses of Chipping Campden and Broad Campden*, (CADHAS, 1998) 25
xiv Leics RO DE3214 181/33
xv Marshall, William, *Rural Economy of Glos*, (2 vols 1789) vol 1, 106; Reprint ed G. Nicol (Alan Sutton 1979)
xvi Crawford, Alan, *Arts and Crafts Walks in Broadway and Chipping Campden*, (Guild of Handicraft Trust, 2002) 64
xvii Trevelyan, G.M., *English Social History*, Longmans, Green & Co, 1944 35
xviii Rushen, op cit 165
xix Bigland, op cit 186
xx Trevelyan, op cit 294
xxi Rushen, op cit 91; Atkyns, Sir Robert, *The Ancient and the Present State of Gloucestershire, Part 1, (1712* reprinted EP Publishing 1977) 321
xxii Rushen, op cit 72
xxiii ibid 81
xxiv Witts, Rev. F.E., *Diary of a Cotswold Parson 1763-1854*, ed David Verey, (Alan Sutton, 1979) .128
xxv Rushen, op cit 165
xxvi Witts, op cit 128

xxvii Bradley, Oliver, 'Overlooked Aspects of the 18th Century Bishops' Palace in Gloucester' *BGAS Trans,* Vol 118, 2000, 162-3; Rushen op cit 141
xxviii Leics RO DE3214 134/27: lease of 'messuage and mansion' 2 June 1699; also DE3214 230/17 'capital messuage and manor house' 20 May 1625
xxix Voters' List, 1811 Rushen op cit 81
xxx Pigot, Directory of Gloucester, 1844
xxxi Atkyns, op cit.321
xxxii Rushen, op cit 80-1
xxxiii Whitfield, Christopher, *History* op cit 153
xxxiv Rushen, op cit 71; *Cranfield Survey: Westington.* Kent Arch Off U269/1 B4; (CADHAS Archives 1995/1R)
xxxv 1841 Census
xxxvi Shakespeare R.O. PR 162: PRO WO 97/346
xxxvii Rushen, op cit 73-77
xxxviii Personal knowledge of writer.
xxxix Bailey's British Directory 1784, Vol IV
xl ibid

14

The Land and Its Management

The much-travelled William Marshall, who towards the end of the 18th century investigated the rural economy of several English counties, wrote of the Cotswold labourer that his wages were 'remarkably low'. Only a shilling a day, they were raised to eighteen pence or two shillings during the harvest, together with six quarts or more of weak beer; the latter, shamefully 'exorbitant' to Marshall, was not merely to quench their thirst but provide food for the body as well. A woman would bring home only half that sum; a bachelor living with the farmer's family, although well fed on bacon and vegetables, earned a mere pittance.[i] Even in 1836, after the enclosures, the usual daily wage on the local Norton Farm (now Attlepin) was 1s 4d or 1s 8d for men, and 6d to 8d for women. Piece work rates were equally low — up to 3s an acre for hoeing wheat, 4d or 6d a perch (16 feet 6 inches) for hedging; 4d a bushel for threshing[ii] and 7s an acre for 'bresplowing'. Breastploughing was common up to the end of the 19th century for paring turf and burying stubble. Gangs of men wearing leather aprons would be employed pushing the blade under the surface, turning the soil to a depth of 2 or 3 inches.

The Stanleys, who lived at Stamford House in Leysbourne, in the Borough, hired Thomas Parker in 1792 at Stow Fair for £4 14s 6d, at the same time buying him a new smock for six shillings. The next year Parker was given a guinea rise, but earned only an extra half guinea in 1794. Betty, an indoor servant, was paid just £3.[iii] Except for the poorest labourers, most married men did, however, have some slight stake in the land on which to grow food, even though it was no more than a minute cottage garden.

Before the Campden Enclosure Act was passed in 1799 the countryside around Campden was unenclosed and very different from today. The farmhouses that today dot the wolds had still to be built; rare were the stone walls that now criss-cross them, and few coverts had been planted to house pheasants. To those unused to the beauty of the open spaces and changing light of those rolling hills, they could appear dull indeed.

Even in 1826 William Cobbett could see the Cotswolds, now mellowed after the enclosures, as 'an ugly country ... having less to please the eye than any other I have ever seen'.[iv] He was not alone in this. The diarist the Rev. Francis Witts, a local man, loved the beauty of north Gloucestershire, and after driving some visiting friends in his phaeton around Bourton-on-the-Water and Little Rissington he wrote:

> They are agreeably surprised with the country: they had anticipated bleak hills, stone walls and all the horrors which the inhabitants of the Vale of Gloucester ascribe to the Cotswolds, and were pleased to find warm valleys, rich meadows, luxuriant hedges and a fine autumnal foliage not yet parted from the trees.[v]

Marshall was another admirer. After riding across much of England, he likened the Cotswolds to the Yorkshire Wolds but 'less magnificent' and as 'subjects of rural ornament ... susceptible of great beauty'.[vi]

By the 18th century some part of the farmland, probably mainly ancient demesne land, was worked by men or women holding it on lease, mostly from a Gainsborough. Some individuals might combine the farming of a mere half yardland (perhaps 8 or 10 acres) with a trade such as collar-maker, mason or inn-keeper. Others could have a couple of yardlands on which a family could make a living. In Campden the terms of the lease were usually for three lives with an initial money payment and an annual rent, but with the relic of the old labour services sometimes hanging on until the early years of the 18th century and with 'the best beast being paid as well as a heriot'.[vii] This hangover from the medieval obligation of the heir on the death of a tenant had become a kind of fee to enter possession of land. 'Husbandman' was the usual name for these small farmers, with a few, usually those with the larger holdings, ranking as yeomen, though there was no fixed difference between the two sometimes fluctuating terms.

However, most of the agricultural land around Campden was still held by customary right by the inhabitants of the hamlets, cultivating their scattered strips. Only recently has that 1722 map[viii] disclosed how the parish looked before being enclosed, although Rushen, writing nearly two centuries afterwards, tried to set down the details from local memories and records.[ix] In Campden's open fields those working the land had a number of often dispersed strips, each a quarter of an acre or so in size, sixty of them counting as a yardland. As was the custom in the West Midlands, half of these fields would lie fallow each year.[x] Those ridge and furrow patterns, as on Dover's Hill and the Hoo, that today can be seen so clearly even in permanent pasture, came about through centuries of ploughing, proof that in the past the grasslands were once open arable fields. The agricultural land in Campden was still divided into the three hamlets of Broad Campden, Westington and Berrington, the agricultural year in each being regulated by its own Court Leet. The 1722 map, together with the description of the lands in the Enclosure Award, allows us to define the boundaries of the open fields.

To the north and east of the town lay the vast Berrington fields. There was Hoo field and Church Field (called in the map The Pothooks). To the east of Church Field was another large field, by then divided into furlongs and quarters, their names including Pound Furlong, where Berrington Pound stood (and where stray animals were impounded); two Bratch Quarters and two Whaddons. To the north of this field were the Bratches (brakes or patches of bushes and briers) probably corresponding to the medieval 'Spinney' noted in 1273. Still in Berrington, between Hoo Lane and Dyers Lane, were the Leasows: five or six enclosed grasslands where hay was cut and cows pastured; and against Kingcombe Lane there were the Berrington sheep runs.

In Broad Campden was the large Greystones field, divided in 1722 into Marbrook Quarter and Fowlfeed Quarter, with meadows and leys along the brook against the Paxford boundary. There were Sedgecombe, and Moorside Quarter, which the Enclosure Award divides into Moorside Furlong and Briar Hill Furlong. South of the 'Cat' Brook was Broad Campden Mill Brook Quarter, which by 1799 seems to have been divided into Catbrook Furlong, Coddle Apple Furlong, Long Close and Puck Pile. To the west and north of the village were the cow pastures.

In Westington hamlet was the Walk Hedge Quarter and Westington Gratten (in Rushen's time remembered as Conduit Hill Furlong),[xi] Westington Pool and Westington Brook Furlongs. Names have changed over the years, but the way in which they ran in pairs is further evidence that the local land lay fallow every other year, rather than every third or fourth year as happened elsewhere.

In the richer land of the valleys and bordering the streams on the Ebrington and Paxford borders, were the meadows of permanent pasture and the leys: in Campden the two terms seemingly near synonymous. The hay grown on the pastures was the winter feed for horses, plough oxen and breeding stock. Its

1782
Oct 24 Orders maide and agreed upon By the Amlet of
Broad Campden a penently 5
We agree that no Body shawld turn upon the Hill Wate
To tin the Hill Wate Imadetly or a penetnlly — 5
To Take the pigs up in one wick
If Hany found upon Trespas shall pay 2 each pig
If Rined If not wringed 6
Not to Hitch nor mow hany Latter math A penantly

The first few lines of the proceedings of Broad Campden Court Leet in 1782. The full transcript (in more orthodox English) shows the amount of regulation necessary in each hamlet before the Enclosures. ***(By kind permission of Gloucester Record Office)***

cutting and use were strictly controlled by the Manor Courts, as was the number of animals that could be kept on the fallow and the stubble. Pool Meadow (below old Campden House), Westington and Berrington Meadows lower down the Cam, and Pye Mill Leys in Broad Campden among others marked on the map, still keep their names.

Above the cultivation were the high open sheep runs with their sparse but valuable grazing, upon which landholders could each graze a certain number of animals. Stretching uphill on either side of Conduit Lane were 'Broad Campden Hill below the Road' on the left and 'Westington Hill below the Road' on the right, both of them running on across the London Road to what were marked as 'The Upper Part above the Road' of the two hills — called in the Enclosure Award Broad Campden Far Hill and Westington Far Hill.

Stretching along the southern side of the brook all the way from Blind Lane to the (two) Coneygrees were a large area of what the Enclosure Award calls 'Ancient Enclosures', and which are shown in the 1722 map as many small closes, sometimes called grounds or leasows, and walled or fenced, where poultry and pigs were reared and oxen stalled at night. Because their names were usually those of their current owners, they could often change but some have

TRANSCRIPT

1782

Orders made and agreed upon by the hamlet of Broad Campden.

We agree that nobody should turn [animals] upon the Hill Wheat on penalty 5s.

To hain [protect or enclose] the Hill Wheat immediately on penalty of 5s.

To take the pigs up in one week.

If any [pigs] are found upon trespass they shall pay 2d. each pig.

If fined (?) if not ringed, 6d. [i.e. pigs' noses had to be ringed.]

Not to hitch [animals on] nor mow any lattermath on penalty £1.

To hain Sedgecombe and the Clover Hill at Old Candlemas [13th February] on penalty 5s.

To mound [enclose] by the yardland from the Upper Wall to Northwick Wall to be done by Old Lady Day [5th April].

To mound Sedgecombe Plain to be done by Old May Day [May 12th] on penalty of l0s.

To sow clover from Witherset Hedge to Sedgecombe Plain.

To sow pulses from the top of Wheelers Gore to the Lower Wall.

To hain the Lowfield pulse on 12th March on penalty l0s.

The Constables to buy the bull as usual.

We agree that if anyone is found overstocked upon horse, cow or sheep he shall pay double common or the cattle to lie in the pound till the money is paid.

We agree that the Constable should have a liberty to pound [animals] at any time upon suspicion.

We agree that nobody should hitch nor bait [animals] upon the highways. If any cattle are found there they shall be pounded and pay a penalty l0s.

Not to turn nor bait pigs till harvest is in. If any are found upon trespass to pay a penalty l0s.

We agree that the cows should be nobbed [hobbled] before they go into the common and to keep them nobbed till the common is done, on penalty l0s.

To sow the fatches [vetches] upon Over Sharcombe.

To stock the Lowfield of sheep, five to the yardland.

To find a hurdle and a half to a yardland, for the Constable to hire the Lowfield shepherd and to be paid by the yardland.

Any person or persons refusing to pay the shepherd or bring their hurdles a penalty 5s.

We agree that the Constable should call the meeting at three days' notice at any time to settle business for the use of the town to be determined by the majority of voices.

We nominate Constables for the year ensuing John Handcock, James Dorill, Richard Handcock, Hayward.

We agree to take horses and cows up at St. Andrews, New Style [October 30th]. If any are found upon trespass after, a penalty £1 1s.

We agree for the cows to have the (?) Lying Closes [Lion Closes].

survived for at least three centuries, notably 'The Crofts' (which late 20th century fashion, following local pronunciation, has started spelling 'The Craves') and 'Paretree Close', as it is marked on Lady Dorothy's map, transformed in the 1970s into a housing estate. This large area probably represents the medieval lord's 300 acre demesne. The Coneygrees date from the time when rabbits were bred as food for the more wealthy, but their rippling ridge and furrow suggest that they might once have been an open field.

Some other land had long been enclosed, especially the 600 acres of Combe hamlet. Combe had for some hundreds of years been farmed separately and since the early 17th century had been leased out by first the Smyths and later the Gainsboroughs. Other ancient enclosures were the closes that lay along the remote Broad Campden Moor.

Until the enclosures the medieval manor courts — the Court Leets — still retained much of their vital powers and influence. The Court Leet officers were carefully chosen: the tythingmen and constables (responsible for closing the meadows at the due date, the upkeep of stock, exacting minor punishments and keeping the bull of each hamlet), the haywards (responsible for mending fences and impounding stray animals) and the fieldsmen (who managed the common fields).[xii] Regardless of the type and size of their holding, as freeholders or leaseholders, large or small, all those who tilled the open fields and grazed their animals on the leys, meadows, stubble and hills, were obliged to work in unison, ploughing, harrowing, sowing and reaping as the farming year demanded. The pages of instructions given at each of the three Court Leets in 1782 seem to have touched on every aspect of farming life: the number of sheep put to a yardland of the fallows; the dry cow and eight dry sheep that the holder of each yardland could stock on the hill land on 1st May; the date that the mowing of meadows could start; when and where wheat, pulses and vetches should be sown; which persons should buy the bull (usually the constables); that horses should be brought in from grass by 10th November. And so it went on, every detail laid down, as were the fines for breaches of the rules, the latter so numerous as to suggest that they were not uncommon.[xiii]

The complexity of the problem can be illustrated by the recorded holdings of a single individual, William Eden in the last decade of the 17th century. This man had land in more than twenty different furlongs in Westington and Combe, all named, most of them in a single land (or strip), but others shown as a complete yardland, a quarter of a yardland or by the acre. To calculate his total holding is not possible, but clearly he was a man of consequence, as was his successor; on that map the Eaden *[sic]* Leasow where the Littleworth Estate was to be built and the Eden Close, adjoining ' Pare Tree Close', indicate two of his smaller fields.[xiv]

A section of a map of Gainsborough lands dated 1818, showing how Hoo field was rapidly enclosed after the Act of 1799 ***(By kind permission of Gloucester Record Office)***

The Lords of the Manor were absent for most of the 18th century. However, Sir Gerard Noel, who inherited the Gainsborough estates in 1798, was interested in Campden and much concerned to implement the major agricultural changes that culminated in the enclosures. It was in the eastern counties that other large landowners, individuals such as 'Turnip' Townshend of Norfolk and Thomas Coke of Holkham (another Norfolk estate), later Earl of Leicester, were the most prominent. They improved crop rotation, grew roots for winter feed, improved light land for wheat, and developed stock breeding on a scientific basis. Sir Gerard followed their lead as did his fellows, setting an example to smaller men and employing highly skilled and forward thinking agents, a prime example being William Westbrook Baker, who served the Noels for forty years, instituting the Rutland Ploughing Match and Stock Show, and continually winning prizes at Smithfield.[xv]

Such improvements could not be superimposed upon the feudal open field system of land holding. Enclosure was the widespread solution and in 1799 Parliament passed Campden's own Enclosure Act. It dealt with 3381 of the 5000 or so acres of the parish. The balance comprised 829 acres of Combe and another 470 that had long before been enclosed, as well as the town itself, the churchyard and the various small closes already walled or fenced.[xvi] The cost of it all mounted to £2 for each acre of the enclosed land for legal fees, walls, fences and roads.

Under the Act commissioners were appointed, and after a series of meetings in Campden, an award was made. The outcome was that 223 acres (in Broad Campden) were allocated to John Rushout, the second Lord Northwick, 145 to Edward Cotterell, 73 to Henry Roberts, 64 to William Postlethwaite, 58 to William Izod, and 92 to Mary Perrins 'as a lessee of Gerard Noel'. In addition 261 acres went to the vicar in lieu of his lost tithes. Of the rest, Sir Gerard Noel had some 2,380 acres.[xvii] Even before the Act was passed some of the old scattered strip holdings had already been consolidated into largish patches,[xviii] some of them worked from High Street buildings such as Grevel House with its fine old barn, or Stamford House. But the crop-raising and stock-rearing of the parish now became centred on a number of large farms, let to solid citizens with the capital to develop them, and worked from new buildings out on the wolds, using the stone from freshly opened quarries and connected by new roads,[xix] rough but with wide verges to avoid their becoming impassable in wet and muddy weather.

Efficient it may have been and good for the nation's economy and the wealth of the nobility and gentry, but the enclosures caused a great change in social structure in the Campden hamlets. The great fields of 150 or 200 acres and their quarters and furlongs were divided up by walls, fences or hedges into smaller enclosures, some of no more than three or four acres and most of no more than 15. The majority of the new owners (the Noels, the vicar, the Cotterells, etc.) leased out their land, not to the many peasants who had been working the land, but to large farmers, in batches big enough to be viable given the new advances in agriculture. It was a tragedy for most of the smaller customary tenants who now either became landless agricultural labourers, working for wages for the new tenant farmers, or were forced to emigrate to the new industrial cities such as Birmingham or Coventry, or to migrate overseas. As the fields were enclosed, some of the new tenant farmers worked from houses in the townships, such as Stamford and Leasebourne Houses, or Westington and Poplars Farm, or Hollybush Farm in Broad Campden, whilst others built new farmhouses in open country. Such farms as Greystones, Briar Hill, Sedgecombe and Lapstone farms, all in Broad Campden, came into existence for the first time.[xx]

Stamford House in Leysbourne was a typical town farm house. Behind it, as far as what is now Griggs Close, lay its orchards and home closes. Their arable and pasture lay nearby in the fields running along Station and Ebrington roads, much of it now housing.[xxi] Some farm labourers might have a cottage and perhaps a garden; others would have lived in the crowded alleys or entries running back off the High Street.

The effect in Campden may have been lessened because some of the strip farming was carried out by tradesmen and craftsmen, but the amount is still unknown. The first population census of 1801 (the new national bureaucracies were getting under way) showed that Campden's population numbered 1,700, but their names were not then recorded. However, an investigation of the state of agriculture, taken at the same time by parish incumbents, possibly inspired by public unrest at the high wartime cost of food, revealed that Campden had 760 acres under wheat, 444 under barley, 186 under oats, 228 under peas and beans and 122 under turnips. Land lying fallow was not included, nor did the cautiously suspicious farmers necessarily always render accurate returns; nevertheless, they do indicate how well balanced Campden's arable was so soon after the enclosures had come into effect. Incidentally, Campden was one of three parishes in Gloucestershire in which the parson complained about the profiteering of middlemen.[xxii]

It was another half century before a reasonably clear picture of the final effect of the enclosure emerges. The 1851 census was the first to give the birthplaces of individuals as well as their occupations.[xxiii] In it, 21 men described themselves as farmers, indicating also the number of men and women they employed and the acreage they worked. Of these farmers no less than nine, together with their 187 agricultural labourers, lived in the borough itself or in Berrington, most of them in or near the High Street with their buildings behind. The largest was William Rimell at the Court House, farming 530 acres with 35 labourers, as well as a carter, a dairy-maid and a general servant living in the house. The smallest existed on just five acres. All were locally born men, unlike many of their craftsmen neighbours, who had moved in from elsewhere. In Westington, Combe and Berrington were another dozen farmers, employing 95 labourers. Every farmer in the parish was a Campden man and all but one or two of their labourers were born there or in a nearby village, as were most of of their wives. It is, however, noticeable how Broad Campden, but not Westington men, often courted wives in Blockley, Paxford or Draycott rather than in Campden. One can also perhaps assume that it would have been difficult for any incoming farmer to have prospered in this closed community.

Periods of comparative comfort in rural England seem always to have alternated with poverty. Pauperism in Campden was nothing new. In 1768, 162 families, say 650 individuals or a third of the parish's population, were receiving alms, an intolerable burden on the ratepayers.[xxiv] Bread and cheese, together with the vegetables, especially potatoes, grown in their gardens and washed down with beer, was the staple diet of the poor; meat was rarely seen except for the bacon from the pig raised by most families. Game or rabbits might be had, poached in the woods, hedges and streams. When wages and prices for produce dropped, starvation threatened. Wages could be indeed low. To keep warm in the winter and to cook was a serious problem. Wood in the parish, as elsewhere, was in short supply, and a ton of coal cost a labourer five weeks wages. The result was the burning of straw for fuel to the detriment of the land. As Marshall put it, 'the poor, on these shelterless hills, must be in a wretched state, as to fuel, ... fortunately for the owners, stone walls will not burn'.[xxv]

In all, the agricultural labourers numbered 282, if we count a very few farmers' sons among them. Many such men could have lacked the initiative to make the effort — or even own the means — to move elsewhere to scrape a living. For some, Birmingham, Coventry or even London beckoned. There, the booming factories of the industrial revolution with their constant need for fresh supplies of labour tempted the often semi-starved landless labourer and his family with the hope of livable wages; fresh Cotswold air and supportive neighbours would be exchanged for a stinking crowded urban basement and intermittent employment. How many Campden people left for the cities we do not know, but local family history research has revealed its frequency.

Notes

i Marshall op cit vol 2, 20
ii *CADHAS Notes & Queries* III Nos 1-3
iii Stanley *Farm Ledger*, op cit 15
iv Cobbett, *Rural Rides* 403-4
v Witts, op cit 80
vi Marshall, op cit vol 2, 15
vii Leics RO, DE/3214 181/41 lease
viii Leics RO, DE/3214 486/6 (copy in CADHAS Archives 2002/052/M)
ix Rushen, op cit 105-8
x Marshall, op cit vol 2, 38
xi Gratten is coarse grass or stubble. Its use here suggests that the land had been left as stubble for longer than the usual year.
xii Nelson, J.P., *Chipping Campden* (Privately printed, 1975) 39
xiii ibid 38-45; *Court Papers*, Gloucs RO D2857/2/2
xiv Nelson, op cit 34-6
xv Noel, Gerard, *Sir Gerard Noel MP and the Noels of Chipping Campden and Exton* (CADHAS 2004) 130-32
xvi Rushen, op cit 99-102; Warmington, *Reconciliation of Campden Inclosure Award*' (unpublished) CADHAS Archives 1990/38/DS
xvii ibid
xviii Leics RO DE3214, various leases
xix Rushen, op cit 99-100 for details
xx CADHAS analysis from Leics R0 DE/3214 of deeds Broad Campden, Berrington, Chipping Campden and Westington. (Paper by Jill Wilson unpublished)
xxi Stanley *Farm Ledger*; Rushen op cit 42
xxii Minchinton, W.E., 'Agriculture in Gloucestershire during the Napoleonic Wars,' *BGAS Trans*, 1949
xxiii Census, 1851
xxiv Atkyns, op cit. 321
xxv Marshall, op cit vol 2, 27

15

Riches and Poverty
'No Squires, Few Gentlemen and Many Poor'

The Noels were the major county landowners of Rutland, owning some 15,000 acres[i] and living at Exton, their main country residence. They were a Staffordshire family, their origins dating from the Norman Conquest, and it was not until the early 16th century that one of them first settled in Rutland.[ii] The Noels' Campden land totalled only one fifth or so of the acreage of their other possessions; it was a subsidiary estate seemingly rarely visited during the 18th century, its supervision left to their local agent. Nevertheless, Dorothy, the Dowager Countess who commissioned that 1722 map, could have inspected it during the minority of her son, the 4th earl, judging from the interest she clearly took in the place. And the fact that the sixth earl did, in 1773, present brass-gilt maces to the town suggests also that he may have known it.

The Noels would eventually do much, as Lords of the Manor and the major landowners, to influence Campden's future, but the heads of another distinguished family, the Ryders, later ennobled as the Earls of Harrowby, were also to become prominent locally. They still are, although they never owned more than a small amount of land in Campden itself. The Ryders' roots and main estates lay in Lincolnshire. The increase of their land ownership to a total of 11,400 acres[iii] began with Sir Dudley, a wealthy lawyer who became Lord Chief Justice and died in 1756, the day before his creation as Baron Harrowby was ratified. Sir Dudley's eldest son, Nathaniel, was to acquire even more land, buying the Sandon estate in Staffordshire and building a new Sandon Hall there in 1776. It was Nathaniel's son, a prominent diplomat and politician, who became the first earl. By 1800 Harrowby land touched that of the Gainsboroughs at Ebrington, Mickleton, Norton and Willersey, with other Warwickshire and Worcestershire holdings of between 3000 and 4000 acres in all.[iv]

Henry Clarke, resident agent to the Noels in Campden, lived at what he described as 'The Court House, Camden' in the grounds of the ruins of the old Campden House. His wife ran a market garden business there. Seemingly with the approval of the Noels, Clarke worked also for the Ryders and others, including the Kytes of Norton. His twenty-year correspondence with the Ryders and their London stewards, ending with his death in 1771, provides a vivid picture of 18th century country life.[v] On the Ryders' behalf Clarke rode to and fro across the West Midlands, investigating land that might be bought, arranging leases with tenants and reporting on their behaviour, before returning home to write by candlelight long reports to his employers, at times twice or thrice weekly. Although his haphazard spelling was of its time, his Gloucestershire accent can be detected in the consistency of his 'woords'. In 1757 he journeyed as far as Somerset and Exeter checking on properties suggested by the steward; however he could 'find no part to compare with this', nor could there be 'any good sporting'.[vi]

The nearby Burnt Norton, on the other hand, Clarke strongly recommended in 1753, encouraging Sir Dudley to come down from London to see it. It was a macabre semi-ruin, the remains of what had been a newly built small mansion in which Sir William Kyte had lived with a mistress and some servants, bankrupt and continually drunk. Twelve years earlier he had burnt himself to death there.[vii] Somehow Clarke arranged for Sir Dudley and his wife to stay in an undamaged wing, organising bed and table linen and arranging for beer to be brewed beforehand.[viii] This visit seems to have produced a quite close personal relationship between Clarke and the future Lord Chief Justice and their respective wives. As well as regular gifts of venison and other game, sent by the regular weekly carrier service from Campden to London, little parcels of black pudding made for Lady Ryder by Mrs Clarke often accompanied them. In his business correspondence the agent often mentions his many problems with his health, so arousing sympathetic responses.

At the end of the 18th century a member of the Noel family began to take a direct and personal interest in Campden. In 1798 the sixth Earl of Gainsborough died without issue, leaving his Rutland, London and Campden estates, together with a million pounds in cash, to his nephew, Gerard Noel Edwards, with the wish that he would assume the surname of Noel.[ix] The title had, however, died with him.

Born in 1759, Gerard Noel Noel, as he became (later he assumed his wife's title of Lord Barham), was a well-rounded man. Although grossly extravagant, beseeching his uncle to pay his debts and later running through much of his inheritance, he was as popular with his tenantry and neighbours as he was with his peers. A poem about him starts:

Now this put me in mind of a jolly good Squire,
High Sheriff this year for a proud little shire,
Whose character rambles all over the county,
For his great love of fun, for his heart full of bounty.[x]

Letters reveal his friendship with the Prince of Wales (later George IV), with whom he played cricket at Brighton against a team of fishermen, and the amusement of the Prince at the impudence of Gerard's young sons, who sailed with their father in soaking weather six leagues out to sea.[xi] His interest in his many children was close and affectionate: by no means always the case in his station and era. He had 18 of them by his first wife, born almost annually between 1781 and 1801.[xii] The threat of French invasion took him into the military sphere, serving first in the Rutland Militia, embodied in 1778-83 and again in 1793; he then raised the Rutland Fencible Cavalry, and equipped it at great cost, running himself further into debt. For fifty years he was a rather independent Whig member of parliament, active in abolition of the slave trade, and in the 1832 Reform Act.[xiii] His failure to get on with its Tory opponent, Sir Robert Peel, was thought to have been the reason why, to his great disappointment, the revival of the Gainsborough earldom was delayed until his son's accession.[xiv] Gerard Noel's masterly portrait by Lawrence,[xv] in the robes of High Steward of the Corporation, graces Campden's Town Hall.

Sir Gerard Noel inherited his vast estates at a time of major revolutions: that of the American colonies which brought about the loss of this country's first Empire; that of the French in 1789 that saw the start of a quarter century of war; the industrial revolution, in which Britain led the West into a new economic era; and the agricultural that helped provide the manpower for the grim new cities in which industry expanded. As well as initiating the enclosure of land, described earlier, Sir Gerard was faced with the decline of local industry, and with it the dying administration of the town.

The Borough of Chipping Campden was defined by a very tight physical boundary.[xvi] Since the reign of James I it had been governed as a corporation by a self-perpetuating oligarchy of 14 capital burgesses, from whom two bailiffs were appointed each year, together with 12 inferior burgesses and a steward learned in the law. It continued to operate in this way at the start of the 19th century. Holding their quarterly courts, the burgesses tried cases for debt and trespass for sums not greater than £6 13s 4d, and they supervised the four annual fairs and the Wednesday market, collecting the dues for the Corporation's expenses. The 1605 Charter had reserved half of those dues to the Lord of the Manor, but the Gainsboroughs had started to lease that share, together with their ancient burgage rents and other manor profits, including those of a horse fair, to the Corporation for a small premium and a rent of some £6 annually; in return the latter undertook to repair the Market Hall and the sheep market wall and pay any taxes that arose.[xvii] This sheep market wall probably enclosed a stretch of land on the High Street used for that purpose.

However, by the middle of the 18th century a serious decline had taken place and self-government was in a rather poor state. The Court Leet and Court Barron for the Borough seems by then to have concerned itself mainly with nuisances, such as (in 1814) repairs of roads, footpaths and drains; stones, timber, dung and other rubbish left lying in the street, and the ever-present problem of cleansing the brook behind Watery Lane.

Those permitted by the burgesses to practice their trades and crafts in Campden were made freemen of the borough, as was the custom in other ancient boroughs and cities. The fee for admittance for those who had learned their trade in Campden was a mere 2s 6d, but those who had done so elsewhere were made to pay two guineas. The fact that the Corporation made two rulings, in 1780 and again in 1784, that anyone with the temerity to disregard this rule should be fined £5 for each month that he did so, may imply that the rule was being ignored. The names of those recorded as admitted as freemen between 1771 and 1785 indicate how people could move around to find work: 23 had served their apprenticeship in the town; 30 were incomers. The latter included men in the rather more skilled trades: four tailors, three blacksmiths and a peruke maker; none-the-less, there was both a home-trained and an imported surgeon.[xviii] This curb by the Corporation on the individual's freedom to work where he would was gradually eroded, and eventually fell into disuse.

That the bailiffs countersigned the churchwardens' accounts during the first decade of the 18th Century suggests their high status.[xix] But by the end of that century much had changed. In Bigland's words:

> From various Causes the magisterial Power is at present much declined, the Corporation defective both in Number and Police, and the Merchandize and Manufactures of early Days totally lost.[xx]

That the Borough's ceremonial at least was functioning wholeheartedly in the latter years of the 18th century is suggested by the presentation of the two new brass-gilt maces by the sixth Earl of Gainsborough to the Corporation in 1773.[xxi] Why he did this is not known: the smaller but more valuable silver maces, dating from 1605, must surely have still been available.

As we have seen, there were in Campden no squires and but few gentlemen, while the Gainsboroughs lived away in Rutland. The absence of local men of both birth and substance ensured that the magistrates responsible for Campden were found from outside the parish, several from the nearby villages, among them at times the squires of Ebrington, Hidcote, Stanway, Moreton and Mickleton.[xxii] Answerable to the monarch and appointed by the lords lieutenant of the county from among its resident squires, the magistrate's primary function was that of keeping the peace, but from their feudal beginnings they had been steadily saddled with a number of administrative tasks. As unpaid country gentlemen, lacking any such staff, the magistrates now passed those chores to the parish vestries.

With a near defunct Corporation and the Court Leets doing little more than ensuring the smooth running of agricultural life, power in Campden rested increasingly in its Vestry. Responsibilities between magistrates, vestries and corporations were not always clear cut. This was certainly so in Campden where the Corporation was becoming ineffective. So it was that St James's Church Vestry gained in power, choosing the parish overseers for the poor, overseeing the Acts of Settlement, and dealing with administrative chores such as road repairs, sanitation, relief of poverty, collection of the poor rate, and a variety of other small jobs. From the start of the 18th century and for the next 150 years, Campden's Vestry was the most powerful body in the parish.

Formally, as is clear from the *Churchwardens' Accounts*,[xxiii] the General Vestry was an assembly of all householders, both male and female. Relief for some of the worst poverty was administered by the Special Vestries, panels of between ten and twenty residents, chosen by the General Vestry and set up in the early 19th century. Those appointed to Special Vestries had to be 'substantial householders and occupiers' and to be approved by a local magistrate. The Vestry almost invariably included the vicar, curate and churchwardens. From among their number a parish overseer was appointed, to whom many of the decisions were delegated.

Typical of the decisions of the Campden Special Vestry were those made at a meeting in March 1822. At that meeting a man and a woman were each given a smock for their sons; others got a shirt and a sheet; one man got 5s advance and another 1s 'on account of an idiot child'; another had the earnings of his daughter made up to 1s 6d in case she could not earn it. At other times there were more unusual items, such as one in 1828 when Joseph Keen had applied 'to be allowed a person to wait on his wife', and it was decided that his daughter be 'liberated from Northleach prison for that purpose'. Occasionally, removal orders such as that 'for the purposes of sending Judith Smith to the Parish of Old Hatfield' were made.[xxiv]

Emigration overseas was becoming a popular solution to poverty.[xxv] In 1832, 77,134 people departed from England and Scotland, thirty times more than went in 1815. By 1850 the annual figure had quadrupled. In compelling detail Campden's vestry accounts indicate how in 1834 the ratepayers lightened their crippling burden by paying for 23 of their paupers to emigrate overseas: to Canada went a man, his wife and four children; to Jamaica sailed a widower and his six children, a motherless family of a man and four children and four single men. All of them were given clothes for their journey, and some were provided with boxes and bedding as well. The detailed accounts show the cost and number of each article bought: four shillings for boy's buckskin trousers and seven shillings for a large bed and pillow; most of them had probably never before been so well clad.

To ensure that everyone got safely on board without selling their new garments and bedding or slipping away, Mr Freeman, one of the Campden overseers for the poor, took them by carrier to Stratford, by canal to Birmingham and on to Liverpool, paying for their and his board and lodging on the way and even standing them a pint of beer before they embarked. The total cost of it all was £67 5s 5d; with the poor relief that year costing £1,524, it was a sound bargain for the parish. What happened to the emigrants we may never know. If they survived the voyage (many such passengers did not), those to Canada may have moved on to the United States; rum or disease or both may have killed those who chose Jamaica. There were other destinations. At the Special Vestry meeting that finally authorised the money for this 'shovelling out of the paupers' (as the procedure was colloquially known), Catherine Tracy, in being granted a passage to Gibraltar to join her husband in the 68th Regiment, would have reduced the burden on the poor rate by yet one more person.[xxvi]

The alternative to the vast expense of poor relief was the workhouse. In 1834, the same year that Campden paupers were 'shovelled off' to the New World, a fresh Poor Law was enacted, replacing outdoor relief with new workhouses, made deliberately harsh and as such exposed in Dickens's *Oliver Twist.* A workhouse had existed in Campden since at least the 17th century, the £40 given by Lord Noel in 1630 'for the use of the poor of the town for ever', having been used by the overseers to enlarge it.[xxvii] A hundred years or so later we know that one was still in use,[xxviii] near the end of Sheep Street, below a field then known as Workhouse Close and the row of houses known until the 1930s as Workhouse Bank (now graced with the name Gainsborough Terrace). In 1837 that building was pulled down,[xxix] to be replaced by the larger and probably much more severe workhouse of the Shipston Union, serving the whole area. The 1834 Act was not universally applied, and parishes had some say in how they cared for the unfortunate. The designation of people as 'paupers' in the 1851 census suggests that Campden was not shipping everyone off to Shipston but that many were supported in their own houses or those of relatives. The previous census is less clear on the subject.

A count of those who were put down as paupers in the 1851 census reveals only 43 names: every one an aged agricultural labourer or his widow, most of them the latter. Only three of the widows and two of the men were middle-aged. No one fit to work appears to have lacked a job. It was a time of comparative prosperity, helped also perhaps by the building of the local railway, of which more later.

By and large, rural people everywhere could be generous to those in trouble, something seldom mentioned by historians as they analyse the miseries of the poor and their possible oppression by superiors. In places like Campden it was not easy for the more prosperous to ignore the plight of hungry neighbours living next door to them, to whom they might even be connected by marriage. In fact, charity towards the unfortunate extended far beyond parochial boundaries. On most Sundays during the late 17th and early 18th centuries, collections, known as 'briefs' were taken in St James's Church for towns in misfortune, often the consequence of fires.[xxx] Such giving extended far afield, at various times as far as the Strand in London or Edinburgh, Dolgelly, and the Hartlepools. In 1717 alone, as many as 37 such 'briefs' were collected. The relief of the 'French prodistance' aroused compassion in 1682, the year King Louis XIV's renewed persecution of the Huguenots provoked another mass emigration to England and elsewhere; again two years later, the large sum of seven pounds was collected for the same cause, equal to a quarter of the annual church rate.[xxxi]

Apart from the relief of the poor, the variety of the Vestry's tasks was astounding. The repair of the church itself, together with its wall and the costs of the graveyard, were the main calls on the church levy. But from the church rate the Vestry paid two pence a dozen for sparrows' heads, the bill in 1743 rising to the large sum of near £5 to cover the deaths of almost 6,000 small birds, perhaps not all sparrows. Not until 1806 was this stopped, long after Romantic writers had begun to record the pleasure bird song gave them. The culling of 'urchins', or hedgehogs, earned a steady bounty of four pence a head until the start of the 18th century, 41 of them in 1684; dead foxes, badgers, an otter and even a raven were also rewarded.

The repair of the parish roads, including those of Broad Campden and Westington, was another burden on the Vestry, at first paid for by the church rate but later by a separate road rate.[xxxii] Other regular outgoings were insurance, from 1845 onwards, with a cover of £1,000, rising each year. The sexton or verger had to be paid, with sometimes the clerk, an organist from 1837 onwards, and always the bell-ringers, their work not seen as a hobby until the 20th century. Churchwardens bought bread and wine for the sacrament, an expenditure apparently watched with care by their colleagues, and in 1697 queried in the minutes. The archdeacon's Visitation also cost money in dinners, wine and the ringing of celebratory peals, until in 1757 the parish exploded in rebellion at a bill of £8 5s, driving them to cancel such spending from funds, together with the costs of celebrating the Gunpowder Plot and Royal Oak Day.[xxxiii]

The Vestry, as well as the Corporation, was manned by solid men, tradesmen or farmers, who tended to be as careful with the public money they safeguarded as with their own. The agent to the Gainsboroughs, himself a working citizen of the town,[xxxiv] together with the vicar, if he were both resident and a strong personality, exercised more influence than their peers. But the near absence of gentry resulted in the parish being governed by men with a stake in the place, men who began to be spoken of before the 18th century ended as the middle classes.

The men who ran the parish were, however, few in number. At the turn of the 17th and 18th centuries the church accounts tended to be signed each year by half a dozen or so citizens who tended to be past, present or future churchwardens. Details of their occupations are sparse, but a comparison with the Gainsborough leases brings a few to life: Anthony Juggins and Thomas White, were both yeomen; the husbandman William Eden also an innkeeper; William Horne a saddler; Price Reade a baker; and John Lane a member of the plumbing family. Of some prominent individuals towards the end of the 18th century, more is known. A comparison of Bailey's 1784 Directory of merchants and traders with signatories of the church accounts and names of Corporation officials shows an attorney, a silk-throwster, two maltsters, a plumber, a grocer and a shopkeeper were or had been churchwardens, and of these, three had also been bailiffs in the borough, as were four more of the tradesmen named in Bailey.[xxxv]

Preferable though living conditions may have been in Campden as compared with the new industrial cities, statistics do suggest that the expectation of life here was much the same. Campden's burials between 1781 and 1787 averaged 44 each year, a death rate of 26 in each thousand.[xxxvi] The annual national rate was exactly the same.[xxxvii] A decade later a statistician had it that the rate had dropped to 22.2 per thousand, still no better than the then national average that included all the new industrial towns and cities. Campden appears to have been especially unhealthy for a rural town. Could it have been the drainage?

For centuries sewage had either run into the Cam, been transported from earth privies to allotments, or used with the pig muck to fertilise cottage gardens. During the 19th century a number of the more prosperous people on the north side of High Street began to install water closets, draining into pits. However, foul water from these inadequate provisions drained across the road towards the brook, and into the wells on the opposite side of the street. For several years a number of cases of fever occurred among those living on the lower side of the street. An unsigned, undated copy letter (probably mid 19th century) in the Noel archives addressed to the Secretary at the Home Office complains of 'Fever about every summer or autumn every one of the cases being of the one principal street'. The Lord Gainsborough of the time was accused of failing to take any steps to abate the nuisance, which was said to be of the typhoid type; at the time of writing 12 of the 14 then sick, of whom one had died, lived on the lower side. Drainage of sewage, the writer declared, was required.[xxxviii] The summer stink in small closes running off the High Street, such as the charmingly named Poppet's Alley, picturesque to romantic Victorians but breeders of disease, must have been overwhelming. The town's high death rate could well have resulted from sanitation even worse than in the average country place. But it was not until 1926 that Campden was to benefit from main drainage, and even then it was not universal.

We have seen how the development of the country's canal system had enabled the paupers to be moved to Liverpool in a mere four days. Canals also changed the appearance of Campden in the early 19th century by allowing roofing slates from the quarries of North Wales to be transported to Campden so undercutting the laboriously made and costly stone Cotswold slates. Thus we have the Regency houses of North End Terrace, built in 1826, efficiently and not unattractively slate-roofed.

The building of the turnpikes from the late 1700s onwards, of which more later, so improved long distance road travel that by 1763 London letters could be sent and arrive daily.[xxxix] By 1838 the postal service had become so dependable that the Rev. Mr Witts complained bitterly when the Moreton postmaster informed him that letters from Gloucester, Cheltenham and parts of the North would take two days to reach him rather than the usual one day.[xl] As each decade passed, Campden was further widening its contacts with the commercial and industrial world. By 1784 Mr Edward Horsman was established in the town as a banker, drawing on a London firm and increasingly used to finance the widespread new building as well as the thriving commercial activity in the town. A mercer and a currier also managed to describe themselves also as bankers. By early in the next century there was business enough for three insurance agents, together with a branch of the Gloucestershire Banking Company that served not just the wholesale trades of the town but a large range of shops, selling not just to the parish but outlying villages, too. Among these were seven butchers, three druggists, two stationers, a hardwareman, a hairdresser and an ironmonger.[xli] Some of these have left their mark in the town with the Regency bow-windows that still grace a number of the shops and private houses in the town.

Notes

i A major source for the Noel family is the Exton Manuscripts that survived the destruction by fire of the family house at Exton in 1810. Recently discovered, they are now held in the Leicester Record Office. Their cataloguing is not yet completed. The papers are discussed by Jenny Clark in Rutland Record, Nos 13 and 19, copies of which with further notes on the family compiled by Carol Jackson are in CADHAS Archive 2002/034/9

ii Noel, Gerard, *Sir Gerard Noel MP and the Noels of Chipping Campden and Exton* 3(CADHAS 2004) 17-20; Noel, Emilia F, *Some Letters of the Noel Family*, St Catherine's Press, 1910 1

iii Notes on Ryder family (File Sandon Estate Archives), CADHAS Archives 2003/105/G

iv ibid Reid 12

v Clarke *Letters*. CADHAS Archives 2003/104/G

vi ibid, 227

vii Whitfield, *History* 168-71 quoting Gentleman's Magazine, April 1774; Court, Doris, Weston-sub-Edge (Privately printed, 1992) 31-3

viii Clarke *Letters* op cit 148, 152, 167

ix Noel, Emilia, op cit

x Jackson, *Notes* CADHAS 2002/034/9

xi Noel, Gerard, op cit 106-7; Noel, Emilia, op cit 86

xii Noel, Gerard op cit Appendix VIII; Noel, Emilia, op cit 25; Rushen op cit 15

xiii Noel, Gerard, op cit, 78-82 & 126-29

xiv ibid 47, 138

xv Sir Thomas Lawrence, 1769-1830, the leading portrait painter of the day. Became President of the Royal Academy in 1820.

xvi The boundary ran roughly behind the houses in Park Road, along Back Ends, and part of Leysbourne, behind the vicarage garden and the almshouses, down Calf Lane to the brook, and up behind the houses in most of Sheep Street and the southern side of Lower High Street. Only a few closes were incorporated within it.

xvii Leics RO, DE3214 61/8

xviii Rushen, op cit 85

xix Bishop, Leighton, (ed), op cit 148, 157v. 167

xx Bigland, op cit vol 2, 286

xxi Rushen, op cit 168

xxii Whitfield, *History* 153

xxiii Bishop op cit see index

xxiv Gloucs R.O. p.81 VE2/1-3

xxv Powell, Geoffrey, 'Shovelling Out the Campden Paupers' *Glos Local History Bulletin*, 13; Bishop, op cit 387-90

xxvi Bishop, op cit 388

xxvii Rushen, op cit 172

xxviii Fendley, John (ed) *Bishop Benson's Survey of the Diocese of Gloucester, 1735-1750*, (BGAS, 2000) 113

xxix Whitfield, *History* 199

xxx Bishop, op cit: (for details see index)

xxxi ibid

xxxii ibid, 339

xxxiii ibid, 229v

xxxiv Henry Clark, agent to both the Ryders and the Noels

xxxv Baileys *British Directory* 1784; Rushen, op cit 83-5; Bishop, op cit index

xxxvi Bigland, op cit 281

xxxvi Trevelyan, G.M., *English Social History*, (Longmans, Green & Co, 1944) 342
xxxviii Leics R.O. DE 3214 662/30
xxxix Rushen, op cit 60
xl Witts, op cit 148
xli Pigot, *Directory of Gloucestershire* 1844

16

Religion, Drink and the Schools

Fortunately a vivid account of the interior of St James's Church survives, written in 1729 just seven years after Lady Gainsborough's map was drawn. Its author was George Ballard, Campden's first known antiquary. His account reveals the contrast between the church's then dilapidated interior and the new dwelling houses rising around it.

From one of his many letters, written to his friend Mr Hearn and forming the basis of his paper on Campden, we learn that 'the inside of the Church has been lamentably defaced of late years by the indiscretion of the Townsmen'. Ballard lamented 'the sacrilegious havock in bursting up and making away with the Brasses; and the shameless and scandalous neglect that is still had of em': When they became loose they were 'Embezeled and lost'.[i] Only four years before, Rowland Smith, a churchwarden, had cut off and carried away more than a third of 'a very fair font, handsomely carved' to make room for a pew for his tenant; it was a 'most scandalous piece of impudence ... contrary ... to all right order and discipline ... there is so little hope of it's *[sic]* ever being repaired'. This ravaged Norman font beside the pulpit, the mutilation of which Ballard himself tried to halt,[ii] remains broken and unused. More successful he was in 1753 when he prevented Mr Weston, the new vicar, recently appointed by the then Lord Gainsborough, from destroying Thomas Smyth's magnificent Tudor tomb. As he wrote to an influential London fellow antiquarian:

> What can infuse such Monstrous Barbarism into his Capricious Brains to Demolish such an Elegant Monument of so worthy a man I can't conceive, or what should my lord to consent to so Dishonourable and unworthy an action ...[iii]

Unlike the majority of his contemporaries Ballard treasured Campden's past and cared little about incurring the disfavour of churchwarden, vicar or Lord of the Manor.

'To preserve from oblivion', Ballard recorded, or drew, the still legible lettering and armorial bearings on tombs and monuments. However, he admitted that 'those that had neither Antiquity, Beauty, Elegance in the Inscriptions; nor the persons in any way remarkable for Birth, Fortune or Merit, I have omitted as not worthy of your Notice'. He also criticised what he found to be 'the faulty copying' by his predecessor, Sir Robert Atkyns.[iv]

It is from Ballard's paper that we have some slight inkling of what 'was formerly a great deal of Curious painted Glass', now lost to us. Surviving in the north chancel were four panes of figures, that of St Werburg standing between St Gregory, St Jerome, St Ambrose and St Augustine. Only the heads of the figures were missing, suggesting to Ballard that they had been removed 'by some Sacrilegious person for lucre'.[v] In the south aisle were the remnants of the Passion of Christ; in the north chapel 'not long since' had been several rich figures; while in the north aisle were St George and St Christopher, 'very prettily represented', although only from the knees upward.

Ballard also mentioned what he saw as more modern glass, and specified that among Baptist Hicks's many benefactions to the Church was the east window of the chancel in which 'are his armes 6 foot in height finely painted which cost 13£'. In 1631, Ballard also recalled, John Fletcher gave the middle window on the south and John Gilby five glass windows on the north side of the nave, thus implying that they were still there at the time.[vi]

The churchyard wall (repairs to which in the last years of the 20th century created contention between Baptist Hicks's descendants and the Parish Council) Ballard mentions also as another of Gilby's gifts, built at a cost of £150.[vii] Otherwise we can safely assume the outside of St James's Church looked just as it did when its soaring tower arose. And, except for the Victorian vicar's vestry and the dozen lime trees representing the apostles, planted in 1770,[viii] so it still remains.

With the arrival of photography we can view the interior of St James's as it was in the early 19th century. But nothing we have shows the three galleries that existed for years: the singing gallery[ix] under the tower given by Baptist Hicks; one built over the south aisle for girls; and a third in 1825 over the north aisle for boys.[x] Photographs also show the newish pews, also made in 1825, that replaced the 'irregular and misplaced' oak settles Bigland knew, some with the coats of arms of medieval woolmen.[xi] The 1884 restoration removed the galleries and replaced the pews once again.[xii]

Also recorded in these early photographs is the overwhelming and vast scroll encircling the east window that declares I AM THE RESURRECTION AND THE LIFE.[xiii] It was a mark of the new evangelicals, the 'vital religion' that had swept not only through dissenting congregations but the Anglican Church as

St James's Church at Easter, 1876

well, its doctrines affecting especially the more prosperous classes of society. In the 1820s, Campden's incumbent, Rev. the Hon. Leland Noel, the 10th son of Sir Gerard Noel, had inspired 'a local blend of evangelical piety, accompanied by improved administration and material progress'.[xiv] The extent of the evangelical movement's popularity in the Cotswolds is revealed by Francis Witts's diary entry for 14th April 1830, written after he had dined with 15 of his 'Clerical brethren' of the Stow Clerical Society. He equated the 'Evangelical principles' of several of his fellow diners with the 'puritanical views' towards which the Dean of Gloucester, who was in the chair, was 'somewhat warped'. A Tory magistrate and broad churchman himself, Witts also developed reservations about the Tractarians. Possibly the Hon. Leland Noel was a fellow diner.[xv]

The Toleration Act of 1689 had granted freedom of worship to all, the governing classes having learned the futility of persecuting their fellow-citizens. The Broad Campden Friends, no longer seen as a danger to the established order, drew their members from a wide area. Nevertheless, there were not many of them, Bishop Benson in the second quarter of the 18th century counting but three Quakers in Campden itself.[xvi] The membership at Broad Campden had, in fact, declined so far that by the time of Waterloo, money could not be found to repair the Meeting House.[xvii] In both 1801 and 1819 Quakers failed to pay their church rate, some twentieth of the total collected,[xviii] but whether on principle or otherwise is not recorded.

William Davison, the leader of the other dissenting church, died in 1711. In 1715 Samuel Knight took the Oath of Allegiance and the Abjuration Oath before the Quarter Sessions at Gloucester. These were Oaths required to be taken by all dissenting ministers under a number of post-Restoration Acts. Then in 1724 a certificate was presented to the Bishop of Gloucester:

> that some of His Majesty's protestant dissenting subjects called Presbyterians do intend to hold a meeting for the worship of God in a New House built for that purpose in the parish of Chipping Campden which they desire may be registered in the Bishop's Court according to an Act of Parliament of 1 William and Mary.

This chapel was built at the far end of the plot of ground that is occupied today by the Baptist chapel, its manse and former graveyard. It was used, first by this group of dissenters and subsequently by the Baptists. Samuel Knight's name leads us to a second connection between the dissenters of Blockley and Campden. He married the daughter of Blockley's first silk throwster, and in 1729 his widow appears as the first Blockley name in a list of members of the Campden church under a new minister.

This Campden meeting house became a Baptist chapel when the Rev. Elisha Smith arrived as pastor in 1785. He not only revived the faltering Campden community but was seen as 'an evangelical apostle who carried his message all over the North Cotswolds', founding the Baptist Church in Shipston-on-Stour and being prominent in setting up another at Stow-on-the-Wold.[xix] Making his home in Blockley, he carried on his living as a grocer and druggist, as dissenting pastors were often obliged to do:[xx] Rarely could the congregations of small places fund the full stipend of their ministers.

In the same century, from John and Charles Wesley and their followers, sprang Methodism, the 'method' of religious life that took root among both Anglicans and dissenters. This movement, its most famous manifestation being the preaching of the Wesley brothers, helped foster philanthropic and educational ideals. Active indeed in the North Cotswolds and the Vale, John Wesley's journals make only one reference to Campden: in 1776, when he noted

> I had been informed that Mr Weston, the minister of Campden, was willing that I should preach in his Church; but before I came, he had changed his mind. However, the vicar of Pebworth was no weathercock, so I preached in his church.[xxi]

This was the same vandalising William Weston, already mentioned, who thus became known as 'the weathercock parson'. Not until 1808 was there a Methodist Society in Campden.[xxii] In 1841 it acquired and converted into its church a recently-built house between West End Terrace and the High Street.[xxiii] There the society stayed, with one mid-19th century break, until it closed in 1975 and the Campden building again reverted to a private house.

Like the Blockley silk mill owners, many of the more prosperous tradesmen and skilled craftsmen of Campden[xxiv] were either Quakers, Methodists or Baptists. It was a time when church- or chapel-going was becoming the mark of an increasing class divide. The congregation of St James's Church, as was often so in the rural Anglican Church, by then amounted to little more than the few gentry, their agents and servants both indoor and outdoor, together with the larger farmers, the few professional people and others who feared to offend their employers or landlords. In the dissenting meeting houses could be found tradespeople and those who depended on them for a living. For the penurious who might feel awkward alongside their better off and better dressed neighbours, the Primitive Methodists held a welcome. In Campden itself, a Primitive Methodist Society existed for some years alongside the Wesleyans around the middle of the 19th century, while Blockley was a centre of Primitive Methodism.[xxv]

There was no Catholic place of worship in Campden until after the conversion of Charles, Viscount Campden (later to become the 2nd Earl of Gainsborough). In 1851 he and his wife moved into the newly converted Campden House, where there was a small Catholic chapel. The convent and St Catharine's school came later, as did the Catholic church, and the Catholic community has gradually built up from that time on.

A mark of all the dissenting churches was their work in attacking social problems, one of the worst of which was drunkenness and its consequent evils. In this they became the springboard for the various temperance movements founded in the 1830s. As William Marshall wrote towards the end of the 18th century:

> Alehouses are an intolerable nuisance to husbandry. They are the nurseries of idleness and every vice. A virtuous nation could not, perhaps, be debauched sooner, or with more certainty, than by planting alehouses in it.[xxvi]

In Campden it was certainly easy to buy a drink, as it was in most similar places. In 1755 the Justices of the Peace had licensed 25 houses of one sort or another; in the next century the total rose at one point to no less than 38.[xxvii] Some were beer retailers run as side-lines to other businesses; others were often the business of wives or widows who brewed the ale or beer themselves (it was, after all, a woman's job), selling it from their front room or kitchen.

Not that there was any lack of proper inns or taverns in which to buy a pint. Eight were listed in Bailey's 1844 directory; five of which survive today. There the business and social life of Campden was run. Farmers and tradesmen bargained there over a drink or a meal, and goods could be stored in their warehouses. Auctions were held in or outside them and election meetings were accommodated. In the larger ones, feasts, small balls and pursuits such as cock-fighting could be enjoyed. For commercial travellers and other visitors there were bedrooms.

Of the five such surviving inns, the main one was the Noel Arms, now known as a hotel. Until 1821 it had been the George, indicated by George Lane which runs up from its yard to the Broad Campden road. It was the main coaching inn of the town as is clear from its wide archway entrance and large yard; the excise office was run from there and it was also the posting house. In the large assembly room behind the oriel window, feasts such as that attended in 1811 by 70 Baptists, and balls and dances, such as the Volunteer ball held later in the century could be enjoyed. Its bowling green, already mentioned, and later in the century a billiard room, brought good business to the tavern.[xxviii]

A much earlier building was the Eight Bells in Church Street, parts of which are Elizabethan or older. But it has not always been an inn. There was another Eight Bells in Leysbourne on the site where the Convent now stands; often called the 'Old Eight Bells'. The masons building the Church tower in the 15th century are said to have given the old inn its name.[xxix]

Like the Noel Arms, the Lygon Arms has changed its name, but more often. Originally the White Hart, it also became the George for a short time before changing to the Hare and Hounds. Only after Waterloo was it given its present name, after General Lygon of Spring Hill who fought in the battle. It also was a coaching inn, as its Georgian arched entrance indicates.[xxx]

The name 'King's Arms' also raises problems. Until the end of the 19th century the name belonged to the Old King's Arms, now the Caminetto restaurant, a well-balanced half-timbered building on the lower side of the street, the creation of Norman Jewson in the 1920s. Previously its frontage showed traces of Elizabethan half-timber, but a muddle of early Victorian windows and brickwork did little for the building until Jewson took it in hand. Only in 1935 was its name moved across the road to Ardley House, now known simply as 'The King's'.[xxxi]

The Red Lion, as with most of the other inns, has a complicated history. Its name was earlier attached to what is now Leysbourne House at the other end of the town. The present inn's buildings are, however, just as old and it is known that beer was sold there before King Charles II returned to his kingdom. For a short time at the turn of the 18th and 19th centuries it was a private house, but Rushen was probably correct in saying that its licensed history was as old as any in the town.[xxxii]

The other three public houses mentioned in 1844 all lost their licences at the end of the First World War. The George and Dragon, now called Dragon House, is marked by its fine sun-dial, from which the Town Hall clock used to be checked.[xxxiii] The Swan, opposite, was taken over by the grammar school during the first half of the 20th century, and retained its name until the end of that century, selling antiques.[xxxiv] The third of these pubs was in Broad Campden but no longer exists; though its name lives on in Angel Lane.[xxxv]

The Volunteer, in Lower High Street, had its licence by the 1860s but was certainly a beer house a century before.[xxxvi] The present Baker's Arms at Broad Campden is of the same late Victorian vintage, when its landlord was selling beer as well as baking.[xxxvii] Thoroughly explored though the subject has been, the names of new licensed houses still come to light. Only recently has the Sign of The Cock surfaced in Broad Campden, an alehouse in 1721.[xxxviii] It sometimes seems that every house in Campden's High Street at one time sold either drink or food or both.

Only in such hostelries could a man find company and refreshment after twelve hours or more hard toil. Marshall's so called 'nurseries of vice' they may at times have been, but they could often be a weary working man's sole refuge from his two-roomed cottage, crammed with perhaps ten children. Nor, as has been touched upon, did many have that much to spend on drink.

In due course, the spread of education was another cause to arouse fervour, especially among dissenters. After Baptist Hicks had revived the grammar school by exposing its corrupt feoffees and putting right its finances, that ancient academy was set again to 'maynteine a ffrescole in the said p'ish. of Campden for ever'.[xxxix] In its early days, as was always the case, the grammar school's headmaster was a priest, sometimes the curate of St James's or the vicar of some nearby parish. Not until 1889 was the first layman, Mr F.R. Osborne, appointed. The headmaster's stipend after Baptist Hicks's reforms was £20 and his house. It had no more than doubled by the start of the 19th century but it was a valuable addition to a curate's stipend. His assistant, or the usher, earned less, at times half that sum and on that he had to exist if he did not also possess a curacy.

It was the ushers who usually provided the free education — the introduction to reading, arithmetic and possibly writing — to most of the sixty or so boys.[xl] The headmaster himself taught advanced subjects, mainly the classics, to boys whose parents were prepared to pay for it, but the raising of the salaries of both masters in 1797 so that they would teach the scholars 'without any fee or gratuity from their Parents or any other person',[xli] suggests that the so-called free school had sometimes charged for its teaching.

It has been said with some authority that most of the fifteen grammar schools in Gloucestershire in the 18th century were in varying stages of decay,[xlii] as was so throughout the country. Campden was perhaps an exception. In 1682 George Townsend had provided in his will for eight scholarships to Pembroke College, Oxford, to be taken in turn by four Gloucestershire grammar schools.[xliii] The usual age for entry to Oxford was then fourteen and the stay there eight years. Full use appears to have been made of these endowments and such was the demand for sound education in Campden that a century later John Freeman, described as a schoolmaster and living 'in a street called Lazebourne', left money for the education of further scholars who were to be taken to the Parish Church each Sunday;[xliv] hence one of the galleries in St James's Church.

Townsend also left money for a schoolmaster to teach poor children and provide them with books. It was the habit of the time for benefactors to endow teachers rather than schools[xlv] and there is no actual evidence that another boys' school was then created. Part of Townsend's endowment was also to apprentice a poor child each year.[xlvi]

At that time lads from all sections of society sat side by side in the grammar school: boys whose parents might rather have seen them working in the fields; tradesmens' sons having a basic education beaten into them; others possibly aiming at a Pembroke College scholarship; and the heirs of gentlemen from neighbouring houses. Boys could board at Campden, to the financial benefit of the headmaster, and some stayed with other families in the town.

Such was the pressure on the grammar school during the 18th century that not until 1812 were free places extended from townspeople to the parish of Campden as a whole.[xlvii] Only for a time does there appear to have been a shortage of scholars, and even then thought was being given and money spent on plans for improving the cramped school buildings. However, it was not until 1863 that £2,500 was raised to enlarge the site and rebuild the old school as the fine Victorian building that still graces the High Street,[xlviii] although now in use as a shop and flats. Its ancient schoolroom with the bust of John Fereby survives (though some say it is Baptist Hicks).

Campden was well in advance of its time in educating girls. Among other bequests to charities that benefited from the will of James Thynne in the early years of the 18th century was a yearly £50 for instructing and clothing thirty poor girls of Campden. Entered between the ages of nine and twelve, they were to stay for four years learning to read, sew and knit; as we have noted, a gallery in St James's was built for their use. Money was also set aside to repair their school building and pay for their apprenticeships.[xlix] The Blue School, as it was to be known, was first built on the site of the present public library, but in 1820 it moved to a new building next to Grevel House, on land given by the then Lord Barham, previously Sir Gerard Noel, with the provision that it should be open to all poor girls of Campden, not just Anglicans. The earlier building then became an infants' school.[l]

Even though some poor boys could take advantage of free education at the grammar school, by the start of the 19th century the demand in Campden was not being met. It was a national problem that led to local Anglican communities founding in 1811 what were to be known as National Schools. In 1833 a very small state grant was paid to suppport them: a benefit that was later extended to Roman Catholic and dissenters' schools. It was the harbinger of Gladstone's Education Act of 1870 that made free elementary education universal.[li]

It was the new young vicar, the Rev. Charles Edward Kennaway, who gave this free education its major impetus in Campden. Married to a Noel bride and ordained in 1832, four years later he arrived in Campden, where he was to stay 37 years, until two years before his death in 1873.[lii] Straight away he became involved. In 1835 he wrote to the National Society asking for financial help, saying that 'I have since my coming here three years ago been obliged to hire a room ... and that a very inconvenient one, in consequence of our having no proper schoolroom'. The next month he wrote again asking for sixty pounds and revealing that there were 140 or 150 boys. In the end the National Society supplied £30 and the Treasury the same amount. The land for the building (now St James's Church Rooms) was given by Lord Barham. The first schoolmaster was Richard Ellis, a local artisan whose parents may or may not have been lettered, but who almost certainly obtained his own education at the grammar school.[liii]

The long delay between the foundation of the National Schools and Gladstone's provision of free universal elementary education was due to rivalry between the Anglican Church and dissenters. The State insisted that such schools should run under Anglican auspices and the dissenters understandably objected.[liv] Although the two bodies had their disagreements, there is no evidence that the local dissenters tried to thwart the founding of the National School in Campden, which over the next two centuries developed into the present fine St James's Primary School.

Notes

i Ballard, *Letters* 1. CADHAS Archive 2002/062/DT
ii ibid 3
iii Rushen, op cit .127, quoting Ballards letters of 31 Mar 1775 to his patron R. West Esq. squire of Saintbury
iv Ballard, op cit 1, 5
v ibid 4. St Werburgh was of course the Patron Saint of Chester Abbey.
vi ibid 17
vii ibid
viii Rushen, op cit 171
ix Bishop, op cit 208. Rushen op cit 179
x Bishop, op cit 308
xi Bigland, *Historical Collections* op cit vol 2, 286

xii Bishop, op cit 385, note 10
xiii ibid
xiv Noel, Gerard, op cit 138
xv Witts, op cit 87
xvi Fendley op cit 113
xvii Wood, Jack V., *Some Rural Quakers* (William Sessions, 1991) 76
xviii Bishop, op cit 226v, 229v
xix Icely, *Blockley through Twelve Centuries* (Paradigm Press 1984) 121
xx ibid 124; Wood, op cit 58
xxi Anon, *A History of Mickleton Methodist Church*, Ch 1; John Wesley, *Journal* 23rd March 1776
xxii Warmington, 'The Methodists in Campden', *CADHAS Notes & Queries* Vol IV No 3
xxiii Rushen., op cit 151
xxiv Icely, op cit 125
xxv Warmington, op cit 1; Shakespeare Memorial Trust Record Office Ref DR 147/2-9
xxvi Marshall, op cit vol 1, 15
xxvii Jones, Celia & Others, *The Inns & Alehouses of Chipping Campden and Broad Campden*, (CADHAS 1998) 4
xxviii ibid 27ff
xxix ibid 10-14, 57-8
xxx ibid 15-19
xxxi ibid 8-9, 19-21
xxxii ibid 30-35
xxxiii ibid 50-53
xxxiv ibid 19-22
xxxv ibid, 60-61
xxxvi ibid 41-3
xxxvii ibid 59-60
xxxviii ibid, Leicester, RO DE3214 230/19 (1722 map)
xxxix Rushen, 157, The author and his successor Cook have between them explored the history of the Grammar School.
xl Cook, Robert, *Chipping Campden School 1440-1990.* (Drinkwater, Shipston on Stour) 1990, 6-7, 27,. 46
xli ibid 27
xlii Platts, A. & Hainton G.H., *Education in Gloucestershire*, (Glos CC, 1954) 11
xliii Rushen, 162; Cook, 22-4
xliv Rushen, 164
xlv Platts & Hainton, op cit 41
xlvi ibid 22
xlvii ibid 30
xlviii ibid 29, 32, 33; Rushen, 161
xlix Bigland, op cit vol 2, 280; Rushen, 163
l Rushen, 163
li Trevelyan, G.M., *English Social History*, (Longmans, Green & Co, 1944) 580-1; Platts & Hainson, op cit chs III & IV
lii Holdsworth, S.D., '*Incumbents of Campden*' (CADHAS Archive 2002/044/DS 2002), 10
liii Ellis, Judith, 'Richard Ellis and the National School', *CADHAS, Notes & Queries* III 3. The author is her subject's great-great granddaughter
liv Trevelyan, op cit Pt IV Chapter 4

17

Keeping the Peace; Brunel's Folly

Poverty was touched upon in an earlier chapter. It was rarely absent, with a third of Campden's people in 1768 living as paupers on levies extracted from the ratepayers. Such hardship was not always accepted without protest by a quiescent peasantry. The previous year Henry Clarke, spelling in his usual idiosyncratic manner, informed Sir Nathaniel Ryder how hard it was to keep away the wood stealers:

> ... if one is not often amungst them, and the only Law is to thrash and drive them off. I dont much care to meddle with them. I am afraid of ther doing mischief. ... The times was so bad with the poor they would a stole it half. I think it is wors this year.[i]

Rarely absent among the more comfortably off was the fear of being at the mercy of 'sturdy and ferocious looking vagabonds that swarmed the roads', as the Rev. Mr Witts put it early in the next century.[ii] Clarke wrote his letter in the year of the outbreak of what was to become the Seven Years War against the French. It was to result in the raising of the Militia, a form of compulsory service in which counties chose men by lot to serve part-time for three years. The quota for Gloucestershire's Regiment numbered 960[iii] and unpopular it was, arousing county-wide rioting. What happened in Campden was again reported by Henry Clarke to his employer. When the lists were brought to the High Constable:

> the moob as come to Camden ... was not less than 6 or Seven Hundred. They took all the lists and burnt them, and put the Town in great faire of being plundered, for my part I durst not stir from home for fare of mischief, but did not much damage, a large number of the moob went to Sir John Rushout to Northwick and was very rude and impudent without any sort of reason on Sir John's side, but they did no damage: except to the Celle. They thretton very much to plunder the country and to pull down all the mills upon the Avon, and the Stillhouses. How it will end I can't tell, I am afraid bad.[iv]

This rural violence, at times reaching levels more usual in the cities, was to occur at intervals during the rest of the 18th and the first half of the 19th centuries, the worst examples in 1795, 1816 and 1830. It often cast its shadow over Campden.

Little has yet come to light about conditions in Campden during what have been described by one historian as the 'quite well-mannered riots' of 1795. We are rather better informed about the troubles of the years after 1815. As always after any major war, munition-making ended, trade patterns were disturbed, and farming and landowning hit by cuts in food production, which had been expanded during the wartime years. Memories of revolutionary France increased the worries of the more comfortably off for their safety. This concern peaked after the Peterloo Massacre, the shameful Manchester tragedy, when on 16th August 1819 the Yeomanry dispersed a peaceful crowd under the orders of the magistrates, killing eleven people and injuring four hundred. The general dismay is reflected in a postscript to a letter of Sir Gerard Noel's, written on 2nd December to his Campden agent, John Hickman:

> I shall be glad to hear what are the politics of the people of Campden and that part of the Country. I mean as to their sentiments concerning the Radical farmers as well as the lower classes — what they think of the Government and the Manchester magistrates and whether they are for an enquiry into their conduct.[v]

In his reply Hickman was to confirm that the recession had continued: 'the distress that prevails', he wrote, 'is beyond description'.

Sir Gerard had good reason for this enquiry. In 1780 he had walked with his uncle, the 6th Earl, among the troops gathered in St James's Park at the time of the devastating anti-Roman Catholic Gordon riots. As the Earl wrote to his sister:

> The mischief those plundering rascals have done is amazing ... last night the sky towards Holbourn, the Fleet Prison, the King's Bench and the Toll barrs on Black Fryers bridge was illumined by their horrible proceedings ... London is full of military, military law is established and Hyde Park full of soldiers in camp. ...[vi]

In that letter to Hickman, Sir Gerard also mentioned that he was 'very happy to hear that the other tenants [one had been troublesome] conduct themselves so well and that Mr Leyland is liked in Campden'. The latter was his young son, the Campden vicar, about to move into the vicarage, preparations for which had just cost his father £3,338, or about half a year's Campden rents.[vii]

Sir Gerard Noel, who was about to inherit his mother's title to become Lord Barham, was by then taking a close interest in his Campden estates. One measure initiated by him was the division of Wolds End Farm into gardens and other small parcels of land for the townsmen, so allowing them to grow their own food.[viii] Barham was himself then short of money and giving thought to selling all or part of his Campden estates,[ix] at a time when, to reduce distress, he had cut rents by a quarter as 'other neighbouring gentlemen have done the same'. Extravagant at the best of times, he had just been faced with the cost of building a new Noel family mansion at Exton Park, the old house having been destroyed by fire in the first decade of the century.

By 1830 the social problems of the country, both urban and rural had deteriorated even further. It was known even locally that fear of mob violence had obliged King William IV to cancel his formal visit to the City of London, where he was to dine in the Mansion House: crowds were waving tricolour flags, and the Duke of Wellington, then Prime Minister, was stoned.[x] In the countryside what were to be known as the 'Captain Swing riots' were spreading. Churches were vandalised, threshing machines broken, fires started, prisoners released from local jails, and money and beer demanded with menaces. Violence to individuals was, however, rare and no one was killed. Around Campden — from Winchcombe to Bourton-on-the-Hill and from Shipston to Evesham — ricks and barns were torched and mobs were blackmailing to extort money.[xi] Only one rick burning was recorded at Campden itself, by a Thomas Cooper who was caught.[xii] But here, according to the Warwick Advertiser,

> the greater part of the respectable inhabitants, amounting nearly to 300, have been sworn Special Constables for the purpose of preserving the peace, and the Magistrates have strongly advised owners and occupiers of land to relieve their workmen by a general advance of wages.[xiii]

With the total population numbering under 2,000, the 300 'respectable inhabitants' would have included most fit men of working age. As for the local landlords, Lord Northwick, possibly recollecting the mob that had threatened his grandfather in the previous century, sent his bailiff to destroy the hated threshing machine of one farmer, an obstinate man who had refused to do so himself.[xiv]

To counter such violence Campden, as elsewhere, depended not just on its own citizens, elected annually as constables, but also on the specials, which in 1830 were recruited in large numbers. What value such levies might have been in a major riot was fortunately never tested. During the next decade, however, when the Mansion House, Customs House and Bishop's Palace of Bristol were all razed by rioting crowds, the need for a proper police force became clear. Sir Robert Peel had already raised his 'Peelers', the London Metropolitan Police, in 1829, highly controversial measure though it was. Ten years later the

Gloucestershire magistrates recruited the first ever county force.[xv] Built around a nucleus of 13 trained constables imported from the Royal Irish Constabulary,[xvi] by June 1840 the force numbered 16 superintendents and 229 constables, one of the superintendents and six officers being stationed at Campden. The Campden strength remained constant at this level until well into the following century.

Drink was then the curse of the British race; not that the failing was confined to the populace. In the first six months of Gloucestershire Constabulary's existence, 17 constables were discharged either for drunkenness or for fighting with a colleague; one was sacked for getting married without permission.[xvii]

Until the police were put in place, serious trouble was tackled by the armed forces, both regular and part-time. In 1824 the more southerly part of the county, around semi-industralised Stroud, needed the presence of a party of the 10th Hussars to help quell what the Rev. Francis Witts, in his capacity as magistrate, described as 'disorderly assemblages, actual Violence and alarming tumult'.[xviii]

Such regular troops were, however, few in number. To support them were the local volunteer force, first raised in 1794 for internal defence because of the perceived threat from revolutionary France. In 1796 the Stow Troop of Yeomanry Cavalry, similar to Sir Gerard Noel's Rutland Fencible Cavalry, was manned by farmers' sons and the like from the area of Northleach, Stow, Moreton and Campden,[xix] their task to suppress 'any tumult or riot within twenty miles of the town of Stow'; or to march 'towards any part of Great Britain in case of invasion, or otherwise, by consent of the Troop'. Men of reasonable substance, these yeomen found their own mounts and were liable to fines — 5s for the first and l0s 6d for any subsequent absence from a parade.[xx] From about 1806 until Napoleon's final defeat, Campden also recruited the Loyal Cotswold Volunteer Infantry Company, about which little is yet known.

In 1860, when another Napoleon caused further concern, similar volunteers were raised, with the North Cotswold Rifle Volunteer Corps operating in Campden and Moreton. As before, for the privilege of serving, men had to pay a half-guinea subscription and take the risk of being fined for absences. The captain was a neighbouring landowner but the lieutenant was William Henry Baker, a Campden man, a churchwarden and seemingly a surveyor. It was an indication that the middle classes were at last thought suitable, if not for a peacetime regular army commission, at least for the Lord Lieutenant's commission.[xxi] Local business people, craftsmen, tradesmen and farmers, with familiar local names such as Ellis, Hathaway, Horne, Haines and Hands were listed as paying voluntary subscriptions for the upkeep of the corps, together with most members of the local gentry, ranging from Lord Redesdale's ten guineas to a Miss Stanley's five shillings.

The Gloucestershire police owed their existence primarily to the danger of public disorder, determined though the ratepayers were to try to avoid paying for them. Such a force was vital also to cope with crime, much of it petty by today's standards but widespread, and understandably so when numbers of badly-paid or unemployed labourers were watching their children starve. In 1830 Job Sermon, a twenty-year old Campden labourer, was condemned to death for stealing a lamb and six fowls; another, Stephen Blakeman, a middle-aged ex-soldier, suffered the same penalty. Both sentences were commuted to transportation to Tasmania for life. Within the next three years, Henry Cotton, an Aston-sub-Edge shepherd, John Davies, a Mickleton labourer, together with Thomas Harwood and Thomas Tomlins, both of Blockley, suffered the same fate: lifetime deportation.[xxii] In April 1836 a Campden woman, Harriet Tarver, was hanged at Gloucester for poisoning her husband with white arsenic, the same penalty exacted for sheep~stealing.[xxiii] Until the police began to enforce the law, only the dread of such vicious penalties kept minor crime in check.

On the other hand, penalties could be quite mild when shopkeepers were caught robbing workmen: in January 1818 the Rev. William Boughton, JP of Bourton-on-the-Hill fined eight Campden shopkeepers 5s or 15s each for using defective weights and three innkeepers 25s or £1 for giving short measure.[xxiv]

However bad conditions might be, people could always find ways to enjoy themselves. For Campden the high point of the year was Dover's Games, ended in the 17th century by a combination of the Civil War and Puritan rectitude. They were revived after the Restoration and in May 1725 a notice for 'The Dover's Meeting' appeared in the *Gloucester Journal* indicating that by then they were again prospering.[xxv] Lasting between one and three days, as their popularity rose and fell, they continued to evoke criticism from the self-righteous, typical being that from a minister at Stow who preached against such relics of paganism as morris and maypole dancing:

> attended usually with ridiculous gestures and acts of folly and buffoonery ... What I have now been desiring you to consider as touching the evil and pernicious consequences of Whitsun-Ales doth also obtain against Dover's Meeting.[xxvi]

For the better-off, public dinners, halls, plays and concerts were enjoyed at the principal Campden inns where mains of cockfighting might be fought in the mornings. On the Saturday, at the end of the Games, the Wake (later to evolve into Scuttlebrook Wake) was held with traditional stalls and roundabouts.

Before the Campden and Weston enclosures, the Games took place not just on today's Dover's Hill but on a larger area running for a couple of miles westwards along the high ground towards Saintbury; it was later that they were moved to the vale side of Kingcombe Lane. There 'Substantial farmers on their long-tailed steeds', as well as members of the local aristocracy, supped ale as they watched wrestling, shin-kicking, back-sword and cudgel playing by teams of men, and enjoyed also the sight of maidens dancing for a Holland shift. Horse racing, the distances of which varied from time to time, gave opportunities for betting; in 1818 the prize money amounted to 35 guineas and the course measured two and a quarter miles. By 1851 'five flights of fair hunting hurdles' had to be jumped.

A Poster for the 19th century Dover's Games

The following year the Games were shut down. The circumstances are disputed.[xxvii] Until recently it was accepted, as Canon G.D. Bourne, magistrate and Rector of Weston-sub-Edge protested, the Games had become:

> a meeting of the lowest classes merely for debauchery — no longer to witness or take part in manly games and true old English sport, but simply for the indulgence of the grossest wickedness — the most sensual crimes. During Whitsun week, the residuum of the 'black country' came there. I have seen as many as 30,000, but I am told that many more were assembled.[xxviii]

Bourne was writing in 1884, an eye-witness of it all. His many successors copied, and sometimes exaggerated his diatribe. Prominent among them was C.R. Ashbee, who specified early in the next century how:

> the scum and refuse of the nearest factory towns shot annually into Campden ... two or three thousand at a time ... and the pleasant valleys of Weston and Saintbury tramped by armed bands of Birmingham yahoos.[xxix]

Uncontrolled crime and the vastness of the crowds were regularly condemned by the critics. Dr Bearman's recent and scholarly research on the subject suggests otherwise.

Not one report of such disorders has come to light in local newspapers; neither are there accounts of criminals being brought before the courts for offences committed at the Games. Feeling so strongly about it, why did neither Bourne, who was already a magistrate, nor anyone else, do anything? The duty diary of Campden's Police Superintendent for the earlier 1840s describes Campden itself being sometimes disorderly at the time of the Games; on the other hand, when he took his six or so constables up to the Hill he nearly always found it reasonably quiet and orderly; the countering of illegal prize-fighting seems to have been his main concern. Surely conditions did not dramatically deteriorate during the next few years. If there had been serious trouble, police reinforcements could have been summoned from elsewhere, as they were on another famous occasion, but they never were.

Nor does the Superintendent mention any vast crowds of 30,000. There was no way such numbers could have been transported to Dover's Hill. Before 1851 only the Birmingham-Bristol line was running, and its nearest stop to Dover's Hill involved a 15 mile walk. No mention is made of any excursion trains that might have had Dover's Games as the destination.

Most accounts of the suspension of the Games in 1852 blame Canon Bourne for obtaining the support of Lord Harrowby, the owner of a significant area of

Weston-sub-Edge, for enclosing the area. The report of the Enclosure Commissioners is, however, dated 1849 and the measure went through without mention of it being needed because of public disorder. One otherwise responsible historian who elaborated on the closure of the Games has, in fact, been accused of misinterpreting and misrepresenting the evidence.[xxx] Canon Bourne appears to have had little if anything to do with influencing the enclosure of Dover's Hill. However, had he done so, he might have had two reasons. The first is the natural alarm, typical among his class at the time, of the danger such gatherings might create. The second is mere self-interest: the Canon had benefited from the allocation of 63 acres, one tenth of the whole, from the Enclosure Act.[xxxi]

Hunting, another recreation popular with all classes, was a major pursuit, not just with the gentry and the many other horse-owners, but with the number of humbler people who followed and watched as best they could on foot. In the mid-18th century both the fox and the stag were the quarry around Campden, and once again Henry Clarke's letters describe it. That he failed to find properties in Somerset and Devon with 'any good sporting' has already been touched upon. In 1754 he informs Mr Dudley Baxter, the London agent of the Ryders, that Lord Byron, the uncle of the poet, had taken Upton Wold, bringing his hounds with him (packs were then all privately owned). Clarke wrote:

> On Tuesday last was the grandes [*sic*] meeting on Snowshill Course. ... There was a great number of noblemen and gentlemen of great fortun [*sic:* the local accent is again clear]. The whole company was computed at 1000 horse and a larger number on foot. The Hinde stood about 12 miles chase and was killed in a millpond.

The letter then discusses the beneficial effect on local property prices engendered by this sporting activity with gentlemen coming from London to hunt.[xxxii] Already the foxhounds were meeting in Campden.[xxxiii] Four seasons later we learn from the same source that a Cornish gentlemen had taken New Combe for five years, had brought a pack of fox hounds and begun to build kennels which would be ready for Christmas.[xxxiv] The division of the open wolds into walled fields by the enclosures brought an end to stag-hunting around Campden. Fox-hunting became even more popular, leading in the end to the founding in 1868 of the North Cotswold Hunt. Although never highly fashionable, its reputation was by the early 20th century such as to attract followers from far afield, to the benefit of the already important tourist trade.

The increased movement of people and goods, in the course of both trade and recreation, emphasised the shocking state of the local roads, especially in winter. The burden of their maintenance had in the past been borne by the parishes through which they passed, at very high cost and therefore skimped. Across the northern part of the county, those roads seem to have been especially bad, the much-travelled William Marshall complaining in 1788:

> Roads of the vale are shamefully kept ... with the ditches on either side full of water to the brim. ... The toll roads are raised much too high but even on the sides of those I have seen full ditches. ... The road between Cheltenham and Gloucester, one of the most public roads in the island, is scarcely fit for the meanest of their Majesties' subjects to travel on.[xxxv]

The rudimentary state of local government made it incapable of coping with such problems, and help was sought from private enterprise. The toll roads Marshall criticises were the result of this radical measure. Turnpike companies, run by trustees, were granted the power to erect tollgates and collect fees, in return for repairing a stretch of highway. A series of Acts of Parliament, three of them in the reign of George II and a fourth in his son's, set out details of the toll roads leading into and past Campden, together with the names of the Commissioners and the charges they could levy, ranging from eighteen pence for a six-horse landau to three half-pence for a mare or an ass.[xxxvi] In the 1836 accounts for Norton Farm, tolls paid for carting included, for example, 5d a horse to Broad Campden and Blockley, 6d to Bretforton and 1s to Evesham.[xxxvii]

These Acts produced a number of tollgates on the edge of Campden. At the junction of Sheep Street and the Broad Campden roads was Tilt Up End Gate, now marked by Pike Cottage; on the Aston Road the red-brick Paul's Pike Cottage, still standing; and White Cross Way gate, close by the turning to Berrington Mill.[xxxviii] There was almost certainly another at the top of Conduit Hill, probably by the junction with the present A44, where the late 17th century signpost known as Four Cross Hands (the original still preserved in the Old Police Station) provides travellers with grossly inaccurate distances to Worcester, Warwick, Oxford and Gloucester.[xxxix]

By 1824 conditions were marginally better, and Witts reported with a satisfied air that the new road from Winchcombe to Cheltenham provided 'a great relief to travelling'. Witts was himself a Commissioner of the local turnpikes.[xl]

As is clear from the surviving Vestry accounts, Campden's ratepayers still carried the high cost of repairing and constructing their other internal roads. Again and again sums had to be found: in 1807 the large amount of £31 13s 3d for Sheep Street Lane; in 1813 a new road at Westington was needed at £8 14s, and another road at Westington Fields in 1820; paving at the pool and from the almshouses had cost £16 11s 11d the previous year.[xli]

Stagecoaches and canals were, however, already doomed. In 1824, as a Turnpike Commissioner, Witts had been warned that the Stratford Railway would be completed in December, and that the money had been raised for another from Birmingham to Liverpool. One was also projected from Moreton to Oxford with a branch towards Cricklade and thence to Bristol. Ideas proliferated everywhere, but many schemes never started: in 1846 alone, Parliament passed 172 Acts for new railways. The financial capital, Witts noted, was available for them; the new discoveries in science and mechanics, he reflected, rendered railways easy and cheap.[xlii] Fortunes were to be made and many more lost in one of the greatest engineering feats ever seen, one that was to spread into every continent. On the Stratford to Moreton line the 'tram-wagons' (as Witts called them) were at first horse-drawn, but he was well aware that steam was in use for the same purpose in Yorkshire. But not until 1836 did the Birmingham to Gloucester line open and it was 1844 before the Oxford, Worcester and Wolverhampton Railway Company was floated with Isambard Brunel commissioned to survey the work. Steam had been long known in Campden as a source of power for the Silk Mill, but it was 1854, late in the day in the proliferation of new lines, before the steam train came to Campden.

The line, as first planned, was to pass from Berrington Mill and by way of the land below old Campden House towards the Volunteer Inn. The opposition of Sir Gerard Noel's son, the first Earl of Gainsborough in the recreated title, combined with the near impossibility of the gradients, prevented this happening and saved Campden from desecration. The landowners themselves did well out of it, Lord Harrowby being paid £1,937, Lord Gainsborough a similar sum, and Canon Kennaway £236 for the land on which the line was built. Lord Northwick, as chairman of the company had stipulated that a station be built at Blockley and Lord Redesdale of Batsford Park, another director, that all London trains should stop at Moreton.[xliii]

Work began on the Campden part of the line in 1846. The most serious task facing the contractors was the Mickleton Tunnel which took six years to complete, so attracting the name 'Brunel's Folly'. Rows with the sub-contractor led to rioting between Brunel's and the contractor's men. Three thousand of them gathered there, the Riot Act was read, police reinforcements brought in from elsewhere in the county, and Brunel's workmen sworn in as special constables.[xliv]

Most of the navvies working on the railway lodged in hutments erected by the contractors on or near the site. Some lived in Campden itself, the result being a temporary increase in the town's population. Steady at under two thousand for the previous 20 years, the figure jumped to 2,351 people living in 490 houses in 1851, but fell again to 1,975 ten years later.[xlv] A few of these 250 or so railway workers were supervising engineers, with the rest describing themselves as miners, railway labourers or craftsmen. Some of the latter can be distinguished from local craftsmen because their birthplaces were far removed from Gloucestershire; others because they were sharing a house with a gang of other railway workers. Some had their wives and children with them, especially the engineers. Tradesmen and miners were better skilled and paid. Although many of the navvies were Irish, only half a dozen or so of those who lodged or rented houses in Campden gave Irish birthplaces. One or two of the men seem to have married local wives, but no more than six or so were locally born men. Did Campden men lack the specialist skills or were the railwaymen a closed shop?

Drink, of course, was their recreation and Campden was nearby. On Saturday night after pay day it was a rowdy place, as the half dozen police well knew, five of them lodging with their Superintendent in his house at the corner of Leysbourne and Cider Mill Lane. Their orders were not to waste their time in arresting the merely drunk. Nevertheless, local memory has it that the bars were inserted into the Grevel House windows to protect them from the Saturday night rowdies. A man was well paid for his ability to move twenty tons of rock and soil a day with pick and shovel: he had a thirst to quench and little else to spend the money on. Those navvies may have made their way up to Dover's Games, but the police diary does suggest that Campden itself may have satisfied their needs on pay day.

Notes

i Clarke, Henry, *Papers*, (extracts) op cit 230 (26 Nov 1757)
ii Witts, op cit 95
iii Chater, Brigadier J.K., '*The Volunteer Soldier of Gloucestershire*', 18 January 1990 (CADHAS 1900/35/DS) 5
iv Clarke *Papers*, op cit 228, 9 Nov 1757
v *Correspondence.... on Estate Matters* Leics R.O DE3214 49/16/1-49
vi Noel, Emilia, op cit 8
vii *Correspondence.* op cit Later Leyland would move to the main Noel living at Exton, Campden being handed over in 1832 to his brother-in-law, the Rev. Charles Kennaway.
viii ibid
ix *Glos Estate correspondence from John Hickman... to Lord Barham* Leics R.O. DE3214/ 38/7/l - 15
x *Warwick Advertiser*, 9 Oct 1830
xi Hobsbawm, E.J & Rude, George, *Captain Swing* (Lawrence & Wishart 1969). 128-9
xii *Warwick Advertiser*, 9 Oct 1830
xiii ibid 11 Dec 1830
xiv Hobsbawm & Rude, op cit 235
xv Thomas, Harry, *History of the Gloucestershire Constabulary 1839-1985* (Alan Sutton, 1987) is the main source for details of the Gloucestershire Police
xvi ibid 12
xvii ibid 13-15
xviii Witts, op cit 45-6
xix Chater, op cit 6
xx ibid 6, 7
xxi *Rules for North Cotswold Rifle Volunteer Corps, 1862.* CADHAS 1990/27/DO
xxii Marsh, Judith, 'A Note on Job Sermon' *CADHAS Notes & Queries*, III, 2, 21 & 3, 28
xxiii Anon, 'Harriet Tarver, the Campden Poisoner' *CADHAS Notes & Queries*, II, 6, 62
xxiv Extracts from files of Quarter Sessions (sic) Gloucs RO, Q/PC/2
xxv Quoted in Burns, Francis, *History of Olimpick Games*, 28. Details about Dover's Games are based mainly on Burns and Whitfield, Christopher, *Robert Dover & The Cotswolds Games*
xxvi Burns, op cit 28
xxvii Bearman, Dr C.J., 'The Ending of the Cotswold Games, *BGAS Trans*, 64, 1996 (copied to CADHAS 1997/067/DS), a closely researched and documented paper disputes some long established aspects.
xxviii Bearman, op cit 132, quoting *BGAS Trans*, 9, 1884-5, 12
xxix ibid quoting Ashbee, C.R, *Last Records of a Cotswold Community*, Chipping Campden, 1904
xxx Bearman, 137
xxxi ibid, 139, quoting Gloucs RO QIRI 156 of 17 Jul 1854
xxxii Clarke *Papers*, op cit 182. 23 Feb 1754
xxxiii ibid 178, 1 Dec 1753
xxxiv ibid 227, 5 Oct 1757
xxxv Marshall, op cit vol 1, 14
xxxvi Road Act 10 May 1768. CADHAS Archives 2000/052/DO
xxxvii 'Work on a Local 19th Century Farm', *CADHAS Notes & Queries* III 3
xxxviii Rushen, 106
xxxix But see Wilson, Jill, 'Izod's Post' *CADHAS Notes & Queries* IV 3 36
xl Witts, op cit 35-7
xli Bishop, Leighton, op cit. See index for details.

xlii Witts, 37-8
xliii Whitfield, *History of Chipping Campden* 210-12
xliv ibid 215-7. Coleman, Terry, *The Railway Navvies* (Pelican 1965) 110-14
xlv 1851 Census

18

Agricultural Depression and Town Celebration

From the 1851 census it is possible to get a glimpse of the parish at that time. The Silk Mill in Sheep Street was by then powered by steam as well as water. It was occupied by John Long, a silk throwster, born in Blockley, one of his nephews being the mill foreman and another an apprentice. Women could find well paid work in the Silk Mill. Long then employed two men, 15 women and four girls. Many of the other 41 girls and women described in the census as silk throwers or workers probably walked each day to Blockley to work in the silk mills there. Most of these were from Broad Campden but at least one lived in the town.[i]

1851 was one of the last years of prosperity for the silk industry: later in the decade it closed, following on the closure of the flax mill and the rope and sack works in Back Ends. The 1851 census shows only one man, a native of Campden aged 62, who described himself as a ropemaker, while a resident of the almshouses was a flax dresser. There was still some home work for women. In 1851 eleven ladies claimed to be occupied as gloveresses and even in the 1881 census, one, aged 25, still declared herself to be a gloveress.

But the main source of employment in the town was the traditional one of agriculture. For the agricultural labourer in the 19th century life was hard and comfortless and holidays, apart from Christmas Day and Good Friday, all but unknown. By some measures the farm labourers' lot improved in the two decades after 1850; an average weekly wage of 9s 3d in 1850 had increased by 21% to 11s 10d in 1870[ii] but their lives in crowded cottages with hungry children remained very poor while incomes of farmers and landlords had trebled in that time.[iii] Pigs were an important factor in the rural economy. The majority of allotment holders and many cottagers owned a pig, which they could feed cheaply from their own produce. The children of both farmers and labourers were expected to help with the tasks they were strong enough to perform. However, there was frequent recourse to charity and the ever-present fear of the workhouse.

After a period of high prosperity in the fifties and sixties, Campden, like most other rural communities, suffered in the succession of agricultural depressions that began in the 1870s and were nationally acknowledged in 1879. They were caused by a number of bad seasons coupled with a surge in foreign competition. 1874 came to be remembered as the last of the really good years for agriculture. 1875 and 1878 saw bleak harvests and so did several years in the eighties and nineties. As a result, rural populations dropped.[iv] The effects upon Campden were inevitably profound. Unemployment and poverty drove many from their homes in search of work, leaving behind them empty houses and cottages which all too soon fell into decay and ruin. The population which in 1881 was 1,861 had by 1891 declined to 1,736 and by 1901 there was an even sharper decline to 1,542, the lowest figure ever recorded since reliable counts began.

There was again a good deal of distress in the town. In the 1880s local churches opened soup kitchens and for a time the Baptist Church ran a clothing club; in 1888 free coal and bread were distributed. Soon after the Guild's arrival in 1902, the guildsman Charlie Plunkett began raising money for the poor, and some of the profits from the Guild's first major dramatic production, Ben Jonson's *The New Inn*, were used for such schemes as to buy coal for the needy.

Trade suffered rather less than agriculture. Shops there were aplenty in the town during the later 19th century. A chemist, grocer and 'Italian Warehouseman' dispensed both human and veterinary prescriptions, sold lubricating, burning and seed oils, shot of various grades, loose gun-powder and cartridges, as well as groceries, home made ginger beer and aerated waters of various colours and flavours. Wixey's, on the opposite corner of Church Street, was established in 1863. They regarded themselves as the most exclusive grocers in Campden. T.W. Colman's premises have alone survived to this day as a grocery store through a variety of changes of ownership, being known variously as Morreys Stores, Burtons Stores, Fine Fare, and Londis, and, in the 21st century, the Co-op. Another grocer and tea dealer was in the Square. The Post Office, later combined with a drapery, was at first in Ardley House (now The King's Hotel) and then London House. There were three or four bakers, and the same number of shoemakers with butchers, drapers, tailors, blacksmiths, plumbers, builders, maltsters, carpenters, masons, a saddler and harness- maker, a bookseller, hairdresser, wheelwright and carriage builder.

The learned professions were well represented. In addition to the clergy, two doctors and a veterinary surgeon, there were at one time no fewer than five solicitors. The best known of these, William Higford Griffiths of Bedfont

House, was also clerk to the magistrates.

The Earls of Gainsborough, the principal landowners in the area, still owned some 2,300 acres at the end of the 19th century. In about 1850 a new Campden House in Combe was converted from a farm house, and into it moved Charles Noel, Viscount Campden with his new bride. There his son was born. For the first time since the 17th century the Noel family began to become closely involved in the life of the town. To celebrate the birth the people of Campden performed a musical serenade outside the house.[v] Viscountess Campden distributed warm clothing at the onset of winter that year to 80 poor people of Campden who 'all appeared with cheerful countenances very grateful for her ladyship's bounty'.

This baby became the third earl, a rather short man and sandy haired, a keen ornithologist who wrote books on the flora and fauna at Exton, where he felt most at home. His wife, sons and daughters, however, preferred Campden to Exton, and during the whole of the second half of the century the family spent much of their time in Campden.

Before the depression set in there was a period of optimism among farmers and traders. On 25th October 1842 the Loyal Cotswold Lodge of the Independent Order of Oddfellows of the Manchester Unity had been established in Campden, mainly by the middle classes. Shortly afterwards a small hall was built for their meetings at the rear of the Swan Inn. By the end of the century the lodge had purchased land on the Big Ground off Station Road, for allotments to help grow food.

At about the same time the Campden branch of the Britannia Benefit Society was founded. Its membership was made up mainly of agricultural labourers who paid a small weekly subscription to the club, which entitled them to medical attention, financial help when unable to work due to illness, and burial with dignity. The weekly subscription was increased as members grew older and the viability of the society rested on the recruitment of young, healthy members and on benefactors. It depended on the support of wealthy honorary members and patrons, including the Earl of Gainsborough.

The annual Club Day became the primary opportunity to publicise the Society as a very important part of the life of Campden and to attract the essential new members. The Society's Club Day was on the Thursday in Whitsun week. The next day was the Oddfellows Club Day and on the Saturday came Scuttlebrook Wake: three consecutive days of general festivity, in some way taking the place of the closed Dover's Hill games. On Club Day, the officers and members of the Society processed through the town to the church for a special service and back to the clubhouse for a formal dinner, speeches and entertainment.[vi]

However, the agricultural depression brought about the decline and eventual collapse of the Britannia and in 1890 its role was largely taken over by a newly formed Campden branch of the Cirencester Conservative Working Men's Benefit Society. Because of objections to the political nature of this, a branch of the apolitical Stroud Mutual Provident and Sick Benefit Society was formed a year later. Both continued the tradition of festive club days.

As in the previous century, poverty brought petty crime. Until the police station was built in 1871, the magistrates met in the Town Hall, which also acted as a gaol. Later, Petty and Special Sessions were held on the first and third Wednesday of each month in the court room. At that time the chairman of the bench was the wealthy and powerful Canon Bourne, rector of Weston-sub-Edge for 53 years, from 1848 to 1901.

The presence of a police force was having its effect in keeping the peace. But there were difficulties. In the 1840s it was not untypical for the police diary to report:

> at 7pm. mob attacked the Police with sticks, stones etc. on their attempting to prevent them making fires in the street (Bonfire night 1840)
>
> Visited patrol on Town duty, from 1am. until 2am. in consequence of several harvest feasts being given this night, a great number of drunken people about the streets (14th September 1842, and similarly on 4th September 1843)[vii]
>
> On town duty from 9pm to 4am this being the annual meeting of various clubs etc., a great many drunk and disorderly people about throughout the night (8th June 1843)

The Licensing Act of 1872 gave the magistrates power to grant (or refuse) licences and fixed the closing hour for country pubs at 11pm. By the end of the 1860s even skittles and dominoes had been banned from the pubs by the magistrates.[viii]

As we have seen, Campden had a disproportionate number of public houses, and men frequently appeared before the magistrates charged with drunkenness.

Occasionally, too, a landlord was required to quit because of cases of drunkenness in his inn. In 1891 the King's Arms was refused a renewal of its licence and closed, partly because it was disgracefully dirty and partly because it was decided that there were too many licensed premises in the town.

Prosecutions for poaching, mainly of hares and rabbits, were also frequent. As early as 1863 a group of boys were fined for poaching 'a large quantity of rabbits'. About 1870 the Earl of Gainsborough conceded to his tenants the right to kill rabbits on their holdings, and this was much appreciated, but as conditions worsened during the depression more and more men were brought before the magistrates for poaching rabbits for their dinner. The justice administered was harsh; in 1887 a Campden case was brought to the attention of the Home Secretary by the local MP, Mr. Winterbotham. Three boys, none of whom had any previous convictions, were found guilty of stealing two pennyworth of apples. For this, each was fined 8s, and two were also sentenced to be birched. This was carried out so unmercifully that the boys had to be taken, badly cut and bleeding, to a nearby hotel where they were revived with the aid of stimulants. The Home Secretary, however, merely replied that 'the flogging was carried out in the presence of ... four Police Officers who positively deny that the punishment was unduly severe'.

In the period leading up to the agricultural depression there were clear and growing divisions in the town, between the more affluent farmers and tradesmen and the poor, particularly the agricultural labourers; between Conservatives and Liberals; and between adherents to the established church and non-conformists. In 1872 at Barford near Wellesbourne, Joseph Arch, son of a labourer, now a Primitive Methodist lay preacher and self-employed hedgecutter and later to become a Liberal MP, was prevailed upon to lead the National Agricultural Labourers Union in protest against low wages, the insecure dependence on the tied cottage, fear of eviction if illness or injury interrupted a man's employment, and the tyranny and arrogance of many farmers. He advocated better wages but also argued for more widespread education, the vote, and emigration for those who would seek a better life elsewhere.

In June that year a union meeting was held in Campden under the Elm Tree, at which an old labourer, Job Benfield, who was called upon to preside, growled over the 'lingering, not living', which he said he had had to endure. A secretary and treasurer were elected and a few signatures obtained.[ix] After a poorly

The Elm Tree that stood near Sheep Street Corner and was the venue for many public meetings in the 19th century

organised meeting in July,[x] Joseph Arch himself came to speak to a successful and well-attended public meeting[xi] under the Elm Tree in September. Mr G.C. Smith, a leading Blockley Baptist, was voted to the chair and put the proposition (which was carried) that 'the meeting would support in every possible manner the interests of the National Labourers Union Association'.[xii]

In April 1873 another mass union meeting was held. The main speaker was 'met by a large concourse, headed by the Broadway brass band, and marched in procession to the Elm Tree where a wagon was drawn up as an impromptu platform'. The speaker, for upwards of two hours, enlarged upon past and present grievances, denounced everyone from the prince downwards, sowing dissension and promoting republican principles. 'Had he been really desirous of doing good between employed and employers, he would have addressed them more in the spirit shown by Mr Arch.'[xiii]

1873 seems to have been a year of dissension. At the annual meeting of the Britannia Benefit Society, chaired by the Earl of Gainsborough, union members vocally expressed their dissatisfaction both with the rules of the society and with their treatment by employers. Toasts were proposed from the floor to Mr Joseph

Arch as a labourer pressed his view that the union offered a better option than local discussions with employers.[xiv] In July the same year, three men disrupted a meeting being conducted by the Rev. Leland Noel under the Elm Tree; they were subsequently convicted of being drunk and riotous and of using blasphemous language.[xv] Two months later a union meeting under the Elm Tree 'abused' the clergy in strong language, but the Baptist Mr W. Godson addressed the meeting and concluded with 'sensible remarks' encouraging labourers to emigrate to Australia.[xvi]

The meetings of the Liberation Society in Campden marked another peak in discord among the local community. This Society advocated the separation of the Church of England from the state. The proposal was not new but the Irish Church Act of 1868, which had disestablished the Church in Ireland, re-ignited the smouldering embers of the argument in England. In March 1874 the Baptist minister, the Rev. W.R. Irvine organised a public meeting on disestablishment that was crowded with opponents of the theme. While the announced lecturer attempted to speak:

> three cheers were given for the Queen, three for the House of Lords and three for the Volunteers, with groans for the promoters of the meeting. Some of the most stalwart of the members of the Volunteer corps marched into the room with 'Church and State forever' printed on a blue ground and wearing it round their hats.[xvii]

Ultimately the chairman dissolved the meeting and vacated his seat. Mr W.H. Griffiths was thereupon elected to the chair and an antidisestablishmentarianist proposition was passed.

Other such meetings followed and in January 1876, at one crowded and stormy Liberation Society meeting, Mr R.B. Belcher of Blockley declared that with disestablishment the country would be more radically and irreversibly changed than by any of the measures enacted so far. The opposition reacted against the perceived threat to their church and the monarchy, and in the uproar that followed the chief ministerial protagonists were said to be standing and shouting at each other, one from a chair, one from a table, and there were accusations from both sides of violent handling among the crowd. This issue created more antagonism than any of the contemporary debates on education—much more so in Campden than in other neighbouring places.

The 1867 Reform Act extended the electoral franchise in the borough to all rate-paying householders and in the country to occupiers of property rated at

£12 per annum, thus meeting the dissatisfaction of many who were not given the vote in 1832; but agricultural labourers were still excluded. However, in June 1885, following the 1884 Act to enfranchise labourers, there took place in the Noel Arms yard the largest political meeting ever held at Campden, in support of the Liberal candidate for the general election. It was attended by about one thousand people. The candidate, Mr A.B. Winterbotham, was successful, beating the County Chairman of the Conservatives, and for a short time thereafter Campden (to the dismay of many) came to deserve the reputation of being 'the most radical place in Gloucestershire'.

In December 1888 a meeting was held in the Baptist Sunday Schoolroom with a 'very good attendance of working men' to discuss representation on the newly formed County Council. The meeting was addressed by Mr J.C. Reynolds, the Liberal president, a farmer and leading member of the church who advocated representation from the ranks of the people, rather than from the 'upper classes or from clergymen of the Church of England'.

In the following year, 1889, Mr Winterbotham gave the principal address at the public service held on the Friday before the harvest thanksgiving service. To a very full church and schoolroom, he preached discontent — divine discontent — and called on his audience not to listen to calls to be thankful in present conditions, and not to be content with that station in life to which God has been pleased to call them.[xviii]

Despite all this excitement, middle-class Campdonians continued to be proud of their town and as the decade progressed, began to come to terms with life in the depression. Accepting that agriculture had become a declining industry, they realised that Campden had a unique and priceless asset in its intrinsic beauty, and sought to promote the new concept of Campden as a resort. This new civic awareness came at a time when people from the towns and cities were seeking refuge and recreation in the countryside.

The annual celebration of the benefit societies' club days have already been mentioned. In 1887 Campden joined in the nation's loyal celebration of Queen Victoria's Golden Jubilee. Flags or patriotic mottoes hung from almost every window and shopkeepers decorated their windows. A peal of bells rang out and at 8.30 am Campden Brass Band, followed by members of the Friendly Societies, paraded around the town to the parish church for the special Jubilee Service. After a dinner of cold meat and potatoes in Cotterell's Orchard, the day ended with grand illuminations and bonfires on Dover's Hill. Dinner for the elderly and infirm was provided in the Town Hall.

By 1888 Scuttlebrook Wake was once again in full swing after an interval of 17 years, and was being advertised as 'Ye Wake of Scuttlebrook', with a programme of 'Old English Games' — an obvious attempt to attract tourists as well as those from nearby towns and villages. During the 1880s people from the world outside had begun to discover Campden, and its residents had begun to see advantages in encouraging such an interest and had themselves begun to appreciate the beauty of the medieval town. The bicycle was already bringing visitors from Cheltenham and even from Birmingham. Campden's new tourist industry was gradually developing and so, too, was an awareness that visitors could bring much needed trade and employment. By 1890 Muriel Neve, daughter of the postmaster, Julius Neve, commented in her journal, 'Campden will beat Broadway yet and be a summer resort for urbanites, such a quantity of people about'.[xix] Indeed in 1893, the *Evesham Journal* even published a Campden 'Visitors List' giving the names of visiting tourists and the hotels and houses in which they had stayed.

It was, however, in 1895 that it was finally resolved to bring the charms of Campden to the forefront of public attention. Following a 'grand floral parade' in Eastbourne, it was felt that Campden could do something even better. The Cirencester Benefit Society lodge expanded their Whit Monday Club Day to involve the whole town in a spectacular festival. The parade represented many aspects of Campden life: the fire brigade, the children of the elementary schools; agriculture with a cart entitled 'Going to Market in Ye Olden Times' and the tradesmen with carts representing their businesses. 'There was scarcely any portion of the town which remained undecorated'.[xx] Later there were sports, dancing and a display of fireworks. The image of a town slumbering in the hills was banished by the fete, which was deemed to have been the most spectacular Whitsuntide entertainment in the district.

A similar event took place the following year when there was a cart bearing a maypole and dancers and the first May Queen in modern times in an open carriage with postillion, accompanied by a bevy of pages and maids of honour. The parade ended with a cart representing the wool merchants of old Campden and a display of the old robes and maces of the former corporation. A third Whit Monday fete in 1897 was the last of the series and it was not until after the arrival of the Guild of Handicraft that elaborate Whitsuntide fetes were once again organised.

The Town Hall before 1897
(By kind permission of Oxfordshire County Council Photographic Archive)

Queen of the May : Floral Celebration, May 1896. One of the three Floral Celebrations organised by the town in the late 19th century, partly designed to attract visitors

In June 1897 two major events followed close on each other's heels: the Whit Monday fete and the Queen's Diamond Jubilee. The celebration of the Jubilee followed very much the same pattern as in 1887, although torrential rain drowned the bonfire on Dover's Hill. This time it was decided that there should be a permanent memorial. There had been a proposal in 1891 to enlarge and refurbish the Town Hall and in 1897 the work was finally undertaken as a fitting memorial to the Queen. A new porch was built and both the lower and upper rooms were renovated, the upper room being made suitable for dances. During the process of the restoration remnants of the 14th century roof were uncovered.

There were humorous incidents, too. On July 8th 1905, while King Edward VII was spending the week-end at Batsford with his old friend Lord Redesdale, the royal car drove through Campden in the early afternoon. The story of how the paper seller, Bob Dickinson, sold a copy of *The News of the World* to the king and won the right to display a plate bearing the royal coat of arms, has remained part of Campden's folk history ever since — a tangible memento of a delightful episode in Campden's history.[xxi]

The great social event in Campden in 1906 was the celebration of the coming of age of another Viscount Campden. Lavish celebrations at Campden House lasted three days. There was a dinner for all the tenants of the estate in a marquee in the garden, another dinner and tea for the employees and cottagers and a garden party for the local gentry and more well-to-do tenants. C.R. Ashbee was invited to this but was decidedly disparaging about the whole event and predicted doom for the English aristocracy.[xxii]

For the visitor Campden was an oasis of tranquillity after the big city. In the High Street little seemed to have changed outwardly since time immemorial. The noise and clutter of traffic was still far into the future and carefree children could still safely roll their hoops from one end of the unmetalled street to the other. In July 1884 the Bristol & Gloucestershire Archaeological Society chose the North Cotswolds area for their summer tour. They were entertained to lunch at the Noel Arms and in the evening the Rev. Canon S.E. Bartleet read a paper on the Manor and Borough of Campden which has come to be regarded as the first serious study of the town's history. An increasing number of people were visiting the town to relax, walk, paint or simply to share its peace and beauty. The age of mass cycling was promoting a new means of escape from the crowded cities.

So here was a Cotswold town whose beauty and antiquity was attracting increasing attention, first among a few writers and painters, then among ramblers, cyclists and other tourists who were seeking and discovering places of escape from overcrowded and polluted cities. Campden had a railway station between London and the industrial Midlands and, therefore, a name on the railway timetable. It had the assets which make for a progressive community: good water, good schools and lively churches. Furthermore it was an underpopulated town with room for more people. There was a surplus of empty houses, not of the highest standards of quality and comfort but capable of being repaired. It also had a redundant silk mill awaiting any group of people who might have a use for it. As the century turned, it must have presented an ideal choice for Ashbee to offer to his doubting guildsmen.

Notes

i Census, 1851
ii *Encyclopaedia Britannica* sv agriculture
iii Ashby, M.K., *Joseph Ashby of Tysoe* (The Merlin Press 1974) 60
iv See, for example: Perry, P.J., *British Agriculture, 1875 - 1914* (Methuen, 1973)
v Whitfield, *History* 208
vi Fees, Craig, *Christmas Mumming in a North Cotswold Town* (unpub PhD Thesis, Univ of Leeds 1988) II.2 44 (copy in CADHAS Archives 1990/08/B)
vii ibid 50 & note 20
viii ibid 50 & note 22
ix ibid 52 & note 26
x ibid op cit 52 & not 27
xi ibid op cit 28
xii Warmington, *Baptists in Campden and Blockley* (unpublished) CADHAS Archives 2002/065/DS 60
xiii Fees, op cit .53 note 29; Wilson, Jill, 'Notes on two Elections in Campden' *CADHAS Notes & Queries* Vol II 24
xiv By contrast at the Oddfellows celebrations the next day farmer William Stanley felt pleasure in being among a class of men who loved order themselves and felt pain to witness how much there was of envy, discontent and evil-speaking spread abroad among the lower orders. He spoke of great unfairness towards the great middle-classes who had long gratuitously assisted in educating the children of those immediately below them but were now compelled to give education to that class who turned round and used the weapon against them.
xv Fees, op cit 58 & note 35
xvi ibid 58 & note 36
xvii *Evesham Journal* 28/3/1874
xviii Warmington, *Baptists* op cit Ch 10
xix Muriel Neve's *Journal*, quoted in Caroline Mason's papers in CADHAS archive
xx *Evesham Journal* 1895
xxi For the best account of this incident see Fees, Craig `(ed), *A Child in Arcadia* (CADHAS 1997) 51-55 and 73-75
xxii For a view of this see Fees, *A Child in Arcadia* op cit 31-2

19

Into the Modern World

Apart from a brief population expansion in the 1850s, due to the influx of workers building the railways, population fell back with the agricultural depression. There were, however, new opportunities. The through train service opened on 4th June 1853, with three passenger trains daily between Dudley and Oxford. New markets were thus opened up, perishable crops could be moved quickly to the cities; livestock could be carried without the losses of weight and value sustained on the old drovers' roads. There were employment opportunities on the railway, too, with better rates of pay and regular employment. A railway porter could receive 15s a week compared with an agricultural labourer's rate of 9s or 10s.

The railway brought other changes. From 1854 the Town Hall clock which had hitherto been set by Mr Wright's sundial was set by 'railway time' until 1886, when it was set by Greenwich time telegraphed to the Post Office each morning at 10 o'clock.[i] The postal services had been operated by the new 'penny post' since 1840 with a stage coach drop at Moreton for delivery by a letter carrier who walked to Campden and returned with the outgoing post. They were now centred on a Campden post office served through the railway system. The last stage coach service, from Banbury to Campden, was withdrawn when the railway opened.[ii] The Wonder-to-Many coach which ran from Campden to Evesham and to Stratford[iii] also ceased, but a horse bus service was introduced from the Noel Arms to Campden Station (by arrangement). The services of the purely local carriers tended to thrive.

Sundial in the High Street. Local tradition has it that this was in use to set the Town Hall clock until 1854. There are six other sundials in the High Street, more than in any other market town. *(By kind permission of Chipping Campden Camera Club)*

A coal merchant's business was established by a siding at the station and Campden's small local livestock market received a boost at the end of the century by this transport link, when at its peak 138 trucks of livestock were handled in a year. H.T. Osborn writes that early in the 20th century he and other small boys could earn a useful few pence by driving sheep to the station after the monthly market.[iv]

The 19th century censuses show Campden as a typical market town, its population made up almost entirely of traders, farmers, landowners and every kind of agricultural worker. Almost everyone served the needs of a small, balanced and prosperous agricultural community. The number of new public buildings erected in the last half of the century bears witness to a spirit of confidence in the town's future. Among these were the rebuilt grammar school in the High Street, the new Baptist Church, with a schoolroom and manse behind it, and the new Police Station, both completed in 1872, St Michael's Church at Broad Campden in 1868, a chapel of ease (later demolished) at Westington, and, perhaps most significant, St Catharine's Roman Catholic Church built in 1891.

The Gas Company was formed in 1869 by the subscriptions of a number of Campden farmers and tradespeople and was said to have been expressly for the public good rather than the benefit of the shareholders. One symbol of this was the differentiation between the prosperous local landowners who were the shareholders, and the more professional directors and officers of the company, one of whom was the Baptist minister, the Rev. W.R. Irvine. The gasworks gained from the benefit of coal delivered at lower cost by the railway and the works could be sited directly by the railway, at a point lower than the town. At the opening banquet, Lord Gainsborough thought that gas should go to the 'lower class habitations' as well as the better, and suggested that he and other landlords should pay the initial expense of the meter and installation, if desired, to be recouped by a temporary increase in rents.

The Campden gas system appears, however, to have been the subject of complaints throughout the years. The pressure could not be relied upon, the quality of gas was thought to be bad and the smell very strong. It also provided excitement. At Christmas, 1890, the *Evesham Journal* reported that:

> A gas explosion in Chipping Campden took place in a shop being fitted out by Mr J.S. Morris, the butcher. A smell of gas had been noticed the previous day and on the morning in question Mr Alfred Edge entered the

> shop about 6 am. with a light and on lighting the gas an explosion occurred. Mr Edge was knocked down and slightly scorched on the face, the shutters were blown out and the meat hanging in the shop was blown all over the place. Fortunately the shutters had holes in them, usually found in butchers shops, and the gas had all got away except the upper stratum next to the ceiling, or else the result would have been very different.[v]

Farming, of course, continued to dominate. In the second half of the century steam power and the mechanisation of harvesting, threshing and winnowing had become more widespread and the horse-drawn scuffler was a useful implement to cut off thistles and other weeds. The first sixty years following the Enclosure Act of 1799 was a prosperous one for the farming community and local trade. Among the leaders of a new generation of Campden farmers was Ulric Stanley who lived at Stamford House in Leysbourne. Politically a Conservative and a pragmatist, in 1889 he helped to form the North Cotswold Farmers Association, where he preached the message that times had changed and farmers needed to adapt. He argued forcefully for useful, as opposed to classical, education and was concerned that the existing system of education creamed off all the more able young people, fitting them for urban rather than rural employment. Other influential farmers of the period were George Haines, remembered as a very fair employer of men; Robert Coldicott, one of the first trustees of the Town Trust; and the Izod family, one of the oldest Campden families that had been in the town since the time of Baptist Hicks.

Local government continued much as before and there was some attempt to preserve old customs. Meetings of the Court Leet & Court Baron for Chipping Campden at the Town Hall and for Berrington at the Court House were convened in December 1865 and 1866 at which officers were appointed in an attempt to revive the courts, in reality defunct since the 1830s. But their functions had been superseded; they were unsustainable and little more than an excuse for annual gatherings.[vi]

The decay of the Corporation, which had started in the 18th century, continued. It may have been hastened by a long dispute between one of the Capital Burgesses, John Kettle, and his fellow burgesses and bailiffs. Kettle was clerk to the Campden solicitor. In 1837 he was already a Capital Burgess, and '... in the absence of the Deputy Steward on business' proclaimed the accession of Queen Victoria from the steps of the Town Hall and at each end of the High

Street.[vii] In 1853 there developed a bitter dispute, focussed on the collection of subscriptions for the repair of the Town Hall roof. Kettle tried to dismiss his fellow members, refused to relinquish the subscriptions collected, tried to seize the Town Hall and rents which were due, and threatened to take the Corporation to the High Court. After years of dispute Kettle removed himself to Birmingham taking with him the mace, robes and record books which were not finally returned until 1866.[viii]

The Commissioners appointed under the 1884 Municipal Corporations Act, having looked at Campden, reported that it would not be expedient to retain the Corporation and it was consequently abolished in 1885. The estate and property of the borough were to be managed by a newly established Town Trust, set up in 1889. The estate consisted of the Town Hall and an adjoining cottage which has since been demolished, the land between the Town Hall and the Market Hall and the rights of the Market Square. The chattels consisted of the four maces, an ancient wooden staff, the Corporation robes and the Lawrence portrait of Sir Gerard Noel. The Town Trust was administered by its own board of Trustees until well into the 20th century. Local government then became the responsibility of the Vestry meetings and the Rural Sanitary Authority, an offshoot of the Board of Guardians, until in 1888 County Councils, and in 1894 Rural District Councils & Parish Councils, were statutorily established. In 1894 Campden elected a mainly Liberal parish council, under the chairmanship of Ulric Stanley.

In 1887 the town was threatened with being absorbed into Warwickshire — a proposal that would have meant the end of Campden as a district administrative centre. The Town fought the proposal and in the end was made the centre of its own non-workhouse union.[ix]

In 1860 'K' Company, 2nd Volunteer Battalion, Gloucestershire Regiment, was established in Campden with their armoury in the building which is now the HSBC Bank. In the summer they would go off for a week under canvas. A great highlight of the year was the annual Volunteer Ball, held in January in the Town Hall, following dinner in the Noel Arms. These balls were regularly attended by the Gainsboroughs, the farming community and leading tradespeople, as well as others from farther afield. By the end of the century 47 Campden men were seeing active service in the Boer War and, as a speaker observed at a dinner of the Stroud Society, Campden sent more men out to South

Africa in proportion to its population than any other town.

Education was the subject of rapid change. Campden, greatly indebted to earlier benefactors, was well endowed with opportunities for education at a time when the state offered little by way of funding or compulsion. In the 1851 census almost all children aged between 4 and 11 years were listed as 'scholar' even if they belonged to large families of impecunious labourers.

In 1850 the grammar school was still housed in an early 17th century building which it had outgrown. This was greatly extended in the 1860s by public subscription and contributions from the local gentry and former pupils, to provide a new house for the master, as well as boarding accommodation for thirty boys.

The headmaster in the 1860s, Dr S.F. Hiron, had been born in Campden and was an old boy of the school. On his retirement, and with the passage of the Endowed Schools Act of 1869, there was considerable resistance to the perceived danger of a 'higher classical teaching' replacing the 'useful' education Dr Hiron had practised. In 1871 the Rev. W.R. Irvine addressed a public meeting, chaired by Dr. Hiron, to consider the future of Campden Grammar School. He proposed that 'the more useful education desired by the majority of the parents' must not be allowed to be superseded 'by a higher classical teaching ... under the Endowed Schools Act.' He argued that a quarter of the students in the grammar school were non-conformists and that section of the community should be fairly represented on the Board.[x]

This was to little avail, and under the next master, the Rev. J. Foster, the school veered towards a more classical approach. In 1889 however, Francis Osborne became headmaster, the first layman to be appointed to that post, and in 1891 a new body of governors modernised the curriculum to include science and technical subjects, shorthand, book-keeping, drawing, French and German.[xi]

With low numbers of pupils, the staff was correspondingly small. In addition to the headmaster there were an assistant master and a mademoiselle responsible for French. The main hall was the classroom, but after the old King's Arms closure in 1891, lessons were also held there. In 1906 Gloucestershire Education Committee decided to award four scholarships to the school, available to pupils from elementary schools in the district. All four scholarships were won by

Campden children.[xii] The pupils were a typical cross-section of the middle classes, consisting of the sons of farmers, professional people and tradesmen, but the arrival of the Guild in 1902 resulted in the admission of some of the guildsmen's sons.[xiii] In 1907 a new requirement was made that secondary schools receiving public grants should make no fewer than a quarter of their places available free of charge to pupils from elementary schools. The governors decided that the time had also come to augment the dwindling numbers by admitting girls. As a consequence, some twenty girls were admitted, bringing the total number of pupils up to about fifty.

However, both educational standards and numbers of pupils were falling and there was a real danger of losing the county grant. A row which had simmered for years between those governors who supported Osborne as headmaster and those, notably C.R. Ashbee, who pressed for his resignation, finally came to a head in 1913. The governors made it clear to Mr Osborne that he had no alternative but to resign. He was succeeded by Mr Matthew Cox, headmaster of a school in Wells, a number of whose former pupils followed him to Campden and became boarders. Under Mr Cox's leadership the grammar school rapidly regained its former reputation and soon had to contend with the problem of overcrowding. In due course, four sets of premises had to be used for classes: not only the grammar school and the old King's Arms, but also the Swan, which ceased to be a public house in 1918, and the Town Hall. This was obviously not an ideal arrangement but it was to be some years before a new building could be contemplated.

In addition to the grammar school, there were the two National Schools, boys and girls, the infants school, and after 1854 a Catholic school. Several private schools also existed, one of which[xiv] called itself the High School for Girls and placed particular emphasis on music, French, German, drawing and painting. The Education Act of 1870, introduced universal education through rate-supported elementary schools. Controversy however arose over a proviso that the curriculum should include religious instruction in the tenets of the Church of England. One non-conformist said 'While I am in favour of religious teaching and in favour of the Bible being read and taught in school, I am opposed to sectarian, denominational, dogmatic teaching ...' There were complaints from both Baptist and Primitive Methodist churches that Sunday School scholars

The Old King's Arms before it was occupied by the grammar school

were being weaned away by promises of places in the new Board Schools if they attended Church of England Sunday Schools.

There was little provision for physical education at the time. Francis Osborne had wanted to establish a Campden bathing lake. The question was raised unsuccessfully as early as 1886 but Osborne brought the matter up again in 1898, proposing that the parish council should consider building one, as his own attempts to build a private one for the school had failed. The resolution was passed but the Earl of Gainsborough vetoed the choice of a site in the Coneygree because access would be too difficult and the site too exposed. A site near Westington Mill was subsequently chosen but the scheme floundered through lack of finance until it was revived and brought to fruition by Ashbee in the early years of the 20th century.

Adult education has had quite a long history in the town. The first move came in October 1877, when a preliminary meeting was held in the boys' National School, 'well attended by young persons of both sexes ... to discuss the desirability of establishing technical classes in the town'. The classes seem to have taken off successfully and in 1878 the *Evesham Journal* reported that a class in connection with the Departments of Science and Art was held during the winter months in the Blue Schoolroom. In the examinations in May, six first class and six second class awards were presented. Evening classes seem to have been held annually and in 1886 the *Journal* reported that the inspector for the Science and Art Departments, South Kensington, had expressed himself highly satisfied with the teaching arrangements and apparatus.[xv]

How much longer these classes continued is not clear but in 1891, with a grant from Gloucestershire County Council, the grammar school opened a technical school which offered evening classes to the public. By 1897 the technical school was offering about twenty-five weekly lessons in such subjects as butter-making, cookery, carpentry, laundry, drawing and woodcarving. Some of the classes proved to be so popular that students had to be turned away. The genesis of technical education thus predated the advent of C.R. Ashbee and his School of Arts and Crafts (successor to the grammar school's technical school) by some 25 years.

The churches were influential, confident and very active at this time. St James's Church maintained a fair degree of stability throughout the period of change. This was reflected in the long incumbency, from 1832 till 1873, of the wealthy Canon Kennaway. Chairman of the Vestry and a magistrate as well as vicar, he left his mark on the town in many ways but most enduringly with the construction of a row of cottages at the bottom of the vicarage garden in Leysbourne, built to house his outdoor staff. He also extended the vicarage, though, not surprisingly, his extension was subsequently pulled down in less affluent circumstances.

In 1884 St James's Church underwent major interior restoration, much to be regretted by future generations. The old carved oak pews were ripped out and replaced with stained deal, and the black and white marble slabs and flat tombstones were removed and terra-cotta tiles laid. The vicar, the Rev. Francis Forster, seems to have been the instigator of that work and was clearly delighted with the co-operation he received from the parish in its implementation. The result according to him was 'that the dear old Church is now externally and internally the glory of the parish'. Mr Forster endeared himself to his flock in 1890 by marrying the daughter of the solicitor William Higford Griffiths. In the

Almshouse residents Margaret Emms and Richard Cooper, 1849. Two of a set of eight delightful coloured drawings presented by Canon C.E. Kennaway to the vicarage, these pictures show the uniform and stag's head badge of almshouse residents.
(By kind permission of Rev. Canon David Cook)

same year the carillon in the church tower was restored by the family of the late Canon Kennaway as a memorial to his widow.

The church, mindful of the diminished population and of continued depression in local industries, did its best to care for the physical as well as the spiritual needs of the people but resources were often stretched beyond its limits. The church operated a Provident Medical Dispensary and collected money for 'Hospital Sunday' each year to obtain tickets for Stratford Infirmary but it is clear that demands greatly exceeded resources.

The Baptist Church in Campden was also strong during the last three decades of the century, under the leadership particularly of two outstanding ministers. In May 1867, after about 90 years, the church had fallen to such a low ebb that it was formally dissolved. However, the following year there arrived in Campden a vigorous Scot, the Rev. W. Ritchie Irvine who achieved a remarkable change. Irvine accepted the pastorate and by 1872 he was able to build and pay for a new church with capacity for 300 people on the site of their old meeting house. A new manse was built soon afterwards.

Mr Irvine took a positive role in the improvement of the lives of his members and in asserting their rights. He served on many committees, including that of the first Reading Room in Campden, established (in the old gaol below the Town Hall) for the benefit of working people. In 1872 he spoke strongly at the Vestry meetings discussing the sanitary condition of the town. However, he died in 1878 aged only 59. He had been held in high regard by all sections of the population. His funeral was accompanied by many signs of respect and was attended by townsfolk of all persuasions.

Seven years later, the Rev. Philip Lewis was inducted and his evangelistic preaching and concern over pressing social problems soon made him the natural leader of the working classes, who largely made up the Baptist community. There were three main aspects to Mr Lewis's ministry: evangelism, as evidenced by a growth in membership; efforts to relieve the continuing distress in the town; and action on a wider political front. Shortly after his arrival in Campden, he became involved in Liberal politics and was soon secretary of the Liberal Association.

Mr Lewis was involved in collecting money and clothing for the poor. As the distress caused by the agricultural depression continued, this relief work increased. In 1888 some unspecified 'very severe events tried our congregation very much' and the Pastor took the lead in distributing coal and bread to the needy. He also preached the cause of temperance. Further, the old Quaker Meeting House at Broad Campden which had earlier been taken over as a Baptist Mission Station was renovated and re-opened. A library, open to all, boasted no fewer than four hundred books. In 1906 his long and successful pastorate ended with his retirement to Broad Campden where he later became a Parish Councillor and J.P.

The Methodists continued their ministry in Campden, although while Mr Irvine was here they seem to have joined in worship with the Baptists. At the end of the 19th century the church sent a travelling 'Joyful News' evangelist by the name of R. Kedward to Campden in an attempt to revive the cause, but his presence and his insistence on preaching in the open air, under the Elm Tree, caused considerable controversy in the town. As reported in an article in 1903,

> 'Concertinas, bells, and other noisy instruments' failing to silence him, his persecutors adopted other means, and, in default of paying the fine imposed, the preacher was imprisoned. Probably he would have served his time but for an accident to his mother ...[xvi]

when Mr Thomas Champness, a leading Methodist minister and founder of the 'Joyful News' movement, paid the fine and secured his release. Mr Champness himself later came to Campden and preached in the open air, having first ascertained that it was lawful to do so.[xvii]

Following the conversion of the second Earl of Gainsborough to the Roman Catholic faith in the 1850s, a considerable Catholic community grew up in and around Campden. Services were held first in the little domestic chapel of Campden House and then in the chapel of the Catholic school in Lower High Street (or Cow Fair as it was then called). In June 1891 an old barn which stood on the corner of Back Ends and Cow Fair was pulled down and the foundation stone laid for a new Catholic Church. The earl paid most of the costs and gave the site and most of the materials used, some of the stone coming from the demolished chapel at Westington.

The small Quaker community, however, had declined in numbers. By the mid 19th century, attendance was very low and in 1871 the Meeting House closed as a place of Quaker worship until its most successful revival in 1962.[xviii]

In 1890 a meeting was held at the Blue School (now the County Library) to discuss the possibility of building a cottage hospital. The vicar, who so often had to refuse requests for 'hospital tickets' for Stratford Infirmary, said that it would be of enormous benefit to the poor — a view strongly supported by Dr Morris who explained how difficult it was to treat patients in their own homes. It was estimated that £400 would be needed and that annual maintenance costs would be between £80 and £100. George Haines chaired a committee to put the matter in hand. The Earl of Gainsborough offered the site of the former Westington Chapel but this was turned down on the grounds of being too far from the centre of Campden. In the event, the plans were shelved.

Other improvements were made in the town. The cracked and broken blue lias stones of the pavements, which were a pitfall to the unwary and had given rise to a number of complaints were repaired, but there were nostalgic regrets and much opposition when in 1893 they were replaced with 'the highest quality concrete' — the high quality indeed being recognised years later when the pavements were lifted for the installation of public utilities. These were still in excellent condition when they were finally replaced in the 1970s.

In 1904 Campden took a major step into the 20th century with the installation of water mains by the Cotswold Water Board. This was a back breaking job, for which men were paid only 4d an hour, but it brought welcome employment to many. However, not all Campdonians greeted this progress with enthusiasm and some refused to allow their homes to be connected to the mains water supply, preferring to continue to pump their water from a well. It was also around this time that the main roads, previously made of local yellow limestone, were metalled with Malvern granite. The doctor was the first person in Campden to own a car: a tiller-steered Stanley steam car; but a year or two later, Mr Benjamin M. Chandler, an American who came to work at the Guild, introduced the first petrol driven vehicle. Horses and farm animals did not take kindly to these noisy, smelly intrusions on their previously quiet roads.

1905 saw the arrival of the first telephone in the town — the doctor's private line to his partner in Mickleton. It was not until 1923 that there was a public telephone. Nevertheless, with the new supply of piped water, with gas lighting, the telegraph, the railway and the bank, Campden was acquiring the symbols of modern life. The journey to and from the station, however, was still made in the same old, yellow horse bus, 'The Mustard Pot', which had been in service since the 1880s and was now driven by Ben Benfield, better known as 'Ben-the-bus'.[xix]

In 1899 Percy Rushen had published privately the first edition of his *History and Antiquities of Chipping Campden in the County of Gloucestershire* with the clear intention of making the history and beauty of Campden known to a wider public.[xx] Rushen was not alone in trying to publicise Campden. As the century neared its end travel publicity increased and various articles appeared featuring the town including one by postmaster and draper Julius R. Neve, who was also an antiquarian.

There are different views on the state of Campden at the turn of the century. Looking back at Campden before the Guild, the former Guildsman H.T. Osborn likened it to 'Sleeping Beauty".[xxi] Lord Redesdale described it as 'fast asleep' before it was awoken by Ashbee and the Guild. In 1906 the town doctor, Dr Dewhurst, claimed that the town was at last 'waking from its long sleep'. The local historian, Christopher Whitfield, called it 'rather moribund'; C.R. Ashbee himself asked why so many fields were covered with thistles and the roofs of so many cottages were falling in, and he never tired of stressing how the Guild, arriving in 1902, brought new vitality to the town. Annette Carruthers, on the other hand, warns that 'the town had never been as moribund as it suited Ashbee to believe'.[xxii]

In 1981, at the age of 89, the Earl of Harrowby, who could remember planting a tree in Campden to celebrate Queen Victoria's Jubilee in 1897, wrote of the town he knew as child and youth: it was, he said, 'choc a bloc full of an intelligentsia which had done an enormous amount for Campden in modern times, and without any of the dangers which in 99 per cent of the cases this sort of influx would have caused; it is a complete revolution in the atmosphere of those days'.[xxiii] It might be added that Campden proved itself particularly good at accommodating, and getting the best out of, its incomers.

The question remains: was the Campden of 1902 sleeping or moribund? It was certainly poor. Farming had not fully recovered from two disastrous decades; landlords could not charge rents that would encourage them to renovate their decaying properties; tourism was still in its infancy. Alec Miller, in his autobiography,[xxiv] spoke of 'many evidences of local poverty'. He was surely right. Dr Craig Fees, however, whose doctoral thesis looks at Campden life in great detail, argues that Campden was awake and alive to the times long before the Guild arrived.[xxv] He points to the development of trade unions in the 1870s, the formation of the North Cotswold Farmers' Association in 1889, the opening of a technical school in 1891, and the plans to open a swimming pool. Further evidence can be gleaned from the *Evesham Journal*: reports abound of social activities that include bellringing, musical concerts, garden fetes, sports, and theatrical entertainments. What the Guild brought were new talents and new energy, often invigorating existing institutions or taking up ideas that were already in the air.

Notes

- i Whitfield, *History* op cit 229
- ii Trinder, Barrie, *Victorian Banbury* (Phillimore & Co Ltd, 1982) 81
- iii Piggott's Directory, 1830
- iv Osborn, H.T., op cit 24
- v Jackson, A.S, *The Gas Works at Moreton-in-Marsh* M-i-M & Dist Local Hist Soc 20
- vi *Evesham Journal* 1st Jan 1866, 22nd Dec 1866
- vii Whitfield, *History* op cit 205
- viii ibid 219
- ix Fees, Craig, *Cotswold Mumming* op cit 70 & note 79

x ibid 53 & note 25

xi Too late for Muriel Neve, who had commented in 1890 in her private journal, 'often I sighed with envy when I saw or heard of the education London children can get so easily.....having to admit that you don't play, sing, draw, know French or German is not pleasant'.

xii The fourth was Harry Warmington, later to become a noted silversmith. Life was not made easy for the first four scholarship pupils when they arrived at the grammar school, and they were quickly dubbed the 'Charity Kids' but this was soon dropped and attitudes changed when they proved themselves to be academically equal to the fee-paying pupils.

xiii See Russell, Gordon, *Designers Trade* (Allen & Unwin 1956) 34. They introduced a lively trade in silver cuff links, fountain pen clips and similar items. Mr. Osborne was less than enthusiastic about the new arrivals from London. He disliked Ashbee and what he described as the 'Cockney invasion' and made no attempt to understand what the Guild was trying to do.

xiv See Chamberlain's *1898 Almanac*

xv Warmington, *The Campden School of Arts & Crafts* (unpublished) CADHAS Archives 2003/079/DS 2

xvi *Methodist Recorder* 1st October 1903

xvii Champness, Eliza M., *The Life-story of Thomas Champness* (Chas Kelly, 1907) 286-88

xviii Wood, Jack V., *Some Rural Quakers*, (William Sessions Ltd. York 1991) 77-8

xix See 'Old Days in and around Evesham' Nos 1076 & 1079 *Evesham Journal* 21 Aug and 27 Nov 1948

xx Percy Rushen is remembered as a little old man with little steel-rimmed spectacles who always wore a morning coat and top hat.

xxi Fees, Craig, *A Child in Aradia* op cit 13

xxii Carruthers, Annette, 'The Guild of Handicraft at Chipping Campden' in Mary Greensted ed. *The Arts and Crafts Movement in the Cotswolds* (Sutton, 1993) 54

xxiii Letter to Fiona MacCarthy 18 March, 1981 (Sandon papers)

xxiv Miller, Alec, *C.R. Ashbee and the Guild of Handicraft* (unpublished, 1941) 93

xxv Fees: *Cotswold Mumming* op cit 136 -44

PART V: THE ARTISTIC INVASION

20

Out of Babylon

While Campden sought to come to terms with the agricultural depression, others in the cities were seeking a solution to the problems created by the industrial revolution. Queen Victoria, in her speech at the opening of the Great Exhibition of 1851, had expressed the pious hope that industry would promote 'friendly and honourable rivalry ... for the good and happiness of mankind'. For many of her subjects, however, it was a cause of poverty and degradation. The poet Roden Berkeley Wriothesley Noel, the grandson of Sir Gerard Noel, was popular in his time and prolific. In one of his best poems, 'The Red Flag', he expresses his anger at the poverty in London in satire that has an Augustan edge. It includes this passage:

> Now trips a dame who lifts her skirt for fear
> Of many a foul contamination here,
> Revealing delicate ankles to the friend,
> Who (to assist) his manly arm may lend.
> 'Think what a desperate misery may slink
> In these low neighbourhoods from whence we shrink?'
> In silver tones she whispers: 'Look! there prowl
> Two terrible ragged ruffians with a scowl.'
> 'Near our town houses! who could fancy it?'
> Drawls out the dandy with more birth than wit.
> She, with a light, quick shiver, half a sigh:
> 'One's heart aches even to *dream* such poverty!'
> (It jarred her nervous sensitivity).[i]

The East End of London in 1900 was much closer to the world of Dickens than it is to the East End of today. There were no large factories in the East End, but there were thousands of small workshops, most employing only a handful of people. In 1890 William Booth, founder of the Salvation Army, asked: 'As there is a darkest Africa, is there not also a darkest England?'[ii] In his monumental survey, *Life and Labour of the People in London*,[iii] Charles Booth estimated that some 50 per cent of the population of Whitechapel lived in poverty, and nearly 59 per cent in Bethnal Green.

A modern historian, Gareth Stedman Jones[iv] has made a useful distinction between 'sweated' labour on the one hand and 'artisans' on the other. The sweated labourer was poor; the artisan usually was not. While the sweated man struggled for life itself, the artisan was responsible for most of the community's energy and inventiveness. He could become quite prosperous, too — as long as he remained healthy and the economy remained sound.

Out of all this poverty grew multifarious movements for reform, from the Salvation Army, the Labour Party and the trades unions to the work of Ruskin and William Morris, George Bernard Shaw, Robert Blatchford, and the Webbs.

In 1856 the designer William Morris came into contact with the Pre-Raphaelites and, under their continued influence, the Arts & Crafts movement in Britain emerged. Its ideals were a high standard of individual craftsmanship and utilitarian simplicity, in marked contrast to the heavily decorated factory-made articles which were the conventional taste of the time. In 1861 the firm of Morris, Marshall, Faulkner and Co. was established and became the inspiration for many Arts & Crafts communities in Europe and in the United States. By the end of the 1880s the firm, now Morris and Co., had taught many artists and craftsmen skills, with which they went on to work independently or to form guilds.

At that time Charles Robert Ashbee, son of a London businessman, was an undergraduate at Cambridge, where, via the influence of fellow student Lowes Dickinson, he encountered Edward Carpenter, then in his early forties and a leader of various socialist reform movements advocating the so called 'simple life'. Through Carpenter, Ashbee came into contact with Morris and a number of like-minded young men. After leaving Cambridge Ashbee went to London to train as an architect, living at Toynbee Hall, the pioneer Oxford University Settlement in Whitechapel. Deeply concerned about all the social evils of the day, Ashbee particularly admired the ideals of Ruskin who had formed a utopian guild, based on a form of romanticised feudalism.

To the young Ashbee this was stirring stuff and he started a Ruskin reading group for working people at Toynbee Hall. It began simply as a study class but before long it turned into something very different: a group of thirty men and boys, experimenting in various crafts. Out of the experience came the idea of a school and workshop which would educate people and give them employment by producing things of beauty: the idea behind the Guild of Handicraft. By 1888, after a season of discussion and money-raising, the Guild, together with its School of Handicraft, was formally inaugurated.

Ashbee was neither original nor alone in his basic beliefs. From John Ruskin he drew the idea that the craftsman should express his creativity in every object he made and that mere imitation and replication were to be rejected. From both Ruskin and William Morris came the ideal of the medieval craftsman who lived at a time when there was no hierarchical division between the arts and the crafts, and who had time to produce the finest work: work, too, that related to the lives of ordinary people. What destroyed this world was not the machine itself — which for Ashbee had its uses — but industrialism, which exploited and debased both producer and user. Ashbee drew his ideals from the medieval guilds but he also embraced Carpenter's theories about comradeship, honest labour and the creation of a new socialist society.

Ashbee was different from the other reformers in that, while others thought on a theoretical level or looked for national, even international, solutions, he sought to realise his ideals in a microcosm of his own making: local, practical, human. In this he went further than even William Morris had done. His Guild would live and develop in its own way, be entire of itself; perhaps in time it would prove the prototype of something much greater. He placed a special emphasis on education, as he believed strongly that training and production should take place simultaneously.

The work of the Guild quickly gathered momentum and soon involved many different crafts. By 1891 it had moved into its own workshops in Essex House in Mile End Road. In 1898, after the death of William Morris, Ashbee acquired the presses of Morris's Kelmscott Press, with some of Morris's printers, and thus began the Essex House Press.

When recruiting for his Guild from the 1880s on, Ashbee looked first for signs of vitality and commitment; talent was a secondary requirement, prior training and experience useful but not essential. Thus he found most of his recruits not among the legions of the derelict and defeated — he was neither Salvationist nor social reformer — but among the class of artisans. Some of them were born outside London — Kelsey in New Zealand, Hill in Australia, Curtis in Hull, Adams in Southampton, Pyment in Royston, Barlow in

Manchester, Jelliffe in Wiltshire, Daniels in Birmingham, Williams in Rochester, and the two Hart brothers on an Essex farm. Many were certainly Cockney by birth, though it is likely their forebears were not. And some, like C.V. Adams and Thomas Binning, came with trade union experience which prepared them for the communal and democratic life of the Guild.

By the turn of the century, Ashbee's Guild had developed into a thriving urban community, democratic, self-sustaining and comradely. His craftsmen produced fine objects of many kinds: furniture and carving, metalwork and ironwork, jewellery and enamelling. The Guild ran lectures and evening classes in many subjects, organised sports, folk-singing and dramatic productions, took members and their families on holidays and river trips, during which they camped, swam and rowed. They later ran a retail shop off Bond Street — 'Essex House is roaring along,' Ashbee wrote to his wife Janet in March 1900,[v] but all around them, a street or two away, were all the squalor and poverty that Booth had written about. And there was another factor: within months the lease on Essex House would be due to close.

Through others, including Morris, his friend Edward Carpenter and the proponents of the Back to the Land movement, Ashbee came to feel that the Mile End Road could not provide the right environment for a simple and healthy life for his guildsmen and that it was better for men to live close to the land. Consequently in 1901, as the lease on Essex House was coming to an end, Ashbee scoured the countryside for a suitable rural setting for his enterprise. His friend and supporter, Robert Martin-Holland (he later changed his name to Holland-Martin), a young director of Martin's Bank, suggested Campden, with its old Silk Mill and many cottages lying invitingly empty and available for low rents. For the romantic medievalist in Ashbee, Campden was Camelot, his dream of unspoilt rural peace and beauty come true, a small moribund town waiting to be caught up in his great social experiment.

When Ashbee took his Guild to the country he called it 'going home', as though it meant a return to a medieval Arcadia. He firmly believed that contact with the elemental things in life was essential to happiness and fulfilment and that these things could not be found in a city. So now was the time when his whole community of craftsmen, their wives and children, their baggage and furniture, their tools and machines, all should move away from London — the existing home of them all — and out into the country. The idea was extraordinary, and only a man of exceptional vision, personal charisma and practical ability could have made it happen. Of course, it was necessary to convince his guildsmen of the need to leave their homes and all that was familiar. And, indeed, the majority of the guildsmen were less than enthusiastic at the prospect of a move into the country. However, just before Christmas 1901, and after various reconnoitrings, the Guild members voted democratically by 22 to 11 (with one unrecorded) in favour of a lock-stock-and-barrel move to Campden. Ashbee was gratified that 'the men themselves have decided that on the whole it is better to leave Babylon and go home to the land'.[vi]

The Silk Mill; an original hand printed wood engraving by David Birch, 1985
(By kind permission of the artist)

Ashbee saw the exodus from Whitechapel to Campden both as a great experiment in socialist living for his men and also as a mission for Campden, which he saw as a cultural desert waiting to be invigorated by the Guild. For all his romantic rural yearnings, Ashbee was irrevocably a townsman and incapable, despite all his intentions, of understanding country people and their way of life. The unfortunate consequence of this was that he grossly underestimated Campden and the intelligence and abilities of its inhabitants, wrapping himself and his followers in a rural myth that has persisted down to the present day.

The guildsmen arrived gradually during the course of the spring, the different workshops each coming in turn. The Silk Mill was leased at £40 a year and structural repairs were carried out. An electric power plant was installed, the first to be seen in Campden. The old building proved to be very suitable for the workshops and the craftsmen quickly settled into their new premises. The ground floor housed the showroom, drawing office, Essex House Press and the general office; the silversmiths, jewellers and enamellers were on the first floor. The woodworkers and carvers were up on the second floor, the smithy was in an outhouse, and a circular saw, band-saw and planer were housed in wooden sheds at the far end of the grounds. These machines were permitted by Ashbee but otherwise work was by hand.

Houses and cottages nearby were leased and repaired by the Guild and sub-let to the men on a temporary basis, while they looked for long-term homes. Only long afterwards did Ashbee learn to his horror that some local labourers had been evicted from their homes by Lord Gainsborough, so that he could obtain higher rents from the incomers.[vii] Some men lodged with local families or at one of the many inns but a number of the younger men and bachelors were housed together in Braithwaite House. Will Hart, an assistant in the woodcarving shop, known as 'the skipper' because he had been in the Navy, was in charge of Braithwaite House. Ashbee liked to call it a Hall of Residence, connoting something between a Cambridge college and an American fraternity house. The men paid 15s a week for board and lodging and this included the services of a resident housekeeper and a cleaning woman. Braithwaite House was also used as an overflow for Ashbee's many guests, so there were constant visitors. Elm Tree House became Ashbee's architectural office and he and Janet made Woolstaplers Hall into their home.

The town meant different things to different people: for Ashbee the atmosphere was medieval, whereas to the young Glaswegian guildsman, Alec Miller, Campden was 'as foreign as Cathay, and as romantic as the architecture of fairy tale'.[viii] Charlie Downer, the young blacksmith, and his friend Fred Brown, who were lodging at the Rose and Crown in Lower High Street, felt particularly homesick. Another guildsman missed London so much that he used to go to the station each day to reassure himself that it was still possible to go back there. George Hart, by contrast, immediately fell in love with the sheer beauty of Campden and, even if he had not later married a Campden girl, it is unlikely that he would ever have left. Communications at first were not always easy, as the local dialect was far stronger and more prevalent than it is today and sounded very archaic to a Cockney ear. Even the guildsmen's clothes set them apart from the local people. The adjustment, however, was easier for the men than for their wives. Most of the guildsmen, whether reluctantly or not, became infected by Ashbee's crusading spirit and caught up in a sense of adventure. It was an exciting challenge to set up their new workshops together and it was a necessity to become active and productive.

All Charles Ashbee's many talents found expression during the twenty-year life of the Guild. He continued to design houses and to renovate old ones throughout the Campden period, in part to raise money in support of the Guild. He was a designer of flare and originality: of furniture, silverware, jewellery, of most things his craftsmen could make. He lectured and wrote prolifically, producing one work in particular of great lucidity and power, *Craftsmanship in Competitive Industry* (1908), in which he expounded the philosophy and ideals that drove him. He was a visionary, but he also had great personal magnetism and could inspire others.

He started a bookbinding shop in the High Street, run by one of the few women associates of the Guild, Annie or 'Statia' Power, and in London he opened a showroom near the existing Guild shop. He took over the evening technical classes being run by the grammar school and set up a new educational establishment, the School of Arts and Crafts. He adapted Elm Tree House in Lower High Street and its malt house to provide a lecture room, two libraries and offices, and the school soon eclipsed the old technical school. At one point it had 330 students attending classes in subjects as diverse as laundry and instrumental music, and hearing lectures on Thomas More and Heraldry and the Renaissance. Soon the production of finely printed books and pamphlets resumed on the old William Morris presses, leading in the autumn of 1903 to the publication of the superb Prayer Book of King Edward VII for which Ashbee provided both the type and the illustrations. Guildsmen constructed a bathing lake that was open to all, and the Guild staged a series of theatrical productions

— mostly of Elizabethan and Jacobean plays — that were remarkable in their ambition and quality of performance. The Guild in Campden began to do well.

Ashbee was almost thirty-nine and becoming increasingly well-known as an architect and designer, when the move to the Cotswolds was made. He was tall and handsome, with a high domed forehead, a large moustache and a small beard. His extraordinary personality, magnetic exuberance and enormous vision inspired loyalty in his friends but there was an undeniable quirkiness in his character, speech and 'arty' appearance which repulsed many others.

Left: C.R. Ashbee by William Strang. Strang was a painter, etcher, engraver and illustrator who worked for Ashbee's Essex House Press and visited Campden, staying at Braithwaite House. *(By kind permission of The Art Workers Guild)*
Right: Janet Ashbee by William Strang *(By kind permission of Rev. Richard Ames Lewis)*

In 1898 Ashbee had married Janet Forbes. It was to be a strange companionate marriage and one to which children only came very late. With a few exceptions, women did not feature significantly in Guild life. Indeed it would be true to say that so far as was possible they were pushed into the background. Comradeship was Ashbee's guiding principle in life and Janet was required to assume the role of 'Comrade Wife'. She was 23, much the same age as most of the guildsmen who all adored her. Janet Ashbee was as strong and determined a personality as her husband. Yet, while he could seem aloof, even forbidding, she was warm and practical, though shrewd, highly articulate and outspoken. She involved herself in many aspects of Guild and Campden life, but particularly in the personal lives of the guildsmen and their families. That she earned their respect and affection is revealed in the many letters written by guildsmen, and in the reminiscences of Archie Ramage, Philip Mairet and Alec Miller. Miller himself described her as 'beautiful, vitally alive, cultured, musical, and quite without affectation'.[ix]

A stream of distinguished well-wishers visited the Guild, some of them already friends of the Ashbees. They came to look, to discuss, to buy, sometimes to take part in Guild activities: George Bernard Shaw, Mrs Patrick Campbell, the Webbs, Hartley Granville Barker, Walter Crane, John Masefield, Maude Royden, Jack London, Lawrence Housman, William de Morgan, Jack Yeats — and the former Prime Minister Arthur Balfour who, according to Janet, 'came, saw and smashed a showcase'.[x] In his later years Ashbee selected from a vast collection of letters, photographs and miscellanea, together with his own and Janet's hand-written observations covering the years 1884 to 1941, and these he gathered into more than fifty volumes which are now held by King's College Library, Cambridge. The entries of both Ashbees make an intimate commentary on the lives of Campden and the Guild.

Ashbee's later claim that the Guild rescued Campden from decay and oblivion was undoubtedly greatly exaggerated. Despite the depopulation, clearly evidenced by the empty dwellings, there was a lot of activity in Campden at that time. Campden, like most other rural communities of the time, was dominated, usually benevolently, by local gentry, farmers and vicar. The Guild, on the other hand, was run on a democratic, profit-sharing and co-operative basis. Working conditions were good and wages were high. Guildsmen like Alec Miller and Archie Ramage conveyed some of the radical and trade union ferment that was spreading from the cities.

The farming population and tradespeople of the town were working hard to find solutions to their difficult problems and they were not remotely interested in utopian dreams of rural socialism, which seemed nothing more than a high flown irrelevance. The townspeople showed their disapproval, as they had done to the railway navvies in the previous century, by charging the incomers a higher price for goods. At first there was some resentment between townspeople and newcomers, a major cause of which was the difference in wages. In 1902 guildsmen were paid between 30s and 40s a week, when farm workers received about 11s or 12s.[xi] On the other hand there was new business in the pubs and shops, and Ashbee's renovations gave work to local builders.

While some shopkeepers put up their prices to profit from the higher wages of the newcomers, and there were other grounds for mistrust, most guildsmen made friends with local people, and within a few years several had married Campden girls. In London guildsmen had gathered daily for work and sometimes for play, but their homes were scattered across the East End and beyond. In Campden their homes and their workplaces were within a few hundred yards of each other, so their lives became intricately linked. Outside the workshops they performed in entertainments, sang together, cycled and swam together, joined the town band, attended classes together, met at church and in the pub.

The driving force, however, remained Ashbee himself. Alec Miller, the outstanding figure apart from Ashbee, has left the best insight into the Guild outside the Journals. He testified that CRA (as the Guildsmen called Ashbee) 'designed almost all the furniture, silverware, jewellery and blacksmithing made by the Guild'.[xii] Ashbee also designed fonts for the printing presses, translated some of the literary texts they used, wrote his books and pamphlets. He lectured and travelled constantly, and when he had time and occasion, he exercised his architectural skills. He was also a fine actor and took leading roles in several Guild plays. He became personally involved in everyday Campden life, as the Journals reveal.

The Guild of Handicraft has been fortunate in its historians: Alan Crawford's biography of Ashbee[xiii] is finely researched and written, and Fiona MacCarthy's account of the Campden years[xiv] traces the intricate consequences when a small country town is suddenly invaded by large numbers of incomers whose outlandish accents, clothes and behaviour must have made them seem like aliens. Alan Crawford suggests that Ashbee's focus was wider than his work as a designer (and that is being seen as more and more important in the history of the Arts & Crafts Movement as the decades pass). He says, 'Ashbee was always more interested in the life of the Guild than in the wares they produced'. That is certainly true. Ashbee was in essence a unifier, of art and craft, town and country, man and nature, the historical and the modern. He was a socialist idealist, but also a conservative with a deep love of the country and a belief in 'the experiment of the British Empire'.[xv] He sought to reconcile man and machine, with man always the master, hand and intellect, doing and learning, rich man and poor man, creator and executant in all the arts. If he exemplified Renaissance man in his own actions, he also wanted other men to share his Renaissance ideal. By no means all the guildsmen shared his vision (though Alec Miller did). The point was that he would take each man with him as far as each man had it in him to go.

Notes

i Noel, Roden, *The Red Flag* (1872)
ii Booth, William, *In Darkest England; the Way Out* (London 1890)
iii Booth, Charles, *Life and Labour of the People in London* First Series (Macmillan 1902-03) vol II, 25
iv Stedman Jones, Gareth, *Outcast London: A Study in the Relationship between Classes in Victorian Society* (Clarendon Press, Oxford, 1971)
v Ashbee, *Journals* (Kings College Cambridge) March 1900
vi Ashbee, *Journals* Dec. 1901
vii Crawford, Alan, C.R. Ashbee: *Architect, Designer & Romantic Socialist* (Yale University Press 1985) 114
viii Miller, Alec, *C.R. Ashbee and the Guild of Handicraft* (unpublished, 1941)
ix Miller, op cit 65
x quoted in Miller, op cit
xi Patrick, George, *A Scotch Boy in Chipping Campden*, an edited memoir of Archie Ramage by his grandson (unpublished) (G of H Trust Archives)
xii Miller, op cit 22
xiii Crawford, op cit
xiv MacCarthy, Fiona, *The Simple Life* (Lund Humphries 1981)
xv ibid 31

21

... *Into Arcadia*

Ashbee and his wife and the leading guildsmen were no respecters of status; moreover, they threatened change, and change threatened a way of life in Campden. Disputes were not long lasting but they were real enough, and the language could be heated. The compositor, Archie Ramage, for instance, a serious and intelligent trade unionist, who had recruited 200 members for his Campden Labour Union, was accused at a public meeting by the local peer, Lord Harrowby, of raising subscriptions in order to line his own pockets.[i] But disputes sometimes had their roots in personality. Commenting many years later on Ashbee's attacks on the same earl, Fiona MacCarthy wrote in a letter to the Earl's son:

> Ashbee's view of your father is, I fear, characteristic. It often suited his convenience to fit people into a ready-made rùle without questioning whether it was in fact a true one. Your father was given the role of haughty landlord; Vicar Carrington was type-cast as the hostile clergyman. Once he took up a stance he could not easily budge from it.[ii]

The Ashbees' view of the Earl of Gainsborough, whose family had been associated with Campden since Stuart times and who had owned most of the land since the Enclosure Act of 1799, was very different, and Janet described him as 'a harmless, gentle creature'. He had aroused Ashbee's ire by opposing his plans for a new School of Arts and Crafts, though he was open-minded enough within a year to change his mind and agree to chair the opening ceremony.

Less forgiving was the headmaster of the grammar school, Mr Osborne. He talked of the Guild as 'the Cockney invasion' and disliked Ashbee from the outset. His classroom window overlooked the High Street and he was in the habit of passing acid comments on passers-by, probably to the joy of his pupils. One victim was Ashbee, whom he dismissed as 'a trap and snare for the unwary'. This was a case of the biter bit, however, when a few years later Ashbee and the other governors dismissed Osborne and replaced him with the more dynamic Matthew Cox.[iii]

Then there were those that the Ashbees distrusted. Louis Dease was Lord Gainsborough's agent, Irish, devious and ubiquitous. 'They say he is the worst liar in Campden,' wrote Janet. 'He is everywhere, all the town knows him. ... The outward and visible sign of the Gainsboroughs. ... Dease keeps his wishes ever before the eyes of the citizens.' And she protests in exasperation at class prejudices in Campden: 'I cannot imagine that we shall be able to break the immense barrier of conventionality which divides us, to form an intimacy with any of them,' and she declares, 'our frank refusal to be classed anywhere in Campden society seems greatly to puzzle its inhabitants'.[iv]

Ashbee was often at odds with the local vicar, Thomas Carrington, 'almost the only person,' Alec Miller recalled, 'with whom he was completely and invariably impatient'. But the vicar 'got the wrong side of the Ashbees and the Guild, regarding us as intruders in his domain, and that breach never healed'.[v] Ashbee accused him of proselytising among the guildsmen. 'Our people are not accustomed to this and they do not like it,' he wrote in a letter of complaint. 'I hope therefore you will pardon the suggestion which as a member of the Church of England perhaps I may be permitted to make, that anything like an inquisitorial search for souls is more calculated to drive them away from church than to attract them thither.'[vi]

After a public meeting called to discuss a political issue of the day, protectionism, Janet was splenetic about the Carringtons: 'The Church was represented in force by the leaden-eyed poppy-cheeked vacuous heavy-dewlapped Vicar, who brings a blight with him wherever he comes; and the wife is even worse than he, a paragon of self-righteousness and Pharisaism, and who purred the whole evening at the glorious hour of life which a considerate deity was awarding her by setting her, in the eyes of all, next to a Countess.'

But Janet was not always as severe as this. She went on in the next sentence to describe the local MP as a 'simple, downright, blue-eyed soldier who made up for his innocence by his obvious good intentions'. Then she warms up again with her picture of 'the ubiquitous truculent ambient-mouthed Mr Davies, the political agent, a man with one green eye and one brown one, neither of which you can trust'.[vii]

Then there were two farmers, nick-named 'old Farmer Bigshilling and old Farmer Nibblecrust, the one because he makes the coin spread over so much, the other because he wastes so little. The one looking like a Normandy pippen, scarlet and wholesome, the other like Father Christmas, with a smile of intricate benevolence.'[viii] Ashbee characterises another farmer, 'old Stanley, Chairman of the Parish Council', as an 'admirable speaker, unsuccessful farmer, theoretical organiser, polite politician'. Ulric Stanley was a prominent figure in local life. He espoused a number of reforms: the admission of farm workers to his North Cotswolds Farmers' Association alongside the farmers, and measures to improve the technical training of the farm worker so that he would both be more useful in his job and less likely to leave for the city in search of a better wage. But Janet accused him of playing at reform: 'He likes to pretend he means it, he knows he does not mean it at all. ... Every bête-noire of ours is for the time being old Stanley's also.' [ix] And she reports the shrewd local teacher, Martha Dunn, as remarking: 'Ah, don't you put too much trust in him — he's one of them as says'. Yet Stanley was a large and eloquent figure in Campden for several decades.

Janet could also be observant and affectionate about local personalities. There was 'old Dolphin, the postman ... who keeps the children's window and has about 15 hats that he wreathes around with flowers and walks along the street with a kitten on his shoulder. Old Dolphin has a sense of beauty and we love him for it'.[x]

Of Martha Dunn, Ashbee wrote: 'She is Campden's staple of woe, a sort of Mrs Poyser, but without Mrs Poyser's acidity and pessimism. Still, it would not be well to quarrel with Mrs Dunn, for her tongue goes a long way. Yet it is a truthful tongue ... she goes for a bit of humbug like a terrier at a rat ... She finishes up the parson with "an' so I tell you straight to your face". And his face bears the mark of her truthful slap.' The Journal goes on: 'The husband of Mrs Dunn, as may be supposed, is the husband of Mrs Dunn. ... Richard knows his place — and his place for the most part is to sit in the ingle of her big cosy kitchen in bewildered admiration of Martha Dunn.' Once, when Janet was away and Ashbee was on his own, he reported: 'Mrs Dunn, dear soul, looks in occasionally to see that the world is treating me properly.'[xi] In later years, in letters to Ashbee, more than one guildsman recalled the kindness and generosity of Mrs Dunn.

An example of Ashbee's contribution towards Campden's life and wellbeing was the construction of the bathing lake[xii] which was as extraordinary as anything else that Ashbee achieved in Campden. The need for a swimming pool had been pointed out a quarter of a century before by J.C. Kingzett, and boys had had to make do with pools along the mill-stream that ran between Haydon's Mill and Berrington Mill, pools they called Eighth Tree, Tenth Tree, and Sluice; girls had nowhere to swim at all. In the 1890s Ashbee's bête-noire, F.T. Osborne, the headmaster of the grammar school, had made several unsuccessful attempts to find a suitable site, and in 1898 had passed the task on to the Parish council.

There the matter might have ended had not Ashbee taken it up soon after the arrival of the Guild. He commented on the unhealthy appearance of Campden school children, and the scheme chimed well with his ideal of the physically and mentally healthy individual within a healthy community. Ironically, he succeeded where the abrasive headmaster had failed. Loans were obtained, special money-raising events arranged. Some of the profits from the Guild's first dramatic production in Campden, Ben Jonson's *The New Inn*, were assigned to it. Janet Ashbee sent carol singers around the town to raise funds so that children could afford to buy tickets when the pool opened — as was hoped — in the summer. South of Campden a path led past Westington Mill to a pool in the brook, some half a mile from the town. Here, upstream of a sluice-gate, volunteers, including many guildsmen, dug out the lake by hand, planning to make it 153 feet long and 105 feet wide with a deep end of 7 feet 6 inches and a shallow end of 3 feet 6 inches. The pool was lined with clay, which cracked later during a dry June, thereby adding to the ultimate cost. In August 1903 the pool was opened.

Ashbee had a military friend, Lieutenant (later Captain) Montague Glossop of Hull, whose pronouncements were scarcely less Wodehousian than his name. He was, however, a keen supporter of the bathing lake project and a passionate campaigner for the revival of the ancient Cotswold Games in Campden. 'What a great day in the athletic world of England and also for history would be ... the reviving of the Cotswolds games', he declared before an audience of townspeople. 'May we in days to come be able to develop many champions at swimming and wrestling fit to compete with the world's greatest athletes. I sincerely hope that I may have many years amongst you, and in future I shall make a point of always being amongst you for them and shall get together the best wrestlers in London and Paris, so that we shall have quite a unique gathering unequalled before or since.' If some of the things he was proposing were a tall order for a small country town, personally he was unfailingly generous when it came to the bathing lake. In 1903 he donated a Swimming Challenge Cup to be competed for annually by men. It was designed and made in the Guild and decorated with enamel plaques.[xiii]

Three years later Glossop donated a silver Challenge Mace, this time for girls.[xiv] The ineffable Glossop 'hoped in future to see ladies from all parts of the country plunge into Campden lake to win the laurels of fame and take back to their village or domain the mace of honour.' And in 1907 he gave a Glossop Shield to be competed for by girls under 18, and a small Glossop Challenge Cup for boys under 18. Both of these are still awarded annually at Campden School.

The Bathing Lake, c. 1905

For five years the bathing lake flourished. The guildsmen taught a good part of a generation of Campden children to swim (one shilling reward was offered for passing a proficiency test). Galas were held and large crowds watched swimming and diving competitions, polo matches and entertainments of various kinds. But when the Guild began to fail so did the bathing lake. By 1911, with Ashbee often away and with serious faults developing in the clay lining, the pool became barely usable. After 1914 it fell rapidly into disuse. In 1998 building work at Haydon House uncovered some old graffiti on a lath and plaster wall, providing the bathing lake with an odd kind of obituary. 'Bathing Sports', it read. 'Sept. 1st 1904. Swam for the Glossop Cup.' Then: 'Won second prize for diving and swimming sports at Campden, Sept. 1st 1906 Roy Haydon.' And last: 'C. Corbin won the Glossop Cup, 1904.' Charles Corbin had worked with the Guild as a metalworker between 1902 and 1905.[xv]

The names of a number of guildsmen stand out among the records of the Campden years. Others have disappeared almost without trace: lives reduced to a name or a line or two only. Bill Hardiman was a silversmith and modeller. Ashbee had found him in the East End selling cats' meat from a barrow, trained him and grew to admire his talent. He was unstable, however. When he died suddenly, Ashbee commented sadly: 'His little life was an object lesson in the condition of modern labour. One of the unfits yet had an exquisite skill and taste.'[xvi] He had come to Ashbee too late, bearing the baggage of his background.

The two blacksmiths, Bill Thornton and Charlie Downer, occupied a forge in the Silk Mill grounds, making screens, fire-irons, lamp fittings and garden gates of high quality. Long after the Guild had gone, Thornton and Downer continued to work together in Campden until the Second World War, with a kind of irritable affection, tossing insults as well as hot iron from one to the other. Alec Miller, carver, modeller and sculptor, had read a book by Ashbee and travelled from Glasgow to Campden, via Dublin and Bristol, to find him. He loved the co-operative nature of the Guild, the comradeship and the sense of common purpose. Ashbee called him 'an ideal craftsman. A fine skill of hand — the firm sensitive touch of the carver and modeller, with a creative power of his own.' With Charlie Plunkett he founded the local Labour Party, became a JP and was elected to the Parish Council. Miller continued to work in Campden up to the late 1930s, although from 1924 he made frequent visits to the United States.

Alec Miller with the Statue of St Michael carved for Coventry Cathedral, 1923
(By kind permission of Jane Wilgress)

Archie Ramage, another Glaswegian, came to visit his friend Alec Miller, and stayed to become a compositor with the Guild. As early as 1904 the Guild was in financial difficulties, and the Press was put on half time. Two years later it was closed completely, and Ramage, penniless, moved to London. Later he gave up printing altogether and became an organiser of university extension classes[xvii] and finally a Presbyterian minister.

Jim Pyment and his half brother Arthur Bunten, cabinet makers, were born in Royston, Hertfordshire but both had joined the Guild during its London days. Jim became the foreman of the woodwork and furniture making shop and it was he who eventually acquired the Silk Mill premises in 1921 after the breakup of the Guild, and set up a building firm which became the leading firm of builders in Campden throughout the 20th century. He also became one of the leading figures in Campden life, reviving and leading the town band and organising many celebrations in the town.

Philip (or Philippe) Mairet was half Swiss. Ashbee brought him to Campden in 1906 as an architectural draughtsman (not a craft in the Guild sense and he never became a guildsman). He produced fine drawings for Ashbee's restoration of the ancient and ruined Norman Chapel at Broad Campden, at that time housing no more than a couple of pigs. He illustrated Ashbee's book *Modern English Silverwork* and extended his skills to become a stained glass artist, producing work for Liverpool Cathedral. Later he became secretary to the new owner of the Norman Chapel, the exotic (in the Campden context) Anglo-Sinhalese geologist, art expert and writer, Ananda Coomaraswamy. In due course, he fell in love with Coomaraswamy's wife, Ethel, herself a weaver of considerable skill.[xviii]

Ethel and Philip left Campden and married. He had at one time been an actor at the Old Vic under the name of Henry Cohen, a name he had seen on a milk cart on the way to the theatre. In later life he became a publisher and editor, and wrote a number of books. He was a friend of T.S. Eliot who dedicated his *Notes Towards the Definition of Culture* to him. He was primarily an intellectual of huge talents and distinction. His wife, who was the sister of guildsman Fred Partridge, finally joined the crafts community at Ditchling in Sussex where Eric Gill also worked.

The Hart brothers, George and Will, silversmith and carver, were countrymen and had been delighted to make the move to Campden. They had joined the Guild quite by chance. George, recently back from serving in the Boer War, had been working in Hitchin in the corn trade and, as a hobby, used to make corn dollies.

His skill with his hands had been noticed by the local parson who had encouraged him to take up metalwork at the boys' club. Some time later both George and Will entered a local craft competition which Ashbee had been invited to judge. Both won first prizes for their entries and Ashbee was so impressed with George's work that he invited him to join the Guild. Ashbee had found in George Hart, with his natural talent at his craft, combined with a love of the land and enthusiasm for sports, his ideal guildsman. He executed some of Ashbee's most demanding designs. Will, the wood carver, was particularly liked and admired. He managed Braithwaite House, the Guild hostel, with tact and efficiency. Ashbee found in him 'English character at its best', but thought that he lacked imagination. He had served seven years in the Navy before being invalided out. When he was turned down by the War Office for service in the Boer War, he enlisted instead in Lord Lock's Horse, and later served with Lord Roberts in Pretoria. '... he just takes command and does things', commented Ashbee. He served in the First World War and returned as a major. Alec Miller in old age mentioned that he and Will had been friends for sixty years. Mairet, however, was less than complimentary about George: 'perhaps the least likeable of this company of artificers',[xix] though Ashbee found him 'always cheerful and genial'.

In 1906 the Harts were joined by their remarkable stepfather, Wentworth Huyshe.[xx] Son of a general, he had been a war correspondent for *The Times*, author of several historical works and translations, expert on arms and armour, heraldic artist, actor, medievalist, composer and raconteur. He produced the last of the Guild plays in 1909, Thomas Heywood's *The Fair Maid of the West*, which seems to have been a fine production of a difficult play. Later, when war broke out, he was to return at the age of 67 to his earlier profession of war correspondent and spent the last months of 1914 on the Belgian border. Huyshe spent some time at Braithwaite House before settling with his family at Pike Cottage in Westington. He had three sons of his own, one of whom, Reynell, became a skilled silversmith and worked for some time in partnership with his half-brother, George Hart, before leaving Campden to become a highly regarded teacher of metalwork in Kent.

Despite the Guild's initial success, the first financial strains were evident within a year of the move to Campden. Janet complained at that time: 'Here is Liberty putting ten thousand pounds into the Cymric Silver Co. and we struggling to get our hundreds, and having to potboil with vile brooches etc. to make ends meet.'[xxi] Firms like Liberty had seen a commercial niche, invested appropriately, and were prepared to use machinery in mass production. The Guild had always used machines in the basic preparation of materials, and, as Janet admitted with some exaggeration, they were willing to lower their standards in order to compete. But the signs were ominous. Other weaknesses began to appear, though decline was gradual. Costs were high: the Guild paid good wages, and there was the expense of the buildings they owned or rented in Campden and London. The education programme had to be paid for and the entertainments to be subsidised. There were other questions. Was the Guild properly managed? Had they over diversified, spread themselves too much? Was Campden not just too far from their suppliers and their main outlets? In London, craftsmen had been able to find occasional work outside the Guild when times were bad; in rural Gloucestershire there were few such opportunities. In Alan Crawford's view: 'It was naive of Ashbee to think that a workshop employing as many as seventy men could be set down in the country all at once and survive; its skills belonged to the city, and so did its patterns of employment; when bad times came in the country, it could not respond.'[xxii]

As the Guild neared collapse, some guildsmen left — because they had to. Others still saw a future in Campden, setting up their independent workshops: Thornton and Downer, the blacksmiths; George Hart and Jack Bailey, silversmiths; Teddy Horwood, jeweller; William Mark, enameller; Alec Miller and Will Hart, carvers. Jim Pyment turned to building and joining him were Bill Wall and Arthur Bunten, cabinet makers, and Charlie Plunkett, polisher and upholsterer. They still called themselves the Guild of Handicraft, still held meetings and kept minutes. Ashbee himself stayed on, advising, helping, but no longer controlling. Alec Miller realised that Ashbee's dream was collapsing but remarked on his courage and extraordinary resilience. He had long encouraged his guildsmen to grow their own vegetables, now he persuaded his friend the generous American millionaire Joseph Fels to buy seventy acres of agricultural land in Broad Campden for the guildsmen's use, and four members agreed to work it. A year after the liquidation of the Guild in 1908, the twelve guildsmen who had decided to remain in Campden gathered to sign the Deed of Trust of a new organisation to replace the Guild, a looser association of independent craftsmen. It called itself the Guild of Handicraft Trust and continued to use the Guild stamp on metalware and to occupy the old Silk Mill. The Trust was to administer both the Mill and the farm at Broad Campden, though George Hart was the only guildsman to persevere with farming.

In the early 1920s, Wentworth and Reynell Huyshe co-designed a village sign for

Campden as their entry for a *Daily Mail* competition. In 1924 the drawing was shown at the Arts & Crafts Exhibition in Campden and in the 1990s it reappeared in the (newly formed) Guild of Handicraft Trust's exhibition in the Silk Mill. It was taken up and in 2002 was executed in metal by a local craftsman, Jeff Humpage, and erected near the Market Hall as part of the millennium celebrations.

Wentworth's stepson, George Hart occupied the old Guild metal workshop in the Silk Mill for the rest of his working life; he also began a dynasty of silversmiths that continued through his sons, Henry and George, and continues still through his grandson and great-grandsons. Paradoxically, George was one of the guildsmen whom Alec Miller felt never fully identified with Ashbee's ideals. Harry Osborn, whose father and uncle both worked for the Guild, wrote of Ashbee in 1982: 'His flock were not all that faithful to him or to his ideas; they were just out to earn a living, whether with handicraft in the country, or in town with mass production. When better prospects presented themselves or the future began to look dim most were ready to take a better job.'[xxiii]

George didn't need to find a better job: he stayed in Campden, proving successful as both farmer and silversmith. In local terms, he was an Establishment figure, willing to accept office in church or parish or farmers' association, conservative, respected but neither idealist nor intellectual. Yet he kept alive in Campden a tradition of fine craftsmanship, and passed it on not only to his sons but also to assistants like Harry Warmington, whom George described as 'one of the finest silversmiths in the country'.[xxiv]

Ashbee was soon busy on projects of his own, writing a new and important book, preparing for a lecture tour in the United States, involving himself with the Garden City Movement. If, in one sense, the Guild had failed, in others it had been a manifest success. It had changed life in Campden, boosting the local economy, reviving old festivals and traditions and starting new ones: Guy Fawkes night, morris-dancing, building the bathing lake, introducing annual theatre, setting up the School of Arts and Crafts, and creating a craft tradition in the town that continues to this day. The Earl of Harrowby, looking back in 1981, wrote: '... for all its immediate failure, the fact is that in less than half a century it turned ... the normal population into the chrysalis of an absolutely roaring success ... Campden came to take a pride in itself and was never content except with the very best and so bringing out the latent virtues of such a community, and this goes on developing the whole time, and it is all a child, or a grand-child, of Ashbee's adventure, and he should be remembered if only for that.'[xxv]

And, indeed, he should be remembered for much more than that: Alec Miller thought the Guild had 'produced work of real importance ... it set standards, and gave dignity and beauty to the crafts'.[xxvi] So true was this that by the end of the century interest in the Guild and its legacy had become appreciated nationally and internationally, and a new Guild of Handicraft Trust, founded in 1990 as an educational charity, was preparing to open a permanent exhibition and study centre in the town, devoted to the Arts & Crafts in Campden and the north Cotswolds.

Many guildsmen simply disappeared from the records when they left Campden. Others kept in touch with the Ashbees, some for many years. Most of these looked back with nostalgia and gratitude to this period in their lives. Several emigrated. William Mark, enameller, returned after 18 years to his native Australia. By the time he died in 1956 there were examples of his work all over Australia.[xxvii] Herbert Osborn, ivory worker, moved to Canada. Alec Miller eventually settled in the United States. He became a highly successful sculptor, his work in demand in both America and Britain. In 1961 he returned to England to meet again with Janet Ashbee. He was staying at St. Nicholas at Wade when news reached him of Janet's death. His daughter wrote: 'The blow to my father was a mortal one ... He died on May 17th, CRA's birthday and the day Janet's ashes were laid to rest.'[xxviii] His funeral was held at St. Nicholas's Church, where he had been married 52 years before.

Bill White, who served the Guild for 17 years, left in 1906, became an art school teacher, then adviser to Northumberland County Council. Walter Curtis, kindly, skilled and meticulous cabinet maker, had served longer than anyone except Ashbee. He became a woodwork instructor with Kent County Council. Walter Edwards, silversmith, took a job making chocolate moulds for Cadbury's, and called his house 'Campden'. Jack Bailey, silversmith, remained in Campden for a time then opened his own workshop in Stratford-on-Avon. If one craftsman, Fleetwood Varley, an enameller, after leaving Campden was prepared to work by a cruel irony for Liberty's, another, Walter Edwards, silversmith, retained his faith in Guild ideals for the rest of his life. When he was over seventy he recalled the inspiration of walking down the beautiful sleepy street of Campden 'and falling under the spell of Ashbee and the Guildsmen who were turning out work equal to anything in the Middle Ages'. He added: 'Industry meant something different, and from that time I have enjoyed every minute of my working life.'[xxix] The Guild had given them not only skills and experience but also self-confidence.

But there were also tragedies, perhaps more than the records reveal. Tom Hewson, silversmith, could not find work and took to drink. Arthur Cameron's case is interesting because it is well documented, largely through the writings of his son, William, who had left Campden as a young child at the time of the collapse.[xxx] Arthur had started as Ashbee's office boy and in time had become an excellent metalworker and a keen performer in Guild theatricals. He returned to the East End to face unemployment and destitution. He lived on the streets for two years, sleeping in parks, while his wife and children lived in the workhouse. In the year in which his father died, William wrote to Ashbee: 'You must have wondered often at my father's silence. Well, you must not think the worse of him for it. I can tell you that the collapse of the Guild was his collapse, too. He was never the same again, and he was unable to discuss his trade without flavouring his words regarding conditions in the trading shops. It was, in your own words, nearer to Utopia than any of you realised at the time.'[xxxi]

The School of Arts and Crafts had closed down in 1916, the bathing lake had fallen into dilapidation as early as 1911.[xxxii] The Ashbees, who had moved into the Norman Chapel after the departure of the Coomaraswamys, remained in Campden throughout the war, though Ashbee was often away. In January 1919 he met with the surviving guildsmen to perform the last obsequies for the old Guild. In truth its essence had long disappeared. As Ashbee himself commented later: 'They had captured the countryside, they had got the confidence of the farmers, they had made friends, they had built up a school of craftsmanship, many had found their wives locally, they had in fact made a country life, and another generation was at hand.'[xxxiii] Seven guildsmen remained, the rest were scattered throughout Britain and beyond, a handful had died in the war. Much had been achieved: much potential had been lost.

Notes

i Powell, Geoffrey, 'An Experiment in English Socialism: C.R. Ashbee and the Campden Guild' *Evesham Journal* 24th and 31st January 1980

ii Letter from Fiona MacCarthy to the Earl of Harrowby, 13th April, 1981 (Sandon papers)

iii Mason, Carolyn, *Notes for a History of Campden* CADHAS Archives

iv Ashbee, *Journals* 1902
v Miller, op cit 23
vi Ashbee, *Journals* 1902
vii ibid 1903
viii ibid
ix ibid
x ibid. There is more of Dolphin in Patrick op cit and in Fees, *A Child in Arcadia*. 52-3
xi MacCarthy, op cit 125
xii Gordon Croot has researched the history of the bathing lake in great detail. I am indebted to him for almost all the information I have used here.
xiii Untraced. A drawing of it was published in *The Studio* for 1903.
xiv The mace can now be seen at Cheltenham Art Gallery and Museum.
xv For details of sports at the Bathing Lake see *CADHAS Notes & Queries* Vol 4 No 3.
xvi Ashbee, *Journals* 1906
xvii Patrick, George, op cit
xviii Coatts, Margot, *A Weaver's Life: Ethel Mairet. 1872 - 1952* (Crafts Council 1983)
xix Mairet, Philip, *Autobiographical and Other Pieces* ed. C.H. Sisson (Carcanet, Manchester, 1981) 32
xx Jones, T.F.G.,: *The Various Lives of Wentworth Huyshe* (CADHAS 1998)
xxi Ashbee, *Memoirs* (a shorter version of the Journals, copies held in the Victoria and Albert Museum Library and elsewhere). Quoted by MacCarthy op cit 173
xxii Crawford, *C.R. Ashbee* 145
xxiii Fees, *A Child in Arcadia* op cit, 37
xxiv Quoted in Mason, Carolyn, *Papers* op cit
xxv Letter to Fiona MacCarthy, 18 March, 1981 (Sandon papers)
xxvi Miller, op cit 126
xxvii See O'Callaghan, J., *Treasures from Australian Churches* (National Gallery of Australia, 1985)
xxviii Wilgress, Jane, *Alec Miller: Guildsman and Sculptor in Chipping Campden* (CADHAS 1998)
xxix Letter to Janet Ashbee quoted in Osborn op cit 57, 58
xxx Cameron, William: *The Day is Coming* (Macmillan, N.Y. 1944)
xxxi Ashbee *Journals* 26 June 1939
xxxii *Evesham Journal* 17 June 1911
xxxiii Ashbee, *Memoirs* op cit. Entry written 1938

22

The Appeal of Catholicism

"...almost all in all to us"

Alongside Ashbee's Arcadian vision of craft in the countryside, another deep well of inspiration for Campden artists in the 20th century was Catholicism. Ashbee identified a link between these two when looking back at his time in the town. In 1924 he wrote to F.L. Griggs: '... I think the dream of you Catholic revivalists and of us "socialistic" humanists had much in common. We both wanted a better world and were both quite out of touch with the one provided us, which the beauty of life — expressed in that Gloucestershire village was almost all in all to us.'[i]

A large part of the town's recent Catholic history was inspired by the second Earl of Gainsborough, Charles Noel. Like many of his generation, he became interested in the Oxford Movement during his time at university and, after a trip to Rome, converted to Catholicism in 1850 with his wife.[ii] Since William and Mary's time, the religion had been virtually outlawed due to strict laws limiting the political and legal entitlements of Catholics in the United Kingdom. A gradual relaxation of these restrictions was made law in the 1827 Catholic Emancipation Act and in 1850 the Catholic church hierarchy was re-established in this country. This produced a flowering of the old religion which was seen by many of its converts as a return to the purity and truth of Christianity and, more importantly for artists, as the national style of Britain. At the time of his conversion, Charles and his wife, as the Viscount and Viscountess Campden, had moved into New Campden House. The small Anglican chapel at the house, which had only been built in 1848, was formally converted to a Catholic Mission.[iii] This chapel was demolished during Norman Jewson's remodelling of the house in 1934 but its east window, from a design by Pugin, the leading architect of the Gothic style and himself a Catholic convert, can still be seen at St Philip's Church in Ilmington.[iv]

The congregation grew and in 1869, Charles, now Earl of Gainsborough, commissioned a Catholic school and chapel in Lower High Street where children were taught by the Sisters of Charity of St Paul. The school chapel soon became too small so the next Earl of Gainsborough, another Charles, provided land in

Lower High Street for St Catharine's Church which was opened on 3rd September 1891.[v] This new church was designed by the Catholic architect W. Lunn of Great Malvern and, as befitting a Gothic Revival church, it was built partly of stone recovered from old buildings in the area. The form clearly shows Pugin's ideal of 'truth' by presenting a combination of building elements including a turret and sanctuary without hiding the parts behind a façade. As with other churches he designed, Lunn favoured ornate tracery with every window having a slightly different pattern and a large wheel East window.[vi] At its opening the church also boasted fine stained glass in the chancel and north chapel windows by the noted London firm of Lavers & Westlake.

These inviting surroundings probably helped Paul Woodroffe decide to move from London to live in Campden. From a Roman Catholic family, Paul Vincent Woodroffe was born in India in 1875, educated at Stoneyhurst and then was trained at the Slade Art School in London. He first came to the town to visit his sister and brother-in-law, Joseph Moorat, who lived at the Cedars (now Abbotsbury) in Westington. Moorat was a composer and music researcher and Woodroffe produced illustrations for his work. Throughout the 1890s Woodroffe visited Campden frequently and used a small cottage next door to the Moorats as a studio. By 1904 his artistic reputation was growing through his stained glass and illustrative work and he felt able to move out of London. He bought the Thatched Cottage, Westington (now Woodroffe House) next to the Cedars. He knew Ashbee through the Art Workers Guild and the Slade and commissioned him to enlarge and adapt the cottage to include a studio and stained glass workshop.

Many of the windows in St Catharine's are filled with Woodroffe's work including the design in the Lady Chapel dedicated to the memory of Lady Edith Noel, who became a nun, and the main window in the South Transept which is in memory of the 2nd Earl and Countess. His most distinguished commission was for 15 windows in St Patrick's Cathedral, New York, which at the time was quoted as 'the biggest single commission for a stained-glass subject that has come to England from another country'.[vii] The First World War interrupted work and the order was finally completed in 1934.

On a more domestic scale, his glass can also be found in houses about the town including Dover's House where there is a Miss Muffet round window on the stairs. Woodroffe continued to work as an illustrator over a wide range of subjects including nursery rhymes, religious primers and historical themes including local work for Ashbee, the Alcuin Press and Shakespeare Head Press.

Woodroffe lived in Campden for thirty years, contributing much to the artistic and community life of the town. It is perhaps unfortunate that the most frequent references to Woodroffe are in the journals and letters of Ashbee and his circle of friends who found this strict, kindly Catholic rather a figure of fun. For example, Ashbee writes to his friend Laurence Housman: 'I think strictly entre nous that the Guild's manners or morals have rather frightened poor Bête Grise.'[viii] Alan Crawford also comments on him in his biography of Ashbee, 'a beaky, austere man to look at, though kindly; he longed to inspire in his own assistants the ... easy camaraderie that prevailed [in the Guild] but he never could.'[ix] Yet as early as 1905 he was teaching life-drawing at the School of Arts and Crafts and in later years would be invited by a former student, Gordon Russell, to give talks to his workforce in Broadway. Woodroffe was a Committee Member of the Campden Society and a long-standing member of the Campden (later the Cotswolds) Arts and Crafts Exhibition committee serving as Treasurer and finally President in 1934. He was also a good sportsman and member of the local hockey team and he helped run the Catholic Guild for men and boys held in Elm Tree House in the 1920s.[x]

Woodroffe moved away from Campden in 1934 and appears not to have settled in his later years. He moved first to Bisley near Stroud, then Axminster and finally Mayfield in Sussex. He died at Eastbourne in 1954.[xi]

The introduction to the Griggs Memorial Exhibition held in 1939 quotes from the artist's Commonplace book which he aptly entitled 'Faith and Work'. In it Griggs had written down these sentences:

> Here lies a failure; he would never learn the art of compromise. He served a cause considered barren. He would rather gain Our Lady's smile than all the world's applause.[xii]

One can understand how the quotation appealed to Griggs. This heart-felt lament contains many elements that made up his complex character and attitude. In his own eyes, Griggs was always doomed to fail. He fought against modernity as it came seeping into his life; he was a perfectionist who couldn't turn out work fast enough to pay for his high expectations; he struggled to save his beloved Campden against local indifference; and above all he did it with a visionary high mindedness that often left everyday practicalities far behind.

Frederick Landseer Griggs was born in Hitchin, Hertfordshire in 1876 and was the son of a baker. Showing artistic talent, Griggs trained as an architectural draughtsman and in 1900 he was commissioned to produce sketches of buildings and scenes to accompany a series of works entitled *Highways and Byways* which were published by Macmillan to feed the growing Edwardian taste for tourism. Whilst working on the *Highways and Byways of Oxford and the Cotswolds* in 1903, Griggs visited Campden. He already knew of the town and the Guild for he was friendly with Wentworth Huyshe who also came from Hitchin. By October 1904 he had taken a room in Westcote House for a studio and had installed himself in Braithwaite House. He joined in the Guild's New Year production of *As You Like It* and in March 1905 was showing at the Guild's own exhibition. He later took a lease on Dover's House in the High Street and lived there until moving into his own house in 1930.

Griggs was not overtly religious when he arrived in Campden. Indeed an early friend recalled 'I did not at first take to him; chiefly, I think, because I disliked some atheistic opinions I heard him expressing ...'.[xiii] He came to the faith during his early years in the Cotswolds through his romantic vision of a rural, peaceful England that had been in decline since Henry VIII's dissolution of the monasteries in the 16th century. He wrote to his friend, Russell Alexander, just before his baptism on 19th February 1912:

> ... think of the Country, the sky + the seasons. Pastoral imagery & how it's derived mainly from the Scriptures, & what is there more beautiful? There's such a *world of beauty* in the Missal. The Mass itself is too wonderful for words - the most wonderful thing on earth ... [xiv]

His old friend, Huyshe, was also a convert and Griggs delighted in the growing Catholicism of the town: 'Must stop now, as some possible converts are coming to tea to meet the Parish Priest. Ps. I expect the Vicar here will resign or have fits soon!' [xv]

For St Catharine's Griggs designed a variety of furnishings including a silver chalice, candle sconces, the pulpit, vestment cupboard, copes and a chasuble. He also designed the Calvary in the graveyard and persuaded his brother-in-law, another recent convert, to pay for two bells.

His artistic vision was closely bound up with his faith and it is interesting that his first serious attempt at etching, the technique that was to make his reputation, was made in the same year he converted to Catholicism. Later, in 1926, Malcolm Salaman, the editor of *The Studio*, contributed to a series on contemporary etchers with a monograph on Griggs and he wrote of the artist as standing 'entirely by himself, a creative artist of essential originality, outstandingly so, ... his etchings are the artistic outcome of this whole emotional and spiritual being.[xvi] Nearly all of Griggs's highly distinctive etchings are architectural scenes of his imagination: ruined churches, looming towers, and gigantic bridges. The few anonymous people that are drawn serve to accentuate the vast bulk of the buildings. The landscapes surrounding these man-made structures with their rounded hills and trees clearly show Griggs's admiration for the visionary pastoral artist, Samuel Palmer, who was little appreciated in Griggs's lifetime. The springboard for these fantastical views sprang from his topographical work for Macmillan and a sketching trip he took to Ireland in 1916.[xvii] As early as 1900 Griggs wrote an article for *Architectural Review* on East Anglian churches and his words could serve as a description for his later etchings: '... their remoteness and melancholy beauty weave a spell of fascination that is irresistible ....' [xviii]

Griggs had to make his living from his art and, although he grew weary of them, Griggs illustrated 13 books in the *Highways and Byways* series between 1902 and 1938. He also undertook other illustrative work for books and magazines. All of these he saw as a distraction from his etchings and his perfectionism meant that his output was small. His Bond Street dealers, Colnaghi's, made a virtue of his slow methods and for a short time during the etchings boom of the late 1920s his work sold well enough to service his needs. But he was never a rich man and, towards the end of his life, his income dwindled so much that he was reduced to selling his own collection of Turner and Palmer etchings and to the support of friends.

Yet Griggs was an uncompromising visionary and so for the most part he simply ignored his financial difficulties and forged ahead to demand the very best from his surroundings. For example, as early as 1912 he was writing to Alexander, 'First then — I'm nearly bankrupt as usual so wish me well! Secondly I wish you to admire the Sir Francis Drake-like courage & sangfroid I have in negotiating for an eighty guinea Samuel Palmer.' [xix] Campden profited from his bravado. He regularly put up money he could ill afford and cajoled wealthy friends to save Campden from architectural disasters. His attitude was fiercely romantic: 'What is this nameless local force or influence? In Campden we call it Campden. It is what in the past gave us the town we know and love, and wish to preserve. While it was always itself, it was always growing and slowly changing. But there are forces at work which, because of their universality, are destructive of local traditions ...' [xx] Under the auspices of the Campden Society, which he founded in 1924, and later the Campden Trust, he bought shops and houses to renovate sympathetically and argued with the District Council and Utility Boards over council houses, wiring and the colour of telephone boxes. He also took on some private architectural commissions such as renovating two cottages on the High Street to create Miles House for his friend and fellow convert, Miss 'Mercy' Macauley, and designing the new Priest's House with Guy Pemberton in 1935. Perhaps his greatest single achievement for Campden was the saving of Dover's Hill from development in the face of local apathy. In 1926 he bid for the land and supported a £2,000 personal overdraft for two years until the debt was paid by Sir George Trevelyan.

On a more domestic scale, his vision and finances came to grief over New Dover's House (now known as Dover's Court). He bought land and outbuildings behind Leysbourne in 1926 intent on creating a house for himself and his family. In his notebooks Griggs writes of: 'The "moral touchstone" as it were — that a building should not be out of harmony with our better ideas & thoughts, ... & thus remind us, by a pleasant progression of thoughts & associations, to the works of God & heaven itself'.[xxi] However, he soon referred to Dover's Court as 'Griggs' Folly' and wrote, 'It's turning out to be a sort of life's job for me, and is as Quixotic as any fool or idealist (...) might wish. ... And I revel in the expensive contrariness.'[xxii] Men worked from his rough drawings. Griggs wanted to oversee every detail and bought the best local materials. He repeatedly called for things to be torn down and rebuilt if they failed to match up to the required standard.[xxiii] The house was praised for its craftsmanship and design but his income could not sustain it. The family moved into an unfinished house in 1930 and the following year he mortgaged it to stave off law suits from builders. By 1935 he had sold his beloved Samuel Palmer prints to stall foreclosure and in 1936 the unfinished house was put up for sale, though a buyer couldn't be found. Ill health, exacerbated by financial worries brought about his early death in 1938 at the age of 64.

Griggs's visionary idealism lives on in his art and in the architectural fabric of Campden. In his Memoirs, Ashbee declared, 'Campden and the Cotswolds owe more to Griggs than it is possible to repay. He was one of the leaders of its communal life, and represented ... the spirit of aesthetic conservatism and living craftsmanship for which the Guild of Handicraft stood.' [xxiv] But whereas Ashbee moved on, Griggs loved Campden with an intensity of spirit few can match. His close friend, Russell Alexander, summed up Griggs's feelings towards the town thus: 'Campden, to Griggs, was a passion — not merely for what it was ... but for what it represented, in his mind, as a survival, in its tenacious hold of what seemed to him to be older and better things than many of the things of today. He thought of Campden ... as a glorious and vanished, or vanishing, England.'[xxv]

An echo of Ashbee's view of Campden's artistic Catholics can be found in Michael Cardew's autobiography, *A Potter's Life.* He observed somewhat wryly that his old college friend, 'Finberg and his friends in Campden maintain the thesis that 20th century Western man ought to cultivate the spirituality of the West and rediscover his own European past, rather than go a-whoring after exotic cults of the far East.' [xxvi] Born in 1900, Herbert Finberg was the son of A.J. Finberg, the leading authority on Turner in his day. In 1921 Finberg's stepmother set up the Cotswold Gallery in London which specialised in work by artists of that region. The exhibitors included Griggs, Cardew, Woodroffe, and the Birmingham School group: Payne, the Geres, Southall and Gaskin. At Oxford Finberg had converted to Catholicism. He developed a strong friendship with Griggs in spite of their 24 year age difference and visited him often in Campden. By 1926 Griggs had found Finberg a job at the Shakespeare Head Press in Stratford. This was run by Bernard Newdigate, a fellow pupil with Woodroffe at the Catholic school, Stoneyhurst. Soon after joining Newdigate, Finberg moved out of Stratford to Campden and lived in Park Road, going to work every morning by train. 'For the next five years, Finberg lived alone in two rooms of a labourer's cottage ... It was a Spartan life — his lodgings had outside sanitation and no bathroom — but it was never dull, for at that time there was an exceptional concentration of artists and craftsmen in the town.' [xxvii]

In 1928 Finberg started his own press in Campden. Called the Alcuin Press, he explained that it was 'named after a friend of Charlemagne, Alcuin of York, whose monastic scriptorium played an important part in shaping the Roman alphabet into its present form'.[xxviii] He hoped the name would hark back to a mixture of monastic learning and good governance and cites a favourable review in *The Times* describing the press as 'making a sensible and successful effort to bridge the gulf between "private" and "commercial" printing'.[xxix] The venture was backed by Ben Chandler, a wealthy American who lived locally. He was a collector of prints and books and, at one time, had planned with Griggs to start a press in Campden. The press was housed in Ashbee's old malt barn behind Elm Tree House, which was now owned by the Catholic diocese of Clifton. On 24th March 1928 the Hon. Charles Noel (second son of the 3rd earl) amongst other trustees, granted a seven year lease at £40 p.a. This malt barn had been renovated and restored as part of the School of Arts and Crafts by Ashbee in 1904 and gave him a lecture hall on the upper floor and workshops below. It is thought that Herbert's printing office and composing room was the old lecture room upstairs, with machines downstairs in the old craft workshops.[xxx]

In *A Specimen of Some Printing Types in use at the Alcuin Press, with a note on the Press and its Aims* printed in 1928, Finberg wrote 'If beautiful surroundings help to promote good workmanship, no craftsman could be more fortunately situated.' The press's work was a mixture of antiquarian and modern books interspersed with diaries, catalogues, letterheads etc. The press gained uniformly good reviews for its simple, unassuming but adequate printing'[xxxi] and 'fine examples of modern typography'.[xxxii] Two books are particularly worth mentioning. The first is a two volume edition of *The Shropshire Lad* and *Last Poems* of A.E. Housman which in September 1929 ran to 325 copies. Many years later Finberg recalled[xxxiii] that Housman was initially very suspicious of private presses as the poet preferred 'ordinary editions of *The Shropshire Lad*, which being legible, are all that I could desire'.[xxxiv] However, through a friend of Griggs, the reclusive and difficult Housman was persuaded to grant permission. Housman wrote: 'Owing to my admiration of Griggs' etchings, I have reluctantly acceded to his wish to bring out a limited edition of both books at the Alcuin Press, which supposes itself to be very first class.'[xxxv]

The second book of which Finberg was especially proud was George Cavendish's *The Life and Death of Thomas Wolsey*, completed in August 1930 to commemorate the 400th anniversary of the great cardinal's death. The title pages were in red and black with decorative initials throughout designed by Woodroffe who had previously worked with Finberg at the Shakespeare Head Press. William Morris had printed an edition in 1893 but the Alcuin edition used a freshly transcribed text which for the first time was reproduced without editorial modification, exactly as Cavendish wrote it. The type chosen reproduced a font designed in Wolsey's own lifetime and special paper was manufactured from unbleached rag in Kent and watermarked 'Campden'. There were also a limited number of bindings in full crimson morocco with gold tooling executed by hand at the Alcuin Press. In a letter to Paul Woodroffe dated 6th November 1930, Finberg wrote: '*Wolsey* is being published this week, and has received nothing but praise from those who have seen it so far. Any merit that it has, however, is the result of your fine drawings. My share in the work has simply been to provide a setting for them, and if the setting is deemed not too unworthy by yourself and others I shall be well content. It has been, for me, a pleasant co-operation, and I hope it will not be the last time we work together in the making of a book.'

In 1930 Basil Fairclough joined Finberg in partnership. Chandler, Finberg's original backer, wanted his investment back and Fairclough was keen to learn the trade. Finberg and Fairclough had been to the same Oxford college, although several years apart, and they met through an Oxford printing club when Fairclough approached Finberg with a view to the Alcuin Press becoming the club's printer. Basil and his wife, Elizabeth, rented Dover's House in the High Street, since Griggs had moved to New Dover's House. They soon got involved with Campden life, becoming close friends with the Griggs and with the Russells. Fairclough also joined the organising committee of the Cotswold Art and Craft Exhibitions as Secretary and Treasurer.

But the relationship between the two men was never comfortable. Finberg's wife recalls Fairclough as 'a quiet young man, but in fact they did not get on well'. Fairclough felt that Finberg had begun to lose interest, leaving him to do much of the work.[xxxvi] Yet, in spite of this, business was growing as the press took on more commercial volumes, novels and some longer runs and reprints. However, the economic depression finally caught up with the Alcuin Press and soon things 'were quite hopeless, there was not enough money'.[xxxvii] This slump, the approaching end of the seven year lease, the death of the press's London agent, coupled with problems over the working relationship finally led to the sale of the Alcuin Press to The Chiswick Press of Welwyn Garden City in 1935. Finberg went on to become a distinguished academic and in 1952 became head of a newly formed department of English Local History at University College, Leicester. Fairclough went to work for Gordon Russell in charge of their printing, photography and exhibitions and later he worked at the Council for Industrial Design (now the Design Council).

The Alcuin Press printed 118 books in its seven years in Campden.[xxxviii] It worked with many of the major publishers of the day, employed modern techniques and machinery and was highly praised in its day for the fine books it produced. The Press was part of Campden's Arts & Crafts life of that era, and, like so much of the artistic life that began here, continued the creative spirit of the Guild of Handicraft and disseminated it far beyond the boundaries of Gloucestershire.

Notes

i Fees, Craig, *Christmas Mumming* 243: Ashbee, *Memoirs*, vol. VII, part 1, 342

ii Noel, G., 'Gerald Noel tells the remarkable tale of the Catholic cathedral of the Cotswolds', *Catholic Herald*, (undated) (2001?)

iii ibid note on 1851, 52,54

iv Verey and Brooks, *The Buildings of England* op cit 242

v 'Catholic Post-Reformation Missions in Gloucestershire: Chipping Campden' (undated) Parish Papers, (photocopy from Gloucester City Library)

vi Lunn was responsible for the large Jesuit church, Corpus Christi, at Boscombe and also Our Lady of the Annunciation, King's Lynn. Parish Papers. Letter from British Architectural Library to Rev. R.E Matus, 22 July 1991. Also Little, Bryan, Catholic Churches since 1623 (London, Robert Hale, 1966)

vii Lady Clarke, 'The Home Industry of Chipping Campden and its individualistic artist-craftsmen: Craftsmanship that flourishes by the creation and export of masterpieces in sculpture, stained glass, woodwork, silverware and textiles', *Illustrated London News* 12 December 1931 968-9

viii Quoted from Ashbee Journals 1st Jauary 1905 to Laurence Housman, MacCarthy, Fiona, *The Simple Life* op cit

ix Crawford, Alan, *C.R. Ashbee*, op cit 130

x Private Papers of Carol Jackson, Peter Gordon's analysis of Elm Tree House Deeds, 1921-8

xi CADHAS Archuives 1966/016/CH. Notes on talk to Campden Historical Society on 18th October 1990 by Peter Cormack, Deputy Curator of William Morris Gallery, Walthamstow

xii P. & D. Colnaghi & Co. Ltd. Memorial Exhibition of F.L.M. Griggs, RA, R.E, FSA, Hon. FRIBA. January 1939. Introduction by Hugh Walpole

xiii Mairet, Philip, *Autobiographical and Other Papers*, ed. C.H. Sisson (Carcanet, Manchester). 34-5 quoted in Moore, Jerrold Northrop, *F.L. Griggs: The Architecture of Dreams*, (Clarendon Press 1999)

xiv Letter to Russell Alexander, Ashmolean, Box 1

xv Letter to Russell Alexander, 19 March 1913, Ashmolean, Box 1 xvi Salaman, Malcolm C., 'Modern Masters of Etching No. 12. F.L. Griggs, ARA, R.E.' *The Studio*, 1926

xvii Moore, op cit Appendix, 270

xviii Griggs, F.L., 'Churches by the Sea: Notes at Some Dead Seaports of Sole Bay' *Architectural Review* Vol. 8, July -December 1900, 69-74

xix Letter to Russell Alexander, 23 October 1912, Ashmolean, Box 1

xx Griggs, F.L., *Campden, XXIV Engravings after Pen Drawings, with an introduction and notes by Russell Alexander* (Oxford. Shakespeare Head Press, 1940) 12-13

xxi Notebooks, 15. Private collection; photocopy in Ashmolean, Box 1

xxii Letter to Matthew B. Walker, 28 October 1927. Quoted in Wright, Harold J.L., *The Etched Work of F.L. Griggs, RA, R.E, FSA*, with a Catalogue by Campbell Dodgson, R.E. (The Printer Collectors Club, 1941) 39

xxiii Moore, op cit 196, note 28

xxiv Ashbee, Memoirs, Vol. VII Part I, 342 (In the Ashbee Collection, King's College Library, Cambridge)

xxv Griggs, *Campden*, 8

xxvi Cardew, Michael, *A Pioneer Potter: An Autobiography*, (OUP 1989) 76

xxvii Gostwick, Martin, *Three Lives in One, A Profile of Prof. H.P.R. Finberg*, unpublished, 1966 (Private Papers of Carol Jackson)

xxviii Finberg, H.L., *An Introduction to the Work & Aims of The Alcuin Press*, 1932, 3

xxix *The Times*, 'An Introduction,' June 8th 1929. 4;

xxx Mrs Josceline Finberg : Interview with Carol Jackson

xxxi *Fortnightly Review*, quoted in An Introduction, 15

xxxii Commonwealth, quoted in An Introduction, 13

xxxiii *Times Literary Supplement*, 17 December 1971

xxxiv Housman, letter to his publisher, 8 November 1908

xxxv Letter to Grant Richards dated 27th 1929 quoted in H.P.R. Finberg, 'Some Unpublished Housman Letters', *Times Literary Supplement*, 17th December 1971

xxxvi 'Most of the administrative and design work fell on Basil's shoulders.' Mrs Ann Porter: Interview.

xxxvii Mrs Josceline Finberg: Interview

xxxviii There existed in 1995 Mr Finberg's own hand-written record of all the books he printed. This lists a total of 118 books printed in Campden, excluding reprints, usually between 1 to 3 per month, the annual breakdown being as follows: 8 in 1928, 12 in 1929, 14 in 1930, 16 in 1931, 17 in 1932, 24 in 1933, 25 in 1934 and just 2 in 1935.

23

Other Artists, Writers and Craftworkers 1920 - 1955

A.J. Finberg, the printer's father, writing an introduction to the Cotswold Gallery's first exhibition in 1921 observed that the exhibitors' 'unity of spirit ... is partly due to the influence of their common surroundings, the silences and spaces of the Cotswold Hills, the freshness and clearness of the air they breathe'. Out of the twelve artists shown, eight either lived in or had a strong connection with Campden. He went on: 'The return to nature, the return to sanity and sobriety, the return to clearness and precision of expression which their work displays ... we may hail them as the heralds of a better and a brighter age.' [i]

These ideas of the cleansing quality of the countryside and the desire to get back to a purer form of artistic expression have already been discussed both in relation to Ashbee and his Guild and the inspiration of the Catholic faith. After the First World War this interest in the rejuvenating quality of 'the silences and spaces' was fuelled by the increasing accessibility of the countryside by the rail network and by the growth of the motor car. Campden, with its artistic roots already established by Ashbee and nourished by Griggs, was ideally placed to attract both more artists and the wealthy touring clients to support them.

This thriving community can be tracked by the Cotswold Art and Craft Exhibitions. In the first catalogue introduction written in 1924, Wentworth Huyshe declared: 'the Campdonian artists and craftsmen, wishing to perpetuate the reputation of the town as an art centre, and to continue as far as possible the work of the Guild founded by Mr Ashbee ... have conceived the idea of holding an exhibition of works ...' [ii] Eleven exhibitions were held between 1924 and 1936 by various bodies including The Campden Society, the Campden Guild of Craftsmen and the Gloucestershire Guild of Craftsmen. The committee members included former guildsmen such as Hart and Miller, and other artists already mentioned: Griggs, Finberg, Woodroffe and Fairclough. The Alcuin Press printed most of the catalogues and their books were exhibited alongside weaving, paintings, silver and furniture from local workshops, both amateur and professional, and from visiting artists who had links with the town.

One loose network of artists who lived in the town were all linked by their study and teaching at the Birmingham art schools and their membership of the Birmingham Group of Artist Craftsmen which started in 1907. The city had a strong Arts & Crafts tradition encouraged by the Birmingham-born colleague of William Morris, Burne-Jones, and a proud history of jewellery making. The Cotswolds could be seen as their place of inspiration and holiday making.

Arthur and Georgie Gaskin, with their two daughters Joscelyn and Margaret, all exhibited in the local Campden shows in the 1920s. They are considered the leading book illustrators and jewellers of the Arts & Crafts movement in Birmingham.[iii] The couple met at Birmingham School of Art and lived for most of their life in the city. Yet they visited their beloved Cotswolds often[iv] and in 1924 moved out to Campden where they spent their last years living at Little House, High Street.[v] Arthur was one of only five artists to work as an illustrator for the Kelmscott Press. He was commissioned by William Morris to produce designs for his romance *The Well at the World's End* and *The Shepheardes Calender*.[vi] Many of his illustrations include Cotswold landscapes or dry stone walls. He was also a tempera painter and a teacher at the Birmingham School of Art. In 1903 he became the head of the Vittoria Street School for jewellers. He appears to have been an excellent teacher, inspiring great affection from all who knew him. He was also a socialist, a pacifist and a teetotaller. In retirement living in Campden, Gaskin found a new style. He moved away from his medievalist Pre-Raphaelite manner of illustration to a much cleaner, more direct approach, inspired by the new artistic sensibilities of the 1920s epitomised by Eric Gill. He presented five woodcuts to the Victoria and Albert Museum in 1927 showing rural scenes with bold designs and exquisite artistry including Chipping Campden.[vii]

Georgie, his wife, 'was very much the stronger character' [viii] and although he was the teacher, she was the organiser and the jeweller: '... I did all the designing & he did all the enamel, and we both executed the work with our assistants'.[ix] Their jewellery was seen by contemporaries as a simplifying, more natural style using much silver and polished stones such as tourmaline, opal and chrysoprase: '... they turned to the East for inspiration ... the more primitive but integrated philosophy behind Eastern jewellery ...',[x] though to our 21st century eyes it seems very intricate with necklaces typically of double or triple chains and stones set in a background of lacy wirework.

Walter Allcott, another painter who studied at Birmingham, settled in Campden in 1919 when he was 39 and was a Chairman of the Exhibition of Arts and Crafts in the 1920s. He married the bookbinder, Maud Bird, whose studio had once been in Birmingham.[xi] She exhibited her bookbinding skills at the shows whilst her sister, Ida, entered examples of her hand woven materials. Ida ran the Weaving Rooms, Broadway. In 1928 the Allcotts moved south to Haslemere, Surrey — another centre for arts and crafts at that time.

A later arrival was Bernard Sleigh. He was another book illustrator, painter and teacher at the Birmingham School of Art and was a student and protégé of Arthur Gaskin. He started a trade apprenticeship with a Birmingham firm of engravers but, drawn to the more artistic side of illustration, came to the attention of Gaskin who arranged for him to teach a class of wood engraving at the Central School. Gaskin also contracted Sleigh to cut his illustrations for an edition of *Hans Andersen's Fairy Tales*.[xii] In his time Sleigh worked alongside many illustrators who knew Campden including William Strang, who had stayed at Braithwaite House and made drawings of the Ashbees and of Guild craftsmen. In 1902 Sleigh was commissioned to cut 13 pearwood blocks that Strang had drawn, to produce *The Doings of Death* published by the Essex House Press.[xiii] He also produced a book entitled *Wood Engraving since 1890 with 80 illustrations from the works of past and contemporary engravers — and many practical hints upon its technique and uses*, which included many artists linked with Campden such as: Gaskin, Gere, Griggs, the Housmans, Payne and Strang.

Following in his old teacher's footsteps, he retired to Old Forge Cottage, Cider Mill Lane, in the late 1930s[xiv] and in 1940 was to help cut some of Griggs's drawings alongside Clemence Housman and others for Griggs's *Campden* book, produced posthumously by his friend, Russell Alexander. Plagued by colourful visions throughout his adult life, in later years Sleigh became increasing drawn to fairies and the occult. He produced several books and murals of his visions which were sometimes augmented by experiments with the hallucinogenic drug mescalin. These fairyland designs were picked up by a textile firm for nursery murals and curtains. It is said that the psychedelic 'Sea Foam' graced the bedroom windows of the Princesses Elizabeth and Margaret at Buckingham Palace.[xv]

Other Birmingham artists in the wider Cotswold area also contributed to the shows, including the Geres and the Paynes. Charles Gere, another Kelmscott

Press illustrator, settled in Painswick with his half-sister, Margaret. They both exhibited in Campden and at the Cotswold Gallery, London. Their sister, Edith, living at St Loes Guild, Amberly, also showed work as did her husband, Henry Payne, another teacher at Birmingham School of Art, whose stained glass work includes the fine east window of St James's Church, dated 1924-5.

Other professional artists living in Campden in the 1920s were exhibition committee members W.K. Hudson and Reginald Sharpley. Hudson was a landscape painter who lived in Lower High Street. Sharpley began life as a civil engineer before turning to watercolours and etchings. His wife also exhibited at the shows with her own paintings and embroideries. There was also Joan Ayling, a miniaturist who studied at the Birmingham School of Arts and Crafts and was taught by Griggs at the Slade.[xvi] She rented Miles House in Leysbourne from him, eventually buying the property in 1926.[xvii] There were also enthusiastic amateurs such as Mrs Winifred and Miss Angela Heaton who collaborated on embroideries for the exhibitions; and the three Ramsay sisters who moved to Wales but still sent their work back to the town for the shows.

Norman Jewson, the architect and designer, was based at Sapperton but examples of his work can be seen all around Campden. He and Griggs formed a loose partnership and they worked together under the auspices of the Campden Trust to repair many houses in the town including the Old King's Arms (later Caminetto) and the Plough. Jewson worked on St James's Church. He refurnished the north chapel and the communion rails and screens are designed by him.[xviii] He also designed The Tithe House opposite the Church for the local historian and poet, Christopher Whitfield.

In the late 1920s, Leo and Eileen Baker set up as the Kingsley Weavers. Eileen had been an apprentice to the great hand weaving expert, Ethel Mairet, who for a time had lived in the Norman Chapel at Broad Campden with her first husband, Ananda Coomaraswamy. The Bakers followed Mairet's principles by taking '... the local girls — who ask to be taken — and set them to learn by experiment and experience, mindful of the days when weavers were made by long apprenticeship and not by class teaching and school design'.[xix] They set up their business at Westcote House, which had been renovated by Jewson and Griggs in 1926, and their looms were in a converted barn on the other side of the High Street, behind Dover's House.[xx] Along with Hart, Russell and others, they were active members of the Rural Industries Bureau, a government body set up to promote rural crafts during the post-war depression.

The Kingsley Weavers, c1931 *(By kind permission of Brian Wheatcroft)*

Leo Baker wrote an article entitled 'Hand-woven' for the Bureau's magazine in September 1927. In it he argues for the education of the consumer in recognising the superior qualities of handspun material.[xxi] This may well have been a plea from the heart, for a local guide book also mentions the Bakers and notes: 'During the Summer months tea is provided and guests are taken.'[xxii] This is a classic example of the inter-war phenomenon of combined tea and craft shops: the tourism propping up the more rarefied craft work, to the disgust of some fellow craftworkers. As Gordon Russell argued in the same Rural Industries' magazine: '... it shows the attitude of mind of many people towards the crafts. Just things in which to interest people at tea-time — secondary to tea, no doubt.'

Although Gordon Russell's commercial premises were based in Broadway and in London, Russell was educated at Campden Grammar School and later commissioned a house for himself and family beside Kingcombe Lane on the outskirts of Campden. The Green Dragon, a building in the High Street was owned by Russell between 1914 and 1923 and it is possible he had planned with the Harts to use the property for a Cotswold Craft Guild.[xxiii] Russell's modern take on Ashbee's craftsmanship was described in 1928 by the editor of *Cabinet Maker* as 'an enlightened alliance between handicraft and machine craft',[xxiv] and resulted during the Second World War in his stewardship of the Utility Furniture Range. Later he became Chairman of the Council of Industrial Design and an organiser of the Festival of Britain in 1951.

Mention must also be made of Robert Welch, the other designer of long standing in Campden, who successfully managed to combine the old crafts like silversmithing with a new commercialism. Welch was born in Hereford in 1929 and studied at the Royal College of Art. As a student, he toured Scandinavia and inspired by their innovative use of stainless steel, Welch began to specialise in the metal. After graduating he was taken on by J. & J. Wiggin, a small family firm based at Bloxwich, north of Birmingham. When he needed a studio to rent nearby, in a pleasing circular story, Griggs suggested the old Silk Mill: the very place where the Guild had first started. Welch rented rooms amongst the former Guild silversmiths and builders in 1955 and stayed there for the rest of his life. In 1969 he took over the shop on the corner of Sheep Street, another of Jewson's renovated buildings, where the family still trade today.[xxv]

As well as artists and craftsmen a number of writers lived in Campden during the first half of the century. In the 1930s writers such as Graham Greene (another convert to Catholicism) lived here, and T.S. Eliot was an annual visitor, staying with friends who, like many people, took a house here each summer. Campden exerted a considerable influence on both writers. Graham Greene, living here from 1931 to 1933, was deeply affected by the drama and comedy of life in the town, which he always referred to as a village, and by the vividness of the characters he came across.

At 5.45 pm on March 2nd 1931 Graham Greene, his young wife, Vivien, and her Pekinese dog arrived at Little Orchard Cottage in Hoo Lane to find mice running up the wainscoting.[xxvi] They were renting the cottage for £1 a week. Greene was 26 and he had just finished a three-year period working as a sub-editor on *The Times* in London and had made enough money to live on for three years. He says in his autobiography, *A Sort of Life*, 'We had found a thatched cottage (that pastoral Georgian dream of the industrial twenties), with a small garden and orchard, up a muddy lane on the edge of Chipping Campden.' [xxvii] That first night the young couple were very frightened, with no sound of traffic, only a hooting owl. After dark there was a knock on the door and an unknown woman was standing on the doorstep, swinging a dead rat by the tail. She just wanted to let them know that there were rats.

They enjoyed home-brewed bitter from the Noel Arms. Edmund Blunden, the poet, visited them for lunch on one occasion in June 1932 and they drank parsnip and cowslip wine from Mr Rathbone, the landlord at the Volunteer, which did not affect the head but had a great effect on the legs.

In August 1932 the Cotswold Exhibition was held in town. There were drawings by Charles Wade, what Greene considered some bad paintings of barns by Rothenstein, the artist who lived at Far Oakridge, and some lovely plates. The Greenes talked to F. L. Griggs 'who was purring over the exhibits, which satisfied his arts and crafts mind'.[xxviii] Generally Greene does not seem to have approved of the Arts & Crafts movement and he did not like what he described as Alec Miller's usual sentimental wood-reliefs of children.

The Greenes knew Charles Wade from the Manor at Snowshill and visited him there, but Graham Greene was afraid of Wade's sudden capacity to insult, and did not really make friends with him. Sometimes they would walk to Snowshill with Fred Hart, and would find people such as Betjeman visiting Wade. Greene liked Fred Hart, the collector brother of George and Will, who would give the young couple his home-made currant and gooseberry wine to drink when they called on him, and very good they thought it. From his collection of objects, he gave Vivien a set of ivory chessmen so they could play on top of her work-table. He was a generous friend to them, usually arriving to see them with gifts. They frequently accompanied him to sales of antiques.

Graham Greene's habit of walking everywhere, to Evesham, or to Moreton, made him concerned about public footpaths and when in 1932 the Hon. Charles Noel closed the Old Gallop he campaigned with Fred Hart to have it reopened, writing to the Society for the Preservation of Footpaths and the Rural District Council. The RDC appointed a committee to look into the matter and the agents of Charles Noel responded by saying they never intended to dispute the right to walk on the path. In February 1933, Greene reports, there was so much sleet and rain that Hoo Lane was impassable, and the High Street like a ploughed field.

Greene finished his novel, *Rumour at Nightfall*, in April 1931, and he completed *It's a Battlefield*, published in 1934, writing at the cottage window, but after his Campden experiences, decided that in future he needed to write more strongly. Vivien was expecting a baby, there was money from the sale of film rights, and they left in June 1933 to live in Oxford. By then Campden had spread its special influence.

The year after Graham Greene left Campden, T.S. Eliot arrived for the first time. At this time in his life Eliot's marriage was causing great distress. He was separated from his wife, Vivienne, who was refusing to accept the situation. In fear of pursuit, he had to keep his address a secret from almost everyone. Meanwhile, his youthful friendship with Emily Hale from Boston, Massachusetts had been revived, and in 1934 she took a year's leave from her teaching post at Scripps College in America to come to England, where Eliot was. Emily Hale joined her relatives, the Rev. and Mrs Perkins who were installed for the summer in Stamford House in Leysbourne, a house they rented from Miss Sunderland-Taylor.[xxix] Emily was to have the adjoining Stanley Cottage and there Eliot was invited to visit her.

Edith Perkins was a dedicated gardener who liked to photograph local gardens and sometimes Eliot went with her on these visits. He loved Hidcote. He also spent much time walking in the countryside with Emily Hale. In 1935 he told Mrs Perkins that he came to feel 'at home' [xxx] in Campden in a way in which he had not felt at home for some twenty-one years. On another occasion, Eliot in different mood observed grimly that Campden suited the Perkinses with its 'olde worlde atmosphere stinking of death'.[xxxi] But mostly he seems to have been happy here with Emily and her aunt and uncle.

Lyndall Gordon quotes a letter from Emily Hale to her head of faculty in the States in which she describes their happy, quiet life in Campden. 'We live a very quiet — to some a too quiet life perhaps — as the residents in a town of 2,000 citizens. All marketing purchases are delivered by hand, the bread comes out of a large basket on the arm of a man too small to carry it, or the milkman stands like a reincarnated Roman charioteer, in his two-wheeled cart, driving his gay sage pony, who knows at just which house he shall wait, or the quiet voiced butcher hands you a leg or a shoulder in a quite callous manner!' Nevertheless, the newspaper articles relating to 'war talk' were depressing. Dr Perkins was sure much was going on in Germany of which they knew nothing. It was difficult to know, as there were few men in Campden who moved 'in state circles'.[xxxii]

Probably in late August or early September Eliot and Emily Hale strayed from their walk into the private grounds of Burnt Norton. The estate is owned by the Earls of Harrowby and in 1936 the 6th Earl and Countess took up residence. When Eliot got lost there it was unoccupied and they explored the garden, which was then a neglected formal garden with box hedges and a processional path leading from a door through a rose garden to a large circular lawn with two empty concrete rectangular pools. The poem, *Burnt Norton*, one of the *Four Quartets*, explores the past, and other selves that might have been, and seems to refer to the love he might have shared with Emily had things not been otherwise. It must have been strange for the Harrowbys to find that their garden had given the title to one of the 20th century's most famous poems, especially when Eliot had been there without their permission. Certainly the Countess of Harrowby was rather indignant that Eliot had thought the house belonged to a Birmingham businessman.

Eliot had not wanted to attract the public gaze when he was in Campden and it is fascinating to think of this world-famous poet quietly walking about Campden, unrecognised.

Campden played a part again in Emily Hale's life in 1957. Vivienne had died by now, and suddenly and surprisingly in January that year Eliot had married again. It was a tremendous blow to Emily. She was able to bear the situation in which Eliot did not respond to her love for him so long as he was not in love with anyone else, but when he married someone else and cut her off she could not deal with the pain it caused her. He had presumably felt too guilty about his feelings for her to be able to consummate the relationship with her. After an emotional breakdown in Boston, she decided in October 1957 to return to Campden, the place where she had been so happy in the thirties. But she appeared disturbed to locals and did not settle. By February 1958 she was back in Boston. This time Campden had failed to work its magic.

Notes

i National Art Library Cat 200.B 140.A
ii Foreword by Wentworth Huyshe, *Chipping Campden Exhibition of Arts and Crafts*, 1924
iii Crawford, Alan, *Arts and Crafts Walks in Broadway and Chipping Campden* (G of H Trust 2002) 65
iv e.g. The New Inn, Willersey dated 11 July 1898. Cat. No. C38 in Breeze, George et al., *Arthur and Georgie Gaskin* (Birmingham, BMAG, 1981)
v Now Camperdene House
vi The other artists were Charles Gere, Walter Crane, Robert Catterson-Smith and Burne Jones. Morris decided upon Burne Jones designs for *The Well at World's End* but *The Shepheardes Calender* with illustrations by Gaskin was published in 1896. Rathbone, N., 'The Gaskins as Illustrators', in Breeze, et al., *Arthur and Georgie Gaskin*, 23
vii Laver, J., 'Campden', *The Studio*, vol. XCV, 1928, 352-3
viii Breeze, G., 'Introduction' in Breeze, et al, *Arthur and Georgie Gaskin*, 10
ix Georgie to Kaines Smith undated letter but early February 1929. File at BMAG. Quoted in Wild, G., 'The Gaskins as Craftsmen', in Breeze et al, *Arthur and Georgie Gaskin*, 62
x Wainwright, 'The Jewellery of Mr and Mrs Gaskin', *The Studio*, vol. LXI, 1914, 296
xi Tidcombe, M., *Women Bookbinders*, 1880-1920 (Delaware, Oak Knoll Press & London, British Library, 1996) 174
xii Cooper, R., 'Bernard Sleigh, artist and craftsman, 1872-1954', *DAS Journal*, no. 21, 1997, 88-102
xiii Sleigh, B., *Wood Engraving since 1890 with 80 illustrations from the works of past and contemporary engravers - and many practical hints upon its technique and uses* (London, Pitman & Sons, 1932) 35
xiv He retired in 1937. Cooper, 'Bernard Sleigh,' 100
xv Cooper, op cit 100
xvi Waters, Grant M., *Dictionary of British Artists Working 1900 - 1950* (Eastbourne Fine Art, 1975)
xvii Peter Gordon's notes, CADHAS Archive 2000/109/DS
xviii Crawford, A., *Arts and Crafts Walks*, op cit 57
xix Lady Clarke, 'The Home Industry of Chipping Campden' op cit 968-9
xx Crawford, A., *Arts and Crafts Walks*, op cit 61
xxi Baker, L., 'Handwoven', *Rural Industries*, September 1927, 3-4, 13
xxii Griffiths, J., *Chipping Campden Today and Yesterday* (Campden, T Elsley, 1931) 10
xxiii Peter Gordon's notes op cit 6
xxiv John Gloag quoted in Harrod, T., *The Crafts in Britain in the 20th Century* (London, Newhaven, c. 1999), 67
xxv Crawford, Alan, Introduction to Welch, Robert, *Design in a Cotswold Workshop* (London, Lund Humphries, 1973) 8, 12
xxvi Webb, Christine, Article in *The Times*, 16 Oct 1999
xxvii Greene, Graham, *A Sort of Life* (Vintage, 1999) 145
xxviii Extracts from Graham Greene's diary quoted in Carolyn Mason's papers, op cit
xxix Gordon, Lyndall, *Eliot's New Life* (OUP 1989), 44
xxx ibid
xxxi Gordon, Lyndall, *T.S. Eliot An Imperfect Life* (Vintage 1998), 315
xxxii ibid

PART VI: THE TWENTIETH CENTURY

24

'Like a Bolt from the Blue'

Although the peace of Campden was about to be brutally shattered by the start of the First World War, few if any of its people had any comprehension of the horrors that lay ahead. Miss Josephine Griffiths, the then middle-aged daughter of Mr W.H. Griffiths, the wealthy solicitor of Bedfont House, was to be accurately portrayed on her death as 'a wit, a saint and a scholar'.[i] Her 'most precious memorial', to quote one of the several historians who have quoted her work,[ii] is her beautiful leather-bound Book of Remembrance, now displayed in St. James's Church. Written in 1923 and decorated with hedgerow and garden flowers, it is inscribed in her ornate calligraphy. In it she recorded the names of 333 Campden men and a single nurse, Minnie Wixey, who between them served in 60 different regiments and 13 ships on 19 battle-fronts of war. On 64 of the deceased whom she had known she wrote short and often moving biographies. Among her various appendices, added later, she includes the names of a further 25 men who served and five who died of their wounds after the war was over.

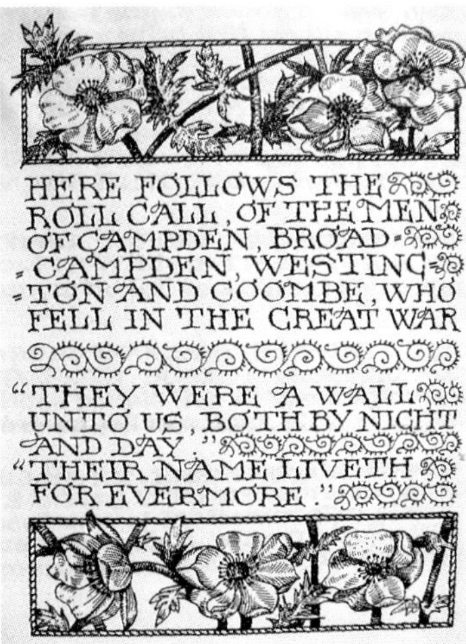

The Introductory page of the Book of Remembrance by Josephine Grifftihs

Josephine Griffiths calculated that 22.6 per cent of those who served had either been slain in action or had died from disease. However, her knowledge was limited and the work of her successors suggests that the number who served may have numbered 450, and that up to one hundred of them may have lost their lives. As Campden's population was 1,608 in 1911, these later figures confirm the proportion of deaths estimated by Miss Griffiths, some one in five of those who served: numbers hard indeed to visualise.[iii]

That sad but vivid book includes a number of sketches of life in Campden during the war years. One of them recalls the eerie lull between the declaration of war and the calling away of husbands and fathers, sons and brothers, a brief moment when the familiar was made unreal by the menace of what might come.

> It was on August 4 1914 that war was declared. That Monday was the August Bank Holiday; and all Campden and the neighbourhood, were gathered together in the pleasant Vicarage garden for the annual Parish Fete, the proceeds of which helped so successfully to finance the many needs of sick and poor during the winter. There were attractive stalls under the trees, tea tables dotted over the lawn; games and other amusements in different parts of the garden; there was the laughter of little people, the scent of flowers and the lovely summer sunshine. The school-children and others, had delighted their audience with a pastoral play; and later on there was dancing on the lawn for the young folk, by the light of Chinese lanterns. Like a bolt from the blue had come the terrible news in the morning; and it had been too late to put off the Parish Fete. The next morning, August 5, the first detachment of Campden men left on active service.[iv]

This 'first detachment' was the regular reservists recalled to the colours. A larger body, members of D (previously K) Company of the 5th Battalion the Gloucestershire Regiment, made up of Territorial Army volunteers from Campden and Moreton, were already in uniform, having hoped to enjoy themselves at their annual fortnight's training camp at Marlow-on-Thames.[v] There was something of a military tradition in Campden, similar to many other small rural places. As touched on earlier, since the end of the 18th century volunteers of one sort or another, usually farmers' or tradesmen's sons, had been raised to protect the country from invasion by the French or to help the regulars, and later the police, in quelling riots. Among the major and long overdue reforms of the British Army, set under way by Edward Cardwell, Gladstone's Secretary of State for War, had been the reorganisation of the late Victorian infantry into two-battalion county regiments, with a training depot and affiliated volunteer units. Thus came about the Gloucestershire Regiment. But the continuing inadequacies revealed during the Boer War of 1899-1902 led to further reforms and the conversion of the Volunteers into a County Territorial Force, of which the Gloucesters were to have three battalions, the 4th, 5th and 6th. The K company of the 5th Gloucester Territorials was raised in Campden and Moreton.[vi]

Left: The Armoury of the 2nd Volunteer Battalion, The Gloucestershire Regiment (now HSBC Bank)
Right: A group of Campden men of H Company, 5th Territorial Battalion, Gloucester Regiment in camp at Beaulieu, about 1910.

The annual training camps, held in such places as Lulworth and Salisbury Plain, gave the working man a paid holiday from his routine work, something previously unknown, together with the chance of seeing a bit of life outside rural Campden. On 2nd August 1914 the 5th Battalion had already left for Marlow, and there it was to be mobilised. In the local company were 41 Campden men, three of them officers, including Edward Noel, Viscount Campden, the future 4th Earl of Gainsborough.[vii] Sent immediately to Chelmsford by way of the Isle of Wight, they left for the Western Front in March 1915. Their families had waved them goodbye in August for what they thought was to be no more than a temporary break. Many were not to see their men again until they appeared for a short embarkation furlough the following year before they left for the Western Front.

Some other Campden men had in fact already seen a lot of life beyond Mickleton or Blockley. There were 37 regulars already with their regiments or ships. The Cardwell reforms had also set radically new terms of service. In the past men had soldiered on until they wore out or died. Now they enlisted for a fixed number of years with a further number on the reserve. Mature men had come home with fascinating tales of life in places as far afield as China, Jamaica, India or South Africa. In the Boer War alone, some 46 local men had served either as regulars or volunteers: 'more men than any other town' according to Canon Bourne of Weston-sub-Edge.[viii] Far more soldiers in South Africa died of disease rather than enemy fire: of these, three Campden men are named in a memorial in St. James's Church, but the names of three others have recently been learned.[ix] Of the 37 local regulars already serving in August 1914, 12 were to lose their lives before that war ended.

The first of the Campden men to follow the regulars were the reservists and the territorials. But for many young men the news they heard on 4th August did not seem quite so terrible as Miss Griffiths remembered, writing as she was when the war was over. For most of the single men war was, as ever, a challenge and an adventure, an appeal to their vivid patriotism. Their womenfolk saw it a different way. Campden's men flocked to enlist for the vast New Armies that Lord Kitchener, the Secretary of State for War, accurately foresaw would be needed to win a long drawn out World War. But as the months passed and more men died or were wounded, such volunteers were not enough. The cherished British voluntary system was abandoned, and in January 1916 the Military Service Act enforced conscription on all unarmed men between 18 and 41. Appeals could, however, be made. George Hart, the silversmith, and no longer a young man, who was mainly working on his farm, employing two men and two boys, was granted conditional exemption,[x] as were many others. Some men who had not been called up, like Charlie Downer and Paul Woodroffe, worked in munitions.

Meanwhile many of the women of Campden were starting to take over their absent menfolk's work, either on the land or in their businesses. Others were tackling the charitable tasks that arose. One of the first was the care of five Belgian families, Campden's share of more than 100,000 women, children and old people, refugees from their country's invasion by the Germans. Press accounts of rape and murder, often grossly exaggerated, aroused overwhelming sympathy for these victims of the war. The first batch of 22 people arrived in Campden in October: but in the end 42 in all found shelter here; five Belgian soldiers also spent their leave from the Western Front visiting their families. Housing was found for them all; food and medical aid was forthcoming; individuals, voluntary groups and local charities all provided money or goods. Some Campden families took individual refugee children into their homes, and a farmer gave them daily supplies of milk. The owner of Norton Hall decorated and furnished one cottage, two other individuals did the same, and Lady Gainsborough made three acres of land available to a Belgian family in Broad Campden. Norton Hall itself became a V.A.D. hospital (a hospital staffed by volunteer nurses). There and elsewhere many local women nursed the sick and the wounded.[xi]

Even the children did what they could, and in September 1916 they were granted a half-holiday to pick blackberries for the Army and Navy: they brought back 223 pounds. However, when the Farmers' Association proposed that nine-year-olds should be released from school to do farm work, there was stern opposition. Alec Miller, who had a malformed shoulder and could not serve, called it 'reactionary and subversive of the nation and of agriculture itself'.[xii]

The war years brought hardships. Farming was seriously threatened by the shortage of labour, there were two severe winters, and inflation was high. Some foods were constantly in short supply, particularly meat, fish, butter and suet, and there was little bread. Janet Ashbee wrote of living mainly on parsnips, potatoes, leeks, onions, and eggs. Many sports and entertainments stopped altogether: hunting, the town band, the Boy Scouts.

Throughout the war everyone was doing all they could for 'the comfort of the brave men at the front', as Miss Griffiths put it. Needles and scissors were busy as women snatched the time to knit and sew; weekly Red Cross meetings were organised to produce further garments and bandages. 'One aged inmate of the almshouses knitted over 400 pairs of socks, besides making two dozen vests and other clothes.' [xiii] Parcels for those away from home, especially before Christmas, had to be filled and packed. The Red Cross always needed money and what were known nationwide as 'Our Days' were held. On 25th September 1918 Miss Griffiths remembered:

> 'Our Day' blossomed out into a wonderful Fete. The beautiful grey old town ... was gay with flags and bunting. It was a great day; for everyone did the utmost to make it a success. There were stalls in the market hall, to which folk contributed whatever they could do without, from sheep and

> pigs; poultry and game; cheese, butter and garden produce; up to rare silks, costly bronzes and china; and Indian gold-embroidered table and table cloths ... and over all was the splendid autumn sunshine.

£300 was raised (some £15,000 in today's money) a large sum indeed when wages provided a bare livelihood. The Soldiers and Sailors Families Association was already active. They brought sympathy and help to those who opened their doors to face a red-coated post-office boy carrying the telegram that would bring the news that their loved ones were wounded, missing or dead.[xiv]

During 1914 the bad news came slowly. Just five men died, including the 39 year old Chief Engine Room Artificer Basil Neve, son of the postmaster, whose ship HMS Pathfinder was torpedoed on 5th September. Each year as the fighting intensified more and more Campden men were drawn in and the reported deaths multiplied: thirteen in 1915, twenty-two in 1916 but just eleven in 1917, when the greatest burden of the Western Front fell on the French. In 1918, however, numbers once again increased to a terrible total of twenty-five in that final year of the war, almost all lost on the Western Front in the spring months; but then more during the summer and autumn with the main losses of the final battles falling on the soldiers of Britain and her Empire. How many Campden men were wounded has not been recorded, but with a national average of three for every one who died, during that last year of the war the sight of those approaching messenger boys must have become even more horrifically familiar.

Most losses occurred on the Western Front, strange names such as Loos, Ypres, the Marne and the Somme becoming known to all. The telegrams were usually followed by letters written by officers or warrant officers who might or might not have known the individuals well. One such letter was addressed in December 1914 to Mrs Ashwin by her son's company sergeant-major:

> I am truly sorry to have to inform you that your son, 9692 Pte. H. Ashwin is dead. He was killed on the 18th or 19th Nov in the woods near Ypres. During one afternoon after some hard fighting Harold was shot and succumbed to his wounds in a very few minutes. He was buried near the place he fell by men of his own regiment, although much firing was in progress. He was very well liked by all his comrades, and everyone was very sorry to learn of Harold's untimely death.[xv]

Others died in even more obscure places. Another Noel, Robert, succumbed to dysentery in 1918 while serving in the East African campaign. The shellshock suffered by Alfred James in Salonika led to paralysis of the throat and heart trouble which he survived until 1923.[xvi]

Letters from the Front hinted at the reality the troops were facing. In September 1915 Lance-Corporal Algy Hathaway, a widow's youngest son, 'a bright and cheerful lad' who worked at the Post Office,[xvii] wrote home from the Dardanelles:

> It is hot out here. We dare not say where we are, but we are in the thick of it. I hope it will soon be over. I hope everything is going on all right at home. I am all right up to the time I post this, and I hope God will spare me to get through safe.[xviii]

A little later Charles Hedges wrote:

> Sorry I have not written before, but we have had a little hell this last few weeks; but it has all come out in our favour. We have had some very terrible weather here, to make it worse for us, up to our knees in mud and water ... I can thank God for bringing me safely through without a scratch. ... I never was in such a mess and so tired in all my life.

Algy Hathaway died fighting the Turks with the 7th Gloucesters at Gallipoli, a few weeks after writing to his mother,[xix] and Charles Hedges only a few days after sending his letter.[xx] Mrs Hathaway had two other sons at the front. Another Campdonian wrote home to his aunt about Hedges: 'He was caught right in the head and was killed outright. I did not see him but I was not far off at the time. You must break the news quietly to his folks. Fancy! I am the only one from Campden left in this Battalion.'[xxi]

Letters like these, awkward, censored, with their understated eloquence, continued to arrive, to be passed around close friends and relatives, often tear-stained, some to be published in the *Evesham Journal*. William Tracey had already lost a son in the Boer War and of his five others who served in this one, two were killed. One of them, Harry, was a reservist who had emigrated to Australia; nevertheless he returned to die with the Worcestershire Regiment in 1915. Harry was one among thousands who had emigrated to the Empire before the war to make new lives for themselves but now returned to fight for their beliefs. Gordon Ellis, Harry Ellis's 'fine looking lad', who had served in the Campden Boys Brigade and then in the local territorials, left for Canada where he joined the Saskatchewan Light Horse; in May 1915 he also fell on the Western Front. Seven other Campden men came back from Canada to fight for the old country, as did others with the South African and New Zealand forces.[xxii]

The war did not prevent people bickering about the town's petty affairs. There was a rambling debate in the Parish Council on whether, because of the war, public houses should close an hour earlier. With happy arrogance, a Mr A.

Walton declared that he 'had studied the working class' and considered that 'working men should be in bed by ten'. To this Mr Keitley added inconsequentially that 'old Jim Court used to sleep in public houses all night and he's nearly 90'.[xxiii] Then there was the government proposal to save daylight by changing the clock. Ulric Stanley thought 'it was all tomfoolery to say people should go to bed an hour earlier ... the only effect was that they worked an hour longer during the day'. And Mr Haines rightly added that 'the Act affected the senders of milk in the morning more than anyone else. Would they get their men to start milking at three in the morning? In haymaking, too, they could not start an hour earlier, because the dew would not be off.'[xxiv] The chairman admitted that 'in his own case his wife wanted to go by the new time and he wanted to go by the old time, and then there was a bother'. Because of an unlit lamp near the chestnut tree pillar-box, someone complained (as ever) of 'darkness lending itself to the committal of nuisances'. Such was the concern about zeppelin raids 'which had come as close as Stratford and Birmingham', that the tops of street lamps were painted. Later they were put out altogether.[xxv]

On 11th November, 1918, the Armistice was signed that ended the war. Campden men continued to be killed and wounded almost to the end. In the weeks and months that followed, a few at a time, the surviving servicemen returned, some of them wounded, many of them mentally scarred. One or two of their stories survive. Frank Voyles, who had been a butcher in Campden, told his neighbour, Lionel Ellis, that he had seen the Angels of Mons: '... there was no doubt about it'. Then there was Charlie Ladbrook who had gone missing in Mesopotamia in 1916: 'Ah, if you'd been shot at like those Turks had been shooting at me, you'd have been missing for two days', he told Lionel Ellis, who added 'he got shot in the ankle and finished up in Russia with the White Army'.[xxvi]

Reynell Huyshe, commissioned in the King's Shropshire Light Infantry, was wounded twice at Ypres. He had once been buried alive by a shell and was rescued in a state of utter exhaustion. He returned suffering from shell-shock and wounds. Jack Newton Horne of the Grenadier Guards was shot through the elbow in 1918. He spent part of his convalescence at the Dormy House, just outside Campden, but his arm was useless and he was discharged. He became a second lieutenant in the Home Guard in the Second World War and died in 1986 at the age of 87. George Howley of the Scots Guards served at Ypres.

George was wounded in the leg; gangrene set in and the leg had to be amputated. Campden people remember him in local pubs constantly massaging his stump. He once told Lionel Ellis how grateful he was to the Guild bathing lake in Campden as there he had learned to swim underwater. At the battle of the Somme, Howley had swum underwater in order to avoid German gunfire and that had saved his life.[xxvii]

Not all who died did so during the war years from bullet, shell, disease or poison gas. Some lingered on for a few more months or years. Seven of them at last found their peace in St. James's churchyard, their graves — like those of their comrades who died abroad — dignified by the plain memorial stones of the Imperial War Graves Commission.

Notes

i West, John, 'A Book of Remembrance', *Local History*, Jan-Feb 1998

ii The first to add to Griffiths's invaluable work was John Macartney, who transferred it to computer in tabular form and filled in blank spaces. At the same time he contacted Paul Hughes who was undertaking a wider project on Campden in WW1. Using the latter's data which included twelve previously unrecorded names of those who had died, Macartney produced his `Revised Book of Remembrance' now displayed in St. James's Church. Details are in Macartney, John, 'Chipping Campden and Two World Wars', *CADHAS Notes & Queries*, Vol II, No 3. West's vivid article (op cit) followed. This chapter is largely based on the work of these three historians, as well as that of Paul Hughes who is writing a book on Campden during World War 1 (West, Note 5), based on his meticulous research. His *Correspondence* is in CADHAS Archive 2003/203/DO. To them all the authors are grateful.

iii Hughes, *Corresp* 13, gives the total of 450. See Macartney, 'Revised Book', for total killed.

iv Griffiths, J., 'Concerning the Declaration of War'. This and later references to Griffiths are to her section headings

v Hughes, Paul, *Corresp* 4

vi ibid 6

vii Griffiths mistakenly states he died in West Africa, not East Africa

viii *Evesham Journal* 16 June 1900

ix Macartney, 'Chipping Campden in Two World Wars', op cit

x Griffiths, 'Roll Call of the Men of Campden'; Hughes *Corresp* 13

xi Griffiths, 'Concerning the Work in Campden during the Great War'

xii *Evesham Journal* 10 March 1917

xiii ibid

xiv ibid

xv *Evesham Journal* 16 Dec 1914

xvi Griffiths, 'Roll Call'

xvii Griffiths, 'Roll Call'

xviii *Evesham Journal* 11 September 1915

xix ibid 11 Sep 1915

xx His cousin, William Charles Hedges, had already died two months earlier at Loos, together with two other Campden men.

xxi *Evesham Journal* 23 October 1915

xxii Hughes, *Corresp* 12

xxiii *Evesham Journal* 4 Sep 1915

xxiv ibid 3 Jun 1916

xxv ibid 12 Feb 1916

xxvi Oral Tapes, Lionel Ellis (CADHAS Archives 1980s)

xxvii Lionel Ellis, Tape 5

25

Between the Wars[1]

As Miss Griffiths remembered how the war started so she recounted its end:

> At 5.30 a.m. on November 11 A.D. 1918 the armistice was signed; and all hostilities ceased at 11 a.m. Was there ever a more glorious Martinmas; or were there ever more wonderful happenings on the feast-day of that soldier-saint? It was hard, at first, to believe the good news; but the wire announcing the fact, received from the War Office, had already been put up in the Post office window, for everyone to see. And suddenly the bells pealed out, which during the war had been silent; and like magic, the streets were bright with flags; and people were laughing and crying at the same time. And at 3 o'clock in the afternoon all hurried to the Parish Church for a great Thanksgiving Service. There, where the men of Campden in the fighting-line, had been daily remembered before the Altar, "it was meet to sing unto the Lord, for He hath triumphed gloriously". The wounded men from Norton Hall V.A.D. Hospital had chairs in the Nave; and in spite of crutches, pain and suffering, their joy was indescribable. This wonderful day ended with a bonfire in the Square, and the singing of the National Anthem with patriotic enthusiasm. But, hush! Amid all that gladness, there were broken hearts, and tearful eyes, and deep mournings.[ii]

In 1918 Campden was a quiet and remote place, affected deeply by the war, and by other national events, but also like many similar small towns, inward looking and focused on its own local politics. Several incidents serve to demonstrate this duality. To national jubilation the Armistice was signed on 11th November. The soldiers who returned had to deal with the trauma of their war-time experience and also with practical difficulties. They received 28 days' pay, but obviously this money would not last long. Inflation was rampant, food and other necessities were in short supply and expensive, and employment was hard to find. Those who had fought for their country were now faced with poverty.

The problems of reconstruction were not helped by the fact that the community leaders of pre-war Campden were no longer there. Ulric Stanley had died in 1918, George Haines died in 1920, and C.R. Ashbee left in 1919 for Jerusalem. In December 1919 a branch of the Comrades of the Great War was formed at a meeting in the Town Hall. Captain Spencer Churchill of Northwick Park was in the chair and over fifty members enrolled at the inaugural meeting.

Earlier in 1919 the War Office had offered the town a German field gun, as a reminder of the bravery of Campden's servicemen. The Parish Council unanimously accepted this war trophy and consulted the Comrades who chose a site next to the Market Hall. On 6th March the gun, brought by a gun team, was formally accepted on behalf of the Parish Council. Unfortunately the ceremony was abruptly cut short by torrential rain and this proved ominous, for it soon became apparent that the presence of a German field gun in the centre of Campden was an emotive and divisive issue. For the children it was an excellent toy for playing soldiers around, and for some it was a symbol of triumph, but for many it was a terrible reminder of the horrors of the war they had been through.

Two weeks after the installation, the annual parish meeting was asked whether the gun could be moved to a less prominent site, but it was explained that the site had been chosen in full consultation with ex-servicemen. Nothing was said but a month later the gun was found ignominiously dumped in the New Pool (the cart-wash opposite the almshouses). Undeterred, the Parish Council replaced the gun and this time the trail and wheels were bedded firmly in cement, or so it was thought. But before the cement could set, a child was sent to go and quietly scratch it out. Then on the Saturday night, shortly before midnight, a group of young people gathered round the gun. Speeches were made opposing the gun's continued presence, and it was claimed that sealed orders had been given, which were to be opened at the church, to remove the gun to a hitherto unknown destination. Meanwhile, a police constable hearing the disturbance, came out to investigate. He was told to return to the Police Station and know nothing, which he did. The sealed orders were opened at the church and the instructions were to drag the gun to the Coneygree and run it into the brook. The gate of the Coneygree was reached with considerable difficulty but great determination. The gun was hauled up to the top of the bank, where the lynch pins were removed and from there it was allowed to run down to the brook, its wheels dropping off as it reached the water.

The Parish Council realised that the cost of retrieving the gun for the second time could not be justified and the subsequent offer by Lord Sandon from Burnt Norton to remove it to his grounds was gratefully accepted, as was his gift of two guineas to the Campden War Memorial Fund.

The German gun mysteriously ends up in the New Pool, c.1920.
(By kind permission of Diana Evans)

Controversy also surrounded the question of establishing a permanent war memorial. As early as 1916 J.W. Pyment and Sons had received permission to erect a wooden war memorial near the Town Hall and had suggested that plans should be made for a permanent memorial. There were six diverse proposals including two different ones for a cross: a simple cross, suggested by Josephine Griffiths, and a more elaborate one by Paul Woodroffe. The other ideas were the extension of the Town Hall by fifteen feet, the construction of workmen's cottages, a drinking fountain, and a nurses' home. In the end, Woodroffe's proposal of a cross in front of the post office, which was then in London House, was agreed. It was to be designed by Griggs. Contention soon arose again, however, mainly because Griggs had not fought in the war (for health reasons) and possibly also because he had been received into the Roman Catholic Church in 1912. In the eyes of some, these things made him unsuitable to design a memorial for the mainly Protestant dead.

The committee was divided and two thoroughly acrimonious public meetings were held. In the end a vote was taken and the proposal to adopt Griggs's scheme was carried by seventy-five votes to five. After so much dissent there was no alternative but to form a third committee which, though democratically based, was sympathetic towards Griggs. Griggs himself was appalled. There was no further discord and the carving was done in 1920 by Alec Miller, who donated his labour. Over £700 was raised to cover the other costs of the memorial, partly through the efforts of a jazz band. The conductor was Tom Hooke, who had been a comedian in London before settling in Campden to run a paraffin business, and later to sell bicycles and electrical equipment.

In 1921 controversy broke out again, this time over the town maces, which dated from the reign of James I. Since the winding up of the Borough in 1886 they had been the property of the Town Trust. They were valued at between £700 and £1,000 and were being kept out of sight and under somebody's bed. When this situation came to light it was generally felt that as they were part of the town's heritage they should be on display in the Town Hall and a cabinet was made for this purpose. The Town Trust, however, feared for their safety in the Town Hall, which was much used by the public, and suggested they should be sent to the Victoria and Albert Museum on long-term loan, with replicas displayed in Campden. Unsurprisingly, the plan received much criticism at a Parish Council meeting; the debate rumbled on, and in January 1922 a public meeting was held to condemn the Trust's plan. The Chairman, Mr Ellison, opened the meeting, stating that although he, like many others, had never seen the maces, he nevertheless objected to their leaving Campden. The Town Trust was criticised for being high-handed. Miss Josephine Griffiths had prepared a history of the maces, which she read to the meeting, lending her support to the popular wish that they should remain in the town. The motion proposing this was carried by fifty-five votes to three. Finally, a compromise solution was found and the maces were lodged in the bank in Campden, with, of course, the end result that they were still out of sight. But the desire for democracy was satisfied.

No-one suffered more from the conflict in Campden, between its potentially important role on the national stage as an exemplary town, and its intense local interests and passions, than F L. Griggs. In many ways he was the person who contributed most to Campden in this period and perhaps in the whole of the century. He did this partly by rising above the local pettiness and partly by keeping his own vision of the town firmly fixed.

In 1923 he persuaded the Post Office to carry the telephone cables underground, and five years later, when electricity came to the town, he succeeded in influencing the Shropshire, Worcestershire and Staffordshire Electricity Company to place their cables undergound. He also designed small street lanterns for the gas lights. Griggs founded the original Campden Society in 1924 to protect the character of Campden and its neighbourhood, but there were the usual jealousies and disagreements. Griggs may also have been 'a little high-handed in his treatment of fellow-members' and in 1927 he resigned. The Campden Society collapsed in 1929, and in that year he was the main influence in the founding of the Campden Trust, whose main activity was to buy derelict shops and houses to renovate sympathetically.

One of Griggs's greatest achievements for the town was the rescue of Dover's Hill from hotel development in 1926. With associations of the 17th century Dover's Games, and a vantage point over the Cotswold Edge to the Welsh mountains, it had always been a visionary place for Griggs. He tried to arouse enthusiasm in the Campden Society but without success, and he raised only £500 before the sale. Deeply hurt and angered, he decided to risk everything and bid for it in his own name. He would then pass it on to the National Trust. The bill came to £4,400. The National Trust appealed for the money but the funds grew very slowly and in the end Griggs was only rescued from ruin by wealthy friends, including the historian, G.M. Trevelyan, who provided the final £1,700. Nationally Griggs was eulogised for what he had done, but locally there was little gratitude.

A similar achievement followed in 1934 when the Coneygree, ridge and furrow land behind St James's Church, was threatened by development. Again Griggs was largely responsible for persuading the Campden Trust to buy the land for £1,500 and hand it over to the National Trust. Two of Campden's most precious open spaces owe their preservation to the vision and determination of this one man.

The 19th century had seen many prosecutions for drunkenness in Campden and at the beginning of the 20th century there were 36 licensed houses, including ale houses, which were private houses where ale could be bought from a jug. With all this alcohol lubricating Campden, attitudes against drinking grew. The war had brought an abrupt change in drinking habits: licensed opening times had been introduced, alcohol was scarce and most of the men were away. The middle class of the town wanted to build on this development and there was a move to close six of the existing public houses. These were the Swan, which was needed to meet the expanding needs of the grammar school, The George and Dragon, the Angel in Broad Campden, The Live and Let Live, The Rose and Crown, and the Plough. Significantly they all catered for labouring folk. Appeals were heard but all six lost their licences. These closures caused obvious hardship to the licensees as most of them lost their homes and livelihoods, and the whole process generated considerable ill feeling, being seen as an example of the vulnerability of working people.

A perhaps biased glimpse of the characters in Campden in the early 1930s can be gleaned from the anecdotes recorded by Graham Greene during his stay in the town with his young wife. Miss Bright, their landlady who had been a schoolmistress, would chivvy them about the state of their flower-beds, and once, 'going black in the face', asked if she could send a gardener at her own expense. She then turned up with a gypsy gardener when they were out and they felt the place was not their home. Nevertheless, Graham Greene got used to this gardener and grew cos lettuces with his help. Buckland, as he was called, gardened for them once a week and put all the snails aside for his own supper. He also gardened for Christopher Whitfield, who based his essay *'The Old Poacher'*[iii], on Buckland, though without naming him. It begins,

> He is a settled gypsy, though when his wandering brothers come to the village in the summer he hardly knows them. He came as a youth, no-one knows why, and lived rough in the district for one summer, doing odd jobs and picking up his living how he could. Then he disappeared one day, and returned a month later with a young wife. ... They settled, took a cottage in the village, and there they live now ... there the family has rooted itself. ... By profession he is a gardener, and he is so good at his work, and has such green fingers, that everyone wants to employ him, especially the old retired ladies; for they love his picturesque air, and at their tea parties they discuss the quaint words he uses. But though he is a good worker, he is independent, and will never go again to a house where he has not been treated with the perfect respect and equal courtesy with which he treats others himself.

Greene found plenty to enjoy and to interest the novelist in him in Campden and often thought that the people he met every day between his muddy lane and the Live and Let Live Inn on the High Street were far more vivid than the sentimental cardboard figures he felt he was peopling his writing with at that time.

Greene had converted to Roman Catholicism on his marriage and he loved listening to Father Bilsborough's sermons. He talked about the Missions and thousands of Zulus coming to Communion. 'We don't see that in England,' said Father Bilsborough. Once when he asked for money to clean his church he spoke of 'Millions of dead flies breeding away on the ceiling,' which would have been something of a miracle.

A troop of strolling players arrived in Campden and held weekly dances in the Town Hall for a living. Mr Cresswell, the architect who lived in Ardley House (now The King's), objected to the noise of motor-cycles and forced them to stop the dances at midnight. He also tried to move the Wednesday sheep market from the Square, because of the smell and the flies. He hunted, and in retaliation the farmers warned him off their land. He eventually left Campden, and Greene thought this was for Campden's good.

The shops and traders sold all manner of combinations of goods, strange to a modern shopper. Vivien Greene wrote in her diary, 'The fish shop sells china on one side and flies on the other. The best eggs come from Foster, the paraffin man, the best strawberries from Keyte, the coal merchant: papers from the ironmonger.'[iv] The ways of the railway station staff amused her husband. Once when he was catching a train to Oxford, the station staff consisted of one man who was giving out tickets at first. Then the train arrived. He ran to the signal box, opened the gates, put down the signal, changed his coat and ran onto the platform to act as porter.

Campden then was full of wandering people. In the pea-picking season there were always a lot of didicoys and travellers about, the colloquial names for gypsies and tramps, and the Greenes would hear them singing in the lane. Sometimes a circus would appear on Badger's field, with horses, ponies, and clowns. On August Bank Holiday there were sports in Broad Campden, with races, and climbing the greasy pole. In February 1933 a different kind of circus put up its booth and caravan in the market place. There were lions, polar bears, and Bengal tigers incongruously sitting in the small quiet lanes around the Town Hall.

Many of the old ways were revived after the war. The town band, which had been led by Jim Pyment before the war, was re-formed and performed regularly at fetes and other events in and around the town. The morris dancers and mummers, renewed with new members, continued to perform at various functions. In the 1920s largely due to the generosity of Mr Arthur Watkinson, a new swimming pool was built at Broad Campden and became very popular. Poverty, however, persisted, especially during the recession of the early thirties, and there was much unemployment, alleviated only by a growth in the amount of building activity.

Change was very noticeable in the town at this period. By the early twenties motor-cycles were ubiquitous, the noise of their engines drowning the country sounds of horses' hooves and animal cries. (Interestingly, Griggs, the great devotee of rural peace, originally arrived in Campden on a noisy motor tricycle.) Although large farm wagons drawn by four Suffolk Punch horses could be seen collecting coal from Campden Station for the Springhill estate, motor transport and cars were becoming increasingly common and in 1921 it was felt that the time had come to tar the High Street. It had been a yellow limestone street for centuries, although for the previous 15 years it had been metalled with Malvern granite. The County Council used a horse-drawn vehicle to tar the street, carrying a tank of melted tar which was poured sparingly onto the ground by means of several taps. This was spread over the surface and chippings were then applied. The job of rolling was left for the traffic. The neighbouring lanes and roads were left as before and remained dusty in summer and muddy in winter. With the County's neglect of the roads and the lanes at the end of the 20th century it may well seem that not much has changed.

The car brought much-needed work to the town. One ex-serviceman started Campden's first garage in a shed behind the Red Lion Inn, while another bought an American car with which he ran a taxi service. The old horse-drawn station bus, known affectionately as the Mustard Pot,[v] was replaced by a Morris commercial bus run by George Haysum. This vehicle looked a mixture of delivery van, shooting brake and hearse and was nick-named 'the flying greenhouse' by visiting troops during the Second World War. Campden people on the whole accepted it as a Campden idiosyncrasy. George Haysum died in 1963 and in memory of him the piece of land behind Sheep Street, near where his garage had been was named Haysum's Close.

Left: Campden Railway Station in the 1930s showing the Research Station on the left
Right: George Haysum with his bus *(By kind permission of Brian Wheatcroft)*

The coming of the motor-car, like the railways fifty years earlier, brought social changes in its wake. New permanent residents could live here and work elsewhere, and week-enders from the cities could drive in. Campden's role as a haven for the better-off and a magnet for visitors grew rapidly. After the war the housing crisis was acute: the pressure of Campden people wanting decent housing was exacerbated by the pressure of outsiders wishing to rent or buy. Considerable bitterness was caused by the new phenomenon of week-enders whose cottages lay empty from Monday to Friday while ex-soldiers needed homes. In 1919 Gloucestershire County Council, with a government grant, built six semi-detached houses for returning ex-servicemen on Aston Road, each with an acre of land attached as a small-holding. This building was followed in 1921-3 by six stone houses lying back behind a service road at the top of Station Road and the first six of the Council houses in Broad Campden (those standing forward). These were all built by Campden Rural District Council. Next, in 1930 came twelve Council houses in Catbrook, followed shortly after by the last two blocks there, each of four houses.

In 1931 Griggs fought a battle against the use of red brick for eight council houses in Station Road and succeeded in reaching a compromise with the council whereby the houses would have stone quoins and be rendered, so making them less expensive than stone building would have been. These houses at the bottom of Station road were built a few years later by North Cotswold RDC, followed a year or two later by Berrington Road, most of which was finished before the Second World War started.

A major change in property ownership came when the Earl of Gainsborough's estate was broken up. At one time it had comprised most of Campden. This process had begun back in 1869 but the pace quickened in the 1920s. In 1922 Top Farm and 100 acres was bought by William Haines for £5,000. In June 1924 a major auction brought three farms, five houses, and twenty cottages onto the market, many of them to be bought by their occupiers. The death of the 3rd Earl in 1926, closely followed by that of the 4th Earl, incurred double death duties and necessitated further sales including Campden House at Coombe. Only the Court House in Calf Lane, the grounds of old Campden House and Westington Mill remained in the possession of the Gainsborough family. Many conversions, modernisations and new building followed these sales, giving rise to considerable (largely unfounded) fears that the town would be ruined.

Proposals for a new public hall caused controversy in the 1920s. In the end the old Town Hall was renovated and a committee appointed to run it. The committee nearly came to blows. Mr Haines asked if it would not be possible to have 'some real Campden people on the committee - Campden born and bred'. Mr Stokes, a farmer from Battledene, replied that Campden was 'in need of the help of all her sons and daughters whether they were born here or adopted'. [vi]

The sewage system, which was in a primitive state, became a pressing problem. Hitherto most people had earth closets, and many had been obliged to share one between two or more families. In 1926 a modern sewage system was installed in the town itself, draining to a sewage farm in the meadows near the bottom of Station road. The digging, all by hand, was mainly done by Welsh navvies. A blacksmith was on the site all the time to sharpen pickaxes. The surplus soil was removed by horses and carts and the surplus water pumped out with a hand pump. The work was hard, with foremen never lasting more than six months and ten to fifteen men being sacked each week. The rest were terrified of losing their jobs. When they reached Westington they hit solid rock and could make no progress so a compressor was seen for the first time in Campden. While the work was under way, the trenches were illuminated at night by a watchman in a hut, trying to keep warm by a smoky charcoal fire. It was one of the delights for children to go and see the watchman and take him a potato to cook.

Everyone complained about Campden's gas supply which was very unreliable. Children often had to struggle to do their homework by candlelight or by the light of oil lamps. There were frequent reports of the smell of gas in the High Street, with the source never located. On one occasion John Brotheridge's son lit a cigarette in the front room of his father's house in the Lower High Street and there was an explosion, which caused considerable repercussions and was followed by a second explosion. There can, therefore, have only been relief when in the 1930s the gas supply system was taken over by Cheltenham Gas Co. and modernised.

In 1928, as we have seen, electricity arrived in Campden. The installation of electricity brought more back-breaking work. Fred Coldicott was one of those who worked on the project and he recalled how each worker was issued with a pickaxe and shovel by the foreman, a little man in a bowler hat, who then marked out three lengths of the pickaxe with chalk, which was each man's allotted length to dig. Mr Coldicott also remembered how his blistered hands responded miraculously to Ted Ladbrook's home-made ointment.

With all these services installed, with the High Street tarred, and the motor-car a frequent sight, Campden had at last entered the modern world.

Notes

i Much of this chapter is taken from the work of Carolyn Mason. Her extensive research notes and draft chapters, *Campden Remembered*, are in the CADHAS archive. End notes indicate where the work is drawn from.

ii Griffiths, Josephine 'Concerning the Armistice'. This was written some years after the events and the author was possibly mistaken about the day this happened. The telegram she mentions (the original is at CADHAS 1994/0761/DO) was handed in at 1025 and received in Campden at 1245 on 11th Nov 1918. There was hardly time to make all these arrangements. Did they all happen on 12th Nov?

iii Whitfield, Christopher, *A World of One's Own*, Country Life Ltd. 1938

iv Sherry, Norman, *The Life of Graham Greene* (Cape 1987) 93

v Barnard, E.A.B., "Old Days in and Around Evesham" Nos 1076 and 1079, *Evesham Journal* 21 Aug and 27 Oct 1948

vi Mason, Carolyn, *Campden Remembered* Draft, 142

26

'Saving their Voices for when the Boys come Home'

The Second World War affected Campden in many ways. Life was very different from the peaceful interwar years. The threat of war had been clear for some time after the Munich agreement in 1938, and particularly with Hitler's later threats to the independence of Poland and the build-up of German forces on the Polish frontier. War preparations in Campden began even before hostilities were declared, with arrangements being made to receive evacuees from the big cities, gas masks being issued to all townspeople, and, in the last few days, orders made for windows to be blacked out and vehicle lights to be dimmed.

The first few weeks of the war was a period of feverish activity and anxiety. After a short time identity cards were issued to every man, woman and child living in the town, and these were followed by ration books with which, in contrast to the First World War, essential food, and later clothes, were distributed equitably to the population at low prices.

A local Territorial unit — an anti-aircraft battalion — had been formed in 1938 and many young Campden men had joined. Four days before the outbreak of war the Territorials were mobilised and departed from Campden to serve for the first part of the war in various towns and cities in the country, after which many men were transferred to infantry units and served overseas. Other Campden men soon volunteered for one of the three services, and still others — both men and women — were conscripted into one of the services or into other essential war work. Altogether, during the war, over 230 men and 30 women went from Campden into the armed forces. The casualties included 18 people who died and 10, including one woman, Angela Heaton, who were taken prisoner of war by either the Germans or the Japanese.[i] Throughout the war, St James's Church said prayers for different groups of individuals on different dates of the month.

On the Home Front, men joined the 'Specials' (the Special Constabulary) or, later, the Local Defence Volunteers and the Home Guard. Others acted as Air Raid Wardens, and the women of the town manned fire-watching patrols in a field above the town. Although Campden itself saw little of the horrors of war that were experienced by servicemen and by those civilians who were recruited to work in the cities, people were continually reminded of it, not least by the frequent air raid warnings, the noise of German bombers crossing the skies overhead after dark, and the raids on nearby cities, such as Coventry, when the sky would be lit up. Nearer to home a number of bombs were dropped within the parish, and one house — a lodge on the Five Mile Drive — was destroyed by a stray bomb, though luckily the family were not injured. On another occasion the destruction by incendiary bombs of the Gordon Russell furniture factory at Broadway created such a blaze that it is said newspapers could be read in Campden by its light.

Ebrington Home Guard parade past the almshouses

The people of Campden, reflecting the spirit of the country as a whole, united together both to make the most of social life in the town, to assist those who had been called away, and to welcome the many visitors — evacuees, members of the forces and land army — now sent to the neighbourhood.

There was much activity in support of the war effort. A Lockheed brake factory in Cutts's garage (a 'dispersed' factory) employed most of the girls and young women of Campden, who were conscripted to work either there or at a pickle factory in a kind of log cabin down by the station. The drive for domestic food production continued throughout the war years and members of Campden Women's Institute preserved a great deal of fruit and made a great quantity of jam, helped by a special sugar allowance available from the Ministry of Food. Families were also constantly encouraged to grow more vegetables: gardens were turned over to vegetable production. Pig clubs were formed and waste food was collected for pigs and poultry. There was a blossoming of beekeeping, both for the fertilising work of the bees and for the honey they produced. Salvaged paper, bones and scrap metal were collected, railings were uprooted and collections were made of pots and pans to be turned into armaments. There were the annual savings weeks — 'Salute the Soldier', 'Warship Week', 'Wings for Victory' and so on, when targets for savings were set — and invariably beaten.

Besides doing much of the work previously done by men, the women of the Campden Women's Institute were doing much to support the war effort. In December 1939 the committee arranged to hold knitting meetings every Tuesday at the King's Arms Pantry in the High Street (then a tea-room, now the restaurant Caminetto). In the summer of 1940 parties were held in members' gardens to knit scarves, balaclava helmets, socks and gloves. Soft slippers were wanted for the soldiers in hospital, and there were soft slipper evenings in the autumn of 1940. The following year slippers were urgently needed by the Rumanian Red Cross and everyone turned to supplying them. An appeal was made for warm clothing for Polish refugees.[ii] The WI helped the Women's Voluntary Service run soldiers' canteens for troops billeted in Campden and those from the RAF base at Honeybourne. The WI members were also asked to increase their National (or War) Savings, and it was agreed that Campden should organise such a scheme. The WI ran a very successful National Savings club throughout the war and for twenty years afterwards.

Apart from the blackout, evacuees were uppermost in everyone's mind in 1939. The town was surveyed and children allocated to hosts according to the number of spare rooms each had. As the Women's Institute minutes say: '...we have had to cater for quite an influx of children ... London has sent us 150 children of school age, two private schools have taken up residence, one at Burnt Norton, the other at the Golden Cockerel.' Anecdotes of the culture shock these children experienced were recorded in Toc H newsletters, complete with attempts to convey Cockney pronunciation: one boy goes excitedly to his teacher - 'Teacher, I sor a rebbet wiv 'is skin on!' One small girl, taken to help dig 'taters' for dinner, asks, when picking them up, 'Did you bury them cos you was afride of airraids?' [iii]

Obviously the natives of Campden wanted to emphasise the strange city attitudes of the evacuees but this was done affectionately and there was little trouble with the children, many of whom stayed in touch with their hosts. Mrs Barbara Smart, née Webb, remembered happy times as an unofficial evacuee in Campden in 1941. She was here with her mother, sister and small brother, first at the Volunteer Inn, and then at Court Piece Farm, occupied by the Prentice family. She recalled much kindness, dark nights, starlit skies, the hooting of owls, and the special treat of riding on the horse-drawn float for the morning milk deliveries in the town.[iv]

The *Evesham Journal* reported on 25th November 1939 that a communal kitchen for evacuees had been set up in the second week of the war, in premises near the Lygon Arms, lent by Mr Griffiths and staffed by local volunteers. A balanced midday meal was provided for 150 evacuee children and 30 local children which took a lot of pressure off their hosts, who paid 1s 6d a week for each child. Fruit and vegetables were donated by Campden people and by the Research Station. The *Journal* praised this outstanding example of voluntary service.

A Campden Forces Welfare Committee was set up which not only distributed warm clothing and cigarettes to those serving overseas, but sent them copies of a weekly newspaper. The Campden branch of Toc H[v] helped servicemen in various ways. It sent monthly newsletters[vi] to the Campden men serving abroad or in other parts of the country to tell them about 'commonplace happenings in their home town'. 'So let us come back to the little Cotswold town you all know so well, and which is constantly in your thoughts' as one newsletter puts it.

The newsletters are filled with jokes and gossip and fulfilled the function of keeping the image of home fresh for the soldiers, a necessary thing when they were fighting far from home. The jokes included many amusing stories of the officials back home. The Special Constables were the butt of many affectionate stories. A Special saw a light in a cottage across some fields and went to tell the owner to put it out. Half an hour later he reappeared asking for the light to be switched back on. 'I can't find my way out of this blue pencil garden.' (All service-men's letters were censored with a blue pencil.) And then Harry rode that tall bike of his, the 'Camel' into the back entrance of the Red Lion. A Yorkshire sentry greeted him with a fixed bayonet and a stern but unofficial challenge 'Wheer art t'gawn?' Harry jammed on both brakes, looped the loop half way, nosed-dived, lay on the ground, looked up and replied 'I byunt'.[vii]

Toc H members also helped man the canteens and opened their 'dugout' at the vicarage daily into a quiet room and club for visiting troops and Air Force personnel from the nearby air bases.

Land Girls in Campden, 1940s

Soon after the start of the war, troops began to be billeted in disused barns, empty and requisitioned houses and other buildings in the district: first a Territorial battalion of the Green Howards and later the RASC and the Gordon Highlanders. After Dunkirk, the WVS and other services were mobilised to welcome hundreds of exhausted men who stayed recuperating for a few weeks before re-forming into new units. Men and women serving in the nearby Honeybourne RAF station came up to Campden when they were off duty. After 1943 until D-Day and beyond, the town was host to American forces. Many of these men were welcomed into homes, pubs and churches and used the canteens and other facilities provided by local organisations. Land Girls, women conscripted into the Women's Land Army, also arrived and were billeted mainly on local farms, where their labour replaced that of men who had joined the forces.

Another experience for Campden people was the arrival of, first Italian, and later German, prisoners of war. During the war a number of Prisoner of War camps were built on the A44, at Springhill Lodges and above Bourton-on-the-Hill, from which prisoners were allocated to work on neighbouring farms. Later a hospital complex built for American troops in Northwick Park became a POW camp. After hostilities had ceased many prisoners lived in dispersed open camps and mixed with local people. One of these camps was situated in Catbrook, where the Fire Station now stands. An example of the relations between Campden people and the prisoners is given in the next chapter.

The town did its best to keep up its usual activities in the blackout. There was a nativity play in the church rooms on Christmas Eve 1939, the mummers performed and the bells rang on Christmas morning (for the only time during the war). The carol singers were quiet though, 'saving their voices for when the boys come home' (as a Toc H newsletter put it). Meanwhile, whist drives and dances collected funds for the soldiers. Through the winters the Debating Society met, there were play-readings, dances and whist drives, showing that even in adversity Campden's rich and varied social life continued. And local history research was going on, with billeted soldiers discovering the old Gloucester Volunteer uniforms in the old armoury (the building now occupied by HSBC bank). On August Bank holiday 1940 there was a horse and comic dog show in aid of the Red Cross and throughout that summer people had been entertained by the Osiris Repertory Company of seven women, under the direction of Nancy Hewins, performing Shakespeare, Shaw and other classics.[viii] Women were filling the gaps left by men in more ways than one.

Correspondence came in to Toc H from Campden men with details of the filth and flies of the desert, or snowdrifts at an Air Force base in Lincolnshire where one man had to dig out aircraft, reminding him of digging out sheep at home. There is a chasm between what we know of the experience of those involved in the fighting and what seems like the fairly cosy activity of those left behind in the town. But this account shows how those in Campden, and presumably in many other small communities in the country, were keeping up their spirits, and with humour and useful effort holding at bay the horrors of world war. As T.S. Eliot put it, 'Human kind cannot bear very much reality.'

At the end of the Second World War large numbers of Polish soldiers and airmen arrived in this country having fought alongside British forces in the Middle East and Europe. Most faced the problem of having to decide whether to return home to a communist regime or not. Whilst some did return, others decided to remain in the West, some emigrating to the USA, Canada and other countries. Many decided to stay in Britain.

As various military establishments and POW camps became vacant, many were converted to Polish resettlement hostels. In all there were 34 in the UK, and the closest to Campden were Springhill Lodges, near the A44 Cross Hands, on the Snowshill road; Northwick Park near Blockley; and Long Marston airfield near Stratford-upon-Avon. Even though the Poles had served heroically with the British, there was not unalloyed support for their settlement in these local camps. There was also a desperate shortage of housing for local people, and an article in the *Evesham Journal* reports the Housing Committee of the District Council as saying that, as accommodation had been allotted to the Polish Resettlement Corps, it was 'regretted that no accommodation [for local people] was likely to be available at the present time though it might be possible to release some of the buildings on the southeast portion [of Northwick Park Camp] at a later date'. In a letter of protest to the Minister of Health, Mr S. Freeman said this was 'a most deplorable state of affairs. ... Britishers were

The Polish Community join in the celebrations, 1953 ***(Roland Dyer/G of H Trust)***

having to take second place to foreigners. It was a terrible setback to their ambitions ...'.[ix]

Fortunately, this attitude did not prevail and by and large the Polish people were welcomed in the district. It seems that where they did come into contact with the local people they were seen as something of a novelty. Moreover, they were seen to have a useful part to play in the post-war Britain because they were a useful source of labour, particularly in the fruit picking and canning businesses in Pershore for women and in the engineering businesses, such as Dowtys in Cheltenham for men.

Springhill Lodges quickly became a self-contained Polish community. In 1947 the last of the POWs were still there, kept apart in the camp. In 1949 the community at Springhill Lodges consisted of 400 people but eventually grew to about 800 in 1958. Although there were English officers and a warden in charge, all the services were performed by the Poles themselves. There was a priest, a doctor, teachers, including one who specifically taught English language. The camp was organised as a community. There was a choice of communal catering or being 'on the rations', i.e. self-catering. Most families chose the latter option. There was a small general store on the camp and once a week a van would come round selling Polish foods such as sausages and other delicatessen products. Many families developed their own allotments and grew flowers and vegetables, while someone even grew tobacco, which was dried, hanging over the covered walkways. There was a small hospital and a primary school. Older children went to school in Campden if they passed their 11 plus exam and their English was good enough. Others went to the Secondary Modern School in Moreton-in-Marsh, some being transferred later as they caught up by acquiring adequate English.

The Polish community was mostly Roman Catholic and each of the camps had its own church. The church and the resident priest played an important role in people's lives and the camp's activities. However, weddings, funerals, baptisms and the like took place in St Catharine's Church in Campden and there are a large number of Polish graves in the cemetery there, as there are in Blockley cemetery.

There was plenty of musical and amateur dramatic activity in the camps, which helped to maintain and celebrate the Polish culture. This also improved links with the English community. Polish dance troupes regularly performed in local events such as the annual Scuttlebrook procession in Campden, when, dressed in national costume, they would dance in the Square. At the Coronation in 1953 the Polish were included in all the celebrations and a group of their children performed on the Coneygree. Everyone swam in the open air swimming pool at Broad Campden.[x]

Northwick Park Hostel was located on the site of the current Business Park and was part of the estate owned by Captain Spencer Churchill. He was particularly welcoming to the Poles, encouraging them to view his extensive picture collection in the main house, and allowing them to swim in the lake in the grounds, which were also open to the Springhill Lodges residents. The Long Marston camp was for single Polish men only, who were employed by the Ministry of Defence and worked on the military stores and army equipment. There was friendly rivalry between the Northwick Park and Springhill Lodges, and the children competed for who could put on the best play. In 1953 General Anders, the Polish hero of the Second World War, and then Head of the Polish Government in Exile, came to Springhill and this was a major event for all the Polish people in the area.

In the late fifties people began to disperse and the camp closed in 1958. While quite a large number of people remained in the area having married locally, and settled in jobs or set up their own businesses, which enabled them to buy houses locally, others left the camps to join Polish communities which by then had become established across the UK.

Notes

i Some details of these service people are given in Hughes, Dennis, *Campden at War 1939-1945* (Campden, Reminisce, 2004). See also Powell, Geoffrey, *The Book of Campden* (Barracuda, Buckingham 1982) 99-100 and Coldicott, F.W. *Memories of an Old Campdonian* (CADHAS 1994) 75 and 77-92

ii Womens' Institute Records (Books and minutes)

iii Toc H. *Newsletters* in CADHAS Archives 1999/089-92/DO

iv Notes from Mrs Barbara Smart, May 2002

v Toc H is a Christian organisation first formed as a meeting place for servicemen during the First World War at Talbot House, near Poperinghe in the Ypres salient. It now continues by bringing people together in friendship and to do voluntary service work. The Campden branch is now disbanded.

vi Toc H. *Newsletters* op cit

vii ibid

viii The story of the Osiris Players is told in the play *We Happy Few* by Imogen Stubbs. After the war they made their headquarters at Willersey, where Nancy Hewins is buried.

ix 'Houses or Polish Army?' *Evesham Journal*, 8th May.1948

x Conversations with Jan Shaw, Ursula Turowicz and Zosia Biegus, June 2002 and April 2003

27

Religious, Educational and Social Life

Religious life in Campden probably changed less dramatically during the 20th century than many other aspects of life. The conflicts and disputes of the mid 19th century had been more or less forgotten by 1900 and the next century saw closer and closer co-operation between the various denominations in the town. Social security legislation reduced the need for local relief, and the outreach of the churches moved towards help overseas. Christian Aid and Cafod became active in the town, and in the eighties moves towards organic unity culminated in the foundation of Churches Together in Campden and District, with a growing number of joint activities being undertaken.

St James's remained the predominant place of worship. Apart from the introduction of the new liturgy it saw relatively few changes over the course of the century. However, there were structural modifications. The great East Window by Henry Payne was designed and installed after the First World War; electric light was introduced, the North Chapel was restored, and oak screens designed by Norman Jewson and made by local craftsmen were installed there and in the chancel. Silver-work by the Guild of Handicraft was added to the church's treasure, both in St James's and later in Broad Campden church, and a new clock and new organ were installed. Major repairs and restoration of the fabric took place in the seventies. In 1986 it was discovered that the wooden frame holding the church bells was no longer safe. In a massive operation the bells were taken down, the wooden frame replaced with steel girders in a lower position, and the bells were hauled back into place. A festival to celebrate the return of the bells was held and the Morris Men danced in the church.

In the early part of the century the Campden vicar was also vicar of Aston-sub-Edge, but that parish was transferred to another group ministry and the benefice of Ebrington was united with Campden in 1975. Monthly services continued in Broad Campden church.

Like St James's, St Catharine's remained fairly static during the 20th century, though influenced by the world wide changes in Catholic theology and practice. As mentioned in an earlier chapter, it benefited from the presence of men from the Arts & Crafts movement in the acquisition of sculpture by Alec Miller and windows by Paul Woodroffe. A new Priest's House designed by F.L. Griggs was built in 1938 and towards the end of the century a new town cemetery was built in its grounds.

Architectural Drawing of St Catharine's Church by the office of JW Lunn of Malvern, c. 1890
(By kind permission of Father John Brennan)

The Baptist church started the century under the influence of its popular minister, Rev. Philip Lewis, who remained in Campden after he retired. However, after the First World War a gradual decline in membership took place until from the sixties to the early eighties the church was without a minister, and membership fell to under a dozen. At that time it was decided to sell Blockley church, and use the finance from that sale to appoint a young minister who immediately began to attract large congregations. Towards the end of the century, under his successor, the church was completely renovated and enlarged. It had become a thriving centre, especially for young people, from a wide area around Campden.

Two other churches have disappeared from the town. The Methodist church, like the Baptists, suffered a decline in numbers and in 1975, after the death of some of its leaders, it was resolved to close the church and transfer the remaining membership to Mickleton. A small congregation of Plymouth Brethren meeting in Park Road has also ceased to meet.

A different story is that of the Society of Friends, which has had a quiet impact on the nature of Campden throughout the centuries. Its 1663 meeting house was the first non-conformist building in Campden. By the 19th century numbers had, however, declined, largely because of rural depopulation, and in 1874 the meeting was discontinued. Some Quaker activity did continue in Campden with meetings in the Town Hall and elsewhere.

During the next sixty years the Broad Campden building was used by various people, first as a meeting place for the Primitive Methodists and later as a Baptist Mission hall. In 1917 C.R. Ashbee wanted to run a school there but the scheme came to nothing. It was used as a village club for a few years, and in 1931 the house and grave-yard were sold to the owner of a large house neighbouring the site. Unrealised proposals were made for it to become a village hall, and it was used as a barn for a time. During the Second World War the army were billeted there. They used the panelling over the stand to hang a dart-board and holes from the darts can still be seen. By the 1950s the building was derelict and a demolition order issued. This would have been a sad end to one of the oldest surviving Quaker meeting houses in the country, albeit one not in continuous use.

In 1957 Charles and Madge Tyson, Quakers from Lincolnshire, came to live in Campden. Charles Tyson started a campaign to have the meeting house restored. He gained some support and an appeal raised £3,500. The owner sold the building back for the amount paid thirty years before. Central heating, a kitchen and lavatories were installed and other alterations made. The restored meeting house was opened in 1962 and the membership soon grew. Charles Tyson's efforts to preserve the building were appreciated by all who knew it. Unfortunately, by the end of the 20th century, numbers had fallen and only a few of the Friends meeting there came from Campden, but certainly the presence of the Friends in Campden contributed throughout to the spirit of the town.

Alongside a comparatively strong religious life, Campden is blessed with many charities. The Home Nursing Trust, founded and organised by Mrs Jessica Brook towards the end of the century to nurse terminally ill people within seven miles of the town, enabled them to spend the last weeks of their lives at home. The Voluntary Help Group was founded in 1991 to look after the sick and the elderly who needed assistance, and to operate a car ferry to the surgery. The Chipping Campden Community Trust raised money for local people's needs and for local projects. Besides these and other locally organised charities, many national charities received strong local support, and the Rotary

Club and the Chamber of Trade did much charitable work.

Ever since the late 19th century primary or elementary education in Campden has been provided in schools maintained by both the Church of England and the Catholic church. In addition there were, in the earlier parts of the century, several private schools run by Campden ladies, to which only a few children went.

In house names along the High Street there are traces of former schools, showing how Campden's school rooms have moved about the town. For the first 70 years of the 20th century the Junior Church of England School, popularly known as the Infant School, was housed in what later became the library in the High Street. This catered for boys and girls from 5 to 8 years old. For the first 20 years of the century, 8 year-old children moved away to either the Boys' School, then in the present Church Rooms, or the Girls' School (the Blue School), in what are now two houses in the High Street. The Girls' School also then incorporated a teacher's house.

The present Library, then the Infant School, on George V's coronation day, 1911

In 1922 the Boys' School closed and the Blue School, or Top School, became the mixed Senior Church of England School. In 1970, with increased investment from the education authorities, the infants moved to a new St James's Church of England school in Pear Tree Close. In 1980 the juniors joined them. That same year St James's School became federated with Ebrington school.

Meanwhile the Catholic St Catharine's School, founded by the 2nd Earl of Gainsborough, remained in Lower High Street, but greatly expanded. Religious affiliation in education was complicated, with many Baptists preferring the Catholic to the Church of England school. By the end of the century many non-Catholic children went to St Catharine's.

Until the 1944 Education Act children at both elementary schools would stay until the school leaving age of 14 unless they passed a scholarship examination for the Grammar School at 11. There were still also fee-paying and boarding places at the Grammar School for those aged 9 and over. This changed with the advent of universal secondary education, and after 1944 the two lower schools, now called primary schools, catered for 5 to 11 year-olds.

The change in social structure and geographical mobility over the century can be usefully illustrated by the changes in the backgrounds of children at school. A local studies pamphlet produced in 1985 by the 3rd and 4th year classes at St James's School[i] shows that in 1881 55 per cent of the children's parents were born in Campden, and only 10 per cent were born more than 15 miles away. In 1985 this was almost exactly reversed, with just 10 per cent of parents born in Campden and 61 per cent born more than 15 miles away.

However, the most obvious educational changes in Campden during the 20th century were those in the old grammar school and its successor, now Chipping Campden School. Founded in the 15th century, the grammar school suffered many vicissitudes during its long history. As already mentioned, the school was rebuilt by public subscription in the 19th century, but the expansion in the early years of the 20th century caused great problems of accommodation. By the early twenties the school had almost 200 students (three-quarters of them still fee-paying) and classes of all kinds were crammed chaotically into the old school, two inns and the Town Hall.

To alleviate the crisis a field behind Cider Mill Lane was acquired and a new school built, designed to accommodate just 180 pupils. The old Grammar School and the Swan were both retained, boys continuing to board in the old school building, while the girl boarders stayed at Seymour House. Boarders came from all over the country and abroad. At the outbreak of war in 1939 the school had about 250 students.

For most of the century there was a wide catchment area for this school and from the twenties and thirties Grammar School children came in to Campden on the train and by bus from Moreton, Evenlode and Adlestrop, and many cycled in from surrounding villages such as Blockley, Paxford and Willersey. Some were provided with bicycles by the authorities.

With the passing of the 1944 Education Act, children who did not pass the 11-plus exam went to a new secondary modern school at Moreton-in-Marsh. However, in 1965, after being 'bilateral' for several years, the Grammar School buildings were greatly extended, the school became comprehensive and changed its name. The Moreton School was closed and its pupils absorbed in Campden.[ii] This merger more than doubled the size of the school to over 750 pupils. More staff were needed and to accommodate them a housing association was set up and with a loan of £40,000 from the County Council it built 12 houses on Barrell's Pitch to provide housing for key workers.[iii] When boarding ceased in the 1960s, flats were designed for teachers in the old school building.

Further expansion both in numbers and in the school buildings continued. In the 1980s the school was in the pilot scheme for the Local Management of Schools and from 1987 it controlled its own finances. It enjoyed much support from its parents' association and at the end of the 20th century attracted pupils from beyond its official catchment area, including some from Worcestershire and Warwickshire.

After the move to the new site the school gradually disposed of its former properties. The old King's Arms was sold in 1929 and converted by Norman Jewson back into an inn. The Swan was sold in the sixties, and in the nineties, amid much controversy, the old Grammar School building itself was sold off to developers who converted it into flats and an antique shop. The old school room with its Fereby fireplace, known as the Baptist Hicks Room, became a private living and dining room, its interior lost to public view.

Adult education has its own story. As was seen in an earlier chapter, at the end of the 19th century technical evening classes under the auspices of the grammar school were taken over by the Guild of Handicraft with its own School of Arts and Crafts. There was a lull from 1916 to 1946, when a few related activities were carried on by former guildsmen and others. Just after the war, a group of enterprising Toc H members, including George Hart, Joe Warmington and Ernie Lockyer, set up a committee called again the 'Campden School of Arts and Crafts' to run craft classes in Campden.[iv] The project took off very successfully. By the 1949/50 session, for example, there were three weekly classes in metalwork, two in jewellery, two in woodwork, and one each in leather work, fabric design, drawing and modelling, embroidery, and cookery.[v] In 1961/2 of 196 students registered, eleven were under 18 years old, and the largest proportion between 18 and 25. Series of lectures were put on each year and exhibitions became a feature of the School.

Accommodation was always a problem for the post-war School of Arts and Crafts. After two years without a regular home, the School had sole use of the former Swan Inn. When the Swan was sold in 1965 the Committee rented rooms in the old grammar school. Despite setbacks, by 1977 there was a record number of students. The School lost its premises in 1985 and classes were then held in the evenings at Chipping Campden School and elsewhere in the town. Adult craft and educational classes still continued, but at the end of the century they were controlled by the Gloucestershire College of Arts and Technology.

Another organisation looking back on Ashbee's legacy of education in craft work was the Guild of Handicraft Trust. Formed in 1989 and registered as a charity in 1990, the Trust's aim was to advance the education of the public in the work of craftsmen and craftswomen in Campden and the North Cotswolds since the beginning of the 20th century. It began collecting together artifacts, drawings and archives relating to the work of guildsmen and of the craftsmen who followed them, and for several years at the end of the century it had a small exhibition of work in the Silk Mill. It expected to open a permanent exhibition and study centre in Church Street early in the 21st century that would be of national significance, and a great benefit to the local community.

Campden has long been a book-loving place. Campden Bookshop was founded in the 1970s by Mary Hill, in partnership with Geoffrey Powell, and flourished for the rest of the century under a succession of owners. For about 20 years until 1986 Seumas Stewart ran a second-hand bookshop known as Serif Books in Harrow House, and later Draycott Books attracted many visitors with its large selection of rare and antiquarian books.

Early in the century there were penny libraries in Church Street and the High

Street. Then in the early thirties the County Library came once a week, first to the senior Church of England school and later to the Town Hall. In addition, there was an unusual children's library at Elm Tree House, known as the 'Elm Tree Library'. Mrs Hargreaves-Beare started her children's library there as a memorial to her daughter who had died in a riding accident. It began in an outbuilding in 1963 and by 1967 it had 2,000 books and over 150 child members. The studio building was equipped with bookshelves, coat hooks and a bench fixed around the square bay window.[vi]

In an article in the *Evesham Journal*, 'The Elm Tree Library, Just for Children',[vii] Mrs Hargreaves-Beare said, 'They are allowed to take two books: one fiction and one non-fiction. They treat the books very well indeed and they are charming children. They really seem to enjoy coming. ... I tell them when they come along that they are free to sit about in the garden for as long as they like, reading or talking, or to sit in the library if it is wet. They are absolutely free to please themselves. We don't normally take children under six but if they are a little younger and they can read and know how to take care of a book, and an older sister or brother has brought them, I don't keep to the rules too rigidly. ... After the age of 14 they tend to go on to the adult library in the Town Hall.'

Mrs Hargreaves-Beare used to give each child a book as a birthday present. The Elm Tree Library closed in 1970 when the County Library opened in its present buildings and set up a children's section. At this point, Mrs Hargreaves-Beare let each child choose two books to take away and keep.[viii]

The County Library moved into the premises vacated by the Infant School in 1970. It underwent refurbishment and extension in 1997 and, from public subscriptions and grants, the Campden Room with IT facilities was established in the building.

One of the attractions of Campden for incomers at the end of the century was the range of societies established in the town; a phenomenon which could be seen to echo Ashbee's vision of community life. This wealth of cultural and social life not only helped to keep the town alive but also involved and integrated new people as they moved to the area, bringing their own contribution with them.

The Debating Society was founded in 1935 by Mark Green, the son of the vicar, and although still at boarding school he became the first secretary.[ix] At the

40th Anniversary Dinner in 1975, Mark Green, by then Bishop of Aston, was the Guest of Honour, and was again present at the 60th Anniversary in 1995. The society flourished, providing interesting debates throughout the winter, latterly including an annual one against sixth formers from Chipping Campden School.

The Music Society, formed in 1961, presented a programme of concerts by professional musicians, and organised visits to opera, concerts and recitals. Charlie Bennett and friends also organised a summer music festival, and other musical events took place under the auspices of churches and schools.

The Campden and District Historical and Archaeological Society was founded in 1984. The society aimed to research the local history and archaeology of the area, published books and papers written and researched by members, maintained an important local archive, and also offered lectures and visits. It had a large thriving membership.

In 1995 a North Cotswold branch of the University of the Third Age was formed, and a great variety of groups flourished in Campden, ranging from the literary to the dramatic to the geological. For the more active there was a wide range of sporting facilities and clubs in the town.

But the Societies provided far more than social life. The Campden Society was formed in 1970, taking over some of the responsibilities of the Campden Trust, which had been founded by Griggs in 1929, for preserving the characteristic buildings of the town, its open spaces, and surrounding landscape. The Society monitored planning applications in the parish and was recognised by the District Council as a conservation body. In 1964 the Council for British Archaeology published a report naming 51 towns in Britain as 'so splendid and so precious that ultimate responsibility for them should be a *national* concern'.[x] Campden and Tewkesbury were the only towns in Gloucestershire to be selected. The Campden Society was able to use this report, along with the important designation of the town as a Conservation Area in 1973, to further its work. It was largely due to the concern and effort of the Campden Society, with help from the district and county authorities, that the special character of Campden had been preserved so well.

The Society also organised a series of winter lectures and summer outings to places of interest. The Campden Trust, which continued independently, initially purchased historic houses and cottages in order to restore and preserve them, afterwards selling them.[xi]

One small episode shows how the collaboration of different groups of people in the town made a permanent mark in Campden. When Charles Tyson died, his family encouraged those who wished to remember him to plant a tree. This led the Campden Society, along with the Music Society and the Quakers, and with the co-operation of the town and county councils, to organise a tree planting scheme. The Gloucestershire College of Art and Technology undertook the planning as an exercise for their students. The major planting was along the Aston Road, where two long rows of lime trees usher people in to the northern end of the town. A ceremonial planting of trees by the Mayor of Campden, Mrs Madge Tyson and Mr Frank Mottershead declared the first phase of the project complete in Spring 1980.

All this activity shows what a strong local community can do, and despite the many changes that took place in the economy and in society, Campden at the end of the 20th century remained a vibrant and desirable place for its inhabitants to live.

Notes

i Fees, Craig (ed), *Local Studies by the Students in ... St James's School* (Privately printed 1985)
ii Cook, Robert, *Chipping Campden School 1440 - 1990*, 46 (Drinkwater, Shipston on Stour 1990)
iii ibid 53
iv Warmington, Allan, *The Campden School of Arts and Crafts*, op cit
v ibid 16
vi Notes from Carol Jackson 1 Dec 2002
vii *Evesham Journal*, 1 Sep 1967
viii Andy Doran talking to Carol Jackson Dec 2002
ix Speech of Mrs Bernice Mills to the Society at the Anniversary Dinner 1995
x Conservation 3 Areas, A Survey by the Civic Trust, 1967
xi The Campden Society in 2002 took over the residual role and resources of the Trust. See The Campden Society leaflet, 2002

28

Farming and Food

For most of Campden's history agriculture, whether growing or marketing, has been the basis of its economy.[i] By the end of the 20th century farming was still an important activity but had become far from dominant. Some of the biggest changes affecting the town during that century took place in agriculture, mirroring the situation across the country. The revolution in methods of growing, marketing and preservation were of enormous significance, not only in farming itself, but also in scientific advance, to which Campden made a national, and indeed an international contribution.

After the First World War there were a lot of farms in and around the town, many still leased by tenant farmers from the Gainsborough or Northwick families. Some farmers lived right in the centre of Campden. For example, there were Haydon's Farm in Church Street, with its nearby mill; Stamford House, or Stanley's Farm in Leysbourne; and the house which is now Badgers Hall, then Home Farm run by Horace Badger. There were farm houses in Westington (Top Farm, Poplars Farm, Izod's and Westington Old Farm), in Combe (Court Piece and Old Combe), and in Broad Campden (Hollybush Farm, Home Farm and Briar Hill Farm). Other farmers lived on outlying farms like Lapstone, Campden Hill, Greystones and Sedgecombe, and even as far away as Campden Ashes on Springhill estate.

At that time Campden was truly a farming community but by the end of the century there had been much consolidation: tenant farmers had left or their leases had been terminated, and just seven large farms were left, all situated away from the centre of town and farmed by their owners or by large estates. This fall in numbers was accompanied by an even steeper decline in agricultural employment and a change in the nature of the town from an agricultural community to one where tourism was the most obvious activity.

Campden traditionally had a mixed farming economy. Cereals were widely grown in the area: wheat for flour, barley for malting and oats to feed horses. Flailing and scything were largely things of the past, though men from the almshouses were still going to London to scythe Hyde Park. However, up to the Second World War most work was still done by men and horses. Good farming was dependent on good horses. It was not possible to work after dark, and it was not permitted to do more than essential work on Sunday: the farmers largely agreed that both men and horses needed a rest. As the horses left for the day's work there was a rush to collect their manure, much in demand for gardens or allotments. When the horses returned after the day's work they called to their fellows in the field.

All kinds of tasks were performed manually. Haymaking was a communal activity and so was the stacking of sheaves into stooks after the horse-drawn reaper and binder had cut the corn. Hedges were laid and trimmed by hand and provided safe havens for wild life. There were many peewits on the Long Ground in Westington and the crows came home at dusk, before modern farming methods destroyed their habitat.

There was some machinery in use. From the 1880s steam threshing engines had replaced some manual labour. Later steam ploughs could be seen on some farms. After the First World War tractors appeared in Campden on contract, but it was not until 1930 that the Haines family bought their first tractor. Modern materials were not then available for clothing and after the First World War men often wore the puttees they had worn in the war. Woollen clothing gave little protection against the rain and there was a saying, 'More rain, more rotten jackets'. Sacks were put over shoulders to protect from driving rain.

Left: Campden men in Kensington with their scythes, c1875
Right: Mr S.F. Gladwin and Mr Bishop with a horse rake in the "Long Ground", Westington, between the wars *(By kind permission of Mary Gladwin)*

After the depression in farming at the end of the 19th century, the horticultural industry developed nationally as an alternative to farming. With its favourable climate and good soil, the Vale of Evesham especially saw the expansion of horticulture.[ii] Fruit growing spread up from the Vale as a major activity and cherries were a big crop in Campden. Cherry minders were employed and tin cans strung up in the trees helped to scare the birds away. The fruit was picked as piece-work in the evenings and as many as thirty tons of cherries would be picked in a season and sold to the shops or exported to markets. There were many orchards of plums and apples, and the allotments known as The Clay (now Grevel Lane) were given over almost wholly to blackcurrants which were sent to Beech's jam factory at Badsey. Fruit and vegetable produce went off by rail from sidings at Campden station.

The ways in which produce was sold was also very different from today. Five or six dairy farmers sold milk, morning and afternoon, from door to door with their horse-driven milk floats. Buckets, filled from churns, would be brought to the door and jugs filled from them. Cream, butter and eggs were also sold on these rounds. Not until 1936 was milk delivered in bottles and the farmer was then responsible for sterilisation of the returned bottles. Farmers raised a good deal of poultry and several reared guinea fowl. Many cottagers kept hens and ducks.[iii]

On the last Wednesday in every month sheep and cattle were auctioned in the market; sheep were hurdled in the Square and cattle and pigs in permanent market stalls in the sale yard behind the Noel Arms. There were lively scenes in the town and on a hot day the stench would be overwhelming. Butchers from Birmingham bought animals, and boys would earn sixpence for driving them down to the station. The pubs stayed open until 2 pm. Wives made huge meat pies for the men and many interesting tales would be told over lunch. Some of the farmers would ride home in their carts, drunk from beer or strong cider, throwing pennies to the children as they went. Market day was a red-letter day all round. On the other hand, Campden butchers would often go to Stratford market, buy the prize beast, and bring it home to their own slaughter-house behind their High Street shop. Most butchers had slaughter-houses in those days. At the end of the 20th century some farmers were campaigning for their restitution.

By the 1920s and 1930s, with the spread of horticulture to this area, acres of peas and sprouts were grown and there was a sprout sale every September during the 1930s. A bonus for Campden farmers was that vegetables grown on top of the Cotswolds are protected from drought because of the way water rises up the limestone. The Cotswold hill farms used to be called 'boys' land' because even boys could farm it: because of the stoniness, tractors would not get stuck.

There were always tramps passing through and gypsies would move up from the Vale of Evesham to pick peas, as the season in Campden, higher up on the hill, was two weeks later than the Vale. In 1938 Mrs Mary Gladwin received a wedding present of tinned meat from some of the gypsies who were working on the family's land. She recalled the horse-caravans which would park on the Long Ground above Westington. Once the District Nurse was called to one of the caravans as a woman was giving birth. Her mother and the mother of the baby's father were both in the caravan smoking clay pipes and instructing her to do the opposite of what the nurse was telling her. In spite of all this confusing advice the baby was born successfully.

Farming at this time was labour intensive and labour was plentiful as local people had no alternative source of employment. At the end of the First World War there was a camp for German prisoners of war at Mickleton. The market gardener Joseph Webb, who had bought farms between Broadway Tower and the Fish Hill road, took men from the camp to work the fields. Prisoners had a big round red patch on their backs to distinguish them as they bent over the land. This supply of labour was renewed during and after the Second World War when prisoners of war from Springhill and other smaller camps were used. The Gladwins had three young men whom they allowed to live in Robin Cottage.

The poverty of the twenties created many problems. In 1926 the agricultural wage fell to 26s a week, very little to support a family. Agricultural workers held union meetings under the elm tree opposite Sheep Street, as they had done in the hard times at the end of the 19th century. Tied cottages were then the norm for farm workers, meaning that if they lost their job they lost their house, too. These have now disappeared, though in 2000 the Haines family still owned some former tied cottages, now occupied by long-serving employees or their widows.

Some farmers went under at this time. Others managed to survive and even to thrive, taking over the smaller farms, so that by 1930 the average size of farms was beginning to grow. George Haines, a butcher from Pimlico Road in London, was one of the successful ones. He had come from London on his hunter called Lloyd George, married a Campden girl, and farmed above Blind

Lane, on land which the family continued to farm for the whole of the century.

By the 1930s many changes had taken place. Lloyd George's 'People's Budget' in 1910 had increased taxation on land and imposed death duties, so that even before 1914 landowners had begun to sell land. After the war, the selling increased, and there was a hunger for land and homes among soldiers returning from the war.[iv] Double death duties led to the Gainsboroughs selling off much of their estate in 1926. Many well-known farming families as well as some smallholders bought their farms at this time. With the advent of cheap corrugated iron in the 1930s Dutch barns became popular. These saved the trouble of thatching ricks and there were some very elaborate barns in Campden.

During the Second World War agriculture was strictly controlled under the War Agricultural Executive Committees. Farmers received much advice from the Government and from the Committees; in some cases inefficient farmers could be displaced and their farms taken over. As many cereals as possible were grown to feed the population and during these years many sheep-runs on the hills were turned over to arable land. In many cases this land was not returned to grazing after the war. The war years were profitable for growers, as the price of vegetables was fixed. At this time the Haines family farmed nearly 200 acres and employed a carter and four ploughboys, a shepherd and two cowmen, and four daymen, one of whom walked to work from Blockley every day.

Some customs continued. There were pig clubs which provided owners with insurance if their pig fell sick or died, showing how important the animal was to the domestic economy. Between the wars farmers would use hams as an exchange commodity for services such as medical treatment. Pig ownership grew in popularity in the 1940s, with wartime shortages. When the time came, animals were got out of the sties, killed, hung up and dressed on the spot and their meat was then taken into the house to be cured. Hams were put in a large tray lined with lead and anointed with saltpetre and brown sugar. As much of the pig as possible was used, brawn made from the head, faggots and chitterlings from the insides. Pigs' trotters made a favourite meal. Even the pig's bladder was used as a football by the children. Until just after the war rabbits were a common meal. They were caught in gin traps or with wire snares, and many a tale is told about poaching the rabbits. The War Agricultural Executive Committees waged war on rabbits believing them to be an unproductive use of land. The Committee had the power to dispossess farmers who 'farmed rabbits' rather than crops of cereals.

After the war change accelerated. Economies of scale became increasingly important and farming became more mechanised. This drive for efficiency combined with rising labour costs and growing competition from abroad had a far-reaching effect on Campden life. For example, pigs were now bred by specialists in large indoor factories and it was no longer viable for farmers, still less for cottagers, to keep just a few. In the 1960s cherries became uneconomic because of the cost of labour, and competition from California. Many orchards were grubbed up and Cherry Orchard Close was built on land which had been a cherry orchard for 150 years.

During the last half of the century farms got larger and began to be farmed 'in hand' by the owner. For example, when the Noel family owned the Campden estate in the 1920s, ten farms were rented out; by the end of the century, under different ownership and with modern methods, what remained of the whole estate was farmed by the owner. A number of factors contributed to the rise of large farms being worked in hand. In the 1960s the tenancy laws changed. Entry into the European Union took place in 1972; the Common Agricultural policy encouraged landowners to farm their own land, so tenants were paid to surrender their tenancies. Then there were legislative changes like the change in capital transfer tax in 1993; death duties were no longer to be paid on 'in hand' farms, which encouraged owners to farm the land themselves. All these combined to begin to turn farming into agribusiness.

As the decline in agricultural employment continued, so jobs in manufacturing increased in surrounding towns. Factory owners sent buses to the rural areas to bring in employees. In the 1950s companies collecting workers from Campden included a mining equipment firm in Cheltenham, the Shipston Engineering firm, an aluminium works in Stratford, and Long Marston army camp.

In the late 20th century, too, the cost of labour increased dramatically in comparison with farm prices, again leading to increased mechanisation and larger farms with comparatively fewer overheads. As an example, at a fair in 1953 the young Jim Gladwin won a pig which he looked after. When it went to be slaughtered several months later he received £21 12s 3d. Agricultural wages were then about £7 a week and the pig was worth three weeks' wages. By the end of the century labour costs were around £200 a week and a pig might fetch £100, half a week's wage. In 1956 a fleece brought in £3 6s 8d. In 2000 a fleece fetched about £1 10p and it cost 80p for the shearing, plus the farmer's own time and overheads. With the advent of man-made fibres, the demand for wool had fallen steeply. By the end of the century local wool was sold for carpets, an outlet that was also declining. China was buying a lot of wool, but by the end of the century demand was being choked off by the strong pound. There was little profit in sheep-farming and diversification seemed the only way forward.

Increasing mechanisation was another cause of change. Whereas in the early days one job was done at a time, by the year 2000 three operations could be done in a single pass over the land: the furrows pressed, the seed bed prepared and the corn sown. In the 1930s it took all day to work over an acre with a three-legged drill; it was now possible to drill a hundred acres a day. Two horses used to plough an acre a day, walking 19 miles. With a modern tractor it was possible to plough 40 acres in the same time. The combined harvester was introduced soon after the end of the war, and by 1952 would do ten acres a day. Seasonal labour was still bought in, mainly for packing and processing food, but now immigrant labourers were brought in from Birmingham.

Scientific advances also changed the face of farming. During the Second World War weapons were developed using chemicals such as organo-phosphates, which further peacetime research turned into pesticides, herbicides and fertilisers. This was a dramatic change, which again reduced the amount of labour needed. Instead of farm workers being paid a shilling an acre to pull docks at night, now contractors were used to spray the fields. At the end of the 20th century organo-phosphates themselves were being phased out, and sprays containing plant-based enzymes were introduced which would be more controllable in their effects and arguably better for the environment. Science continued to propel changes. Clothing for farmers and farm workers also made advances in the latter half of the 20th century. Wellingtons made a great difference after the Second World War, and there was a revolution in waterproof clothing in the sixties.

Legislation, foreign competition, mechanisation and scientific discovery all changed the shape of Campden's agriculture in the 20th century. The final big development to affect farmers was the advent of supermarkets. By 2000 the Haines family were selling some of their sprouts prepared ready for supermarket shelves. They had to employ people to prepare them, and needed different forms of accommodation. They likened their business to a manufacturing business: new demands had to be anticipated and margins had to be maintained by economies of scale.

Towards the end of the century supermarkets increasingly required farmers themselves to take charge of a section of foods: the approach known as category management. The manager of this side of the family business, responsible for legumes, brassicas, and cucurbits, for example, had to ensure an all year round supply of these for two or three years at a time. He travelled abroad, often to Spain, to see crops there and to negotiate with Spanish growers. The logistics required a large depot in Campden to store all the produce transported here as well as locally grown produce.

In this way, some farmers moved with the times and took up the challenge of the new retail environment. Farming at the end of the 20th century was becoming minimally local. One Campden farmer looked to France to sell his wool, and his lambs also went to France. The traceability of livestock became a key concern. There were concerns, also, about the distances food travelled - a problem that was likely to become a serious political issue.

Nevertheless, some food was still grown for local consumption and a trend towards more 'natural' food had begun. Sometimes things go full circle, as has happened to the marketing of peas. For example, peas, popular up until the 1970s, became less sought after as they had to be prepared by hand. Then, thirty years later, it became fashionable to buy peas in their pods. The Haines family had two fields of peas which were a very successful crop. Agency labour was brought in to harvest the crop. The greengrocer's and butcher's stocked local produce in the High Street; and one local smallholder reared pigs.

The Cotswolds were now an environmentally sensitive area and farmers received grants to maintain walls and hedges and look after the landscape. In the future there could be a trend for farmers to become protectors of the countryside and estate managers, with an increasing focus on the environment and the tourist industry, rather than absolute productivity. This could be the new challenge for the men and women who earn their living from the land.

Alongside the technical and economic changes in agricultural practice during the 20th century came a parallel development in techniques of food preservation. What was founded in 1919 as the Campden Experimental Factory had become a leader in its field. It provided steady employment and under its various guises, put the name of Campden firmly on the map in many different places throughout the world.

In 1911 a tall red brick factory was built with red Honeybourne bricks by Mr J.H. Clarke between the Battle brook and Campden railway station. He had been the head game-keeper for the Earl of Plymouth. Using this experience, he decided to set up in business producing pheasant eggs, dog meal, dog biscuits, and animal medicines. He was looking for land near a railway, the preferred method of transport at the time. The station yard was a hive of industry: sheep, cattle, vegetables and fruit went by rail, and at Campden station, typically, there was a coal yard and a gas-works. Mr Clarke found just what he wanted down by the Battle brook.

He built Battledene House in 1912 for his family, overlooking the factory, and four red-brick cottages for workmen. His daughter, Phyllis, told the story of an occasion when her mother was waiting for a train at Campden and overheard two gentlemen on the platform. One said to the other, 'Ghastly, hideous, all this red brick. Built that house too, all red brick. Hideous. Hideous man as well, all that red hair.' Her mother was very amused.[v]

Mr J.H. Clarke's Factory at Battlebrook which was to become the research station.
(Jesse Taylor/G of H Trust)

Mr Clarke had a siding and a loading platform by the factory and the building had large sliding doors above the railway. He had three teams of horses and wagons to move things around the land. There was a huge wired pen for the pheasants which produced 2,000 eggs a day, a luxury product. The factory was in business, selling pheasant feed and dog food, milling flour and making dog biscuits. 'Only one thing can bring me down and that's a war, and there's no sign of one,' he said.

However, war came in 1914 and the factory was commandeered by the government. The machinery was adapted to make biscuits for the armed forces. There were already special ovens and dough mixing apparatus for the dog biscuits which were so good that children would come in and ask for one hot from the oven, but the biscuits he was ordered to make for the soldiers did not please Mr Clarke. 'I'd be ashamed to give them to my dog,' he said.[vi] Compensation for the requisition was promised but when the fighting was eventually over there was no money for any factory owners.

At that time there was virtually no preservation of food in this country. Just before the war two experimental factories had been set up at Broom Junction and Dunnington Heath, both on the edge of the fruit and vegetable growing area of the Vale of Evesham, with the object of experimenting in the production of canned food. However, by the time they had been completed, they had to go into full wartime production without any idea of advancing the science of food preservation. At the end of the war, government again sought a place where experimental food preservation research could take place. Still conveniently close to the Vale of Evesham, the empty Game Food Factory was purchased by the Ministry of Agriculture and the Campden Experimental Factory was established in 1919, and engaged on the domestic preservation of food.

In 1920 a brilliant Scotswoman, Miss Margaret Watson, was appointed as a demonstrator. She conducted experiments in the preservation of fruit and vegetables, and gave summer courses. In the course of her work she discovered a new method of preserving fruit in bottles. A dilute solution containing sulphur dioxide was introduced as an alternative to the more usual method of heat treatment. This became known as the Campden Solution. It worked as a sterilising agent, killing micro-organisms in the fruit. Later the same results were produced from sodium metabisulphate tablets called Campden Tablets, which converted into sulphur dioxide in liquid. They are still used for sterilisation purposes by makers of home-made wine.[vii]

In 1921 what had by now become the Research Station was taken over by the University of Bristol as part of the Agricultural and Horticultural Department of the University. Two years later the first two scientists, Alfred Appleyard and Fred Hurst, were appointed, the latter becoming Director and later Secretary of the Canning Trade Association. During the twenties and thirties a canning industry was established in this country and given much practical help by the Research Station staff. During the Second World War the station controlled the inspection of canned food production nationally and from 1945 on it oversaw the rapid expansion of the food preservation industry, including the introduction of frozen foods. The name and status of the Association has been changed many times to indicate that research was moving into other areas. By 1960 it was no longer associated with Bristol University but had become the headquarters of the Food Industry Research Association.

In 1972, when a Grant of Arms was made to Chipping Campden, the blazon included an ear of corn and a wheatsheaf, references both to the agriculture of Campden and to the Research Station. The Association was authorised to use the blazon on documents because they had been instrumental in applying for the Coat of Arms and had contributed towards the cost.

The Association was the only national research establishment working with processed fruit and vegetables, and it acted as a process adviser to the world. Funding, membership, residential courses, contract work, Ministry research projects, and overseas commissions all flourished. One of the Campden scientists, Dr David Arthey, reported to *The Grower* in April 1982, 'Campden is making progress on all fronts - agricultural production techniques, quality improvement, processing techniques, studies of new packaging materials, plastic containers, and chilled foods.' The association also helped industry with quality control.

On 1st January 1995 the Association became the Campden and Chorleywood Food Research Association, having merged with the Flour Milling and Baking Research Association from Chorleywood, Hertfordshire. The following year staff from Chorleywood relocated to Campden. At a cost of £2 million the new Chorleywood Building was completed to house the 50 increase in staff numbers. Its scope and influence were to spread further when in 1998 the Association established a subsidiary company in Hungary, taking over a research organisation in Budapest that had dealt with frozen and chilled foods. In 1999 Campden Research Association had well over 200 staff and 12,500 visitors, many of whom stayed in hotels in Campden, bringing trade to the town. American members particularly would often continue their visit to the station with a tour of the Cotswolds.

In 2000 work began on a new £2.5 million building programme, which would provide offices, microbiology laboratories and new training facilities. The old red brick factory from the beginning of the 20th century had turned by the beginning of the 21st into an impressive new complex of modern buildings full of the most up-to-date equipment. Mr Clarke would be surprised to see the changes, and perhaps even more surprised to know that his vision had eventually become an institution of international importance. Campden and Chorleywood Food Research Association is renowned throughout the world, far more than most Campden people realise.

Notes

i Much of this chapter is based on conversations with Fred Coldicott, Jim Gladwin, Mary Gladwin, Eric Haines and Martin Haines

ii Perren, Richard, *Agriculture in Depression* (Cambridge University Press 1995) 13

iii Notes from Nevill New, CADHAS archives (to be catalogued)

iv Perren, op cit. 33

v Oral history tapes of Mrs Dorrie Ellis

vi ibid

vii Miss Watson wrote a book based on her experiments, *The Home Preservation of Fruit and Vegetables*, (OUP 1925). Adams, W.B., *History of the Research Association 1919-65*, CCFRA archive

29

Coping With Change: Visitors and Incomers

As employment declined in farming, Campden residents looked elsewhere for means of livelihood. One strong trend throughout the 20th century was the rise in tourism and this was taken advantage of by shops, hotels, restaurants and bed and breakfast establishments in the town. It has already been noted that the town's beauty and rural situation had attracted an increasing number of visitors since the 1880s. From the 1970s onwards this grew into an all-year-round phenomenon.

Tourism led to one of the most striking changes in Campden during the 20th century. On 17th August 1890 Muriel Neve, the 19 year old daughter of the postmaster, who lived in London House on the High Street, wrote in her diary:

> Campden will beat Broadway yet and be a summer resort for urbanites, such a quantity of strangers about, a party of the Lanes have been staying at the Noel, another lady and gentleman there too, another at the Lygon, and a whole family at the Court ... we are quite lively.[i]

The excitement, however, did not last into the winter months and on 4th December 1891 she wrote:

> Life is so small in Campden, too small to carry one out of oneself, so monotonous and at times its dullness weighs me down and I feel the want of a larger, freer life, excitement, change, anything, anyhow to wake me up from the apathy and lethargy of these fits of dumps.[ii]

It is debatable if Campden beat Broadway in the tourist stakes, but certainly by the end of the next century tourism had come to be a major part of the economy of Campden. Muriel Neve would have been surprised to hear discussions about keeping tourist coaches out of the town, and heated arguments over car parking as Campdonians tried to strike the right balance between preserving the character of the town whilst welcoming visitors As far as her feelings about the dullness of Campden were concerned, she would have been amazed to find that a host of societies and activities kept the town alive at the end of the 20th century, and she would surely have been incredulous to hear the retired population constantly sighing because there was just too much happening in Campden and one could not do everything.

In his introductory essay to *Arts and Crafts Walks in Broadway and Chipping Campden*[iii] Alan Crawford traces the changes in attitude to the Cotswolds at the beginning of the century. Reacting against industrialisation, people sought escape in the countryside, which took them back to their roots. An idealisation of the English landscape developed, based on a southern landscape which was gentle, fertile and domestic. The Cotswolds fitted this myth very well, and drew artistic and literary people to their golden stone towns and villages. Both Broadway and Campden, with their beautiful main streets, were magnets. Edwin Abbey and Frank Millet, both painters, had visited Broadway in the 1880s, taking houses there in the summer, and in 1885 they brought with them the famous American writer Henry James, and John Singer Sargent, who painted his impressionist-style *Carnation, Lily, Lily, Rose* there. Indeed, a little colony of artists grew up in Broadway. A few years later, James published an article about the village in *Harper's New Monthly Magazine*. All this of course put Broadway on the map. Then the architects came. At the end of the 19th century the architect Guy Dawber stirred a new interest in Cotswold houses, and young architects came to draw, learn and copy.

In 1900 Macmillan launched the *Highways and Byways* series of well-illustrated guide books to interesting areas and it was as an illustrator for the *Oxford and The Cotswolds* volume[iv] that F.L. Griggs came to Campden in 1903. In the following years Edwardian tourism was under way. The tourists tended to be well off, able to afford the railway or the motor car, and usually educated and cultured. Gordon Russell's father saw the ways that tourism was developing and had the foresight to buy the large old coaching inn on the High Street in Broadway and turn it into a grand hotel for American visitors and other wealthy tourists. He furnished the Lygon Arms with antiques, setting up a separate workshop nearby to repair and restore them. This eventually became the Gordon Russell furniture business in Broadway. Later, Sir Gordon Russell built Kingcombe House in Campden, lived there with his wife and contributed in many ways to the town.

The coming of the Guild of Handicraft in 1902 brought an influx of friends and visitors with an interest in the arts and crafts. In December 1907 for example T.E. Lawrence, then an undergraduate at Oxford, visited Campden by bicycle with a friend one snowy weekend and called at the Norman Chapel in Broad Campden, where they knew there was a disciple of Morris. They were 'gladly taken in to see the Morris treasures'.[v] The disciple was Ananda Coomaraswamy, an exotic and attractive presence in Campden who had gained an international reputation in oriental art and theology, and in turn his disciples visited him here.[vi]

Of course parallel developments were happening elsewhere in the country. The Arts & Crafts movement was flourishing in the Lake District, too, at the beginning of the 20th century, and with it tourism there was growing.

There was a lull in Campden during the First World War but in the interwar years 'cultural tourism' developed apace.[vii] Some visitors stayed and became residents in Campden: early middle-class incomers to the town. Mrs Martha Dunn wrote to Ashbee in 1928: 'The old town goes on receiving more folks - married and single - quite a motley crew. I do not know half I meet on the street.'[viii]

Books started to appear: both guide books and books based on characters and local stories. Of course the locals played up to this, inventing themselves as characters. In 1931 H.J. Massingham spent a year in the area writing about the Cotswolds and frequenting the Eight Bells Inn. There were many there who knew he would buy them a drink if they told him some good stories, some of which are told in *Wold Without End*, published by Cobden-Sanderson in 1932. Campden was discovered by the BBC in its programme *Microphone at Large*. Visitors came out of curiosity and again many of the visitors settled here. Campden's photogenic background made it a desirable setting for films, which in turn brought it to the attention of visitors. Filming went on throughout the century. For example, *Sorrell and Son* was made here in 1933, *The Franchise Affair* in the fifties, and Pasolini's *Canterbury Tales* in the seventies.

The Second World War called another halt to tourism, though incomers continued to arrive. Now they were evacuees and a number of intellectuals and artists escaping from the city during the war. There were also soldiers and airmen, including US soldiers, billeted about the town in barns and empty dwellings. There were also Italian, and later German, prisoners of war in the camps at Northwick Park and Springhill, and in various smaller camps, including the one at Catbrook. Polish people came to the Springhill camp after the war.

The country recovered in the fifties and in the latter half of the 20th century the town prided itself on a community spirit rising above local tensions. In 1951, as part of the Festival of Britain, Dover's Games were brought back to life after 100 years in abeyance. The communal nature of the town is expressed annually through the Games (also known as the Cotswold Olimpicks) and Scuttlebrook Wake. These two highly local events link to the town's natural love of pageantry and to Griggs's instinct to preserve local custom. Their revival developed into another tourist attraction and by 1966 they were a regular and widely publicised feature, giving the town the image of a place of old traditions and festivals.

The Morris Men dancing the Stick Dance outside the almshouses for the residents, 1976
(By kind permission of Sue Morrey)

At the beginning of the century Scuttlebrook Wake was a traditional Whitsuntide Fair, of the type found throughout the country. There was a queen, with her page and attendants, and a procession of carts, some pulled along the High Street by donkeys, led by men of the town, with tents and side shows in the High Street. In 1938 and 1939 it was decided to organise the events more formally and a small committee was set up under the chairmanship of Reg Smith, the fruit and vegetable grower. (Later his son, Dick Smith, became Chairman). During the war years the fair was suspended and replaced with money-raising events for the war. In 1942 the celebrations started again with a procession led by a horse-drawn decorated trailer. After some years it was decided that the horse was perhaps not an entirely safe form of transport, and the Morris Men pulled the cart. Scuttlebrook Wake took place annually at Whitsuntide and it was a principle of the organisation that neither content nor style should change, in the hope that anyone who returned to Campden after some time away would at least find something that had not changed. Dover's Games, which took place the evening before Scuttlebrook were run by a separate committee, though in consultation with the Scuttlebrook Committee.[ix]

Campden's tradition of pageantry, started in the 19th century, was strengthened by the interest of Ashbee and the Guild. Coronations and jubilees have always been celebrated in elaborate style. As well as the two coronations before the First World War, the Silver Jubilee of King George V in 1935 was marked by a parade of horse-drawn vehicles through the town, a fete in the recreation ground, and a free tea for all the children of the town. The coronation of George VI two years later started with an open air service, followed by the same kind of events, and in 1953 the Queen's coronation, this time watched by many on newly acquired television sets, was the occasion of a pageant in the Coneygree.

Although Campden lost its railway station in 1965 under the 'Beeching axe', by the sixties, with growing affluence and ease of motor transport, tourism took off again. So much so that people complained that there were not enough bed and breakfast establishments. The *Cotswold Chronicle*, the journal of the parish council, recorded in 1966 that the town was thronged with tourists. The parish council saw its role to encourage tourism as a basis for the town's prosperity and the town guide, sponsored by the Chamber of Trade and the council, was sent out all over the world.

In the latter half of the 20th century people's appreciation for the countryside began to be formalised. The Cotswolds was first designated an Area of Outstanding Natural Beauty in 1966, and in 1968 the Volunteer Cotswold Wardens were established. The long distance path, the Cotswold Way, from Campden to Bath was opened in 1970. A new kind of tourist, the hill walker, was attracted to the area and required accommodation in the town and parking spaces in the streets. In 1970 much of Chipping Campden had been declared a conservation area, and Broad Campden followed soon after. Here was another reason for people to visit and indeed move to the area. However, unlike some other local towns and villages, there were severe planning restrictions on the growth of Campden, and although these helped it retain much of its character, they limited the number of resident incomers, while affecting the price of houses.

Out of season the town was still quiet. In March 1970 a photographer came to illustrate an article for *New Society* with reference to the reorganisation of Local Government. The *Chronicle* observed: 'His modern unisex clothing made him noticeable in our quiet streets.'[x]

In the early 1970s television discovered the attractions of Campden. A series about a doctor, *Owen MD*, was filmed here and Grevel House, then the town surgery, was used as his residence in the programme. The local television news programme *Midlands Today* often focused on Campden. More visitors came to see the settings they had seen on television. However, there was still a shortage of bed and breakfast places and in 1974 there were only two in the town. By the end of the century there were 16 such establishments, eight hotels or inns, and ten self-catering cottages. By the seventies, the *Chronicle* again reported that the town was flooded with visitors. A car park was called for in the centre of Campden, and lavatories at the St James's end of town. Neither of these facilities had been provided by the end of the century.

A popular area for visitors to the town to explore and sit in was the Wilson Memorial Garden, opened in 1984. In the seventies a decision was taken, at the suggestion of Sir Gordon Russell, that a garden be created as a permanent memorial to Ernest Henry 'Chinese' Wilson, the distinguished botanist. Wilson, much of whose life was spent plant-hunting and botanising abroad, was born in Campden in 1876. In 1980 the town acquired the lower half of the large vicarage garden opening onto Leysbourne and the plot was laid out after a design by Sir Peter Shepheard, with plants selected from the 1200 or so that Wilson had introduced. Money was raised locally for maintenance and an annual lecture, and many of the plants were donated by individuals and nurseries.

The eighties saw the refurbishment of hotels and a burgeoning of restaurants. For some years tourist information was provided in Woolstaplers Hall, Ashbee's former home on the High Street, which was also a museum of bygones. In 1996 the museum and hence the tourist office closed down, to the detriment of the bed-and-breakfast providers. A committee was formed to set up a local tourist office and after negotiation a grant was made available, an office was opened and at the end of the 20th century about 35,000 people had asked for information in one year.[xi] St James's Church, one of the great attractions for visitors, regularly had over 40,000 visitors a year by the end of the century. A rota of volunteers for Church Watch made it possible for the church to be open to visitors every day. Events like Cheltenham Races and the Royal Show at Stoneleigh brought visitors to the town; theatre-goers at Stratford stayed here and actors became regular customers of the shops. Obviously these numbers brought great amounts of business and income to the town.

So by the nineties the town was relying heavily on income from visitors. Ironically, however, Campden had become a victim of its own success. Coaches, tourist buses and cars threatened to ruin the old stone with pollution and vibration, and the peace of that famous High Street had long gone. Houses to rent for the summer months had been available throughout the century, but the increase of tourism brought the increase of holiday homes to rent, with the drawback of empty houses in the town for at least some of the year. However, a positive development in the closing years of the century was the gift to Landmark Trust of the grounds of Old Campden House. Using skilled craftsmen they restored and converted the two Banqueting Houses and the Almonry to provide luxury holiday accommodation.

But a phenomenon which caused more distress to the full-time residents was that of the 'sterilised house': the sharp increase in property values encouraged people to buy houses simply for investment, leaving them empty for most of the year. Several houses on the High Street fell into this category. This deprived the residents of accommodation, the town of income and the neighbours of security and friendliness.

Supported by the growth in tourism, other businesses developed. In the first half of the century Campden High Street was characterised by butchers, bakers and grocers shops, fruiterers, fishmongers, shoemakers, drapers, haberdashers and tailors. There were a very few craft shops, the offshoot of the Guild of Handicraft, but that was all. By the end of the century Campden fortunately still had a butcher, a baker, grocers and a fruiterer. However, encouraged by the presence of wealthy American tourists and the backdrop of period buildings, antique shops and art galleries were flourishing in the High Street. Indeed when many people thought of Campden they had in mind gleaming copper and brass, polished oak, silver, and a colourful array of china in old shop windows. As a spin-off from the antiques trade, other businesses, like furniture restoration, jewellery and picture framing were established.

In the latter part of the 20th century Campden became famous as a centre for needlework which created another draw for tourists.[xii] The Campden Needlework Centre was opened in 1972. At the time there were no specialist needlework shops in the country. Knitting as a craft was declining and the time was ripe for a boom in the needlework market. In the late seventies the first kits were produced which led to an upsurge of interest in the craft. An enthusiastic staff was employed, including some younger people who had read for degrees in embroidery. The proprietress visited graduate shows and followed the latest developments.

Until the late eighties classes were held above the shop. Summer schools and public lectures were also run. People came from all over the country for these courses, staying in Campden and bringing trade to the town. In the eighties exhibitions were also held above the shop. The Needlework Centre also supplied churches, cathedrals and ecclesiastical workshops with materials for their embroideries, including materials for the kneelers in St James's Church in Campden. For all their success and international outlook, the shop's staff were part of the local community.[xiii]

Among other businesses was a shop selling furnishings and interior décor;[xiv] an upholstery business and the Campden Weavers. This group of businesses shows how this small town was able to survive by building up a specialist economy. A similar example was Campden's famous wine shop, housed in a 1727 building in the High Street. This building had been in the same family since 1931 when Enoch Bennett purchased it to expand his rapidly growing bakery business. His son, Harry continued to run the bakery until 1968 after which the premises were turned into a health food shop and delicatessen. In 1979 Harry's son obtained a wine licence and after 1985 concentrated on wine. The shop became nationally known.

This was another example of a business carried on in Campden by generations of the same family, like the Harts, silversmiths, whose workshop was still in the old metal workers shop in the Silk Mill, but whose name had become known nationally. Silversmiths working there include the grandson and two great-grandsons of guildsman George Hart. People can respond in business to the changing nature and tastes of the area, and in some cases can expand beyond the local clientele to an international one.

At least equally renowned, especially in America, was the family business of the well-known industrial designer and silversmith, Robert Welch, whose founder worked in the Silk Mill from the 1950s until his death. Both design work and the business of selling were carried on by his descendants, in the shop at the corner of Sheep Street.

Incomers continued to move into Campden in increasingly large numbers. The town's geographical location attracted many. Some people commuted to Birmingham or London; many retired here, drawn by the beauty of the architecture and the countryside, the shopping and other facilities, and the vast amount of activities available.

To house all these people much new building went on. Throughout the first twenty years after the Second World War, as incomers took over and restored houses and cottages in the main street, many local people were forced to move to less expensive accommodation at the outskirts of the town. Council housing, begun after the First World War, proceeded apace. The estate at Littleworth, built in the early 1950s, was a particularly good development. Then came more houses in Berrington Road, Coronation Close and in Broad Campden. Finally there were also the Badger's Field old people's housing, the shared leasehold houses at The Bratches and at the end of the century a Housing Association development behind Catbrook.

Newly built houses in Littleworth showing first crop of potatoes in front garden, c.1952
(Roland Dyer/G of H Trust)

In addition there was much building for private sale. The first major development was Cherry Orchard Close, followed by Pear Tree Close in the sixties. In an account of the Campden Society strategy adopted in 2002, the

President listed and commented upon private building that had taken place within the historic settlement in the last quarter of the 20th century.[xv] The award- winning Wold's End housing was started in 1975 and was developed very much in association with the Campden Society. Griggs Close, Haysums Close, Badgers Field, and Haydons Close were all built before 1985. After that, as well as a great deal of infilling, numerous small group developments had taken place. These included Seymour Gate and Rolling Stones (Back Ends); Glebe Fold, the Old Grammar School Mews, Noel Court, Coldicott Close and Grafton Mews; new houses at Littleworth and Dovers Orchard (Hoo Lane); other housing in Aston Road; also Weighbridge Court, Berrington Orchards, Poplars Close, two groups in Park Road and at Top Farm in Blind Lane.

In 1945 the number of houses in the historic settlement was about 450; in 1970 this had risen to about 580, and in 1982 the figure was about 640. By the end of the century the number was over 800. So from the early seventies to the end of the century the housing stock increased by 40 per cent. However, in spite of the building growth, population in the town stayed at around 2000: demographic and social changes meant fewer people lived in each house, and the number of holiday cottages and second homes grew. In 1985 the Cotswold District Council adopted the Chipping Campden Planning Policy, which sought to limit development and retain the green spaces and the character of the old town. This was an important advance, but nevertheless much development occurred after 1985, and at the end of the century as house prices soared, there was pressure on the remaining sites.

Apart from building, other major works to the fabric of the town were carried out in the 20th century. Throughout the 19th century, if not earlier, Campden had suffered from occasional flooding, mainly caused by the overflowing brook, the Cam. Park Road (formerly called Watery Lane) and Sheep Street have always suffered from prolonged rain or flash flooding. In the 1980s localised summer storms caused widespread flooding in the town. A report made for the Cotswold District Council[xvi] led to very considerable work on improving the drains and the town appears at last to be free of the danger.

One project which illustrates the care for Campden's special character is the renewal of the town centre's pavements. In the 1890s concrete footpaths had been laid down through the High Street and other streets in the centre of the town. However, as a result of the use of unsuitable materials for repair over many years, large parts of the footways were becoming unworthy of the quality of the town. In 1973 the Campden Society, together with the Town Council, sourced grants of £40,000 and made an appeal which produced a further £11,000. With this the footpaths in the High Street were all relaid by 1982. There was some opposition to the project on the grounds that Campden would become too gentrified, but others thought the town would be enhanced. In 1985 the District Council drew up planning policy for the town and this proved a significant milestone in bringing planning issues to public attention, and in defining boundaries and controlling development.

Street lighting was a matter of controversy in Campden throughout the 20th century. In the early part of the century it was a question of gas or electricity, and changes between the two were made several times. In the latter half of the century it was design of the lights in the town. In the 1980s there was some dissatisfaction with the lights then installed, which were thought not to be in keeping with its character. However, after some years of planning and a generous donation from Frank Mottershead, new lights were installed in 1994.

Curiously, despite all this development, Campden lost its last resident policeman towards the end of the century. The Police Station had been built in the 1870s to provide a magistrates court, with its cells, as well as accommodation for a superintendent and a sergeant and offices for a number of constables. Little more than a hundred years later it stood more or less abandoned for some years. A campaign was launched in the last decade of the century to acquire the Police Station for communal use. As the century closed it was planned to turn the magistrates court into a meeting room with a display of Campden history, and to house many other social and commercial activities there, including the Town Clerk's office, Tourist Information Office, the Historical Society archives, an education room and a room for voluntary help groups.

No history of Campden in the 20th century would be complete without reference to a publication which had in many ways been the life-blood of the town, the *Campden Bulletin*. Organised and edited by Jeremy Green, the *Bulletin* announced and reported on the town's activities and had a lively letters page. It was funded by advertising which means that it was not beholden to any benefactor and could, and did, exercise freedom of expression. From 1966 its predecessor, the *Cotswold Chronicle* had been published under the editorship of the Clerk to the Parish Council. However, that ceased publication in 1978 with the death of its founder.

In 1982 it was realised that people were reluctant to go to Town Council meetings and trouble arose because they did not know what planning decisions had been made. It was thought that if everyone knew what was happening some disputes would be avoided. William Barnes, a young man from Broad Campden was persuaded to start the *Bulletin.* In 1983 Jeremy Green took it over, attended Town Council meetings and reported on the decisions of elected representatives on planning and other matters. The *Bulletin* grew in size and was eventually delivered free to every house in Campden, Ebrington and Weston-Sub-Edge, with copies to Aston-Sub-Edge and Mickleton. It quickly attracted advertisers. The town had many people to thank for this newspaper which, written in a witty, entertaining and often provocative way, can be said to have helped to keep the town together.

At the end of the 20th century Campden was now officially once again a town with a Town Mayor replacing the Chairman of the old Parish Council. It was a special place with a strong community spirit and many active townsfolk. Its beauty was much admired and much sought after. But it was not without problems. Traffic was perhaps the greatest of these, and the question of a car park and its site was argued hotly throughout the later decades, without a solution being found. Over-development was feared, as was the loss of essential shops and services. The town had always been resilient, however, and would no doubt adapt to change as it had done throughout the centuries.

Campden as a community is a product of its history. Over the centuries it has passed through many phases, from a small Saxon agricultural community to a market town; through periods of decline followed by prosperity in the late 20th century. Often renaissance was stimulated by successful incomers such as William Grevel, Baptist Hicks and C.R. Ashbee. One remarkable characteristic is stability in population and until very recently in the number of houses and in the economy as a whole. Even in the 19th century, despite the advent of the railway, gaslight, the telegraph and the penny post, Campden's fortunes continued as ever to rely on agriculture but by the end of the 20th century there had been striking changes. Although there was still some successful farming, Campden had become dependent on tourism.

"The most beautiful" High Street *(Jesse Taylor/G of H Trust)*

Its community spirit has enabled the town to cope with the stresses of change, the development of tourism and the impact of the motor car. Traditions such as Scuttlebrook Wake and morris dancing have continued and some useful shops have been preserved. In addition Campden has maintained a lively cultural and social life and thriving leisure activities to meet the needs of all sections of the community. Increasingly the townspeople have become stewards of the architecture and the beauty of its surroundings, which attracted benefactors like Griggs to the town and which prompted G.M. Trevelyan justly to call the curving High Street ' ... the most beautiful village [*sic*] street left in the island'.

Notes

i Muriel Neve's Journal, quoted in Caroline Mason's *Papers*, op cit
ii ibid
iii Crawford , Alan, *Arts & Crafts Walks* (Guild of Handicraft Trust, 2002)
iv Evans, Herbert A., *Highways and Byways in Oxford and the Cotswolds* (London,

Macmillan 1919)

v Stewart, Desmond, *Biography of T.E. Lawrence* (London, Hamish Hamilton 1977), 29

vi Mairet, Philippe, *Autobiographical papers*, 19, quoted by Mason, Carolyn, Papers IIA Ch.1. CADHAS archive

vii Fees, Craig, *Christmas Mumming* op cit 'Tourism' 99

viii ibid. Incomers 112 (Interestingly enough, the Campden dentist, Mr John Payton, having lived in Campden since 1975 remarked at the end of the 20th century, 'I don't know half the people I meet on the street.' Both comments reveal the expectation that in a town this size everyone will know everyone else.)

ix Conversation with Dick Smith, 24th April.2003

x Mason, Carolyn, *Papers* 'Tourism' notes op cit

xi Hart, Dorothy, details from Tourist Information Office

xii Conversation with Judy Lusty, April 2003

xiii Conversation with Helen Kirkup, 13th Feb. 2003

xiv Conversation with Judy Lusty, April 2003

xv For more information on the work of the Campden Society see Ch 27

xvi The report was prepared by Brigadier David Atkinson.

APPENDIX I

The Descent of the Manor from 1232 - 1540

The four heirs of Sir Roger de Somery who inherited Campden in 1273 were Sir John le Strange, Henry de Erdington, Sir Walter de Sully and Ralph de Crumwell. Sir John le Strange soon took over Henry de Erdington's share, but died in about 1274. In 1286 his son granted this half of the manor to one Sir John de Lodelowe.[i] Lodelowe and his descendants were wool merchants, probably based in Shrewsbury. The Abbot of Bruerne in Oxfordshire acknowledges in 1286 and again in 1289 and 1290 large debts to the Lodelowes for wool.[ii] According to R.H. Hilton, a John Lodelowe held property in Coventry, a centre of the wool trade, in 1275.[iii] The Shrewsbury connection continues, however, for in 1327 Bogo de Lodelowe, then lord of Campden, was murdered there.[iv]

This half of the manor remained in the hands of Lodelowes and their descendants for some 200 years. In the Poll Tax returns of 1381, Thomas Lodelowe and his wife Elizabeth, the then holders of the moiety, were living in Berrington, presumably in the manor house there. He died in 1391. His son, Edward Lodelowe, had close relations with William Grevel, whose daughter he married. Edward died in 1409 leaving as his heir, a 14 year old daughter, Margaret.[v] Thereafter the succession to this part of the manor becomes complicated, possibly due to the mortality caused by successive recurrences of the Black Death.

Margaret Lodelowe married Baldwyn Straunge,[vi] who was put in possession of the manor. Straunge died in 1431 leaving a daughter, Elizabeth, who later married Robert Molyneux. Elizabeth was succeeded by her son John Molyneux, who died in 1473 aged only 26, leaving a baby daughter, Cecily. At this stage an allegedly fraudulent trust was set up and the half manor was enfeoffed to three Molyneux brothers, ostensibly in trust for the baby girl, but in fact was taken over by one of the trustees, another John Molyneux, who died in possession. Cecily then succeeded. She married, first, John Fitzherbert and then John Josselyn. She died quite young, in 1502, and her second husband was then seized of the manor for life.[vii] He passed it to his stepson, Eustace Fitzherbert, and from him it went to Eustace's daughter, Elizabeth Fitzherbert, whose second marriage was to Sir Thomas Smyth, of whom much more in Chapter 7.[viii]

Walter de Sully, an associate of the earls of Gloucester, was the inheritor of one of the other quarters of Campden. He died in about 1286, and Gilbert de Clare, then Earl of Gloucester, claimed the whole of Campden for himself, but succeeded in obtaining only de Sully's share. A number of de Clare's descendants held this share until, in 1314, another Gilbert de Clare was killed at the Battle of Bannockburn, and it passed first to Nicholas de Clare[ix] and then to his sister, who was married to Hugh d'Audley, later himself created Earl of Gloucester. Hugh d'Audley joined the Earl of Lancaster's rebellion against Edward II soon after succeeding, and for a time his lands were committed to Bogo de Lodelowe, who then held the Lodelowe moiety.[x] When Hugh was pardoned in 1327 his lands were returned to him. He died in 1347, leaving as his heir a daughter, Margaret, who was married to Sir Richard de Stafford.[xi]

Meanwhile Sir Roger de Somery's son-in-law, Ralph de Crumwell, the holder of the fourth portion of de Somery's estate, had died in 1299, to be succeeded by his son, also Ralph.[xii] When Ralph junior died about 1316 his widow married Ralph Bassett of Drayton. Bassett died in 1343 and a few years later this portion also fell to Sir Richard de Stafford. How Stafford succeeded is not clear and there seems at one stage to have been a dispute over custody between him and the Earl of Warwick.[xiii] Stafford was a kinsman of Ralph Bassett and possibly succeeded on the early death of his son. This quarter of the manor was thus united with the d'Audley quarter, under Sir Richard de Stafford. From this time on the manor of Campden was divided into just two moieties, known as the Ludlow Manor and the Stafford Manor.

When Richard Stafford died there was a hiatus, as Richard's son Edmund was a priest who later became Bishop of Exeter. Edmund only succeeded when Richard's wife died in 1399.[xiv] He himself died in 1419 and thereafter the succession seems confused. For a time Campden was in the hands of Edmund's nephew, Thomas, but when he died in 1425, the moiety was taken into the king's hands. At this stage John Stafford, Bishop of Bath and Wells, with others, claimed Campden,[xv] but Thomas's widow seems to have continued the tenancy until she died.

In a rather obscure way the succession of this half of the manor then seems to have fallen first to Sir William Norreys, a dissident during the reign of Richard III, who was deprived of the lordship by the king,[xvi] and later to

Thomas Stanley who had married a niece of Thomas Stafford. From him it passed successively to Sir John Stanley, to another John Stanley and to his daughter, Ann, who married Christopher Savage. In 1544, Savage's son, another Christopher, sold half his moiety to Thomas Bonner, a wealthy Campdonian, and half to the same Sir Thomas Smyth who had succeeded to the Ludlow moiety. As will be seen later, Bonner's son in turn granted it to Sir Thomas Smyth, who thus after 250 years reunited de Somery's manor, though it still excluded both Broad Campden and Combe.

Notes

i *Cal. Close Rolls* 28 April 1286. The reason for these transactions is obscure, but it appears that both John le Strange and his son had many debts, and the grant to Lodelowe may have been made to clear some of these. Sir John was a marcher lord and this may explain the connection of the Lodelowes with Shrewsbury.

ii See *Patent Rolls* 1272 692; *Close Rolls* 8 May 1289 1290

iii R.H. Hilton, *Stoneleigh Leger Book* (Dugdale Soc 1960) and *Unprinted Hundred Rolls for Coventry* (Leigh Collection in Shakespeare Record Office)

iv *Cal Patent Rolls* 1327; 15 March & 13 June

v *Inq post mortem* 11 Henry IV No 18; see also the will of Edward Lodelowe, proved January 1410

vi *Cal Pat Rolls* 20 Feb 1410 (159); & *Cal Pat Rolls* 11 Henry IV Part 1 (1420) 20 Feb. There was some irregularity in this marriage, and in 1415 the Pope issued a declaration on their petition that the two had contracted a lawful marriage, but without the Banns, and had offspring.

vii *Cal Inq p. m* 18 Henry VII Series II Vol 16; 11 July

viii *Cal Inq.p.m.* 19 Henry VII; 24th Jan 1504

ix *Abbrev Rotuli Originalis in Curia Scaccarii*, Vol I; (8 Edw II) Estreat of the gross fines etc

x *Abbrev Rotuli Originalis* Vol I 14 Edw II 255

xi *Cal Close Rolls* 16 Nov 1347; *Cal Patent Rolls* 16 Nov 1347

xii *Patent Rolls* 8 Mar 1257; Close Rolls 1267; *Cal Genealogicum* 27 Edw I No 26; 565

xiii *Cal Close Rolls* 1343 - 17 Edw III; 28 Dec (Calendar)

xiv *Cal Close Rolls* 3 March 1403 (4 Hy IV)

xv *Cal Pat Rolls* 12 Jan 1427

xvi *Cal Pat Rolls* 29 Aug 1484 (472)

APPENDIX II

400 Years of Separation: Combe and Broad Campden

When the monks of Bordesley Abbey were granted Combe in 1150 they held it as a 'grange' in *frank almoin*, an ecclesiastical form of tenure that released the land from any obligations of homage or service to a superior lord (other than spiritual duties such as the offering of prayers). The abbey was to maintain six monks there perpetually, to pray for the health of the grantor's soul, the soul of his father, his grandfather, his mother, and of all Christian souls.[i] Confirmations of the grant were made by Henry II and Richard I.[ii]

Although Earl Ranulf's grant had intended that a group of monks would reside there and work the land, we do not know whether, or for how long, any religious house (a cell of Bordesley for instance) was in fact established at Combe. By the 14th century the abbey had begun to lease out the land at Combe. In the early 14th century for instance the abbot leased the 'manor' of 'Cumbe next Campedene' to one Adam de Hervynton for 10 marks a year. This lease was confirmed by a local inquisition in 1342, where it is restated that 'the abbot of Bordesley holds the manor of Cumbe from the heirs of Ranulf, formerly earl of Chester, in *frank almoin*'.[iii]

The grant to Adam de Hervynton was not an isolated one. Rushen[iv] refers to other tenants of Combe: Henry de la Rever in the early 15th century and Rob Jefford of Weston later in the same century.[v] Then sometime in the 1530s one Ralph Sheldon of Beoley was granted a lease of Combe for a term of at least 25 years. Ralph was succeeded by his son, William, a Member of Parliament and supporter of the first English tapestry weaver, Richard Hicks.[vi] Sheldon may have continued as lessee of Combe for a time after the Dissolution, but in April 1553, the new lord of Campden, Thomas Smyth and his second wife, Katherine, were granted Combe Grange by Letters Patent of his former master, Henry VIII.[vii] From that time on Combe has been treated as part of Westington — although memories of the old dispensation persisted for some time. It was treated as the freehold property of the lord of the manor, even before the Enclosures, and was leased out as an 'old enclosure' to farmers or farmed in hand from the 16th century on.

The history of Broad Campden after it was separated from the rest of Campden is equally complicated. As we have seen in Chapter 2, Ranulph de Blundeville had granted it in 1199 to the guardian of his new wife, who in turn passed it to one of his own knights, Guiomar le Breton, or Brito. The royal confirmation of this grant reads in part:

> John, Dei Gratia, etc. Know that we have granted, and this present charter confirms, to Guiomar Breton and his heirs the gift which William de Feugieres has given him, that is to say all the manor of Twyford with all its appurtenances and all the land which he had at Campden of the gift of the earl of Chester, to him and his heirs to hold from him and his heirs by the service of a quarter of a knight's fee.[viii]

This land is recognised to have been the hamlet of Broad Campden. It is probable that Guiomar was entitled to the rents and service of the tenants of his land, but did not have any demesne lands there. He did not hold Broad Campden long. He fought alongside his lord in Prince Arthur's rebellion against King John, was captured at the siege of Mirabeau in 1203 and imprisoned at Corfe Castle in Dorset. And here lies the source of another story. For, as the historian Powicke says:

> The less important prisoners taken at Mirabeau were ... massed together in England at Corfe, where they were sufficiently free and sufficiently numerous to conspire and for a short time to capture the keep.[ix]

Guiomar may have been among the leaders of this revolt, for after it was put down he was transferred with four others to Caen in Normandy,[x] to be kept there with the more important prisoners from Mirabeau. He lay in prison for some years, until a ransom of 82 marks and 'ten large beautiful and good greyhounds' was arranged.[xi] No doubt he forfeited Twyford and Broad Campden as a result of his support for the rebellion.

Broad Campden seems then to have reverted into the king's hands for a time, and we next hear of it in April 1216 when the Earl Marshal granted 60s worth of land at Parva Campden to Walon de Cotes, a knight in King John's household.[xii] Walon and an associate, Everard de la Beverie, had fought with King John throughout his wars in France and in Scotland and were given rather insecure grants of land from time to time as part payment for their service. However, Walon died about 1219, and the land at Broad Campden presumably reverted once again into the king's hands.[xiii]

Broad Campden's subsequent history is clouded. By 1238 a Richard de Greinville was the tenant-in-chief, but how he obtained this position is not clear.

Greinville (who was possibly one of the king's favourites) had been acquiring land in Devon and Somerset and as early as 1200 a dispute between him and the Abbot of Tewkesbury over the advowson of two churches in Devon was settled by a gift from Greinville to the king of 40 marks and one palfrey.[xiv] Then in 1238 an agreement signed in the king's court at Launceston between Greinville and the Abbot of Tewkesbury settling another long-standing dispute, ended by Greinville granting to the abbot and convent 62 yardlands (about 2,000 acres) in Broad Campden, yielding 5 marks (£3 6s 8d) annually in rent. After the death of the then tenant :

> all his land in Parva Campedene shall be extended according to the provisions of the aforesaid justices and is ceded by right to the use of the abbot and convent in perpetuity.[xv]

This land included the Norman Chapel, which had now become the Chapel of St Mary Magdalene.

Richard de Greinville, who remained tenant-in-chief of the hamlet, died in 1240[xvi] and although his widow brought a case against the abbot 'for the restitution of her dower of our land of Campedene', the case was quashed.[xvii] In 1259 a rather obscure note in the abbey's annals notes that :

> Egidius Scissor died, who held Parva Campedene and connived much ill to the chamberlain of Theokesberie.[xviii]

It appears likely that Egidius Scissor (whom Rushen calls Giles Carver) held another part of Broad Campden from the Greinvilles. It is clear, however, that the Greinvilles continued to hold the hamlet, for when Sir Roger de Somery died in 1273 another Richard de Greinville and Richard de Croiville jointly held Broad Campden by one knight's fee, and paid suit at the court of the lord of Campden every three weeks.[xix] Evidently, Broad Campden was at that time still feudally attached to Campden rather than being a separate manor.

Two rolls of Broad Campden names were taken during the 14th Century. In the first, the 1327 Subsidy Roll, 14 names are listed. However, no lord of the manor is named there. The 1381 Poll Tax returns are more complete. They name 78 persons, living in about 35 households. Of these, 21 households have the description 'cultor terre' or peasant farmer. The heads of two households, both surnamed Weoley, are described, as 'frankleyn' or freeman.

From that time until the 16th century Broad Campden almost disappears from the records. The abbey however continued to hold land there and is referred to from time to time.[xx] Meanwhile the lordship of this manor passed to the Russell family. At the end of the 15th century it was held by Robert Russell and then by his widow, Elizabeth, who left it to her son, another Robert.[xxi] By the 1520s it was held by Sir Thomas Russell. At that time Broad Campden was said to be held 'of William Norreys knight and John Josseleyn as of their manor of Chepyngecampeden', so it appears that during the whole of this time the hamlet paid suit to Campden, as it had done in 1273.

Broad Campden remained separated from the rest of Campden, until it was bought by Anthony Smyth in 1602 and combined back with the rest of the manor of Campden. From that time on, after 300 years of division, and in the case of Broad Campden and Combe, 400 years of separation, Campden was once again unified as a single manor under one lord.

Notes

i See Dugdale, *Monasticon* Vol V 407 - 413

ii For the inspeximus and confirmation of these charters see *Cal Charter Rolls* 51 Henry III; Membrane 10; 28 Dec 1266

iii Madge, S.J., *Inquisitiones Post Mortem for Gloucestershire* (Record Society) 1342 .298/99: Combe.The use of the term 'manor' in these documents is anomalous. The landholdings of Cistercian abbeys were usually on vacant land or recently cleared land, worked by the lay brothers themselves, or by hired labourers.

iv Rushen, op cit 14

v ibid 12

vi For further details of the Sheldon tenure, see 'Bordesley Abbey & the Land at Combe' *CADHAS Notes & Queries* Vol II no 6 & Vol III No 1

vii Rushen, op cit 13. This may originally have been another lease, for another document quoted in the *Monasticon* (Roll 30 of the Deeds in the Augmentation Office of 1595 — Accounts of the King's Ministers in the time of Henry VIII) — says, 'Combe the revenue from the Grange : £20 0 0d.' (Dugdale *Monasticon* Vol 5 143)

viii Hardy, T.D., (ed): *Rotuli Chartarum in Turri Londinensis* (Records Commission London 1837) 1 John, 1199; 21. Both Rushen and Whitfield have misread this charter.

ix Powicke, F.M., *The Loss of Normandy* (Manchester 1913) 360

x Hardy, T.D. (ed) *Rotuli Litterarum Patentum* (London, Records Commission, 1835) 6 John 1204, Memb 8 (46)

xi *Rot Litt Pat.* 8 John, 1206 Memb 3 (68) and 8 John, 1207 Memb 1 (71)

xii *Rot Litterarum Clausarum* 1 ; 17 John, 261

xiii For details see Warmington 'Some Knights of the household of King John' *Trans B & G Arch Society* 1986

xiv *Rot de Oblatis* 2 John 1200 (76)

xv *Annales of Theokesberie* 1238 108; *Feet of Fines for Gloucs* 315

xvi *Annales of Theokesberie* 1240 118; *Close Rolls* 1241

xvii *Annales of Theokesberie* 1249 138

xviii ibid 1259 168

xix *Chan Inq p.m.* 1 Edw I No 15

xx The Taxatio of Pope Nicholas in 1288 reports that Tewkesbury Abbey held 66s 8d in rent in Broad Campden, and the Valor Ecclesiasticus at the time of the Dissolution values the holding there of Bro Andrew, chamberlain of Tewkesbury Abbey at £4. In 1546 Tewkesbury Abbey conveyed a 'moiety of Broad Campden' to James Gunter and Willm Lawes for 8s.

xxi *Chan Inq p.m* 18 Henry VII 20 May: C Series II Vol 16

SELECT BIBLIOGRAPHY

Printed Books

1. Campden History

a. General Histories

Nelson, J.P., *Broad Campden* (privately printed, 1971)

Nelson, J.P., *Broad Campden*, A Supplement (privately printed, 1972)

Nelson. J.P., *Chipping Campden* (privately printed, 1975)

Powell, Geoffrey, *The Book of Campden: History in Stone* (Barracuda Books, 1983)

Rushen, Percy C., *The History and Antiquities of Chipping Campden* (privately printed 1911; 2nd edition)

Whitfield, Christopher, *A History of Chipping Campden* (Shakespeare Head Press, 1958)

b. Particular Subjects

Ashbee, C.R., *Last Records of a Cotswold Community* (Chipping Campden, 1904)

Bishop, Leighton, ed., *General Accounts of the Churchwardens of Chipping Campden 1626-1907* Campden Record Series, 1992)

Burns, Francis, *Heigh for Cotswold : A History of Robert Dover's Olimpick Games* (Robert Dover's Games Society, 2000; revised edition)

Burns, Francis, *Robert Dover's Cotswold Olimpicks - the Twentieth Century Games* (Robert Dover's Games Society 2000)

Clark, Sir George, ed., *The Campden Wonder* (OUP, 1959)

Coldicott, F.W., *Memories of an Old Campdonian* (CADHAS, 1996)

Cook, Robert, *Chipping Campden School 1440-1990* (Shipston on Stour, Peter I Drinkwater, 1990)

Crawford, Alan, *Arts and Crafts Walks in Broadway and Chipping Campden*, (Chipping Campden, Guild of Handicraft Trust, 2002)

Fees, Craig, ed., *A Child in Arcadia; The Chipping Campden Boyhood of H.T. Osborn* (CADHAS, 1986, 1997)

Griffiths, Josephine, *A Book of Remembrance*, (privately printed, 1923)

Griffiths, Josephine, *Chipping Campden Today and Yesterday*, (Campden, T Elsley, 1931)

Hughes, Denis, *Campden at War 1939-1945* (Campden, Reminisce, 2004)

Jones, Celia and others, *The Inns and Alehouses of Chipping Campden and Broad Campden*, (CADHAS, 1998)

Noel, Gerard, *Sir Gerard Noel MP and the Noels of Chipping Campden and Exton* (CADHAS, 2004)

Wood, Jack V., *Some Rural Quakers*, (York, Willam Sessions Ltd., 1991)

2. Artists, Craftworkers and Writers Associated with Campden

Breeze, George et al., *Arthur and Georgie Gaskin*, (Birmingham, BMAG, 1981)

Carruthers, Annette, Greensted, Mary, ed., '*The Guild of Handicraft at Chipping Campden*' in *The Arts and Crafts Movement in the Cotswolds* (Sutton, 1993)

Coatts, Margot, *A Weaver's Life : Ethel Mairet. 1872 - 1952* (Crafts Council, 1983)

Crawford, Alan, *C.R. Ashbee : Architect, Designer & Romantic Socialist* (Yale, 1985)

Gordon, Catherine, *Chipping Campden* (Alan Sutton, 1993)

Jewson, Norman, *By Chance I did Rove* (Kineton, Roundhead Press, 1973)
Jones, T.F.G., *The Various Lives of Wentworth Huyshe* (CADHAS, 1998)
MacCarthy, Fiona, *The Simple Life, C.R. Ashbee in the Cotswolds* (London, Lund Humphries, 1981)
Mairet, Philip, Sisson, C.H. ed., *Autobiographical and Other Pieces* (Manchester, Carcanet, 1981)
Moore, Jerrold Northrop, *F L Griggs: The Architecture of Dreams* (Oxford, Clarendon Press, 1999)
Russell, Gordon, *Designer's Trade* (Allen & Unwin, 1956)
Sleigh, B., *Wood Engraving since 1890 with 80 illustrations from the works of past and contemporary engravers - and many practical hints upon its technique and uses* (London, Pitman & Sons, 1932)
Welch, Robert, *Design in a Cotswold Workshop* (London, Lund Humphries, 1973)
Welch, Robert, *Hand and Machine* (privately printed, 1986)
Wilgress, Jane, *Alec Miller: Guildsman and Sculptor in Chipping Campden* (CADHAS, 1998)
Wright, Harold J.L., *The Etched Work of FL Griggs*, RA, RE, FSA, with a Catalogue by Campbell Dodgson, Hon. R.E., (The Printer Collectors Club, 1941)

3. Other Books

Atkyns, Sir Robert, *The Ancient and the Present State of Gloucestershire, Part 1, 1712* (EP Publishing, 1977; reprinted)
Bigland, Ralph, Brian Frith ed., *Historical Collection Relative to the County of Gloucester*, Part 1, Vol 2 (BGAS, 1989)
Derrett, J.D.M., ed., *A Second Blockley Miscellany* (privately printed, 1994)
Dyer, Christopher, *Everyday Life in Medieval England* (Hambledon Press, 1994)
Dyer, Christopher, *Making a Living in the Middle Ages* (Yale, 2002)
Finberg, H.P.R., ed., *Gloucestershire Studies* (Leicester University Press, 1957)
Gissing, Algernon, *The Footpath Way in Gloucestershire* (Dent, 1924)
Hilton, R.H., *The Medieval Society: The West Midlands at the End of the Thirteenth Century* (Weidenfeld & Nicholson, 1967)
Hoyle, R.W., ed., *The Military Survey of Gloucestershire, 1522* (BGAS, Gloucestershire Record Series Vol. 6, 1993)
Icely, H.E.M., *Blockley Through Twelve Centuries* (Bungay, Paradigm Press, 1984)
Jones, Anthea, *The Cotswolds* (Chichester, Phillimore, 1994)
Lane, Geoffrey, *Lanes of Campden* (Ealing, 2000; 2nd edition)
Marshall, William, *Rural Economy of Glos*, Vols 1 & 2, 1789; (Reprinted: ed G. Nicol, Alan Sutton1979)
Moore, John, ed., *Domesday Book: Gloucestershire* (Philimore, 1982)
Noel, Emilia F., *Some Letters and Records of the Noel Family* (St Catherine Press, 1910)
Prestwich, Menna, *Cranfield : Politics and Profits under the early Stuarts* (Clarendon Press 1966)
Smith, John, ed., *Men and Armour for Gloucestershire in 1608* (Alan Sutton, 1980)
Tennant, Philip, *Edgehill and Beyond*, (Alan Sutton, 1992)
Thomas, Harry, *History of the Gloucestershire Constabulary 1839-1985* (Alan Sutton, 1987)
Trevelyan, G.M., *English Social History* (Longmans, Green & Co, 1944)
Verey, David, and Bowls, Alan, *The Buildings of England, Gloucestershire 1: The Cotswolds* (Penguin, 1999)

Verey, David, *Cotswold Churches* (Batsford, 1976)
Vyvyan, E. R., ed., *Annalia Dubrensis Upon the yeerely celebration of Mr Robert Dover's Olimpick Games upon Cotswold Hills* (The Tabard Press, 1970)
Witts, F.E., Verey, David, ed., *Diary of a Cotswold Parson 1763-1854* (Alan Sutton, 1979)

Journal Articles

1. Campden History

Anon, 'Harriet Tarver, the Campden Poisoner', *CADHAS Notes & Queries* II, 6
Bartleet, 'The manor and borough of Campden', *BGAS Transactions* (1884)
Bearman, C.J., 'The Ending of the Cotswold Games', *BGAS Transactions* 64 (1996) (CADHAS 1997/067/DS)
Ellis, Judith, 'Richard Ellis and the National School', *CADHAS Notes & Queries* III, 3
Granger, Denis, 'The 1851 Census and the Railwaymen', *CADHAS Notes & Queries* IV 5
Granger, Denis, ' The Navvies Moved On - the Trains Awakened Campden' *CADHAS Notes & Queries* IV .6
Holdsworth, Donald, 'Two 17th Century Vicars of Campden - William Bartholomew & Henry Hicks, Father and Son-in-Law', *CADHAS Notes & Queries* III
Macartney, John, 'Chipping Campden and Two World Wars', *CADHAS Notes & Queries* II, 3
Marsh, Judith, 'A Note on Job Sermon' *CADHAS Notes & Queries* III, 2, & 3
Noel, Gerard, 'Gerald Noel tells the remarkable tale of the Catholic cathedral of the Cotswolds', Catholic Herald, (undated, 2001?)
Powell, Geoffrey, 'Shovelling Out the Campden Paupers', *Gloucestershire Local History Bulletin* 13
Powell, Geoffrey & Wilson, Jill, 'The Chipping Campden Altar Hangings', *BGAS Transactions* CXV (1997)
Warmington, Allan, 'Some Knights of the household of King John', B*GAS Transactions* CIV (1986)
Warmington, Allan, 'A Medieval Dispute', *CADHAS Notes & Queries* IV, 2
Warmington, Allan, 'Where is Campden?', *CADHAS Notes & Queries* IV, 1
Warmington, Allan, 'Bordesley Abbey & the Land at Combe', *CADHAS Notes & Queries* II, 6 & III, 1
Warmington, Allan, 'Work on a Local 19th Century Farm', *CADHAS Notes & Queries* III, 1 - 3
West, John, 'A Book of Remembrance Belonging to the Church of Chipping Campden', *Local History*, (Jan/Feb 1998)
Whitfield, Christopher, 'Lionel Cranfield and the Rectory of Campden', *BGAS Transactions* LXXXI (1962)
Wilson, Jill, 'Campden in the Second Half of the Seventeenth Century - What was its County or National Importance?' *CADHAS Notes & Queries*, III 4
Wilson, Jill, 'Notes on two Elections in Campden', *CADHAS Notes & Queries* II, 2
Wilson, Jill, 'Sir Henry Bard, Adventurer, Traveller, Soldier and Diplomatist', *CADHAS Notes & Queries*, I, 1 & 2
Wilson, Jill, 'Sir Henry Bard - Political Assassin?', *CADHAS Notes & Queries* III, 6?
Wilson, Jill, 'The Spiriting away of William Harrison', *CADHAS Notes & Queries*, I, 6?
Wilson, Jill, 'What Happened to Campden's Chantries?', *CADHAS Notes & Queries* IV, 5

2. Artists, Craftworkers and Writers

Baker, L., 'Handwoven', *Rural Industries*, (September 1927), pp. 3-4, 13

Clarke, Lady, 'The Home Industry of Chipping Campden and its individualistic artist-craftsmen: Craftsmanship that flourishes by the creation and export of masterpieces in sculpture, stained glass, woodwork, silverware and textiles', *Illustrated London News* (12 December 1931), pp. 968-9

Cooper, R., 'Bernard Sleigh, artist and craftsman, 1872-1954', *DAS Journal* 21, (1997), pp. 88-102

Griggs, F.L., 'Churches by the Sea: Notes at Some Dead Seaports of Sole Bay', *Architectural Review*, 8 (July - December 1900), pp. 69-74

Laver, J., 'Campden', *The Studio*, XCV (1928), pp.352-3

Powell. Geoffrey, 'An Experiment in English Socialism: C.R.Ashbee and the Campden Guild', *Evesham Journal* (24th & 31st January 1980)

Powell, Geoffrey, Frederick Griggs, RA and Chipping Campden' *Gloucestershire History* (1989) Reprinted, CADHAS (1996)

Salaman, Malcolm C., 'Modern Masters of Etching : No. 12. F.L. Griggs, ARA, RE.' *The Studio* (1926)

Wainwright, 'The Jewellery of Mr and Mrs Gaskin', *The Studio* LXI (1914), pp. 296

Unpublished Papers

Adam, W B., *History of the Research Association 1919-65*, Campden & Chorleywood Food Research Association Archive

Articles of Agreement between Edward Greville and Lionel Cranfield; Kent Archive Office (U269/1 T19)

Ashbee , C.R., *Journals*, (National Art Library, V&A)

53 Deeds relating to Chipping Campden, Castle Ashby Archives (46 & 47)

Catholic Post-Reformation Missions in Gloucestershire: Chipping Campden (Gloucester City Library)

Charter of Incorporation of Chipping Campden Leicestershire Record Office (DE3214 / 156)

Chater, Brigadier J.K., *The Volunteer Soldiers of Gloucestershire*, 18 January 1990, CADHAS Archive 1(900/35/DS)

Clarke, Henry, *Papers*, Sandon Estate Archives

Daunt, Henry M., *History of Campden*, 1894, CADHAS Archive (1996/108/DO)

Estate & Family Papers of the Noel Family, Leicestershire Record Office (DE3214 267/23)

Fees, Craig, *Christmas Mumming in a Cotswold Town*, Leeds University, PhD Thesis, 1988, CADHAS archive

Gostwick, Martin, *Three Lives in One, A Profile of Prof. HPR Finberg*, 1966

Griffiths, Josephine, *Ecclesiastical Records*, St James's Church Muniment Room

Griggs, F.L., *Campden*, Ashmolean collection

Holdsworth, S.D., *Headmasters of Chipping Campden School 2002*, CADHAS Archive (2002/043/DS)

Holdsworth S.D., *Incumbents of Campden*, 2002, CADHAS Archive (2002/044/DS)

Mason, Carolyn, *Campden Remembered*, 1991, CADHAS Archive

Mason, Carolyn, *Notes for a History of Campden*, CADHAS Archive

Miller, Alec, *C.R. Ashbee and the Guild of Handicraft*, 1941
North Cotswold Rifle Volunteer Corps, Rules of and Donations, CADHAS Archive (1990/027/DS)
Patrick, George, *A Scotch Boy in Chipping Campden*, an edited memoir of Archie Ramage by his grandson, Guild of Handicraft Trust Archive
Sandon Hall Papers, CADHAS Archive 92003/105/G)
Stanley, *Farm Ledger*, Transcript by Diana Evans, CADHAS Archive (2004/129/DT)
Survey of Campden carried out for Lionel Cranfield 1607-1609, Kent Archive Office (U269/1 B4 & CADHAS Archive 1995/1R)
Viner, Linda & David, *The Guild: Historical Assessment*, (Guild of Handicraft Trust Archive)
Warmington, Allan, *Baptist Church History*, Draft, 2000, CADHAS Archive
Warmington, Allan, *The Campden School of Arts and Crafts, A History of Adult Education in Campden, 1870-1980*

INDEX

Numbers in italics indicate illustrations